Studies in Logic and Computation

Series Editor

D. M. GABBAY

Nonstandard Queries and Nonstandard Answers

Edited by

R. DEMOLOMBE
Département d'Études et de Recherches en Informatique
Centre d'Études et de Recherches de Toulouse

and

T. IMIELINSKI
Department of Computer Science
Rutgers University

CLARENDON PRESS • OXFORD
1994

Oxford University Press, Walton Street, Oxford OX2 6DP

Oxford New York
Athens Auckland Bangkok Bombay
Calcutta Cape Town Dar es Salaam Delhi
Florence Hong Kong Istanbul Karachi
Kuala Lumpur Madras Madrid Melbourne
Mexico City Nairobi Paris Singapore
Taipei Tokyo Toronto

and associated companies in
Berlin Ibadan

Oxford is a trade mark of Oxford University Press

Published in the United States
by Oxford University Press Inc., New York

A catalogue record for this book is available from the British Library

Library of Congress Cataloging in Publication Data
(Data available upon request)

ISBN 0 19 853852 9

Typeset by Jane Spurr, Imperial College
Printed in Great Britain on acid-free paper
by Bookcraft Ltd, Midsomer Norton, Avon

Preface

This book is the result of the workshop on Nonstandard queries and answers organized at ONERA-CERT in Toulouse, France in July 1991 and contains a subset of papers, formally refereed, presented there as well as some papers which were solicited later.

Future Data and Knowledge Base Systems will require new functionalities: richer data modelling capabilities, more powerful query languages and new concepts of the query answers. Future query languages will go well beyond the power of relational algebra or SQL and include functionalities such as hypothetical and subjunctive reasoning, temporal and modal reasoning, and metareasoning involving knowledge and belief. Answers to queries will no longer be simple collections of tuples - but will include predicates and rules. Intentional answers will lead to cooperative query answering in which the answer to a query takes under consideration user's expectations. For example, if the user is asking for a train connection to New York and if there is no train, but there is a bus connection, he may get this is a part of the query answer. Such a process requires much more intelligence and knowldge of user's expectations (user modelling) - for example we would not want to get the information about the plane to Hawai, when asking for the train to NY!. In a similar way, intentional answers may provide summaries of the large collections of data which may be more useful to return than flat collections of tuples. For example, the part of the answer to a query who can teach undergraduate coursed could be "faculty" and "Senior Graduate Students". Therefore, intentional answers return definitions rather than instances. These definitions may, of course, be further expanded upon user's request.

Non classical logic plays an important role in this book for the formalization of new problems. It is shown how logic allows to give precise definitions for concepts like: intensional answers, subjunctive queries, or reliable sources of information, and gives a precise framework for reasoning about these complex concepts. It is worth noting that adavances in knowledge management are not just an application domain for existing results in logic, but also require new developments in logic.

The book is organized into 10 chapters which cover the areas of cooperative query answering (the first three chapters), metareasoning and abductive reasoning (chapters 5 to 7) and finally, hypothetical and subjunctive reasoning (last three chapters).

The first three chapters deal with cooperative query answering. The first of these papers "An Overview of Cooperative Answering" by Gaasterland, Godfrey and Minker discusses and reviews the area of cooperative query answering and is an excellent introduction to the field. The next paper "CoBase: A cooperative Database System" by Chu et. al. propose to use the type abstraction hierarchy for deriving cooperative query answers. The paper proposes a cooperative extension of SQL and describes experimental results obtained in CoBase project at UCLA. The third chapter "Exploiting User Models to Avoid Misconstruals" by Hemerly et al. addresses avoiding user's faulty inferences which are due to the incomplete and often faulty knowledge.

The chapter 4 serves as foundation for the other chapters which use modal logic approach to model hypothetical and epistemic reasoninig. In "Modal Logics for Practical Reasoning" R. Nossum reviews the basic concepts of modal logic including logics such as KD45, a logic of general awareness and a logic of local reasoning. Chapter 5 entitled "Deriving Answers to Safety Queries" by R.Demolombe and A.J. Jones deals with reasoning about reliablity of information in the database and makes a connection with the theory of signalling acts. In chapter 6 on "Abductive Reasoning in Three-valued Logic for Knowledge Bases" P.Mathieu and J.P. Delahaye discuss the role of abductive reasoning in expert and knowledge base systems. In chapter 7 Dov Gabbay et al. discuss a new way of expanding the human - database interaction based on abductive reasoning, and formalized in the labelled Deduction System.

In the chapter 8. entitled "Hypothetical Reasoning with Inutitionistic Logic" Anthony Bonner provides a formal background for hypothetical reasoning in database systems. Craig Boutillier in "Modal Analysis of Subjunctive Queries" contributes to the theory of knowledge and belief revision by providing a connection between subjunctive queries and updates. Finally G.Grahne and A.Mendelzon in "Updates and Subjuctive Queries" discuss a new semantics for subjunctive queries and complexity of their execution.

R. Demolombe and T. Imielinski
January 1994

Contents

Contributors

Anthony Bonner
University of Toronto
Department of Computer Science
Toronto, Ontario M5S 1A4
Canada
bonner@db.toronto.edu

Craig Boutilier
Department of Computer Science
University of British Columbia
Canada V6T 1Z2
cebly@cs.ubc.ca

Marco A. Casanova
Centro Cientifico Rio
IBM Brasil
Av. Presidente Vargas 824/844 Centro
20071 Rio de Janeiro RJ
Brasil
CASANOVA@RIOSC.bitnet

Quiming Chen
Computer Science Department
University of California, Los Angeles
Los Angeles, California
USA

Wesley W. Chu
Computer Science Department
University of California, Los Angeles
Los Angeles, California
USA
wwc@cs.ucla.edu

Jean-Paul Delahaye
Laboratoire d'Informatique Fondamentale
de Lille
URA 369 CNRS
Universite de Lille I
59655 Villeneuve d'Ascq Cedex
France
delahaye@lifl.lifl.fr

Robert Demolombe
ONERA-CERT B.P. 4025
31055 Toulouse Cedex
France
demolombe@tls-cs.cert.fr

Antonio L. Furtado
Departamento de Informatica
PUC-RJ
R. Marques de Sao Vicente 225 Gavea
22453 Rio de Janeiro RJ
Brasil
furtado@inf.puc-rio.br

Terry Gaasterland
Argonne National Laboratory
MCS Division
Argonne, Illinois 60439
USA
gaasterl@mcs.anl.gov

Dov Gabbay
Department of Computing
180 Queen's Gate
Imperial College
London SW7 2BZ
United Kingdom
dg@doc.ic.ac.uk

Parke Godfrey
Department of Computer Science and
Institute for Advanced Computer Studies
University of Maryland
College Park, Maryland 20742
USA
godfrey@cs.umd edu

Gosta Grahne
Department of Computer Science
University of Helsinki
Teollisuuskatu 23
SF-00510 Helsinki
Finland
grahne@cs.Helsinki.FI

Andrea Hemerly
Centro Cientifico Rio
IBM Brasil
Av. Presidente Vargas 824/844 Centro
20071 Rio de Janeiro RJ
Brasil
ANDREASI@RIOSC.BITNET

Tomasz Imielinski
IBM Almaden Research Center
650 Harry Road
San Jose, CA 95120
USA
imielins@aramis.rutgers.edu

Andrew Jones
University of Oslo
Department of Philosophy
Postboks 1024
Bindern, Oslo 3
Norway
jones@hedda.uio.no

Ruth Kempson
Department of Linguistics
School of Oriental and African Studies
London WC1H 0XG
United Kingdom

Philippe Mathieu
Laboratoire d'Informatique Fondamentale
de Lille
URA 369 CNRS
Universite de Lille I
59655 Villeneuve d'Ascq Cedex
France
Mathieu@lifl.lifl.fr

Alberto O.Mendelzon
Department of Computer Science
University of Toronto
Toronto, Canada M5S 1A4
mendel@db.toronto.edu

Matthew Merzbacher
75 Berkshire Drive
Williamstown, MA 01267
USA
matthew@cs.williams.edu

Jack Minker
Department of Computer Science and
Institute for Advanced Computer Studies
University of Maryland
College Park, Maryland 20742
USA
minker@cs.umd.edu

Rolph Nossum
Agder College P.O. Box 607
N-4601 Kristiansand
Norway
rolfn@adh.no

Jeremy Pitt
Department of Computing
180 Queen's Gate
Imperial College
London SW7 2BZ
United Kingdom
jvp@doc.ic.ac.uk

1

An overview of cooperative answering*

Terry Gaasterland, Parke Godfrey, and Jack Minker

Abstract

Databases and information systems are often difficult to use because they do not explicitly attempt to cooperate with their users. Direct answers to database and knowledge base queries may not always be the best answers. Instead, an answer with extra or alternative information may be more useful and less misleading to a user.

This chapter surveys foundational work that has been done towards endowing intelligent information systems with the ability to exhibit cooperative behaviour. Grice's maxims of cooperative conversation, which provided a starting point for the field of cooperative answering, are presented, along with relevant work in natural language dialogue systems, database query answering systems, and logic programming and deductive databases.

The chapter gives a detailed account of cooperative techniques that have been developed for considering users' beliefs and expecations, presuppositions, and misconceptions. Also, work in intensional answering and generalizing queries and answers is covered. Finally, the cooperative answering system at Maryland, which is intended to be a general, portable platform for supporting a wide spectrum of cooperative answering techniques, is described.

1 Introduction

Whenever we ask a question, we expect to receive a worthwhile answer in reply. This is certainly true in conversation, and this expectation remains whenever we interact with information systems. While people have always built databases and knowledge bases with this intention in mind, they have not necessarily succeeded.

*This chapter first appeared as an invited paper in the *JIIS*: Terry Gaasterland, Parke Godfrey, and Jack Minker. An overview of cooperative answering. *Journal of Intelligent Information Systems*, 1:293-321, 1992. It is republished here with the permission of Kluwer Academic Publishers.

Databases and information systems are often difficult to use because they do not explicitly attempt to cooperate with their users. Unlike people, they answer literally the queries posed to them. Answers will be correct, but can often be misleading. Responses to queries may not contain the information the user really wants. A user may need more information, or might even need different information, than the query requests. The user may have misconceptions about the database and what the database knows.

If we are to build information systems that meet users' expectations, it is first necessary to determine what it means for an answer to be appropriate. Grice [28] proposes a number of maxims that characterize a *cooperative answer*. According to his maxims, a cooperative answer should be a correct, non-misleading, and useful answer to a query. As we seek to endow information systems with cooperative behaviour, the maxims can be used to serve as a measure of the cooperative performance of our information systems. A number of researchers have used Grice's maxims as guidelines in their work. The maxims describe fundamental properties of cooperative behaviour. They describe what people do in conversation.

The *maxim of quality* requires that each contribution to a conversation be valid. One should only say things that one believes to be *true*, and one should not say anything for which one has inadequate evidence. In other words, one should not lie or overstate what one knows. Joshi [32] extends this maxim to state that one should never say anything which may imply to the listener something that oneself believes to be *false*. Given this cooperative maxim, both Joshi and Kaplan [35, 36] consider how to apply it to information systems and databases. In particular, a system should never give an answer which might mislead the user. If a literal answer to a query would lead the user to *false* assumptions, the system must provide further information to prevent this.

The *maxim of quantity* states that a contribution to a conversation should be as informative as required. However, it should not be more informative, or more detailed, than necessary. As databases become more complex and very large, an answer to a query can result in a huge table, much larger than is possible to read. In deductive databases, research has been carried out on *intensional answers*, which are succinct logical formulas that entail the answer. An intensional answer will often be as informative to the user as the table would be, and will often be much easier to understand. Intensional answers can also be more informative than the table itself by informing the user of general facts about the table.

The *maxim of relation* says that a contribution should be relevant. In particular, an answer should be relevant to the user who asked the question. Much work [1, 2, 42, 43, 55] has been done to model users and to determine a user's goals and intentions. This work provides a basis for determining whether an answer is relevant.

The *maxim of manner* states that one must avoid obtuse expression and avoid ambiguity. Also, one must be brief. When an information system provides an answer, it ought to be presented in a form that is easy for the user to understand. It should not be ambiguous, leaving the user with choices to make about its meaning. Otherwise, the answer could be misleading. The answer should be as succinct as possible without encroaching on any of the other criteria.

In part, Grice's intent in introducing a set of conversational maxims was to show that first-order logic suffices to model cooperative dialogue. The maxims describe what should happen in a natural conversation. They also serve to explain when a conversation fails to be cooperative. One can evaluate whether an answer is cooperative with respect to the maxims and generates cooperative responses by adhering to them.

Others have held the view that more powerful logics, such as logics of intensionality and modality, are needed to handle cooperative discourse. Many of the philosophical considerations expressed in [61] reflect this concern. Of course, whether or not first-order logic can serve as an adequate ontology for cooperative answering is an open question. Much research is being conducted on non-classical and higher-order logics. These may play a role in future cooperative answering work.

Once we have established the criteria for an answer to be cooperative, we must determine how to build information systems that exhibit cooperative answering behaviour. Databases, and information systems in general, satisfy the standard of providing *correct* answers, insofar as the system contains valid information. However, for answers to be useful to users, they must ask the appropriate queries in order to arrive at the desired information. To do so, the user must know something about the database's schema, and just what it is that the database knows. When a user's suppositions about the system are inaccurate, most information systems do not do much in the way of correcting the user. Once users do ask the queries that comply with the database organization, the answers returned may still be misleading, less informative than desired, or ambiguous.

To address these problems, specific cooperative techniques have been developed to identify and correct *false presuppositions* and *misconceptions* apparent in the question. Other techniques ensure that answers are *relevant* with respect to the user's intentions. When an answer consists of several parts, it is important to try to make the answer *cohesive* across these parts, and *coherent* as a whole. Finally, if the answer is presented in natural language, the response should exhibit an appropriate conversational organization.

Our focus in this survey is on the nascent field of cooperative answering for query/answer systems. Some of the key topics involved are

- maxims and criteria for cooperative behaviour (as seen above);
- techniques to evoke cooperative behaviour in query/answer systems;
- issues of the computational cost of such methods and methods for containing that cost; and
- knowledge representation needs for constructing cooperative answers.

In the next section, we review foundational efforts in cooperative answering. In Section 3 we look at specific cooperative answering strategies and systems. These strategies are universal in that any system ought to support them and all users require them. In Section 4 we consider when an answer ought to be tailored for a particular user or class of users. This is necessary to attend properly to a user's particular needs and requirements. In Section 5 we review the work on cooperative answering at the University of Maryland at College Park. Finally, we attempt to outline the directions in which the field of cooperative answering is evolving, which direction we should go, and further problems to be solved.

2 Query/answer systems

Research in cooperative answering has grown out of three areas in which question-and-answer discourses arise:

1. natural language interfaces and dialogue systems built for the purpose of studying natural language exchanges between users and computers;
2. databases; and
3. logic programming and deductive databases.

In this section, we discuss each in turn.

2.1 Natural language interfaces

Much of the initial work on cooperative answering focused on natural language dialogue systems [32, 33, 38, 56]. Researchers sought to endow their information systems with the same normative cooperative behaviour described by Grice as occurring in human conversation. Many of the systems we discuss in this survey employ natural language interfaces or are tightly integrated with natural language facilities. The focus on natural language within the nascent field of cooperative answering can be considered as both distracting and beneficial in different ways.

Some researchers are interested in modelling human conversation. Others hope to use human discourse as a normative standard for information systems' behaviour. Many believe that natural language dialogue systems ought to be subject to the same cooperative conversational maxims as human discourse. Such systems are ideal settings for evaluating a systems' behaviour against the conversational maxims.

Natural language interfaces, along with more fully integrated natural language query/answer systems, are important in another way, too: for information systems to be accessible to lay users requires an easily understood interface language. Many hope that natural language, or a subset thereof, will fulfil this need. As information systems become ever larger and more complex, we all become lay users, and the need for natural interfaces becomes even more vital. One cannot expect all users to understand a complex database's schema. Natural language conversation techniques are also useful for answering queries in an interactive fashion when answers become long and complex. One cannot expect users to understand overly complex answers expressed in arcane formalisms or expressed all at once.

While the research in natural language systems is important in its own right, it risks confounding the issues faced in cooperative answering. The tenets of cooperative answering ought to be universal to queries themselves, regardless of whether the queries are cast in natural language, in logic, or in *SQL*. (Of course, there are many other issues particular to natural language.) The same maxims for cooperation discussed above ought to apply to all information systems.

This chapter covers specific topics in natural language research when they relate directly to cooperative answering systems. There are many more topics indirectly related to cooperative answering with extensive literatures that we do not cover. We look at a number of natural language systems of importance to the cooperative answering field in Section 3.1. However, our focus is on the cooperative issues they tackle. We attempt to clarify the relation between natural language and cooperation in such systems as best we can throughout the survey. We do not consider the particulars of the natural language components in cooperative systems.

2.2 Databases

A number of researchers in the area of databases [11, 12, 36, 46] have recognized the practical need for cooperative answering behaviour in standard, widely available information systems. This need has led people to consider how to adapt and develop cooperative techniques specifically for databases.

Kaplan [36] built a cooperative system on top of *CODASYL* (a network-model database) [13, 62]. He pays special attention to making his system *portable*: the cooperative answering behaviour is independent of the information system's knowledge and domain. His system was portable not only between databases using the network model, but also between other types of information systems, too, such as relational databases and expert systems. Mays [41] builds on Kaplan's work and considers how to use a relational database's schema to correct *false presuppositions* in a user's query.

Motro [46] considers modifications to the relational model which would be easy to incorporate into a relational database system to allow for certain cooperative behaviours. In [49] he considers a user interface for relational database systems that would allow users to interact with the database in more cooperative ways. The database can correct queries that have apparent mistakes or that return no answers, and yield to the user *corrected* queries with which to proceed. He also explores the notion of returning to a user related queries that may match the user's intended question more closely.

Chu, Chen, and Lee [11, 12] explore methods to generalize and refine queries to generate new queries related in direct ways to the user's original. Such related queries can find answers which may be of interest to the user outside of the scope of the original query.

2.3 Deductive databases

A large portion of the work in cooperative answering has been carried out within deductive databases. The logic model both subsumes and extends the relational model [62] for databases. The logic model offers a uniform representation for data, knowledge,[1] and queries. Logic also offers a suitable representation for expressing cooperative answers, whereas *SQL* and other database languages must be extended to do this. Finally, the rules and integrity constraints of deductive databases allow for a rich semantics, which plays a vital role in generating cooperative response. In the remainder of this section, we provide basic definitions about deductive databases that will be used throughout this chapter.

A deductive database [25, 27, 45] employs the *logic model* instead of the *relational model* as its data model [62]. A deductive database consists of three parts: *facts*, *rules*, and *integrity constraints*. We denote this by the tuple $\langle EDB, IDB, \mathcal{IC} \rangle$. A *rule* is of the form

$$A_0 \leftarrow A_1, \ldots, A_n. \qquad (\mathcal{C}_1)$$

A rule is a clause, and C_1 is equivalent logically to $\forall.\ A_0 \vee \neg A_1 \vee \ldots \neg A_n$.The A_is, $0 \leq i \leq n$, are atoms. In this chapter, a clause contains a single positive atom, A_0, and some negative atoms, $A_1, \ldots, A_n$, $n \geq 0$.

[1] *Data* and *knowledge* are differentiated. See Section 3.4 for a discussion.

An *atom* is a predicate instantiated across variables and constants. (*Logic programs* are more general in that they also permit functional terms.) For instance, *student*(*chris*) and *student*(X) are atoms of the unary predicate *student/1*. The former is over the constant *chris*, the latter over the variable X.[2] Each variable appearing in a clause is considered to be universally quantified across the clause.

The atom A_0 in C_1 is called the *head*, and $A_1, \ldots, A_n$ the *body*. The atom A_0 is necessarily a logical consequence of the database if each A_i, $1 \leq i \leq n$, is a logical consequence of the database. A *ground* atom is one that contains no variables. A *fact* is a ground clause with an empty body, $n = 0$.

The set of all facts constitutes the *extensional* database (*EDB*), the set of rules the *intensional* database (*IDB*). It is assumed that a given predicate either appears only in facts or in the heads of rules. The *EDB* predicates are equivalent to relations from the schema in a relational database, and individual facts to individual tuples. The rules for the *IDB* predicates are analogous to views, but are more powerful than views as they admit recursion. Clauses and facts as we have defined them constitute *DATALOG*, and a finite set of such clauses and facts is a *DATALOG* database [62].

A relational database is conceptualized as two parts: its *schema* and its *state*. The schema is its relations and views. The state is the database's collection of tuples, the data. Databases are designed on the assumption that the schema seldom changes and remains fairly constant through time, but the state will change rapidly as new data are added and old data are revised. Likewise, in a deductive database, it is assumed that the *IDB* and the $\mathcal{IC}$ are mostly static. The *EDB* will change often as new facts are added and old ones revised.

The type of question permitted in a deductive database is an existentially quantified conjunction of atoms. For instance, if one wanted to know whether there is a student who has passed *CMSC 420*, the logical formula would be

$$\exists X.\ \textit{student}(X) \wedge \textit{passed}(X,\ \textit{`CMSC-420'})\ ?$$

It is standard to take the negation of the question, which is then called the *query*, to resolve against the database. A query, then, is a clause, and has the same form as a rule but without a head. For instance, our question above is represented as

$$\leftarrow \textit{student}(X),\ \textit{passed}(X,\ \textit{`CMSC-420'}). \qquad (\mathcal{Q}_1)$$

[2] We shall write constants beginning in lowercase or 'quoted', and write variables beginning in uppercase.

An *answer* to a query is a substitution of the query's variables such that (the negation of) the substituted query is a logical consequence of the database. For instance, $X = chris$ is an answer to Q_1 if *student* (*chris*) and *passed* (*chris, 'CMSC-420'*) follow from the database.

The third component of a deductive database is an associated set of integrity constraints, $\mathcal{IC}$. An *integrity constraint* (*IC*) is a logical formula that must be *true* of the database.[3] We often limit our concern to *denial* constraints, *IC*s which state facts that cannot be simultaneously *true* in the database. For example, the following *IC* states that no one can be both a student and a professor:

$$\subset \textit{professor}(X),\ \textit{student}(X). \qquad (\mathcal{IC}_1)$$

One may note that (denial) integrity constraints have the same syntactic form as queries,[4] but a different meaning with respect to the database. We may write other *IC*s in the same form as denials, but allowing for negation in the body. For instance,

$$\subset \textit{student}(X),\ \textit{not enrolled}(X) \qquad (\mathcal{IC}_2)$$

states that all students must be enrolled. In other words, if someone is a student, then it is not possible that he or she is not enrolled. This *not* is not classical negation,[5] but negation as failure [39, 59]. Thus, *not enrolled* (*chris*), say, is *true* if *enrolled* (*chris*) cannot be proven. Such constraints are more expressive and we use such *IC*s in some of our examples.

We now turn to a detailed overview of cooperative techniques that have been developed and explored in each of these three areas over the past two decades.

3 Foundational work in cooperative answering

The cooperative answering techniques that have grown out of research in each of the areas that were reviewed in the previous section can be separated into five categories. The techniques in each category are differentiated by the following capabilities:

1. consideration of specific information about a user's state of mind;

[3] This has the same meaning as *static* integrity constraints in relational databases, a statement that must be *true* of the state of the database. We do not consider *dynamic* integrity constraints, which must be preserved across a database transaction.

[4] We use the symbol '⊂', which is also commonly used for logical *if*, instead of '←' within integrity constraints to distinguish them typographically from queries.

[5] We write classical negation using the symbol '¬'.

2. evaluation of presuppositions in a query;

3. detection and correction of misconceptions in a query (other than false presuppositions);

4. formulation of intensional answers; and

5. generalization of queries and of responses.

This section describes each in turn.

3.1 Beliefs and expectations

The genesis of the field of cooperative answering can, for the most part, be traced to work by Joshi and Webber at the University of Pennsylvania. In May of 1978 a workshop entitled *'Computational Aspects of Linguistic Structure and Discourse Setting'* was held, sponsored by the Sloan Foundation at the University of Pennsylvania. Several topics discussed were: question–answering—intensional verses extensional responses, direct and indirect answers; meaning representations—logical representations and their role in natural language processing; and inferences in context. A book ensued, *Elements of Discourse Understanding*, in 1981, edited by Joshi, Webber, and Sag, based upon the articles presented at the workshop [33].

Most of the articles in the book fall under the following topics:

1. Utterance meaning
   (understanding the questions and answers)

2. Discourse models
   (following the query/answer discourse)

3. Models of participants' beliefs
   (mutual ground between user and system)

For query/answer systems, topic (1) concerns whether the system can understand and interpret the query properly. This covers a number of important issues. For instance, natural language queries can be ambiguous and must be rendered unambiguous to be answered. Lehnert [38] has noted that a given query might be asked with different intentions in mind. Thus a user's intentions and goals must be taken into account. (See Section 4.) Even with logical queries (not asked in natural language), proper interpretation of the query is necessary. Cuppens and Demolombe [17] consider rewriting queries to include more information in the answers than would be gathered through the original query in order to match a user's intentions and to provide generally more informative answers. (See Section 3.5.)

Topic (2) concerns whether a system is able to model its dialogue with a user. A system should account for a user's goals changing over time and what the user has learned through previous dialogue with the system (a building of *mutual knowledge*). Also, the system should gain a better understanding of a user's intentions as the dialogue progresses. Webber is interested in how aspects of discourse might shape the mental model that a listener has. In [64] she considers how people understand (definite) anaphora. McKeown [44] and Gaasterland [18, 19] have both considered such issues as involved in the presentation of answers, which are crucial to the user's understanding of the answers.

In general, Webber's work considers user beliefs in order to anticipate user expectations (topic (3)). She explores how to provide extra information to prevent misconceptions. For example:

Q: *'Is Sam an associate professor?'*
User believes most associate professors have tenure.
Sam is not tenured. Sam is an associate professor.

A: *'Yes, but he doesn't have tenure.'*

Pollack, Hirschberg, and Webber [56] consider the effects that a user's interaction should have on the reasoning of expert systems. Joshi, Webber, and Weischedel [34] consider how to generate expert responses that match the user's expectations. Webber and Mays [65] focus on detecting and correcting misconceptions (Section 3.3).

Joshi [32] considers some of the abstract problems of establishing mutual knowledge in question/answer systems. The paper appears in the 1982 collection *Mutual Knowledge*, edited by N. V. Smith [61].[6] The book is a philosophical treatise on mutual knowledge: what mutual knowledge is, its ramifications in dialogue, and how it is established. Joshi, in his article, considers the ramifications for cooperation in dialogue.

Lehnert in [38] has devised a system to analyse questions within an ongoing discourse between a user and a computer in order to determine the user's intent behind the questions. Her system strives to answer questions in a cooperative manner. Her system, called *QUALM*, parses its English questions into a conceptual dependency representation [58] which represents the question's meaning. It analyses the question and surrounding context in the conversation to decide the question's intent. The analysis helps to determine the type of answer that the system should provide.

One might respond to the question below with any one of the following answers, depending on what intent is behind the question:

[6] This book is incorrectly referenced as *Mutual Beliefs* in many papers.

Q:	*'How did John take the exam?'*	(intent?)
$\mathbf{A}_1$:	*'He crammed the night before.'*	(enablement)
$\mathbf{A}_2$:	*'He took it with a pen.'*	(instrumental/procedural)
$\mathbf{A}_3$:	*'He took it badly.'*	(emotional)[7]

Lehnert points out that her system is more than a natural language front-end. The conceptual dependency representation also serves as the core knowledge representation, and for her system there is necessarily no clear distinction between translating the query and answering it.

Many of Webber's and Joshi's students have worked in this area, and established many cooperative answering techniques. Mays [41] considers how to employ the database's schema to detect user misconceptions (as discussed in Section 2.2). Kaplan [35, 36] detects presuppositions in queries, and Hirschberg [29] accounts for implicatures in answers. (See next section.) McKeown [44] considers natural language response to database queries. Pollack [55] studies how users' questions fit with their plans. (See Section 4.)

3.2 Presuppositions

A student asks an appropriate university database

'Who passed CMSC 420 in the fall semester of 1991?'

The database returns with the answer *'No one'*, leaving the student to think, possibly, that *CMSC 420* is a very difficult course. The student then asks

'Who failed CMSC 420 in the fall semester of 1991?'

Again, the database returns with the answer *'No one'*. Finally, the student is suspicious and asks

'Who taught CMSC 420 in the fall semester of 1991?"

The database answers again *'No one'* [36].

Kaplan calls this behaviour *stonewalling*. If the initial question had been asked to a person instead, he or she would have probably answered immediately with a reply such as *'Oh, there was no such course taught last semester.'* Databases stonewall. They will answer a *yes/no* question with a *yes* or a *no* regardless of whether the answer is misleading. As Grice said, though, correct answers are not enough. Clearly a cooperative answer would be an explanation of why the query fails (why the answer is *no*), exposing any false presuppositions. Kaplan states that one should

[7] We have added this one to the example.

consider the presuppositions in a query to be statements that must be *true* for the query to have an answer [35, 36]. If any presuppositions are *false*, the query is nonsensical.

Kaplan built a system called *CO-OP* (A Cooperative Query System), a natural language query system that operates with a *CODASYL* database management system [13, 62]. *CO-OP* provides cooperative responses to simple natural language questions, requesting the relevant data from the database. The system runs as two processes: a FORTRAN process of the *SEED* database system (*CODASYL*) with a query processor and a LISP process of the natural language front-end with a report writer. The system has been tested over a real database from the National Center for Atmospheric Research on both users and programmers.

Kaplan devises and employs an intermediate representation for queries that he calls the *Meta Query Language* (*MQL*). A query is represented as a graph structure in *MQL*, consisting of sets at the nodes and binary relations between sets (the arcs). The graph is a semantic network, and the query is re-expressed in a binary notation. The query answering system checks that each connected subgraph is non-empty. If any is empty, this is a failed presupposition that ought to be reported.

Presumptions are distinguished from *presuppositions*. All presuppositions of a query must hold for the query to make sense. However, the query may contain presumptions, too. If a presumption does not hold, then the query will have only one answer (usually *no*). For example,

'What day does Mary have her lesson?'

presupposes that Mary has a (weekly) lesson. If she does not, the query cannot be answered adequately. In other words, no day of the week can be given in reply. The reply *'Mary has her lesson on no day.'* would not be a correct response since it, too, seems to presuppose that Mary has a lesson. (But when?) The query

'Did Mahler complete an 11th symphony?'

presumes that he began one, but it does not *presuppose* that he began one [36]. We can answer meaningfully and correctly *'No'* even if he never began his 11th symphony, albeit *'No, Mahler never began an 11th symphony.'* would be a more *informative* answer.

Presumptions are a wider class than presuppositions. They are also much more difficult to handle. For instance, the query *'Did it rain yesterday?'* could be answered *'No, there were no clouds yesterday.'* This entails a fair amount of reasoning and domain knowledge, and can be considered a type of explanation. A system must be able to conduct such reasoning, and an appropriate explanation for the user must be chosen from many

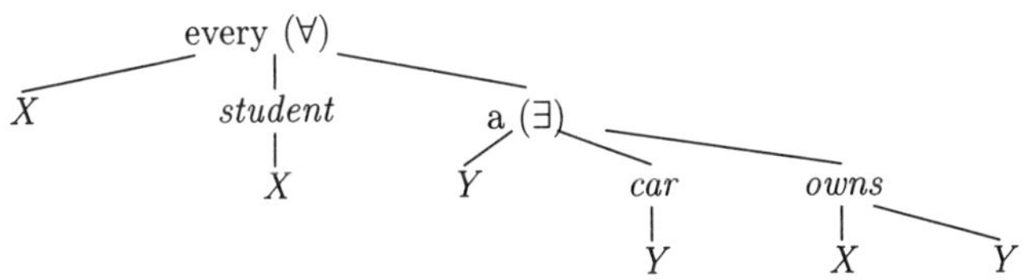

'Every student owns a car.'

$$\forall X.[student(X) \longrightarrow \exists Y.[car(Y) \wedge owns(X, Y)]]$$

Figure 1: Quantifier tree representation.

potential explanations. We explore these issues next in Section (3.3) when we discuss the closely related topic of misconceptions.

A query containing a false presupposition can be considered to have no answer, positive or negative, even though the database may be able to deliver a 'literal' answer. Colmerauer and Pique noticed this dilemma in their work on translating natural language queries into a logical formalism [14]. They employed a three-valued logic that allows a sentence to be marked *undefined* when such false presuppositions occur. (But in their work they do not develop a means to identify false presuppositions to the user.)

In particular, in a natural language sentence, a speaker assumes the existence of the subject and objects (the noun phrases) of the sentence. If any of these do not exist, then the sentence does not have any clear meaning. Colmerauer and Pique translate natural language sentences (and queries) into a logical tree representation called *three branch quantifier trees* (*3BQs*). The first branch is a variable introduced in the sentence, the second a translation of the subject (this can be recursive), and the third a translation of the rest of the sentence (which can also be recursive). In Figure 1 the statement *'Every student owns a car'* is represented as a *3BQ* tree. Once a sentence is translated, they check that none of the typing relations (for instance, *student/1* and *car/1*, unary predicates) representing the noun phrases are empty. If there are no students, then the sentence from Figure 1 is deemed to be nonsensical.

Usually when one asks a query, one not only presupposes the existence of all the components of the query, but one also presupposes an answer to the query itself. For instance, suppose one asks *'Which employees own red cars?'* (query $\mathcal{Q}_2$, see Figure 2). Colmerauer and Pique are concerned that there be cars and employees known to the database. Otherwise, there would be a false presupposition in Q_2, and so no valid answers.

On asking a query, one assumes there are answers to the query, too. If there are no answers, this deserves an explanation. For instance, if there are no employees who own red cars, the database can answer literally *'No one'* to query Q_2. To be more informative, if there is some reason why there are no answers, the database should say so. (We discuss this in the next section, 3.3.) At least, the part of the query responsible for failure ought to be identified. There may be no employees owning red cars because no employee owns a car at all. Thus, the subquery $\langle \leftarrow \mathit{employee}(X),\ \mathit{owns}(X,\ Y),\ \mathit{car}(Y).\rangle$ would fail, too.[8] Reporting this failure is more informative than just reporting the failure of Q_2.

Janas in [31] studies the feasibility of yielding such informative answers. His idea is to report the smallest subqueries that fail. If we consider a conjunctive query as a set of atoms to be satisfied, then the subqueries are the elements of the power set. In all, there are $2^n - 2$ subqueries for a conjunctive query with n atoms, disregarding the query itself (which has already been seen to fail) and $\emptyset$, the empty query. Query Q_2 has four atoms, so there are 14 subqueries to consider. The naïve approach is to test all of them. This incurs exponential cost over the length of the query. More clever algorithms would cut this cost, especially for the average case, but cannot reduce the worst case behaviour to better than exponential.

Janas shows that for most queries, many of the potential subqueries may be discounted. He defines that two atoms in a query are *joined* if they share a variable. The relation *connected* is then the transitive closure of *joined*. Janas defines a query to be *connected* if every two atoms in the query are connected.[9] It is reasonable to insist that queries be connected. (A user can always ask any disconnected parts as separate queries.) In searching for failed subqueries, it is only necessary to consider connected subqueries. For instance, consider the subquery $\langle \leftarrow \mathit{employee}(X),\ \mathit{car}(Y),\ \mathit{red}(Y).\rangle$. This query is not connected. It can only fail if $\langle \leftarrow \mathit{employee}(X)\rangle$ or $\langle \leftarrow \mathit{car}(Y),\ \mathit{red}(Y)\rangle$ fails. These latter subqueries are connected and will be considered anyway. It is not necessary to properly compute answers for each subquery considered; it is only necessary to compute if it has *an* answer.

Even if the cost of this processing remains high, it may be offset by the benefits that these answers offer. When informed of the part of the query that fails, the user will not waste time asking many follow-up questions that will also necessarily fail while looking for the information that he or she is still trying to find. The overall reduction in cumulative query–answering cost could be significant, especially if the user were to ask many spurious

[8] Each subquery in Figure 2 *logically subsumes* each query that it points to. A formula $\mathcal{F}$ *logically subsumes* $\mathcal{G}$ *iff* $\models \mathcal{F} \rightarrow \mathcal{G}$.

[9] He does not define *connected* in [31] in quite this way, but to the same effect.

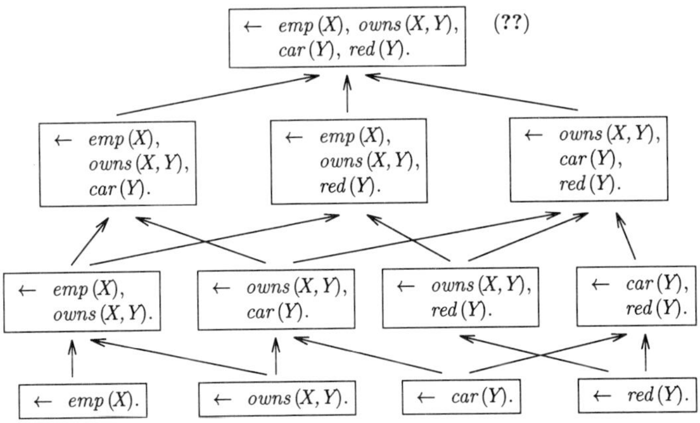

Figure 2: A lattice of subqueries.

queries (as in Kaplan's stonewalling) to obtain the desired information. The user can quickly become frustrated and dissuaded from his or her goal.

Kaplan [36] also considers the necessity of finding the smallest failing subqueries and devises an algorithm very similar to Janas's that operates over a query translated into his *MQL*, but he does not consider the computational issues involved. He points out that his (as does Janas's) algorithm to find presumptions (failed subqueries) is independent of domain specific knowledge. These are techniques that are applicable over any domain. Kaplan also introduces the notion of generalizing a query: if a query fails due to a failing subquery, the failing part can be removed, resulting in a new query that will have answers. This can serve as a tool in correcting possible errors in users' queries, and to give the user information *related* to the query asked. (We elaborate on this last idea in Section 3.5.)

The statement *'No employees own red cars'* implies that employees do own cars. Otherwise, a stronger assertion should have been made according to the maxim of quantity. A response should be as informative as necessary, but no more so. In particular, Janas's queries and subqueries lie on a scale: if a subquery has no answers, then the query cannot have any answers either since the subquery logically subsumes the query. Such a tacit implication is called a *scalar implicature*.

Hirschberg [29] considers how scalar implicatures are involved in obeying the maxim of quantity. Many such implicative scales exist and are employed in conversation. Consider the following piece of dialogue, which takes place between, say, an engineer and an assistant across a remote radio link:

Engineer:	*'Did you loosen the hose?'*
Assistant:	*'I have detached it.'*

If the assistant were to have (truthfully) answered *'Yes'* (he or she did *loosen* the hose in the process of detaching it), this would mislead the engineer, who assumes that the whole story has been told, as in *'Yes, I have loosened it (but no more).'* Going from *loosen* to *detached* is a scale, the latter implying the former. It is assumed in conversation that one always give the response *highest* on such a scale that is true, that it implies the most possible, and that all implications are true.

Q: *'Are mushrooms poisonous?'*
A: *'Some are.'*

Degree of existence is also a scale. To the question above, one cannot answer correctly *yes* or *no*. Some mushrooms are edible, others are poisonous. The answer to the universal question *'Are all mushrooms poisonous?'* could be *'No,'* but this would be misleading. The cooperative response would be *'No, but some are.'*

3.3 Misconceptions

A query may be free of any false presuppositions, but still harbour misconceptions. False presuppositions concern the schema of the knowledge base. In contrast, misconceptions concern the domain of the knowledge base, and what is and is not possible within the domain. Misconceptions can mean that a query will not have any answers, or that some subquery will not lead to any answers. Misconceptions can lead to logical redundancy in a query, so the query overspecifies the solutions, indicating the possibility that the user is unaware of certain properties of the domain. While false presuppositions usually occur with respect to the database's state and schema, misconceptions usually occur with respect to the database's semantics. Misconceptions arise when the user has a false or unclear understanding of what is necessarily *true* or *false* in the database.

Mays [41] employs schema information of a relational database to correct false presuppositions. By employing schema information, he introduces aspects of the database's semantics into answers and can detect and correct misconceptions of the user with respect to the database schema.

For instance, say that only students *take* courses, whereas professors *teach* courses. Even though the following query is destined to fail, having no answers, it is more informative to correct the user's misconceptions of the database by explaining why there are no answers.

Q: *'Which professors take CMSC 620?'*

A: *'None.'*
'Professors teach courses.'
'Students take courses.'

McCoy [42] uses world (or general) knowledge to correct *object related* misconceptions that a user might have, misconceptions about the properties of a given object or class. For instance, a user might ask:

Q: *'Where are the gills on a whale?'*
The system knows the user probably thinks whales are fish because fish use gills to breathe.

A: *'Whales do not have gills. They breathe through lungs.'*

Whenever the user asks a query that *cannot* have an answer, the system infers the probable mismatches between the user's view of the world and the knowledge in the knowledge base. The system then answers with a correction to rectify the mismatch.

Looking at [31] again, Janas considers the use of *ICs* to eliminate subqueries from consideration. He shows how *ICs* that apply to a query can be used to rule out presuppositions that are certain to be *true*. An *IC* might reduce a query to a subquery. For instance, a constraint

$$\subset \mathit{car}(X),\ \mathit{not}\ \mathit{red}(X).$$

stating that all cars are red would reduce Q_2 (page 15) to $\langle \leftarrow \mathit{emp}(X), \mathit{owns}(X,\ Y), \mathit{car}(Y).\rangle$ If something is a car, it is certain to be red. An *IC* can logically subsume a query, meaning that the query cannot have answers. For instance, say

$$\subset \mathit{emp}(X),\ \mathit{owns}(X,\ Y),\ \mathit{car}(Y)$$

were a constraint itself, meaning that employees do not own cars. This is a necessarily failing subquery of Q_2, thus Q_2 itself must fail. The *SEAVE* system of Motro [50] also uses integrity constraints together with false presuppositions, in order to provide additional information about failed queries. Consider the query

$$\leftarrow \mathit{professor}(X),\ \mathit{enrolled\_in}(\text{'CMSC-420'}). \qquad (Q_3)$$

in a database with the following integrity constraints

$$\subset \textit{professor}(X),\ \textit{student}(X). \qquad (IC_1)$$
$$\subset \textit{enrolled\_in}(X,\ Y),\ \textit{not student}(X). \qquad (\mathcal{IC}_3)$$

IC_1 states that professors cannot be students (and the contrary as well) and IC_3 states that all students are enrolled. The query Q_3 violates these *IC*s. Semantic query optimization techniques [4, 5, 6] apply a set of contraints to a query. If any constraint, or set of constraints, is violated, the query is known to fail before any database search takes place. Not only do the constraints identify failed queries, but they also provide information about why the queries fail. Furthermore, they notify the user that if the same query is asked again in the future, the query will still fail, even if the state of the database has changed.

The realization that failure assured by *IC*s is more meaningful than just exhaustive failure motivated the work in cooperative answering by Gal and Minker [22, 23, 24]. They used the semantic optimization techniques [4, 5, 6] to determine when *IC*s applied to a query. The system developed by Gal [22] identifies the *IC*s that guarantee failure. It then includes the constraints in an answer to the user. For the example above with query Q_3, a cooperative response could say

'No one is both a professor and a student.
Anyone who is enrolled in a class is a student.
So no one is a professor and enrolled in a class.'

Gal's work also addresses some of the difficulties encountered when *IC*s are used for explanation. Sometimes several sets of *IC*s can explain the failure independently. In this case, Gal's system uses heuristics to select the best explanation to provide for the user. Sometimes explanations can be quite complex and involved, to the point that they would tax a user's attention and interest. The user is allowed to impose a limit on the content of an explanation prior to asking a query.

*IC*s can be used to do more than explain failed queries. Gal and Minker use them to summarize very large answers. When an *IC* indicates that a query must be *true*, the *IC* can be returned as a summary. For example, the query *'Which professors teach classes?'* would be answered by an *IC* that stated *'All professors teach classes.'* This is a type of *intensional* answer, as will be seen in the next section. In addition, *IC*s can identify logical redundancies in a query or subquery. For example, consider the query

$$\leftarrow \textit{student}(\textit{susan}),\ \textit{enrolled}(\textit{susan}). \qquad (\mathcal{Q}_4)$$

to a database that has the associated *IC*

$$\subset student(X),\ not\ enrolled(X). \qquad (IC_2)$$

which states that all students are necessarily enrolled. This means that the query is overspecified. Simply asking

$$\leftarrow student(susan). \qquad (\mathcal{Q}_5)$$

would be equivalent. If Susan is indeed a student, a cooperative response would say

'Yes, Susan is a student.
By the way, all students are enrolled.'

3.4 Intensional answers

Instead of always responding to a query with a substitution for the variables in the query, it is sometimes more appropriate to provide the user with an *intensional* answer. An intensional answer denotes the complete set of answers, or some subset thereof, to a given query. Query Q_4, which stated *'Which students are enrolled?'* was overspecified since all students were necessarily enrolled. Enumerating the answers, say, *chris*, *terry*, *josé*, *carol*, ... is misleading, unless it is believed that the user knows that this enumeration constitutes the set of all students. Thus, the answer $\forall X.student(X)$ is better. Such an answer is called a *universal* answer as it is a universally quantified formula.

Motro [48] draws a distinction between *data* and *knowledge*. In deductive databases, the data are represented in the *EDB*, and *knowledge* in the *IDB* and $\mathcal{IC}$. Knowledge is the semantics of the database, that which must be *true* of the database's state, and the logical conclusions that must follow from given data. Usually, answers to a query are only in terms of data. Cooperative answers incorporate knowledge in the response. In particular, *IAs* are in terms of knowledge, not data.

Intensional answers (*IAs*) can be more informative than enumerated answers. They can teach users about the structure of the database and of the domain and help to clear up misconceptions. Intensional answers can be more succinct than concrete answers; this is an important cooperative behaviour when databases contain huge stores of data. Users are often overwhelmed by the size of the responses to their queries. In logic programs, it is possible for a query to have an infinite answer set. *IAs* can be used to characterize answer sets of infinite cardinality [10].[10] Intensional answers can be provided in lieu of concrete answers when the database system is under time and computational constraints [30].

[10]This will not occur in the case of deductive databases, which contain no function symbols, but can occur in the case of logic programs, which do allow function symbols.

Let us formalize the notion of *IA*s. Let the query be an existential query (Section 2.3), $\exists\vec{v}.\mathcal{Q}$. ($\mathcal{Q}$ here is not the negated formula for refutation.) Let $\vec{v}$ be the vector of all the variables of $\mathcal{Q}$. Let $\mathcal{F}$ be a formula over $\vec{v}$ and $\vec{u}$ where $\vec{u}$ are the variables that occur in $\mathcal{F}$ but not in $\mathcal{Q}$. The vector $\vec{u}$ can be empty. Three definitions are considered: $\forall\vec{v}, \exists\vec{u}.\mathcal{F}$ is an intensional answer of the query $\mathcal{Q}$ *iff* **I**, **II**, or **III** alternatively:

$$\begin{array}{rll} \mathbf{I}.\forall\vec{v}\,\exists\vec{u}.\ \mathcal{F} \Longleftrightarrow \mathcal{Q} & & \text{(equivalence)} \\ \mathbf{II}.\forall\vec{v}\,\exists\vec{u}.\ \mathcal{F} \Longrightarrow \mathcal{Q} & & \text{(sufficiency)} \\ \mathbf{III}.\forall\vec{v}\,\exists\vec{u}.\ \mathcal{F} \Longleftarrow \mathcal{Q} & & \text{(necessity)} \end{array}$$

First, we must consider how *IA*s can be computed. The number of potential *IA*s for a query is infinite since an *IA* is a formula over the (non-empty) theory of the database, and there are an infinite number of tautologies. We want to find only the interesting ones. One notion of *IA*s is that they are partial evaluations of the query. In a resolution based refutation proof procedure such as *SLD-resolution* [39], the query is *rewritten* at each step (in a deductive, sound manner) by a clause from the database until the empty clause remains. (A goal atom is removed from the goal list when it unifies with a fact.) The resulting substitution is an answer:

$$\begin{array}{ll} \textbf{Rules:} & B \leftarrow C_1, C_2. \\ & \vdots \\ \hline \mathbf{G}_0\textbf{:} \leftarrow A_1, A_2, \ldots, A_m. & \\ \mathbf{G}_1\textbf{:} \leftarrow (C_1, C_2, A_2, \ldots, A_m)\,\theta_1. & A_1\theta_1 = B\theta_1 \\ \vdots & \\ \mathbf{G}_n\textbf{:} \leftarrow \Box \quad \text{Answer} = \theta_1 \cdots \theta_{n-1} & \end{array}$$

The query is $\mathbf{G}_0$ above. The substitution $\theta_1 \cdots \theta_{n-1}$ at step $\mathbf{G}_n$ is an answer to the query. Once the definition for answer is revised to be any formula (meeting criterion **II** above) rather than simply being a substitution, any of the partial solutions above, $\mathbf{G}_1, \ldots, \mathbf{G}_{n-1}$, may be considered as *IA*s. These are intermediate answers between the concrete answers found at the leaves of the solution tree and the query at the root. These *IA*s are dependent on the search (proof) tree. Another notion of intensional answer is that it characterizes a set of answers (substitutions) in some natural way, independent of the search tree.

Imielinski [30] started the work in intensional answers. He defined an intensional answer to be a rewrite of the query that preserves its semantics. This satisfies the strict equivalence definition (**I**) for *IA*s. In the degenerate case, a query is an intensional answer to itself. The rewritten formula, the *IA*, denotes the same answers as the query. For an *IA* to be an adequate answer, it must satisfy the user as being a sufficient, understandable characterization of the ground answers to the query. Obviously, the query itself is an *IA* by Imielinski's definition; however, it is not an adequate answer, since otherwise the user would not have asked the query.

EDB: *prerequisite* ('*MATH-300*', '*MATH-350*').
prerequisite ('*MATH-350*', '*MATH-400*').
teaches (*smith*, '*MATH-400*').

IDB: *teaches* (*X*, *Y*) ← *teaches* (*X*, *Z*), *prerequisite* (*Y*, *Z*).

Q: *Q* (*A*) ← *teaches* (*smith*, *A*). $(\mathcal{Q}_6)$

IA: *Q* (*A*) ← *prerequisite* (*A*, *B*). $(\mathcal{C}_2)$
Q ('*MATH-400*'). $(\mathcal{C}_3)$

The *IA* in response to the query Q_6 is composed of the clause C_2 and the fact C_3. If C_2 and C_3 were added to the database and the query $\langle \leftarrow Q(A).\rangle$ asked, the same answers would result as do with query Q_6.

Cholvy and Demolombe [8, 9] consider *IA*s under the sufficiency criterion (**II**). An *IA* represents sufficient conditions for a query to be *true* if all ground substitutions of the *IA* are correct (ground) answers to the query. They focus on *IA*s that are *invariant*. An *IA* is *invariant* if it implies the query by the sufficiency criteria under *any* state of the database [48]. If an *IA* is based only on the *IDB* and $\mathcal{IC}$ (does not include any facts from the *EDB*) and would still remain an answer to the query regardless of any changes to the *EDB*, then the *IA* is an invariant answer to the query. The intensional answer to query Q_6 above is not invariant because it includes extensional information, *Q* ('*MATH-400*'), derived from a fact in the *EDB*, namely *teaches* (*smith*, '*MATH-400*'). Consider the following database and the query about who receives bonuses:

EDB: *started* (*michael*, *1979*). *commended* (*carol*).
started (*josé*, *1985*). *commended* (*chris*).
started (*susan*, *1987*).

IDB: *bonus* (*P*) ← *started* (*P*, *D*), *today* (*N*),
elapsed (*N*, *D*, *Y*), $Y \geq 10$. $(\mathcal{C}_4)$
bonus (*P*) ← *commended* (*P*). $(\mathcal{C}_5)$

Q: ← *bonus* (*P*). $(\mathcal{Q}_7)$

A's: '*Everyone who has worked here for 10 years or more.*' $(\mathcal{A}_1)$
'*Everyone who has been commended.*' $(\mathcal{A}_2)$

The ground answers to query Q_7 are {*michael*, *carol*, *chris*}. However, these three do not receive bonuses for the same reason. Carol and Chris get bonuses because they were commended, A_2, while Michael gets a bonus because he has been employed for more than ten years, A_1. Answer A_1 is a paraphrase of rule C_4, answer A_2 of rule C_5. These are invariant answers that will always be true with respect to query Q_7 (until the *IDB* changes). These answers may be better in the sense that they explain the semantics behind who gets a bonus rather than just listing the people.

The *IA*s that Cholvy and Demolombe can find may be less direct than A_1 and A_2 above. This is the simplistic case in which each *IA* derives directly from a rule. Rules and *IC*s may interact to result in new *IA*s. The *IA*s may not be obvious, but they still offer correct, and often insightful, characterizations of answers to the query.

It is necessary to find a small finite set of *interesting IA*s from among the potentials for a given query. One criterion Cholvy and Demolombe use is to find only *IA*s that are not logically subsumed (a syntactic check) by any others. This will result in a finite set. They introduce other criteria as well. Their *IA*s are limited to a vocabulary of interest (predicates and constants) defined for a user. Spurious *IA*s that are not meaningful to the user will not be produced.

Motro in [47] and Pirotte, Roelants, and Zimanyi in [53, 54] also consider intensional answers based on the residues as seen in Chakravarthy, Grant, and Minker's work [4, 5, 6] and Gal and Minker's work [22, 23, 24]. They use the residues to identify necessary conditions of answers (criterion **III**) and report these conditions along with the answers as a cooperative style. Like Gal, Pirotte, Roelants, and Zimanyi note that the residues from semantic compilation are knowledge in Motro's sense and are a type of intensional answer. Their work is subsumed by [4, 5, 6, 7, 22, 24].

Another approach is taken by Shum and Muntz [60], who consider *IA*s under the necessity criterion (**III**). Answers to queries which consist of exhaustive lists of values may be represented more succinctly by class descriptions. For example, the query *'Who works from 9 to 5?'* might have {*tom, sue, ann, mary*} as its answer set. If these people constitute all the employees except for Carol and José, then $employee(X) \wedge X \neq \text{carol} \wedge X \neq \text{josé}$ is an *IA*. A simpler, alternative answer would be {4/6 *employees*} since the set constitutes four out of six employees in total in the database. Schum and Muntz's technique requires an explicit type taxonomy over the database domain. This considers the notion of intensional answers as *necessary* conditions on answers as well as sufficient conditions.

Say that Tom and Sue constitute all the secretaries and that Ann and Mary constitute all the technicians in the database above. Then the answer may be represented as {*secretaries, technicians*}. Corella [15, 16] describes how to obtain expressions that are equivalent to the extension of the query (criterion **I**) by finding a set of *types* (unary predicates in the first-order predicate calculus) that when joined together cover all the answers and only the answers.

3.5 Generalizations

Another type of cooperative strategy is to rewrite a query in a generalized form. The scope of the query is extended so that more information can be gathered in the answers. One might seek and include information on related topics, using heuristics and past queries to deduce which topics are of interest to a user. Alternatively, one might look for answers that are related to the original answers, but are not necessarily literal answers to the original query.

Cuppens and Demolombe [17] give methods to rewrite the query so that variables are added to the query vector which carry relevant information for the user. For example, the query

$$\leftarrow \textit{travel}(\textit{washington},\ \textit{toulouse}).$$

might be modified so that its answer reports cost. They define a meta-level definition of a query that specifies the query in three parts: *entity*, *condition*, and *retrieved attributes*. Answers to queries provide values for the variables designated by the retrieved attributes. Methods are defined to extend the retrieved attributes according to heuristics about *topics of interest* to the user. All attributes from the original query along with any new added attributes appear in the rewritten query.

Cuppens and Demolombe [17] also introduced the notion of loosening some of the 'constraints' in a query to find answers close to those asked for. For instance, someone might ask

$$\leftarrow \textit{flight}(\textit{No},\ \textit{'Orly'},\ \textit{'Dulles'},\ \textit{Time}),\ \textit{Time} \geq \textit{17:00},\ \textit{Time} \leq \textit{21:00}.$$

An answer could be returned *flight*(*delta714*, *'Orly'*, *'Dulles'*, *21:05*), even though it does not strictly match the query. It is assumed that the user might be interested in this 'close' answer.

Wahlster, Marburger, Jameson, and Busemann in [63] allow for over-answering of yes/no questions when further questions are anticipated from the user on the same topic. Just as Janas's answers [31], which identify the part of the query that fails, may save the system processing time by eliminating futile follow-up questions, these responses can eliminate the need for many queries to be asked. Their method provides the user with the information he or she probably needs without necessitating that the user engage in an exhaustive question/answer session. Their system employs domain knowledge to ascertain which types of follow-up questions are likely.

Q: *'Has a yellow car gone by?'*
The system adds that the user will want to know where it went by.

Q′: *'Has a yellow car gone by? If so, where?'*

A: *'Yes, one went by on Hartungstreet.'*

In the relational database community, Chu, Chen, and Lee [11, 12] have explored an *abstraction/refinement* method for providing related answers to the original query, pursuing this notion of close answers. A query is abstracted into a more general query that is then refined into a set of new queries to be evaluated against the database. The abstraction and refinement rely on the database having explicit hierarchies of the relations and of the terms in the domain. Chu *et al.* [11, 12] define such a structure, called the *type abstraction hierarchy.* A query rewrite is accomplished by replacing relations and terms from the query by corresponding relations and terms from higher in the hierarchy. The resulting query is considered more general than the original.

Along similar lines, we have introduced a cooperative method called *relaxation* for expanding deductive database and logic programming queries [20]. The relaxation method expands the scope of a query by relaxing the logical constraints implicit in the query. Thus, the database may return answers related to the original query as well as the literal answers themselves:

$$\begin{aligned} &\mathit{travel}(\mathit{From},\ \mathit{To}) \leftarrow \mathit{serves\_area}(A,\ \mathit{From}),\ \mathit{serves\_area}(B,\ \mathit{To}), \\ &\qquad\qquad\qquad\qquad \mathit{flight}(A,\ B)^{*}. \end{aligned} \qquad (\mathcal{C}_6)$$

$$\leftarrow \mathit{flight}(\text{'Dulles'},\ \text{'JFK'}). \qquad (\mathcal{Q}_8)$$

$$\begin{aligned} &\leftarrow \mathit{serves\_area}(\text{'Dulles'},\ \mathit{From}),\ \mathit{serves\_area}(\text{'JFK'},\ \mathit{To}), \\ &\quad \mathit{travel}(\mathit{From},\ \mathit{To}). \end{aligned} \qquad (\mathcal{Q}_9)$$

Query Q_8 seeks a flight from Washington's Dulles airport to New York City's JFK. If no adequate flights can be found,[11] then the query can be relaxed to query Q_9 to look for other means of travel. The clause C_6 is marked as a *reciprocal* clause (marked with a '*' in the body), meaning that it can be used in an abductive direction to relax a query to a more general query, for instance Q_8 to Q_9. (The marked atom, *flight* $(A,\ B)$ in C_6, unifies an atom in the query and is replaced by the head of the clause and the other atoms in the body. See [20].)

Our relaxation method is a general approach to seek additional answers to a query that may or may not be of direct interest to the user. We plan to extend this work to consider user models and user preferences to help determine when a query relaxation might be relevant. In the system *FLEX*, Motro proposes allowing the user to select directions of relaxation, and thus to indicate which relaxed answers may be of interest [49]. We have

---

[11] A real query would specify much more, such as time, date, and cost.

also considered meta-interpreter methods to provide users with choices of relaxed queries, allowing the user to navigate the database [20].

4 User goals and models

In query/answer systems, user interfaces, and human–machine interactions, much attention has been paid to classifying and characterizing users. Knowing more about a given user, a system can better attend to a person's questions. We do not attempt to survey the area of user modelling fully. This is a large and rich field, much outside the limited scope of this survey. In this section, we review the work that is relevant within cooperative answering.

In the previous section, the focus was on cooperative answering styles that are universal: they pertain to all users and questions in the same way. For instance, Grice's maxims should be adhered to in all cooperative dialogue. But, beyond these basics of cooperative response, different users have different interests, needs, and intentions. The better the system can detect these, the better the response and service it can provide the user. This requires the system to know of particular users and to have models of users. It requires the system to be able to detect interests, needs, and intentions in the dialogue with the user. The system must be capable of employing this information to tailor answers to best satisfy these criteria.

Three types of knowledge about a user are relevant to cooperative answering:

1. interests and preferences;
2. needs; and
3. goals and intent.

Interests and preferences (1) direct the content and type of answers that should be provided. Cuppens and Demolombe [17] rewrite queries to include more information than would the original query that is of interest to the user. (Refer back to Section 3.5.) They claim extensibility of their work to incorporate user models. The models would identify *topics of interest* for different users and classes of users. The query rewrite mechanism would be directed to rewrite queries in order to include the relevant information of interest to a particular user, but directed to avoid explicitly including information that is not of interest.

Preferences (soft constraints) are met if possible, but are abandoned when they are at odds with the hard constraints of the query. If answers are provided sequentially (in a top–down manner as in *PROLOG*), then preferences can dictate the order in which answers are found and presented.

Answers that meet the preferences *best* are presented first, while those meeting the preferences most poorly are saved until last.

Needs (2) may vary from user to user as well. A user may be well-versed or may be naïve in the system's domain. The type and level of detail of answers will depend on the user's experience. The appropriateness of different potential responses can be evaluated with respect to the user's needs. Paris in [51, 52] addresses the user's level of expertise in the content of the answer.

Q: *'What is a telephone?'*

System knows user is an engineer. Then
A_1: *(technical description of parts and how they work)*
System knows user is an eight-year old. Then
A_2: *(visual description of object and what it does)*

The two answers use different vocabulary and describe different properties of the telephone.

User constraints are introduced in [21] and formalized in [18]. The notion of user constraints (*UC*s) is analogous to that of integrity constraints in deductive databases. A *UC* is of the same syntactic form as an *IC*, but does not have the same meaning; an *IC* needs to be logically consistent with the database, whereas a *UC* does not. A *UC* dictates what answers are acceptable to the user and filters out unacceptable answers. To a certain extent, the same mechanisms for finding residues from *IC*s in semantic query optimization can be used for *UC*s. Unlike residues from *IC*s, these *UC* residues will block search space that does contain answers, but only answers that are not of interest to the user anyway.

Goals and intent (3) do not vary inherently from user to user; rather, they vary from session to session and depend on what the user is attempting to accomplish at the time. Past dialogue, user models, and other factors can help a system to determine the probable goals and intents of the user. A number of researchers [1, 2, 34, 55, 63, 65] try to determine user goals in order to choose cooperative information.

Of course, it is possible for the system to assume things incorrectly. Short of the ability to ask the user directly why certain information has been requested (and the ability to comprehend the user's response), the system will be prone to mistakes. So, while accounting for users' goals and intent can be a powerful addition to a cooperative answering system, it can also be dangerous. The risk is that when the system is wrong about what the user really wants, the answers it gives can be more uncooperative than if the system did not consider the users' goals and intent at all. Special care must be taken to minimize the costs of such mistakes.

Allen and Perrault [1, 2] seek to detect user goals to help identify potential obstacles to the user meeting the goal. Allen's interest is in temporal issues and knowledge about time and how assumptions about time should affect responses to a user. His work conceptually extends Cuppens and Demolombe's idea [17] in which user models dictate what information to add to the answers (via rewriting the query) by accounting for the user's current goals. For instance,

Q: *'When does the Windsor train leave?'*

A: *'At 4:00 p.m. (five minutes from now), at gate 7.'*

The answer offers two cooperative pieces of information beyond the literal answer. First, it warns the user that the train is leaving in five minutes, an obstacle if the user is trying to catch the train. Second, it tells the user about the gate number, potentially important if this is not the usual gate or if it is somewhat distant from the user's current location.

Pollack [55] detects how the questions that users ask fit into their plans. Then answers that facilitate a user's plan will be given. The answer should, in essence, help to solve the user's problem. Suppose a user has typed a *cntl-Z* during a **vi** editing session and wants to *undo* the results. The user might ask:

Q: *'In the* **vi** *editor, how can I delete cntl-Z?'*

A: *'Cntl-Z has stopped your* **vi** *process.*
Type 'fg' *to resume it.'*

Once the system realizes the goal, it can reinterpret the query and give a response that helps in achieving the goal.

Carberry [3] emphasizes the dynamic construction of a model of the user's current task-related plan during the user/system dialogue. Such a model can be used to identify conflicts that arise between a user's questions and supposed plan. Misconceptions as considered in Section 3.3 arise from conflicts between the user's world view (as indicated by his or her queries) and the system's world knowledge. With a model of the user's task, possible further misconceptions can be identified when the user's queries and task at hand do not align. Care must be taken to try to determine when such an alignment is due to a misconception and when it is due to changes in the user's plan or to mistakes in the system's assumptions and modelling of the plan.

These ideas have been incorporated in the *IREPS* system (Intelligent REsPonse System), part of a research effort at the University of Delaware to provide a robust natural language interface for information systems. A component called *TRACK* infers the user's task-related plan. The heuristics and processing strategies employed are domain-independent; only the domain-dependent plans and goals must be provided for a given application domain.

McCoy in [43] extends her work as discussed in Section 3.3 to consider user models and to respond to misconceptions that a given user may be known to hold. A model of what the user believes cues the system about misconceptions that this user may have. The system has a set of basic, general strategies to resolve misconceptions of the user. Given a particular misconception, a suitable strategy is chosen to resolve it by adding appropriate statements to the response.

Quilici, Dyer, and Flowers [57] also seek to recognize and respond to plan-oriented misconceptions. They consider advice-seeking dialogues between an advisor (an automated system) and a novice (the user). A cooperative response consists of explaining the beliefs of the system that conflict with the user's supposed beliefs in order to resolve the user's misconception. Similar to McCoy's explanation strategies [43], they provide a taxonomy of domain-independent explanations as strategies for resolving different kinds of potential misconceptions.

Quilici, Dyer, and Flowers present a UNIX advisor based on their system for answering UNIX users' questions when they do not understand the results of their actions [57]. This is based on a system called *AQUA* developed at the University of California Los Angeles. The *AQUA* system infers users' beliefs, determines which are incorrect, and attempts to trace the cause of the beliefs. The system has an extended representation schema in order to store information about users' plans.

5 Cooperative answering at the University of Maryland

At the University of Maryland at College Park, we are engaged in building a cooperative answering facility for deductive databases. The system adds many of the cooperative behaviours and methods discussed previously to the deductive database query interface. Goals are that it

1. be a uniform system;
    - defined in, and implemented through, logic
    - a uniform representation and support for all the cooperative methods;
2. be portable, and
    - a general approach for relational and deductive databases and for logic programs;
    - domain-independent—applies to any relational or deductive database schema and state, and to any logic program;

3. have a natural language interface;
   - accept natural language queries;
   - provide cohesive and coherent responses in natural language.

Most of the cooperative methods we have considered in this chapter have been implemented independently and employ different computational strategies. The need remains to integrate these methods and behaviours into a uniform system. All should rely on the same representations and the same computational strategies.

Our platform is deductive databases. Data is stored as the *EDB*, *knowledge* via the *IDB* and $\mathcal{IC}$. The semantic query optimization technology of Chakravarthy, Grant, and Minker [4, 5, 6] provides a general strategy for finding conflicts and interactions between queries and *IC*s. This yields a uniform approach to handling misconceptions. Logic programming (we are using *PROLOG* for our implementation) offers us not just a uniform knowledge representation, but also a viable programming platform for handling the different cooperative methods in a general, uniform manner.

Deductive database and knowledge base systems often use an *interpreter* to read queries and to apply a proof procedure to find answers. For knowledge bases in *PROLOG*, this is usually just *PROLOG*'s interpreter. A *meta-interpreter* in such systems is used to supercede the *PROLOG* interpreter and can effect specialized behaviour over the interpreter. A meta-interpreter reads clauses, queries, and *IC*s as data and can manipulate them to affect different control and query answering strategies. A meta-interpreter is often called a *shell* after the user-interactive shells of operating systems and interpreted environments. The following shell, *relax_solve/1*, is a simple *PROLOG* shell that enacts query relaxations as discussed in Section 3.5:

```
relax_solve(As)  ←  relaxing(As, Bs),
                    solve(Bs).

relaxing([A|As], [A|Bs])  ←  relaxing(As, Bs).
relaxing([A|As], Bs)  ←  clause(relax(A), Cs),
                         relaxing(Cs, Ds),
                         relaxing(As, Es),
                         append(Ds, Es, Bs).
relaxing([], []).
```

This shell is very simplistic, but it illustrates how cooperative behaviour can be achieved for logic programs. In reality, we would want relaxation to occur breadth-first. Also, this shell relaxes the query automatically once the original query's solutions have been exhausted. It would be better to provide the user with a menu of relaxation choices [20]. Of course, relaxation is just one of the cooperative behaviours that we want in our shell.

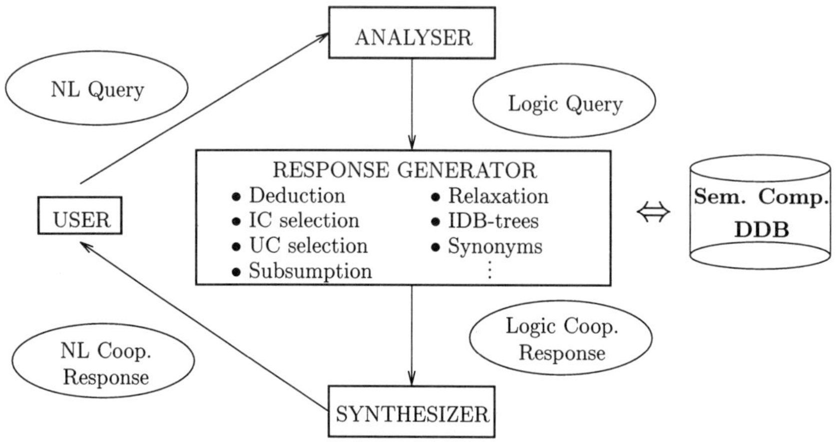

Figure 3: Flow chart of the cooperative answering system at Maryland.

We combine such meta-interpreters for the different cooperative behaviours into a single system.

Our cooperative answering system (Figure 3) is a comprehensive meta-interpreter for *PROLOG* deductive databases that affects many of the cooperative behaviours discussed. The meta-interpreter employs the *IC*s and rules of the database to produce cooperative answers. The system builds on the earlier systems of Gal and Lobo described in [22, 40].

The cooperative answering system is portable. The methods and strategies employed for producing cooperative answers are domain-independent and no special tailoring is needed for a given database domain. The system is easily used with a relational database system since a simple deductive database interface can be implemented on top of any relational system. The shell can also provide cooperative response in more complex knowledge bases represented by logic programs.

The system supports limited natural language input for some domains. Some queries can be posed in natural language text. (Others must be posed in logic.) As discussed in Section 2.1, this becomes important when databases are too big or complex for a user to have a clear picture of the whole schema. The natural language translator builds a logical query. The interface has a dictionary to map natural language terms into the proper database predicates and constants.

The system can produce natural language responses. This is the more important direction. Cooperative responses can be cumbersome since they may incorporate knowledge as well as data from the database. When presented as logical formulas, they can be difficult to understand even for seasoned logic programmers. Answers can be large, full of notation, and connections between concepts may not be clear.

Natural language can alleviate many of these problems [18]. A linguistically motivated natural language back-end is developed to provide cooperative natural language responses to queries. Anaphora helps remove notational redundancies and makes the answer text much more readable and, hence, understandable. Coordination collapses parallel structures into more concise sentences. Cohesion is a global property that assures the answer sentences form a cohesive response in which the components are related in clear, obvious ways and each contributes towards the answer. We have a response generator that uses these linguistic tools, as well as others that produce good natural language response.

The cooperative answering shell handles the following types of cooperative response:

- natural language interface [18, 22, 23, 24]
    - handles natural language queries
    - generates natural language responses;
- false presuppositions (see Section 3.2)
    - finding minimal failed subquery
    - maximal failed relaxation;
- misconceptions (constraint violations) (see Section 3.3)
    - *EDB* search
    - violations with respect to previous answers;
- explanations of derivation paths (proofs);
- positive cooperative information;
- employs heuristics to select best cooperative information [22];
- detects redundancy in the query;
- uses *UC*s to filter answers [18, 21];
- relaxation (menu-driven) [20]; and
- query decomposition.

Any violation of an *IC* by a query indicates a possible misconception on the user's behalf. The most general *IC* necessitating that the query fails is found. These *IC* violations are detected and reported to the user. Sometimes, a query may not conflict with any one *IC* from the $\mathcal{IC}$ set in particular, but the query having an answer would be in violation of the *IDB* and $\mathcal{IC}$ together. In this case, the query will conflict with a *derived* constraint, an *IC* that can be deduced from the *IDB* and $\mathcal{IC}$ and is thus *true* over the database. Then, the derived constraint is presented, along with its derivation. Different subgoals of the query may fail for different causes (each conflicts with a different *IC*). This requires that the failure of each subgoal be explained, and an explanation of the proof tree is also required to explain how these subgoals arose.

Sometimes, *IC*s may interact without indicating a cause for failure. Instead, such *IC*s offer semantic information about the query, other conditions that must be true for there to be an answer to the query. At times, it may be pertinent to include certain parts of this information in the answer.

A query may be overspecified. Some subquery may find all the answers that the query would find. Such a case may also indicate a misconception. This situation can also be detected by the shell when *IC*s show a query and a subquery to be semantically equivalent. An example of this is seen on page 18 in Section 3.3. Query Q_4 is equivalent to the subquery Q_5 due to IC_2.

If there are no misconceptions but the query still fails, false presuppositions are present in the query. The shell informs a user of false presuppositions. The minimal failed subqueries are found as in Janas's method. (Refer back to Section 3.2.) Once a failed subquery is identified, this query is relaxed to find the most general query that still fails. This failure is reported to the user.

There may at times be too much potential cooperative information to provide to the user. To provide all of it would violate the maxim of quantity and overwhelm the user. Choices must be made as to which information is to be included. For instance, a query failure due to a misconception is more pertinent than failure due to a false presupposition. A query that fails due to a misconception *must* fail, whereas a query that fails due to a false presupposition happens to fail given this state of the database, but it would not necessarily fail in some other state. Gal [22] presents a number of heuristics for deciding which cooperative information to include, abiding by the cooperative maxims as closely as possible.

*UC*s provide a means for modelling the user in the system [18, 21]. They are used to eliminate answers for a query that would violate the *UC*s of the particular user. Applicable *UC*s are attached to the query in an analogous manner to semantic query optimization for *IC*s. This effects a query rewrite, but unlike semantic query optimization it changes the meaning of the query in such a way that the rewrite only finds the answers that do not violate the *UCs*.

The system provides relaxed queries to the user once the original query has been exhausted. This way, if the user did not find the answers from the original query to be adequate, he or she may continue to navigate the database by selecting related (relaxed) queries to find related answers. The shell handles relaxation in an efficient manner. Also, repeat answers to the relaxed query are suppressed (avoided in the computation) since the user has already seen (and rejected) them [20].

A query is *disjoint* whenever it can be subdivided into two or more independent subqueries. The shell detects this and decomposes the query in such cases. This, and other such syntactic checks and optimizations, help catch users' mistakes and help to reduce the cost and overheads of the other cooperative techniques.

In our continuing research, we plan to

- integrate the mechanisms supporting the cooperative behaviours more fully
    - develop clear semantic support (in deductive databases) for cooperative answering
    - implement more efficient mechanisms for the different cooperative behaviours;

- provide a better user interface, and
    - provide a sophisticated, integrated natural language response generator
    - develop further the explanation facilities;

- add more cooperative behaviours and facilities
    - allow for useful *IAs*
    - incorporate Cuppens and Demolombe's style of query rewrites
    - further develop the theory of *UCs* and user models.

Work on the cooperative answering system at Maryland is an ongoing project. We shall continue to extend its functionality, improve its performance, and to research new cooperative techniques. We are also engaged in foundational research to map out the requisite knowledge and semantics needed to support cooperative behaviour at large, the requisite representations, and the requisite computational strategies for yielding cooperative response. Although the many cooperative behaviours discussed in this chapter may at first seem disparate, we are seeking a general classification for cooperative response and the universal representations and strategies that will be able to provide them.

6 Summary

In this chapter we have given a brief overview of the field of cooperative answering. Cooperative response is crucial to the success of automated query/answer systems. History has shown that providing *correct* answers to users is simply not enough. Ambiguities, misconceptions, and irrelevances plague such systems. As information systems play a more vital role in society, it is necessary that these problems be addressed.

Fortunately, a good deal of research has already been directed towards these ends, and exciting, promising work is underway. We have reviewed a number of disparate cooperative behaviours. Most of these cooperative techniques have been developed, but each in a different system, reliant on a different representation, and affected by different computational means. While much work remains to explore and develop new cooperative techniques, the current collection of cooperative response work needs to be pulled on to common ground.

Deductive databases offer a suitable platform for the development of uniform cooperative systems. Deductive databases provide a powerful, uniform representation via logic, semantics, and a computational means for effecting efficient cooperative response. Much high-quality work has been carried out in cooperative answering within the deductive database paradigm due to this natural fit. Both the fields of cooperative answering and deductive databases have benefited as a result. The cooperative answering system we have developed, based on logic, is indicative that it is a unifying framework for such systems.

Acknowledgements

This work was supported by the Air Force Office of Scientific Research under grant number AFSOSR-91-0350 and by the National Science Foundation under NSF grant number IRI-89-16059.

References

[1] J. Allen. *Natural Language Understanding.* The Benjamin/Cummings Publishing Company, Inc., Menlo Park, California, 1987.

[2] J. F. Allen and C. R. Perrault. Analyzing intention in utterances. In B. J. Grosz, K. S. Jones, and B. L. Weber, editors, *Readings in Natural Language Processing*, pages 441–458. Morgan Kaufmann Publishers, Inc., Los Altos, California, 1986.

[3] S. Carberry. Modeling the user's plans and goals. In Kobsa and Wahlster [37], pages 64–78. Special Issue on User Modeling.

[4] U. Chakravarthy. *Semantic Query Optimization in Deductive Databases.* PhD thesis, University of Maryland, Department of Computer Science, College Park, 1985.

[5] U. Chakravarthy, J. Grant, and J. Minker. Semantic query optimization: additional constraints and control strategies. In L. Kerschberg, editor, *Proceedings Expert Database Systems*, pages 259–269, Charleston, Apr. 1986.

[6] U. Chakravarthy, J. Grant, and J. Minker. Foundations of semantic query optimization for deductive databases. In J. Minker, editor, *Proceedings Workshop on Foundations of Deductive Databases and Logic Programming*, pages 67–101, Washington, D.C., August 18–22, 1986.

[7] U. Chakravarthy, J. Grant, and J. Minker. Logic based approach to semantic query optimization. *ACM Transactions on Database Systems*, 15(2):162–207, June 1990.

[8] L. Cholvy. Answering queries addressed to a rule base. *Revue d'intelligence artificielle*, 4(1):79–98, 1990.

[9] L. Cholvy and R. Demolombe. Querying a rule base. In L. Kershberg, editor, *Expert Database Systems*, Tysons Corner, VA, 1987.

[10] J. Chomicki and T. Imieliński. Relational Specifications of Infinite Query Answers. Technical Report CS-TR-2177, Department of Computer Science, University of Maryland, College Park, Md 20742, Jan. 1989.

[11] W. W. Chu, Q. Chen, and R. Lee. Cooperative query answering via type abstraction hierarchy. In S. M. Deen, editor, *Cooperating Knowledge Based Systems 1990*, pages 271–290. Springer-Verlag, University of Keele, U.K., 1991. *Proceedings of the International Working Conference on Cooperating Knowledge Based Systems*, 3-5 October 1990.

[12] W. W. Chu, Q. Chen, and R. Lee. A structured approach for cooperative query answering. *IEEE Transactions on Knowledge and Data Engineering*, 1992. To appear.

[13] CODASYL. *CODASYL Data Base Task Group April 71 Report.* ACM, New York, 1971.

[14] A. Colmerauer and J. Pique. About natural logic. In Gallaire *et al.* [26], pages 343–365.

[15] F. Corella. Semantic retrieval and levels of abstraction. In L. Kerschberg, editor, *Proceedings of the First International Workshop on Expert Database Systems, Volume II*, pages 397–420, 1984.

[16] F. Corella. *Mechanizing Set Theory.* PhD thesis, Corpus Christi College, and RC 14706, IBM Research Division, T.J. Watson Research Center, Yorktown Heights, New York 10598, 1989.

[17] F. Cuppens and R. Demolombe. Cooperative answering: a methodology to provide intelligent access to databases. In L. Kershberg, editor, *Proceedings of the Second International Conference on Expert Database Systems*, pages 333–353, George Mason University, April 25-27, 1988.

[18] T. Gaasterland. *Cooperative Answers for Database Queries.* PhD thesis, University of Maryland, Department of Computer Science, College Park, 1992. Dissertation work in progress.

[19] T. Gaasterland. Cooperative explanation in deductive databases. In A. Quilici, editor, *Working Notes: Symposium on Producing Cooperative Explanations*, AAAI Spring Symposium Series, Stanford University, Palo Alto, California, 1992.

[20] T. Gaasterland, P. Godfrey, and J. Minker. Relaxation as a platform of cooperative answering. In T. Imielinski, editor, *Proceedings of the First International Workshop on Nonstandard Queries and Answers*, pages 101–120, volume 2, Toulouse, France, July 1991.

[21] T. Gaasterland, J. Minker, and A. Rajasekar. Deductive database systems and knowledge base systems. In *Proceedings of VIA 90*, Barcelona, Spain, October 1990.

[22] A. Gal. *Cooperative Responses in Deductive Databases.* PhD thesis, Department of Computer Science, University of Maryland, College Park, 1988.

[23] A. Gal and J. Minker. Informative and cooperative answers in databases using integrity constraints. In V. Dahl and P. Saint-Dizier, editors, *Natural Language Understanding and Logic Programming*, pages 277–300. North Holland, 1988.

[24] A. Gal and J. Minker. A natural language database interface that provides cooperative answers. *Proceedings of the Second Conference on Artificial Intelligence Applications*, December 11-13, 1985.

[25] H. Gallaire and J. Minker, editors. *Logic and Databases.* Plenum Press, New York, Apr. 1978.

[26] H. Gallaire, J. Minker, and J.-M. Nicolas, editors. *Advances in Database Theory, Volume 1.* Plenum Press, New York, 1981.

[27] H. Gallaire, J. Minker, and J.-M. Nicolas. Logic and databases: a deductive approach. *ACM Computing Surveys*, **16**(2):153–185, June 1984.

[28] H. Grice. Logic and conversation. In P. Cole and J. Morgan, editors, *Syntax and Semantics.* Academic Press, 1975.

[29] J. Hirschberg. Scalar Quantity Implicature: A Strategy for Processing Scalar Utterances. Technical Report MS-CIS-83-10, Department of Computer and Information Science, the Moore School, the University of Pennsylvania, Philadelphia, PA 19104, May 1983.

[30] T. Imielinski. Intelligent query answering in rule based systems. In J. Minker, editor, *Foundations of Deductive Databases and Logic Programming.* Morgan Kaufman Publishers, Washington, D.C., 1988.

[31] J. M. Janas. On the feasibility of informative answers. In Gallaire *et al.* [26], pages 397–414.

[32] A. Joshi. Mutual beliefs in question answering systems. In Smith [61].

[33] A. Joshi, B. Webber, and I. Sag, editors. *Elements of Discourse Understanding.* Cambridge University Press, 1981.

[34] A. K. Joshi, B. L. Webber, and R. M. Weischedel. Living up to expectations: computing expert responses. In *Proceedings of the National Conference on Artificial Intelligence*, pages 169–175, University of Texas at Austin, Aug. 1984. The American Association for Artificial Intelligence.

[35] S. J. Kaplan. Appropriate responses to inappropriate questions. In Joshi *et al.* [33], pages 127–144.

[36] S. J. Kaplan. Cooperative responses from a portable natural language query system. *Artificial Intelligence*, *19*(2):165–187, Oct. 1982.

[37] A. Kobsa and W. Wahlster, editors. *Computational Linguistics*, volume 14(3). MIT Press for the Association of Computational Linguistics, Sept. 1988. Special Issue on User Modeling.

[38] W. Lehnert. A computational theory of human question answering. In Joshi *et al.* [33], pages 145–176.

[39] J. Lloyd. *Foundations of Logic Programming.* Springer Verlag, second edition, 1987.

[40] J. Lobo and J. Minker. A metaprogramming approach to semantically optimize queries in deductive databases. In L. Kerschberg, editor, *Proceedings of The Second International Conference on Expert Database Systems*, pages 387–420, Tysons Corner, Virginia, Apr. 1988.

[41] E. Mays. Correcting misconceptions about database structure. In *Proceedings of the CSCSI '80*, 1980.

[42] K. McCoy. Correcting object-related misconceptions. In *Proceedings of COLING10*, Stanford University, California, July 1984.

[43] K. McCoy. Reasoning on a highlighted user model to respond to misconceptions. In Kobsa and Wahlster [37], pages 64–78. Special Issue on User Modeling.

[44] K. McKeown. *Generating Natural Language Text in Response to Questions about Database Queries.* PhD thesis, University of Pennsylvania, 1982.

[45] J. Minker, editor. *Foundations of Deductive Databases and Logic Programming.* Morgan Kaufmann Pub., 1988.

[46] A. Motro. Extending the relational model to support goal queries. In *Proceedings from the First International Workshop on Expert Database Systems*, pages 129–150. Benjamin/Cummings, 1986.

[47] A. Motro. Using constraints to provide intensional answers to relational queries. In *Proceedings of the Fifteenth International Conference on Very Large Data Bases*, Aug. 1989.

[48] A. Motro. Responding with Knowledge to Database Queries (Tutorial and Survey), July 1991. Presented at the Proceedings of the First International Workshop on Nonstandard Queries and Answers held in Toulouse, France.

[49] A. Motro. FLEX: a tolerant and cooperative user interface to database. *IEEE Transactions on Knowledge and Data Engineering*, **2**(2):231–245, June 1990.

[50] A. Motro. SEAVE: a mechanism for verifying user presuppositions in query systems. *ACM Transactions on Office Information Systems*, **4**(4), October 1986.

[51] C. Paris. Combining discourse strategies to generate descriptions to users along a naïve/expert spectrum. In *Proceedings of IJCAI*, pages 626–632, Milan, Italy, August 23-28 1987.

[52] C. L. Paris. Tailoring object descriptions to a user's level of expertise. [37], pages 64–78. Special Issue on User Modeling.

[53] A. Pirotte and D. Roelants. Constraints for improving the generation of intensional answers in deductive databases. In *Proceedings of the Fifth IEEE International Conference on Data Engineering*, 1989.

[54] A. Pirotte, D. Roelants, and E. Zimanyi. Controlled generation of intensional answers. *IEEE Transactions on Knowledge and Data Engineering*, 1990.

[55] M. E. Pollack. Generating expert answers through goal inference. Technical report, SRI International, Stanford,CA, October 1983.

[56] M. E. Pollack, J. Hirschberg, and B. Webber. User participation in the reasoning processes of expert systems. In *Proceedings of the American Association of Artificial Intelligence 1982*, 1982.

[57] A. Quilici, M. Dyer, and M. Flowers. Recognizing and responding to plan-oriented misconceptions. [37], pages 38–51. Special Issue on User Modeling.

[58] R. C. Schank. *Conceptual Information Processing.* North-Holland, Amsterdam, 1975.

[59] J. Shepherdson. Negation as finite failure: a comparison of Clark's completed database and Reiter's closed world assumption. *J. Logic Programming*, **1**(15):51–79, June 1984.

[60] C. Shum and R. Muntz. Implicit representation for extensional answers. In L. Kershberg, editor, *Expert Database Systems*, Tysons Corner, VA, 1987.

[61] N. V. Smith, editor. *Mutual Knowledge.* Academic Press, 1982.

[62] J. D. Ullman. *Principles of Database and Knowledge-Base Systems, Volume 1.* Principles of Computer Science Series. Computer Science Press, Rockville, Maryland, 1988.

[63] W. Wahlster, H. Marburger, A. Jameson, and S. Busemann. Over-answering yes–no questions: extended responses in a NL interface to a vision system. In *Proceedings of IJCAI 1983*, Karlsruhe, West Germany, August 1983.

[64] B. L. Webber. Discourse model synthesis: preliminaries to reference. In Joshi *et al.* [33], pages 145–176.

[65] B. L. Webber and E. Mays. Varieties of user misconceptions: detection and correction. In *Proceedings of the Eighth International Joint Conference on Artificial Intelligence*, pages 650–652, Karlsruhe, Germany, Aug. 1983.

2

CoBase: a cooperative database system*

Wesley W. Chu, Q. Chen, and M. Merzbacher

Abstract

This chapter proposes the use of the *type abstraction hierarchy (TAH)* as a framework for deriving *cooperative query answers* (CQA). The TAH integrates abstraction with the subsumption (is-a) and composition (part-of) semantics found in the type hierarchy. This framework provides a multi-level object representation that is an important aspect of cooperative query answering. *Patterns*, which specify one or more conditions on an object, are introduced as a small granularity structure with specific semantic information. Cooperative query answering uses the TAH and patterns to provide query relaxation, generalization, and specialization. Relaxation can be explicitly controlled by the user, implicitly performed by the system, or both. An explanation system is also included to present the relaxation path, as well as a nearness measure between the approximate answer and the exact answer.

The operations required for CQA may be added to any conventional query language. As an example, we present *CSQL*, a cooperative extension of SQL used in the CoBase project at UCLA. Experimental results reveal that the proposed type abstraction hierarchy and relaxation control provide an organized structure for representing concepts at different knowledge levels in various domains, and offers a systematic and efficient method for cooperative query answering.

1 Introduction

When making daily decisions, humans seldom have complete or exact information. Yet, traditional query processing systems accept only precisely specified queries, requiring users to fully understand the problem

*This work supported by DARPA contract N00174-91-C-0107.

domain and the database structure and content. Further, traditional systems offer only exact answers, returning limited null information if the precise answer is not available. *Cooperative query answering* (*CQA*) [4, 5, 6, 9, 11, 13, 20] is an extension to the classical database notation that remedies these shortcomings.

Cooperative query answering provides neighbourhood or generalized information relevant to the original query and within a certain semantic distance of the exact answer. To do this, the CQA system enlarges the scope of the query by broadening the search range to areas near to the original query. Queries with no exact answer can be broadened until an approximate answer is found; even queries with limited answers can be extended to find additional approximate answers. For example, in response to a query about a specific flight departing at 9 a.m. from LAX airport in Los Angeles to Dulles airport near Washington, the system may return all the *morning* flights from airports within the Los Angeles *area* to airports within the Washington *area*. Using the same techniques, cooperative query answering is also able to answer imprecisely specified queries.

A cooperative query answering system requires the support of different knowledge representations at different abstraction levels and query transformations between these levels. Enlarging and shrinking a query scope is accomplished by shifting the queried objects between different levels of abstraction. Thus, our solution to cooperative query answering uses a multi-level knowledge representation.

Although the link between object representations at different knowledge levels can be made using explicit rules [9, 21, 14], such rules lack a systematic organization to guide the query transformation process. As a result, it is difficult to scale-up or combine rule based systems. We propose the *type abstraction hierarchy* (TAH) data structure as an efficient organized framework for coupling data and knowledge for cooperative query processing.

In this chapter we introduce the type abstraction hierarchy and demonstrate its use for neighbourhood and conceptual query answering. We introduce the cooperative extension to SQL, *CSQL*, and show how it can be used to control relaxation and search in the TAH. Based on query context and the user profile, a relaxation manager trims the TAH to limit the search scope and reduce the number of relaxed query answers. Finally, we present an implementation of CoBase.

2 Cooperative answering via abstraction hierarchies

There are three kinds of objects in a relational database, each of which may be abstracted. Attribute values, tuples, and relations can be abstracted separately or in conjunction.

Attribute value abstraction, or *value abstraction*, is a method for changing a single attribute value into a range of nearby values. A query is relaxed by taking one or more of its conditions and relaxing it to an approximate range. For example,

$airport$ = 'LAX'

can be abstracted to the conceptual attribute

$area$ = 'Los Angeles'

and then specialized back to a set of values

$airport$ = 'LAX', 'Burbank' or 'Long Beach'

Multiple levels of abstraction are allowed, so the *area* conceptual attribute may be generalized further to

$region$ = 'Southern California'

then specialized back, and so on.

Tuple abstraction organizes the tuples in each relation into abstraction groups. A tuple may belong to multiple abstraction groups. To find the tuples near to a given target tuple, first determine the abstraction groups to which the tuple belongs and then find the other tuples in those abstraction groups. Those tuples are valid approximations of the target.

Tuple abstraction is approximated in CoBase by simultaneous relaxation of the attributes forming the tuple using value abstraction. For example, in an airline database with each airline storing its flights in a separate relation, the American Airlines tuple,

AA_flight(LAX, Dulles, 10am, 6pm, #076)

may be relaxed by respectively relaxing each of the attribute values to:

AA_flight(Los Angeles, Washington, morning, afternoon, any flight)

Since a higher-level and more abstract object representation corresponds to multiple lower-level and more specialized object representations, querying

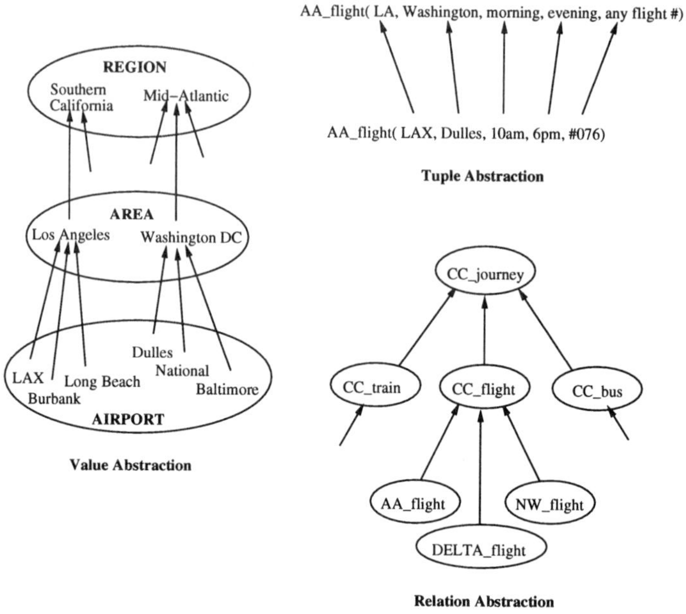

Figure 1: Abstract representations.

an abstractly represented object is equivalent to querying multiple specialized objects.

Relation abstraction allows the relation itself to be approximated. In the example above, the relation 'AA_flight' might be relaxed to the abstraction cross-country flight ('CC_flight'), which also represents flights in the relations for other airlines. Further, since CC_flight is a conceptual relation, it only need contain the attributes distinguishing it. The flight number attribute can be dropped, since it may have any value at this level of abstraction.

CC_flight(Los Angeles, Washington, morning, afternoon)

As in the other cases, multiple layers of abstraction are possible. CC_flight may join with cross-country Bus and Train trips to form:

CC_journey(Los Angeles, Washington)

In this case the departure and arrival times have been removed from the abstraction. Queries conditions on departure and arrival will be ignored at this level of abstraction, but enforced when the query is specialized back down to the instance level.

Together, the three kinds of abstraction (shown in Figure 1) form the *Type Abstraction Hierarchy*, the principal data structure for cooperative query answering used in CoBase.

The notion of multi-level object representation is not captured by the conventional semantic network and object-oriented database approaches. Grouping objects into a class and grouping several classes into a superclass only provide a common 'title' (type) for the involved objects without concern for the object instance values and without introducing abstract object representations. Grouping several objects together and identifying their aggregation as a single (complex) object does not provide abstract instance representations for its component objects. Therefore, an object-oriented database deals with information only at two general layers: the meta-layer and the instance layer. Since forming an object-oriented-type hierarchy does not introduce new instance values, it is impossible to introduce an additional instance layer. In the type abstraction hierarchy, instances of a supertype and a subtype may have different representations and can be viewed at different instance layers. Such multiple layer knowledge representation is essential for cooperative query answering.

The type abstraction hierarchy is instance-representation-based and consists of the following key aspects:

- The value abstraction mechanism for atomic and composed object representations.
- An abstraction relationship between all layers in the hierarchies. In all cases, a supertype object conveys a *more abstract representation* than its subtype object. For example, attribute type *area* is a supertype of attribute type *airport*, and tuple type *CC_flight* is a supertype of tuple type *AA_flight*.
- A formalism for integrating the abstraction view of type hierarchy with the subsumption (is_a) and composition (part_of) views of the type hierarchy, described in Section 3.1.

As shown above, our notion of abstraction originates from different representations between atomic values at different levels. Context based relationships are stored in the database and can be combined to form an abstraction of complex values. Rewriting mechanisms are provided to transform object representations between different levels.

Translating a query between different abstraction levels is achieved by *query abstraction* and *query refinement*. This consists of converting object types, attribute names, and domain values between different knowledge levels. In general, a *query abstraction process* converts a query Q into a more abstract representation Q' through the following steps:

1. Identify a target to be abstracted. The target will usually be an attribute value, but can be a tuple or relation.

2. Find the appropriate supertype object for the target.

3. Convert any subparts of the target to their corresponding types (attributes associated with the same type may be named separately). This may be necessary for complex objects at any level.

4. Transform attributes referred to in the query to that of the supertype object through type generalization rewrite.

5. Transform conditions referred to in the query to those related to the supertype object through both type generalization rewrite and term generalization rewrite.

A *query refinement process* converts a query Q to more specific query representations $Q_1, Q_2, \ldots, Q_n$ according to the type abstraction hierarchy through the following steps:

1. Find the set of subtype objects through type specialization rewrites.

2. Provide conversions between the attributes and the corresponding types.

3. Based on each subtype, use type specialization rewrite to transform attributes referred to in the query to those in the subtype object.

4. Based on each subtype, use both type specialization rewrite and term specialization rewrite to transform conditions referred to in the query to those related to the sub-type object.

The query modification, either upward or downward, is invoked recursively depending on the requirement and knowledge availability. In the following sections, we shall present two typical cooperative query answering mechanisms based on the notion of type abstraction hierarchy.

2.1 Neighbourhood query answering

We first discuss the use of type abstraction hierarchy for supporting neighbourhood query answering. Instead of providing exact answers, neighbourhood query answering provides information of a wider range which may be helpful for the user. For example, assuming that a user tries to reserve a flight on DELTA airlines from LAX airport in Los Angeles to National airport in Washington D.C., if the request flight is unavailable, then an alternative but similar flight on DELTA or other airlines may be provided.

A neighbourhood query answer is obtained by transforming the given query Q up and down along the type abstraction hierarchy to reach the neighbouring objects. For an original query Q, the general processing steps are:

1. Search the exact type of objects required by the query Q. If this fails then go to the next step.
2. Move upward along the type abstraction hierarchy and rewrite the query to a more abstract one through a query abstraction process, i.e., $Q \to Q'$.
3. Move downward along the hierarchy and rewrite the query to more specific ones through a query refinement process, i.e., $Q' \to Q'$.

Three kinds of tables are used for neighbourhood query processing: the *relation_abstraction hierarchy* which describes the subtyping relationship among relations; the *domain-mapping table* which gives the relationship between attribute names and domain names, allowing attributes from the same domain to be named differently; and the *attribute value abstraction* which shows the mapping of instances for each pair of supertype and subtype or the corresponding instance values between a supertype and a range of subtype (e.g. 'morning' corresponds to '7am to 11am'). These tables describe knowledge representations at different knowledge levels which are stored in and managed by the database. Certain additional query language constructs to SQL are introduced, such as **within** for indicating set membership, **between** for indicating a range with an upper and a lower bound, and the relaxation operation '$\sim$' for object types or attributes.

We will show some examples based on the relation abstraction hierarchy shown in Figure 2, where 'DELTA' is the abbreviation for 'DELTA Airlines' and 'NW' for 'Northwest Airlines'. The notation '$\sim$' following an object type or an attribute in the original query indicates that it is relaxable. The domain-mapping table and the attribute value abstraction mapping tables partially illustrated in Tables 1 and 2 are used in these examples.

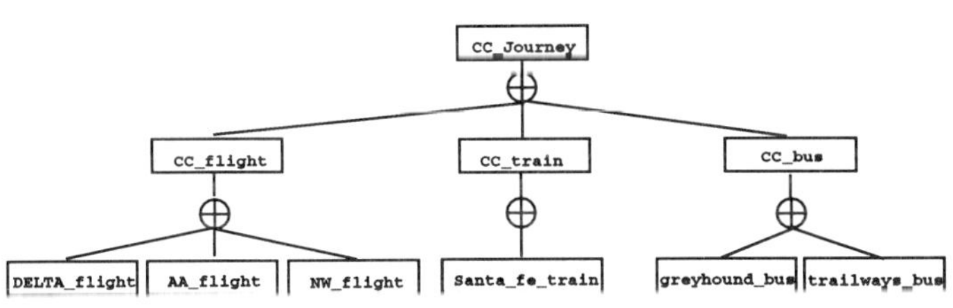

Figure 2: A relation abstraction hierarchy.

Table 1: Domain mapping table

Attribute name	**domain**
departure_time, arrival_time	time
departure_period, arrival_period	period
departure_airport, arrival_airport	airport
departure_area, arrival_area	area

In this example, only attribute relaxation occurs. **9am** on attribute *departure_time* is relaxed to **morning** on attribute (type) *departure_period* through a **query abstraction** process, which is further refined to **between <7am, 11am>** through a **query refinement** process. Since the resulting query condition **between <7am, 11am>** has wider coverage than the query condition **9am**, it provides query answers with a wider range.

Original query

select * from AA_flight
where *departure_time* ~= 9am
and *departure_airport* = 'Dulles'
and *arrival_airport* = 'LAX'.

Query abstraction

select * from AA_flight
where *departure_period* = 'morning'
and *departure_airport* = 'Dulles'
and *arrival_airport* = 'LAX'.

Query refinement

select * from AA_flight
where *departure_time* **between** < 7am, 11am>
and *departure_airport* = 'Dulles'
and *arrival_airport* = 'LAX'.

In the next example, both the attribute values and the relation of queried objects (airlines) are relaxed, and therefore the information returned covers more options on airlines, departure and arrival airports, and fares.

Table 2: Attribute value abstraction tables

time	**period**
<7am, 11am>	morning
<11am, 1pm>	noontime
<1pm, 7pm>	afternoon
<7pm, 11pm>	evening

airport	**area**
LAX, Burbank, Long Beach	Los Angeles
National, Dulles, Baltimore	Los Angeles

fare	**flight_cost**	**cost**
<301, 400>	flight_cost_low	reasonable
<401, 600>	flight_cost_medium	high
<601, 800>	flight_cost_high	high

fare	**train_cost**	**cost**
<251, 300>	train_cost_low	low
<301, 350>	train_cost_medium	reasonable
<351, 400>	train_cost_high	reasonable

fare	**bus_cost**	**cost**
<201, 250>	bus_cost_low	low
<251, 300>	bus_cost_medium	low
<301, 350>	bus_cost_high	reasonable

Original query

select * from **DELTA_flight** ~
where *departure_airport* ~= 'Long Beach'
and *arrival_airport* ~= 'Dulles'
and *fare* ~**between** <320, 350>

Query abstraction

select * from **CC_flight**
where *departure_area* = 'Los Angeles'

and *arrival_area* = 'Washington'
and *flight_cost* = 'flight_cost_low'

Query refinement

select * from **DELTA_flight**
where *departure_airport* **within** {'LAX', 'Burbank', 'Long Beach'}
and *arrival_airport* **within** {'National', 'Baltimore', 'Dulles'}
and *fare* **between** <301, 400>

select * from **AA_flight**
where *departure_airport* **within** {'LAX', 'Burbank', 'Long_Beach'}
and *arrival_airport* **within** {'National', 'Baltimore', 'Dulles'}
and *fare* **between** <301, 400>

select * from **NW_flight**
where *departure_airport* **within** {'LAX', 'Burbank', 'Long_Beach'}
and *arrival_airport* **within** {'National', 'Baltimore', 'Dulles'}
and *fare* **between** <301, 400>

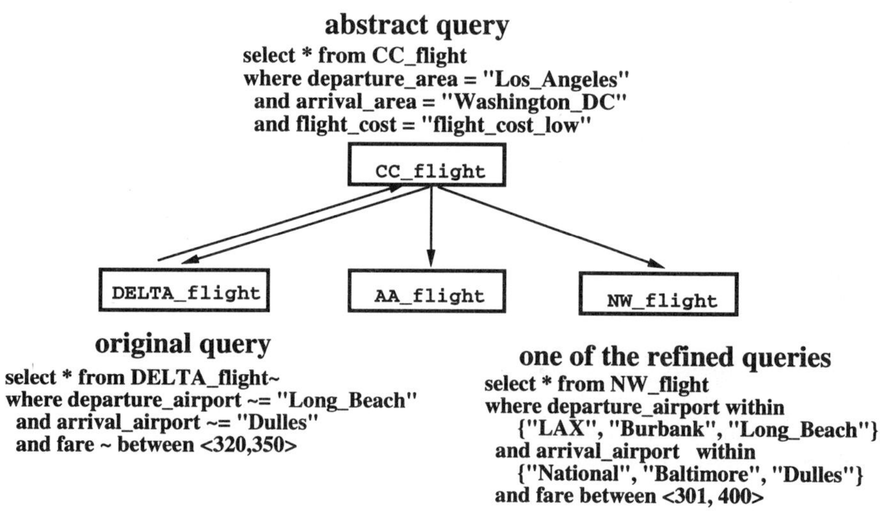

Figure 3: An example of neighbourhood query answering.

As shown in Figure 3, the last example can be extended to a two level query abstraction and refinement. First the query on **DELTA_flight** is abstracted to **CC_flight** that also covers airlines of type **AA_flight** and **NW_flight**, then the modified query is further abstracted to cover **CC_journey** that includes not only **CC_flight** but also **CC_train** and **CC_bus**. As a result, even more options may be provided by answering the queries refined from the above abstract query as shown in the following.

Original query

select * from **DELTA_flight** ~
where *departure_airport* ~= 'LAX'
and *arrival_airport* ~= 'National'
and *fare* ~**between** <320, 350>.

First step of query abstraction from DELTA_flight

select * from **CC_flight**
where *departure_area* = 'Los Angeles'
and *arrival_area* = 'Washington'
and *flight_cost* = 'flight_cost_low'.

Further query abstraction from CC_flight

select * from **CC_journey**
where *departure_area* = 'Los Angeles'
and *arrival_area* = 'Washington DC'
and *cost* = 'reasonable'

First step of query refinement from CC_journey

select * from **CC_flight**
where *departure_area* = 'Los Angeles'
and *arrival_area* = 'Washington'
and *flight_cost* = 'flight_cost_low'

select * from **CC_train**
where *departure_area* = 'Los Angeles'
and *arrival_area* = 'Washington'
and *train_cost* **within** {'train_cost_medium', 'train_cost_high'}

select * from **CC_bus**
where *departure_area* = 'Los Angeles'
and *arrival_area* = 'Washington'
and *bus_cost* = 'bus_cost_high'

Further query refinement from CC_flight

select * from **DELTA_flight**
where *departure_airport* **within** {'LAX', 'Burbank', 'Long_Beach'}
and *arrival_airport* **within** {'National', 'Baltimore', 'Dulles'}
and *fare* **between** <301, 400>

select * from **AA_flight**
where *departure_airport* **within** {'LAX', 'Burbank', 'Long_Beach'}
and *arrival_airport* **within** {'National', 'Baltimore', 'Dulles'}
and *fare* **between** <301, 400>

select * from **NW_flight**
where *departure_airport* **within** {'LAX', 'Burbank', 'Long_Beach'}
and *arrival_airport* **within** {'National', 'Baltimore', 'Dulles'}
and *fare* **between** <301, 400>

Further query refinement from CC_train

select * from **santa_fe_train**
where *departure_train_station* **within** {'Los Angeles', 'Long Beach'}
and *arrival_train_station* **within** {'DC', 'Fairfax'}
and *fare* **between** <301, 400>

Further query refinement from CC_bus

select * from **greyhound_bus**
where *departure_bus_station* **within** {'LA Downtown', 'Hollywood', 'Long Beach'}
and *arrival_bus_station* **within** {'DC Downtown', 'Rockville', 'Fairfax'}
and *fare* **between** <301, 350>

2.2 Conceptual query answering

In addition to neighbourhood query answering, the type abstraction hierarchy supports conceptual query answering. Often, a user has a question in mind but does not know *exactly* how to formulate the query. For example, if a user wants to obtain information about travelling from Los Angeles to Washington D.C., but is unfamiliar with the airline, bus, and train schedules, he cannot expect to phrase his queries accurately. The type abstraction mechanism is able to answer conceptual queries. With

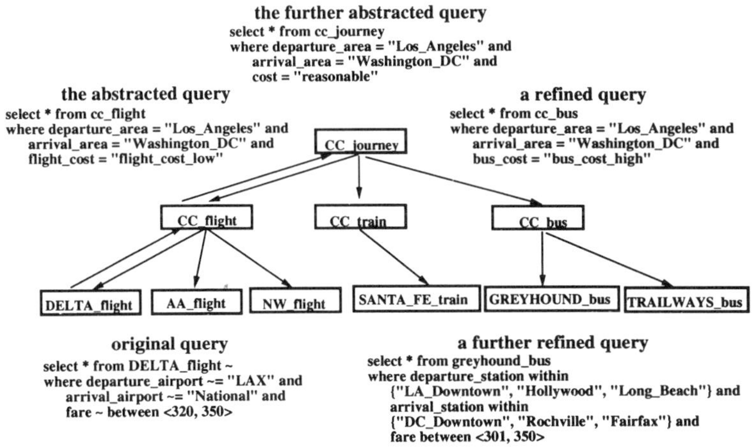

Figure 4: Example of neighbourhood query answering with two-level abstraction/refinement.

this approach, the user may ask a more general question about 'How to travel from Los Angeles to Washington D.C. at a reasonable cost',

select * from **CC_journey**
where *departure_area* = 'Los Angeles'
and *arrival_area* = 'Washington'
and *cost* = 'reasonable'

Using the *hierarchy* in Figure 5, such a query can be automatically refined to the following queries:

select * from **CC_flight**
where *departure_area* = 'Los Angeles'
and *arrival_area* = 'Washington'
and *flight_cost* = 'flight_cost_low'

select * from **CC_train**
where *departure_area* = 'Los Angeles'
and *arrival_area* = 'Washington'
and *train_cost* **within** {'train_cost_high', 'train_cost_medium'}

select * from **CC_bus**
where *departure_area* = 'Los Angeles'

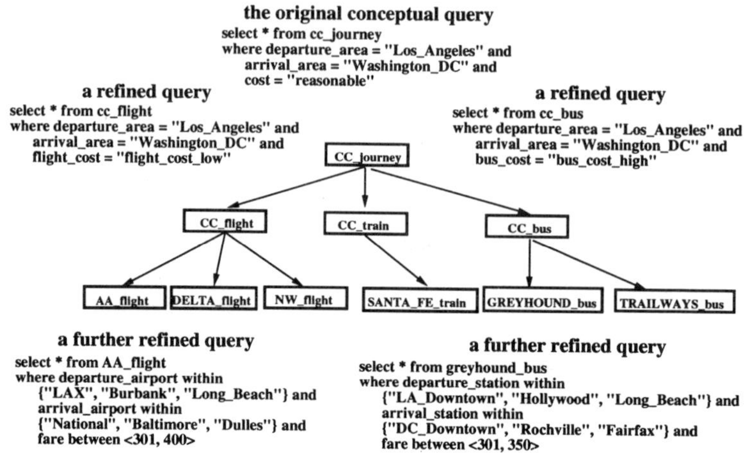

Figure 5: Refining a conceptual query.

and *arrival_area* = 'Washington'
and *bus_cost* = 'bus_cost_high'

Note that in the above refined queries, **CC_journey** is 'refined' to **CC_flight**, **CC_bus** and **CC_train**. These three queries can be further refined to

select * from **AA_flight**
where *departure_airport* **within** {'LAX', 'Burbank', 'Long Beach'}
and *arrival_airport* **within** {'National', 'Baltimore', 'Dulles'}
and *fare* **between** <301, 400>

select * from **santa_fe_train**
where *departure_train_station* **within** {'LA', 'Long Beach'}
and *arrival_train_station* **within** {'DC', 'Fairfax'}
and *fare* **between** <301, 400>

select * from **greyhound_bus**
where *departure_bus_station* **within** {'LA Downtown', 'Hollywood', 'Long Beach'}
and *arrival_bus_station* **within** {'DC Downtown', 'Rockville', 'Fairfax'}
and *fare* **between** <301, 350>

and so on.

Based on the hierarchy of knowledge, a conceptual query can be processed to derive a set of more specific queries which can be answered by a conventional query processing system.

3 CSQL – a language for cooperative query answering

CSQL is an extension of the SQL query language containing cooperative operations to support cooperative query answering. *CSQL* has general purpose syntactic constructs but domain-oriented interpretation. We provide, on top of an existing data schema, a type hierarchy specification based on the proposed abstraction notion and store the corresponding supertype and subtype domain values in a table. This information is used to associate various concepts at different knowledge levels and to interpret *CSQL*. Based on the user's interest, the set of typical queries, and the expected answers, we can construct the desired type abstraction hierarchies in selected problem domains to provide a structured organization for concepts. The system can then provide cooperative query answering in those domains.

3.1 Foundations of CSQL semantics

The semantics of *CSQL* is based on type abstraction hierarchy, match relaxation, and query pattern relaxation as discussed in this section.

3.1.1 Type abstraction hierarchy

The type abstraction hierarchy (TAH) combines the notions of subsumption (is_a) and composition (part_of) to form an integrated hierarchy. In the TAH, *abstraction* is achieved by different representations of an object at different levels of the hierarchy; *subsumption* is a special case of abstraction where the abstract representation of an object under a supertype is the same as its representation under a subtype; and *composition* is introduced by defining the structural subtype relationship. Therefore, our extension also takes complex objects into account. In general, type T is a subtype of T' means:

1. The domain of T' is abstract over the domain of T.
2. The domain of T' subsumes the domain of T (as a special case of the above).
3. The type structure of T' is contained in the type structure of T.

Formally, a type can be an atomic type, a tuple-type $T : (T_1, \ldots, T_n)$, or a set-type, $T : \{S\}$, where $T_1, \ldots, T_n$ and S are types. Based on the type abstraction notion, a type T is a subtype of a type T', denoted as $T \leq T'$, if,

Subtyping

1. For atomic types T and T', if each value in $dom(T')$ represents a single or multiple value in $dom(T)$, then $T \leq T'$, where $dom(T)$ denotes the domain of type T.

2. For tuple-types $T : (T_1, \ldots, T_n)$ and $T' : (T'_1, \ldots, T'_m)$ where $n \geq m, T \leq T'$ iff $\forall i \in \{1, \ldots, m\} T_i \leq T'_i$.

3. For set-types $T : \{S\}$ and $T' : \{S'\}, T \leq T'$ iff $S \leq S'$.

The above definition integrates the subsumption composition views of type hierarchy with subsumption as a special case of abstraction. For a given class, multiple type hierarchies may be formed based on different views.

Let $\Rightarrow$ denote logical implication. By combining object instances and variables of the basic types, the notion of terms can be defined as follows.

Term

The set of terms of type T, Γ_T, is defined recursively as follows:

1. For a constant value c and an atomic type T, $c \in dom(T) \Rightarrow c \in \Gamma_T$.

2. For a variable v of type T, $v \in \Gamma_T$.

3. For a tuple-type $T : (T_1, \ldots, T_n), \forall i \in \{1, \ldots, n\} t_i \in \Gamma_{T_i} \Rightarrow T(t_1, \ldots, t_n) \in \Gamma_T$ (tuple-term).

4. For a set-type $T : \{T_0\}, \forall i \in \{1, \ldots, n\} t_i \in \Gamma_{T_0} \Rightarrow T\{t_1, \ldots, t_n\} \in \Gamma_T$ (set-term).

Query abstraction and refinement are based on the mechanisms of *generalization rewrites* and the *specialization rewrites* of types and terms for converting object representations between different abstract levels. The type generalization rewrite converts a type to a more abstract type, and the term generalization rewrite deals with both types and domain values for transforming low-level object representations to higher-level ones. Their definitions are given below where $\rightarrow$ denotes rewrite or mapping, *type(t)* denotes the type of a term t, and *gen* represents the relation between values of atomic types and their subtypes such as 'Los Angeles' and 'LAX'.

Type generalization rewrite
The set of *generalization rewrite* of type T, Ω_T, is defined as:

- For atomic types T and S, $T \leq S \Rightarrow T \rightarrow S \in \Omega_T$.

- For tuple-types $T : (T_1, \ldots, T_n, \ldots)$ and $S : (S_1, \ldots, S_n)$ where $T \leq S$, $T_1 \rightarrow S_1 \in \Omega_{T_1}, \ldots, T_n \rightarrow S_n \in \Omega_{T_n} \Rightarrow T : (T_1, \ldots, T_n, \ldots) \rightarrow S : (S_1, \ldots, S_n) \in \Omega_T$.
- For set-types $T : \{T_0\}$ and $S : \{S_0\}$ where $T \leq S$, $T_0 \rightarrow S_0 \in \Omega_{T_0} \rightarrow T : T_0 \Rightarrow S : S_0 \in \Omega_T$.

Term generalization rewrite
The set of *generalization rewrites* of term t, ω_t, are defined as:

- For atomic types T and S, if $T \rightarrow S \in \Omega_T, t, s$ are instances, *type*(t) $= T$ and *type*$(s) = S$ and $s =$ *gen*(t), then $t \rightarrow s \in \omega_t$.
- If $T \rightarrow S \in \Omega_T$, t is a variable of T and s a variable of S, then $t \rightarrow s \in \omega_t$.
- For $t = T(t_1, \ldots, t_n, \ldots), s = S(s_1, \ldots, s_n), T \rightarrow S \in \Omega_T$ and $t_1 \rightarrow s_1 \in \omega_{t_1}, \ldots, t_n \rightarrow s_n \in \omega_{t_n} \Rightarrow t \rightarrow s \in \omega_t$.
- For t $= T\{t_1, \ldots, t_n\}, s = S\{s_1, \ldots, s_m\}, T \rightarrow S \in \Omega_T$ and $\forall i \in \{1, \ldots, n\}(\exists j \in \{1, \ldots, m\} t_i \rightarrow s_j \in \omega_{t_i}) \Rightarrow t \rightarrow s \in \omega_t$.

The notions of type specialization rewrite and term specialization rewrite can also be defined similarly. For a type abstraction hierarchy, the specialization rewrite from an abstract type or term may yield a set of refined types or terms which provide refined information for searching for neighbourhood objects. In general, cooperative query answering is based on query modification via term rewriting.

In general, the proposed cooperative query answering is based on query modification which is just a term rewrite. For instance, a query modification from

select * from **AA_flight** ∼
where *departure_airport* ∼= 'LAX'
and *arrival_airport* ∼= 'Dulles'
and *departure_time* ∼= '10am'
and *arrival_time* ∼= '6pm'
to a more abstract one

select * from **CC_flight**
where *departure_area* = 'Los Angeles' and *arrival_area* = 'Washington'
and *departure_period* ∼= 'morning'
and *arrival_period* ∼= 'afternoon'
is a term rewrite from the term

AA_flight(LAX, Dulles, 10am, 6pm, X)

to the following more abstract term

CC_flight(Los Angeles, Washington, morning, afternoon, X)

where X is a variable for the flight identifier. Since a more abstract term has a wider coverage than that of a more specialized one, when a query represented by a specialized term is modified to a query represented by an abstract term, the scope of the query is enlarged. When a query represented by an abstract term is refined to multiple queries represented by specialized terms, the query is split into multiple goals for database access.

Query abstraction/refinement offers the operational view to cooperative query processing. The nature of cooperative query processing can also be described denotationally. Below we will discuss it from the *query matching* and *query pattern* points of view.

3.1.2 Match relaxation

Traditional query answering aims at finding the objects that match the query condition exactly. Cooperative query answering aims at finding the objects that only match the query condition at an abstract level, namely, the abstract representation of the query condition. In other words, objects returned in a cooperative query answer have the same representations as the objects returned by an exact query answer, but at a higher level of abstraction.

For example, while the object being queried

AA_flight(LAX, Dulles, 10am, 6pm, #076)

is abstracted to a more generic representation

CC_flight(Los Angeles, Washington, morning, afternoon)

and then refined to a set of objects which might include

DELTA_flight(LAX, National, 11am, 5pm, #024).

There is an approximate match between the queried object of type AA_flight and the object of type DELTA_flight in the answer. This relaxed match characterizes the semantics of *CSQL*.

Under conventional typing, a precondition for two objects to match is that the types of their component terms at respective argument positions be identical. In a subsumption-based hierarchical typing system, two objects can also match if they are in a subsumption relationship. Thus,

AA_flight(LAX, Dulles, 10am, 6pm, #076)

matches

CC_flight(LAX, Dulles, 10am, 6pm, #076).

since CC_flight subsumes AA_flight. But

AA_flight(LAX, Dulles, 10am, 6pm, #076)

does not match

DELTA_flight(LAX, National, 11am, 5pm, #024),

because there is neither a match, nor a subsumption relationship. However, the type abstraction notion underlying *CSQL* has extended this concept one step further. The fact that type T_2 is a supertype of type T_1 implies the existence of abstract representations of objects of type T_1 under type T_2, so that 'Dulles' on attribute *departure_airport* has the abstract representation 'Washington' on attribute *departure_area*. The goal reformulation facility realizes the relaxable match between an object of T_1 and its abstraction representation of T_2 where $T_1 < T_2$. Therefore,

AA_flight(LAX, Dulles, 10am, 6pm, #076)

and

DELTA_flight(LAX, National, 11am, 5pm, #024)

match each other approximately via

CC_flight(Los Angeles, Washington, morning, afternoon).

3.2 Query pattern relaxation

The proposed cooperative query answering mechanism can also be viewed as a *query pattern relaxation mechanism* [12]. To show this we introduce the notions of pattern and pattern instance.

A pattern is defined on a type by specifying a *condition* [3]. For example, given the following schema definition:

AA_flight(*departure_airport*, *arrival_airport*, *departure_time*, *arrival_time*, *flight#*)

conditions such as

departure_airport = 'LAX', or
departure_time = '9am'

define patterns on the type AA_flight. The objects of the type that satisfy the pattern are said to *match the pattern*, and the identifiers of those objects form a **Pattern Instance (PI)**. Since it is formed of conditions on attributes, a query can be viewed as a pattern called a **query pattern**. The set of identifiers of the objects matching a query pattern is the **Query Pattern Instance (QPI)** for that pattern, while the set of identifiers of objects that are actually included in the query answer is called the **Answer Pattern Instance (API)**. Exact query answering means that the API for a query is identical to its QPI.

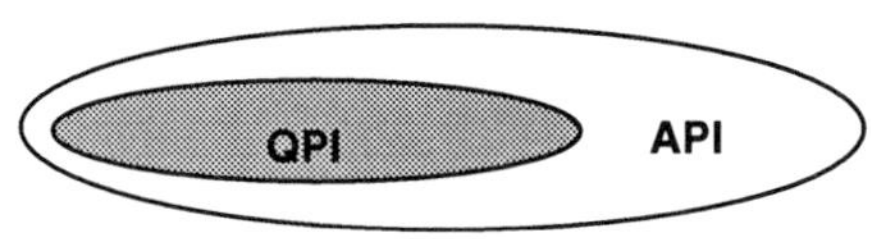

Figure 6: Relaxed API subsumes QPI.

Exact match is a special case of cooperative query answering. Very often the API of a relaxed query contains the QPI of the original query. Thus a cooperative query answering is made through **relaxing the query pattern**. For example, when 'morning' is used as the abstract representation of '9am', the query pattern with condition '*departure_time* = 9am' is relaxed to the query pattern with condition '*departure_time* between <8am, 11am>' and 'morning' may be viewed as the *name of the relaxed range* <8am, 11am>. This offers a quantitative view to the type abstraction based cooperative query answering mechanism.

The query pattern relaxation view provides a general way to express an abstract object by a range. It is typical for those attributes whose values form a *total ordering*, such as attributes of time, space, or numerical numbers, but their ranges are often *difficult to name*. For instance, it is difficult to find an *abstract representation* for 'between 10am to 1pm'. Note that using type abstraction representations may not be suitable for relaxing a query on condition *departure_time*

between <10am, 1pm>,

since 10am falls into the abstract time period *morning* which can be refined to (7am, 11am), and 1pm falls into the abstract time period *afternoon* which can be refined to (1pm, 6pm). Obviously we do not prefer relaxing it to

between <7am, 6pm>

since 10am nears the right limit of (7am, 11am) and 1pm is the left limit of (1pm, 6pm). Instead, the system should take into account the position of 10am within (7am, 11am) and the position of 1pm within (1pm, 6pm) and yield a closer range

between <9am, 2pm>

as the default range.

By viewing the query abstraction/refinement function as a black-box and only concerning ourselves with its input and output ranges, the type abstraction approach to cooperative query answering is a special kind of range relaxation. Using an abstraction-type hierarchy to guide range relaxation is necessary when the range can only be expressed conceptually, and not quantitatively.

3.3 Language constructs

CSQL provides the following extended query language constructs to allow query relaxation:

- Relaxation symbol '∼' for marking the relaxable relations, attributes, and values for which an approximate query answer is tolerable. For example,

  select * from *AA_flight*
  where *departure-airport* = 'Dulles'
  and *arrival-airport* ∼= 'LAX'
  and *departure-time* ∼= 10am

  means arrival-airport and departure-time may be relaxed which rewrites the query to,

  select * from *AA_flight*
  where *departure-airport* = 'Dulles'
  and *arrival-airport* **within** { 'LAX', 'Long Beach', 'Burbank' }
  and 9am < *departure-time* < 11am

- **Relaxation order** specifying the ordered preference of attribute relaxation. For example, after the above query,

  relaxation-order (*arrival-airport, departure-airport*)

indicates that if no exact answer is found, *arrival-airport* is relaxed. If an answer is still not found, *departure-airport* is relaxed. If no single-attribute approximate answer is found, both attributes are relaxed.

- Syntactic relaxable predicates **between** and **within**. **between** indicates a range of values and **within** indicates set membership. Both operations can include the ~ operator, as specified below:

arrival-time **between** <7am, ~11am> becomes
7am < X < ~11am, which is
7am < X < Noon

within ~ {'LAX', 'Burbank'} becomes
within {~'LAX', ~'Burbank'} which is,
within {'LAX', 'Burbank', 'Long Beach'}

- Context sensitive predicates which are relaxable based on given contexts, such as

  near-to ('Redondo Beach')
  similar-to ('McDonalds') **based-on** (cost, w_1; type-of-food, w_2)

  near-to maps to Euclidean distance that is less than a threshold based on the query context. In general, this predicate returns values with a context-based semantic distance that is less than the specified threshold.

  similar-to requests a set of objects semantically similar to the given object. Similarity is a multiple attribute operator with a weight assigned to each attribute in accordance with the relative importance of that attribute. Each object fulfilling the query conditions is evaluated against the given object by calculating the weighted mean-squared error [19] over the list of attributes. The similar objects are listed in ranked order, along with their measures.

- Control commands such as **nearer** and **further** which control the relaxation scope of **near-to** interactively. **nearer** reduces the threshold by a prespecified percentage, while **further** increases the threshold value by that percentage.

3.4 Context based interpretation of CSQL

The relationship between the semantic distance and the actual distance of objects is context sensitive. For example, scales for flight distances and for urban commuting distances should be assigned differently. The nearness relations also vary from case to case. For example, **near-to** has different meaning in different situations as shown by Table 3. Such domain knowledge is stored in the knowledge base for supporting cooperative query answering.

Table 3: Context sensitive nearness measure for different attributes

attribute	nearness measure
departure_time	1 hour
flight_time	10 minutes
airport_distance	50 miles
restaurant_distance	2 miles

Unlike SQL interpretation, *CSQL* interpretation depends heavily on the database content. Language constructs for *CSQL* allow the user to specify the context of type abstraction hierarchy, e.g. 'business trip', and the context-dependent nearness measure, e.g. 'relaxation range for *departure_time* is 1 hour'. Such a specification is then converted to the domain-specific nearness measure used by *CSQL*.

3.5 Relaxation control

When a query is not answerable, some of its attribute values are relaxed to provide a wider search scope. As a result, approximate answers are derived. However, without control over relaxation, we may generate too many approximate answers for the user. Further, if the user fails to constrain the query sufficiently, too many answers may be generated. For example, if the user asks for flights from Los Angeles to Washington on Thursday, then he will be inundated with hundreds of answers. Suppose we know in addition that the user is a frequent flier on United Airlines and that he probably has an early Friday morning meeting. With that extra information we can further constrain the query search to United flights arriving before 9 pm. If it is known that he has many friends in Washington, and that his company will pay for an extra night in the hotel if it leads to a lower airfare, [1] his return may be postponed to Sunday morning to reduce cost. He can, of course, override this modification if he needs to arrive back before then.

The *relaxation manager* combines such rules to restrict the search for approximate answers. The rules are provided from several contexts, including the user profile and query context. After the rules are applied,

[1]Staying over Saturday night usually yields much lower airfares.

relaxation can proceed with only a fraction of the possible tuples under consideration. In addition to constraints on the search, the user can specify the number of answers as well as rules that combine restrictions on multiple attributes.

The RM has three functions. As presented above, it applies rules to constrain the relaxation of attributes by trimming the type abstraction hierarchy as necessary. Next, the RM determines how to direct the search through those hierarchies. For example, there may still be many flights with low fare from LAX and Burbank to New York. Based on application- and user-specified demands, the RM selects the order to relax the attributes. Further, if the user overconstrains the system and no tuples are available after full constrained relaxation, the RM may decide which rules to ignore so that some answer can be obtained. A trimmed type abstraction hierarchy for the coast-to-coast travel example is shown in Figure 7.

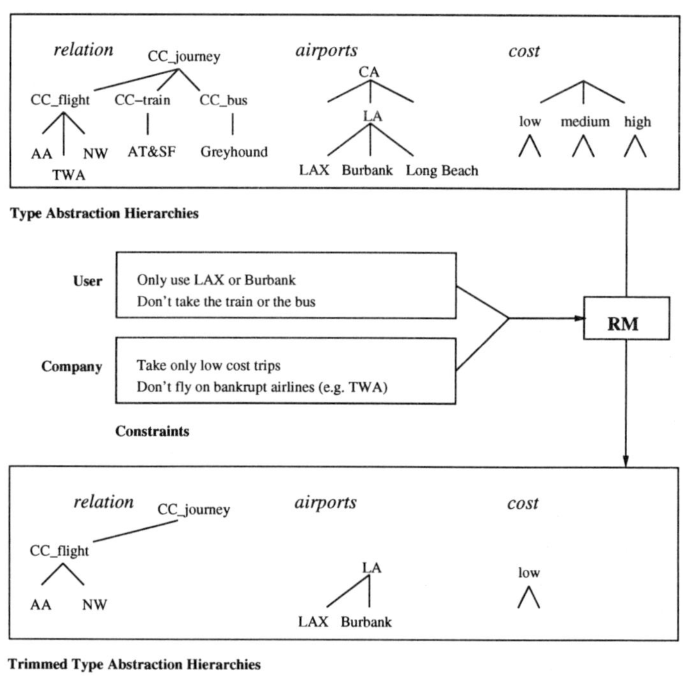

Figure 7: An example of the relaxation manager trimming a type abstraction hierarchy.

3.5.1 Relaxation rules

There are several types of relaxation specifications. Although more general rules give the user more flexibility of relaxation specification, using general rules may severely limit the amount of trimming possible on the type abstraction hierarchies. Less trimming means more tuples retrieved for evaluation and a slower system. Thus we recommend against using general type rules and present several special rule classes, below:

Attribute relaxation order A list of attributes in the order which they should be relaxed, as described in the explicit **relaxation-order** operation in *CSQL*. Multiple attributes can be relaxed simultaneously by specifying them together in the list. For example, *food, fare, food and fare, departure time, departure airport, food and departure time, ...* .

Relaxation level The schedule of successive relaxations for each attribute. For example, *fare: (10%, 30%, 50%), departure time: (20%, 30%), ...* indicates that the first time *fare* is relaxed, it should only be by 10%. If no approximate answers are found, the next relaxation of *fare* is by 30%. Relaxation level only specifies how far to relax each attribute; the order of relaxation is specified by the attribute relaxation order.

Desired answer set size The desired size of the answer set.

Meta-rules Rules that hold in general, rather than being about specific attributes, such as *relax no more than two attributes at a time*, and *Don't relax any attributes more than 50%.*

The query language may restrict which categories of rules are possible. For example, the current implementation of *CSQL* allows only the relaxation order to be specified.

3.5.2 Contexts

Relaxation rules come from several sources, called contexts. There may be one set of rules for the user's company, another for the user himself, and still another one for the particular application domain. In the example of Figure 7, the user context has two rules and the company context has two rules. For a particular query, the user may decide to override some of the rules if, for example, he wishes to take the train instead of flying this time.

The relaxation manager gathers rules from the different applicable contexts. There are four context classes:

Explicit specification

Constraints specified within the current query, such as 'Find a non-stop flight to Tokyo, and *do not relax the non-stop*'.

User profile

Preferences of a particular user, such as, *United is preferred over American.* The user profile may actually consist of several sub-contexts. For example, a user may have personal preferences, as well as rules from the company where he works and other outside constraints.

Domain specific

Rules related to a particular application domain, such as, *flight cost is more important than the in-flight meal*

Default strategy

A general set of rules to guide relaxation when none of the other constraints is appropriate. For example, a default rule says to relax attributes until an answer is found. Further, the default rule to relax multiple values simultaneously is to minimize the sum of the semantic distances between the values in the approximate and exact answers.

3.5.3 Using multiple contexts in relaxation

The relaxation manager can combine rules from multiple contexts, but the rules in the contexts may interfere with one another. To handle this problem, the user must select one of the following policies for selecting which rule to apply:

Default order policy

Use the following precedence to relax the query:
Query Specification > User Profile > Domain Specific > Default Strategy
Thus, restrictions specified in the query will override any other rules. This is the strategy used in the current CoBase implementation.

User specified policy

Instead of using the default order policy, the user may specify a different order to apply the rules.

Separate policy

Apply each context separately to derive different answer sets for each context. This policy will offer answers which satisfy one or more of the contexts, but not necessarily all of them.

Apply-all policy

Apply all rules simultaneously. When there are no conflicting rules, stronger rules will supersede weaker rules. Therefore, this is the most restrictive policy. If no answers are found, then the RM switches to one of the other policies to remove certain rules until a solution is found.

4 Implementation

We have implemented a prototype cooperative database system at UCLA (see Figure 8) to validate the concepts presented in this chapter. Our modular design divides the control section of the relaxation manager from the individual cooperative operator modules. There is a module for each cooperative operator, as well as separate modules to handle general query modification and join queries. The join module coordinates the simultaneous relaxation in multiple hierarchies by alternating between the two (or more) hierarchies. CoBase uses LOOM [15, 16] as knowledge representation and inference system and supports relational databases (e.g. Oracle and Sybase) and LIM (the Loom Interface Module) [17, 10]. Access to distributed databases is made possible through SIMS, a transparent multidatabase access layer [1]. The CoBase engine, written in LISP, controls query relaxation and modification based on the user-provided relaxation constructs, the type abstraction hierarchy, and direction from the relaxation manager. The engine uses the RM to trim the type abstraction hierarchies for query relaxation, as well as translating the relaxation constructs included explicitly in the query. The cooperative primitives presented have been implemented both in *CSQL* and in *CLOOM*, a cooperative extension to the LOOM query language.

When a query is presented to CoBase (see Figure 9), the system first relaxes any explicit cooperative operators in the query. The modified query is then presented to the underlying database system for execution. If no answers are returned, then CoBase, under the direction of the relaxation manager, relaxes the queries by query modification using the trimmed type abstraction hierarchy. The relaxed query is executed, and, if there is no answer due to overtrimming the type abstraction hierarchy, the relaxation manager will deactivate certain relaxation rules, restoring part of the trimmed TAH to broaden the search scope until an answer is found.

When an approximate answer is returned, the user may wish for an explanation of how the answer was derived. An explanation system is included in CoBase to present an annotated relaxation path to the user. When possible, the semantic nearness to the exact answer will be given for each approximation and the approximations will be ranked by their nearness to the exact answer.

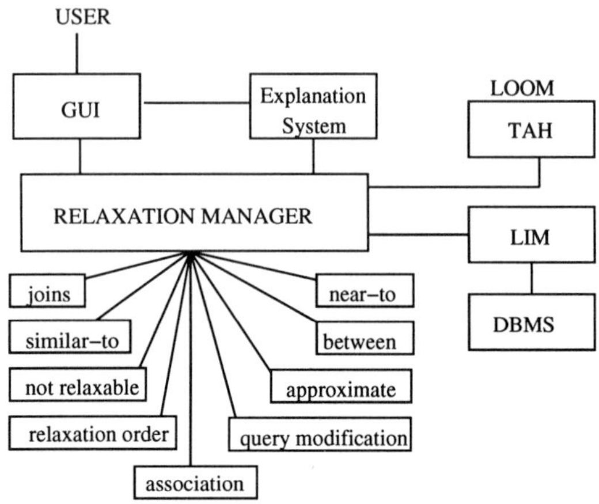

Figure 8: CoBase system architecture.

A graphical user interface (GUI) allows interactive control over system parameters and displays the TAHs and the relaxation path. The GUI is menu-based, providing control to allow explanations of the relaxation choices at the desired level of detail.

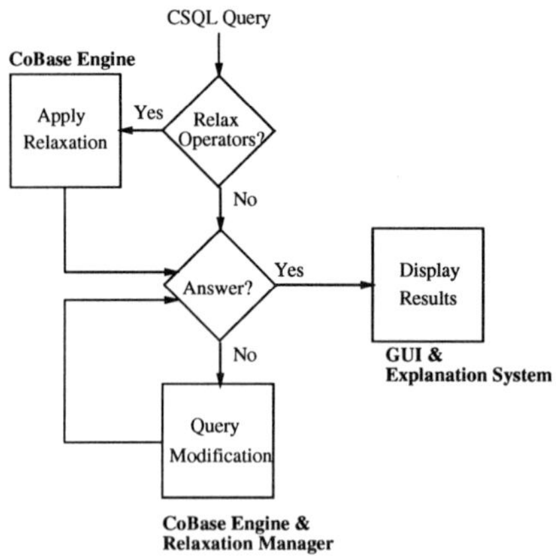

Figure 9: Data flow in CoBase.

5 Technology transfer

We have demonstrated the feasibility and functionality of CoBase in several different domains, including a Transportation Planning Database [8] and a Medical Imaging Database System [2].

The transportation planning system includes information about military cargo, vehicles and locations throughout the world. CoBase can answer cooperative queries on this database, such as

Q_1 : List the airports with the parking capacity *approximately* equal to 200 000 square feet, and

Q_1 : Find the airports in Tunisia *similar to* the Bizerte airport. Use the attributes *runway_length_ft* (with weight 2.0) and *runway_width_ft* (with weight 1.0) as the criteria for similarity. Provide the best n answers.

In medical databases that store X-ray and MR images, images need to be retrieved by object feature or contents rather than patient ID. The queries asked are often conceptual and not precisely defined. We need to use knowledge about the application (e.g. age class, ethnic class, disease class, bone age, etc.), user profile, and query context to answer such queries. Further, exact matching of features is very difficult, if not impossible. For example, if the query 'Find the treatment methods used for tumour x on 12-year-old Korean males,' cannot be answered, based on the TAHs for tumours, age, and ethnic groups, we can relax 'tumour x' to 'tumour class X', and '12-year-old Korean male' to 'pre-teen Asian', which results in the relaxed query, 'Find the treatment methods used for the tumour class X on pre-teen Asians.' Further, we can obtain such relevant information as the *success rate, side effects,* and *cost of the treatment* from the association operations.

The number and size of the type abstraction hierarchies for the transportation planning database are too large to be constructed manually. Thus we have devised methods for automatically constructing TAHs from the database directly. Pattern-Based Knowledge Inference [18] is a bottom-up method that uses rules derived from the database instance to cluster attribute values into a hierarchy. DISC [7] is a method for building hierarchies for numeric domains based on the distribution and frequency of data values. Together, these methods can generate the type abstraction hierarchies from a given database. Further, both of these methods provide a quantitative measure of the nearness for each node in the hierarchy. This measure can also be combined to derive the nearness distance for multiple hierarchies.

The CoBase engine is currently over 8,000 lines of LISP code, excluding user-interface code. The GUI consists of an additional 8,000 lines of

LISP code. To measure performance, we have a sample test-suite of 19 queries using different aspects of CoBase. The response time varies with the queries. On a Sun SPARCstation 10, response time ranges from a few seconds to nearly 20 seconds, with an average time of ten seconds per query. However, over 80% of that time is spent calling the underlying relational database and presenting the results. The overhead added by CoBase averages about 20% which is less than two seconds per query in the current environment.

6 Conclusions

In this chapter, we proposed a cooperative query answering system that is structurally organized on the basis of the type abstraction hierarchy and functionally represented by the extended query language *CSQL*. Based on such a framework, type abstraction hierarchies express concepts at different knowledge levels and in various domains, and *CSQL* introduces additional language constructs to SQL that use these concepts for cooperative query answering. The interpretation of *CSQL* is based on the knowledge of type abstraction hierarchy and is transparent to the users. Thus, *CSQL* provides cooperative query answering not only by extending the functionality of *SQL*, but also by modifying the query evaluation process to include logic inferencing, rewriting, and heuristic searching. These extensions are far beyond the ones in object-oriented and relational databases.

A relaxation manager controls the system using user profile and query context to trim the type abstraction hierarchy and restrict the search space. An explanation system provides the user with reasoning for the relaxation path taken and the nearness of the approximate answers provided.

With the proposed cooperative query answering capability, a database system can provide approximate and conceptual query answering, tolerate imprecisely specified queries, and support object association. This approach can also be used to improve the availability of distributed databases during network partitions by providing relevant information when the exact information is inaccessible, and can be used to support negotiation between multi-agents by determining the joint requirements that are relaxed from the original ones made by these agents.

We have implemented a prototype cooperative database system, CoBase, and the extended query language *CSQL* at UCLA to validate the proposed concept. We have also applied CoBase to two domains—transportation planning and medical imaging. The type abstraction hierarchies for these domains are generated automatically from the databases. We find that it is an essential stage for applying CoBase to large-scale problems. The explanation system is useful for informing the user about the relaxation process, as well as providing the nearness measure of the approximate answer. Our experimental results reveal that our structured approach provides an efficient and scalable methodology for cooperative query answering.

References

[1] Y. Arens and C. Knoblock. Planning and reformulating queries for semantically-modelled multidatabase systems. In *Proceedings First International Conference on Information and Knowledge Management (CIKM)*, pp. 92–101, Baltimore, Maryland, 1992.

[2] W. W. Chu, A. F. Cardenas, and R. K. Taira. A Knowledge-based Multimedia Medical Distributed Database System — KMeD. Technical Report 93–005, UCLA Computer Science Department, 1993.

[3] W. W. Chu and Q. Chen. Neighborhood and associative query answering. *Journal of Intelligent Information Systems*, 1(3/4):355–382, 1992.

[4] W. W. Chu and Q. Chen. A structured approach for cooperative query answering. To appear in *IEEE Transactions on Knowledge and Data Engineering*, 1994.

[5] W. W. Chu, Q. Chen, and A. Hwang. Query answering via cooperative data inference. *To appear in Journal of Intelligent Information Systems*, 1994.

[6] W. W. Chu, Q. Chen, and R. Lee. Cooperative query answering via type abstraction hierarchy. In S.M. Deen, editor, *Cooperating Knowledge Based Systems*, pp. 271–292. North-Holland, Elsevier Science Publishing Co., Inc., 1991.

[7] W. W. Chu and K. Chiang. A Distribution Sensitive Clustering Method for Numerical Values. Technical Report 93–0006, UCLA Computer Science Department, 1993.

[8] W. W. Chu, M. Merzbacher, and L. Berkovich. The design and implementation of CoBase. *SIGMOD '93*, pp. 517–522, May 1993.

[9] F. Cuppens and R. Demolombe. Cooperative answering: a methodology to provide intelligent access to databases. In *Proceedings of the 2nd International Conference on Expert Database Systems*, 1989.

[10] T. W. Finin, D. P. McKay, and A O'Hare. The intelligent database interface. *Proceedings of the 7th National Conference on Artificial Intelligence (AAAI)*, 1990.

[11] T. Gaasterland, P. Godfrey, and J. Minker. An overview of cooperative answering. *Journal of Intelligent Information Systems*, 1(2):123–157, 1992.

[12] T. Gaasterland, P. Godfrey, and J. Minker. Relaxation as a platform for cooperative answering. *Journal of Intelligent Information Systems*, 1(3/4):293–321, 1992.

[13] A. Hemerly, M. Casanova, and A. Furtado. Cooperative Behavior Through Request Modification. Technical report, IBM Brasil, Brazil, May 1991.

[14] T. Imielinski. Intelligent query answering in rule based systems. In J. Minker, editor, *Foundations of Deductive Databases and Logic Programming*, pp. 275–312, Washington, D.C., 1988. Morgan Kaufman.

[15] R. MacGregor. A deductive pattern matcher. In *Proceedings of the National Conference on Artificial Intelligence (AAAI 88)*, pp. 403–408, Cambridge, Mass, 1988. MIT Press.

[16] R. MacGregor. The evolving technology of classification-based knowledge representation systems. In *Principles of Semantic Networks: Explorations in the Representation of Knowledge*, 1991. J. Sowa, ed.

[17] D. P. McKay, J. Pastor, and T. W. Finin. View-concepts: knowledge-based access to databases. In *Proceedings First International Conference on Information and Knowledge Management (CIKM)*, pp. 84–91, Baltimore, Maryland, 1992.

[18] M. Merzbacher and W. W. Chu. Pattern–based clustering for database attribute values. In G. Piatetsky-Schapiro, editor, *AAAI Workshop on Knowledge Discovery in Databases*, Washington, D.C., July 1993. AAAI Press.

[19] A. Motro. VAGUE: a user interface to relational databases that permits vague queries. *ACM Journal Transactions on Office Information Systems*, **6**(3):187–214, July 1988.

[20] A. Motro. FLEX: a tolerant and cooperative user interface to databases. *IEEE Transactions on Knowledge and Data Engineering*, **2**(2):231–245, 1990.

[21] S. Su. Sam*: A semantic association model for corporate and scientific-statistical databases. *Information Sciences*, 29, 1983.

3

Exploiting user models to avoid misconstruals

Andrea S. Hemerly, Marco A. Casanova, and Antonio L. Furtado

Abstract

When interacting with a database, a user is typically tempted to infer further information from that explicitly obtained from previous queries. However, his inferences are not necessarily valid, because his model of the world is often incomplete or even faulty. This chapter addresses the problem of avoiding users' faulty inferences or misconstruals. It describes a cooperative interface to deductive databases that alters the processing of users' requests to include additional information that will block faulty inferences. The interface is governed by predefined user models, created during the design of the database. It also maintains a log of previous interactions with each user that records all information he has already acquired in his current session. The inferences of a given user are identified with those possible from the user model and the information in the log. The main result of the chapter says that, given any user model and any deductive database, all logs produced by the interface indeed contain sufficient information to block all misconstruals.

1 Introduction

When interacting with a database, a user is typically tempted to infer further information from that explicitly obtained from previous queries. However, his inferences are not necessarily valid, because his model of the world is often incomplete or even faulty. For example, after consulting the database, a traveller may find out that his flight arrived on time and unadvisedly infer that it will depart on time, when in fact the flight has been delayed because the airport at the destination is closed. A more cooperative database system would have informed the traveller that the plane has indeed landed, assumed as the original question, and would have added that the flight has been delayed. To achieve cooperativeness, the system would naturally have some model of typical travellers.

In this chapter we describe a cooperative interface to deductive databases that includes additional data along with the answers to the queries when it perceives that the user has gathered enough information that will lead to a faulty inference, sometimes also referred to as misconstrual [Web86].

The results described here are part of Project NICE [CF90, HCF91a], whose purpose is to investigate cooperative query processing methods to reduce the cost of developing 'help desks' and similar advanced database interfaces. Cooperative query processing has been explored, for example, in [BJ86, CCL90, CD89], through the use of richer conceptual models, and in [Mot84] via the generalization of failed queries. A natural language database query system, which recognizes users' presuppositions about the application domain, is also described in [Kap82]. The problem of detecting and responding to plan-generation misconstruals is investigated in [Qui89]. A good survey of user model techniques can be found in [KW89].

This work is organized as follows. Section 2 contains an informal introduction to the environment we propose for addressing the problem of misconstruals. Section 3 presents the logic programming concepts that we will need in the chapter. Section 4 formally introduces the environment and describes the cooperative interface. Section 5 proves the correctness of the cooperative interface. Section 6 summarizes the chapter.

2 An environment for addressing the problem of misconstruals

To address the problem of misconstruals, we propose a *cooperative interface* that passes additional information to the user when it discovers that he has gathered enough data to infer information that contradicts the database. The interface essentially simulates the user's inferences and compares the result with what can be inferred from the database.

In this work, the environment of the cooperative interface consists of a deductive database, a log, and a user model. The generalization of this environment, including a more sophisticated user/domain model [CF90, HCF91a], is simple. In addition, there are two theoretical concepts, called the certification criterion and the cooperativeness domain, created to guide the design and prove the correctness of the interface.

We assume that, in the context of a given session, the user remembers his past interactions with the deductive database and that he can use the information thus obtained in his (real world) inferences. The results of past interactions in the current session are kept in a *log*, which will indicate that certain facts hold and that certain other facts do not hold in the database.

For simplicity, we consider just one class of users, which isolates our problem from that of classifying users. Thus, from now on, when we refer to the user, we mean any user in this class. The *user model* is a theory, designed together with the database, that abstracts out the rules that the user adopts to reason about the domain of discourse in question. We stress that we use the term 'user model' to mean a model of how the user reasons, which is somewhat different from the use of the term in the literature.

We model the user's inferences during a session by the deductions from the user model and the positive facts that the current log indicates to hold. In particular, we assume that the user reasons about negated facts only through *negation as finite failure.* This intuitively means that, in a given session, we model the inference of a negated fact $\neg A$, by the failure, in a finite number of steps, to find a proof for A from the user model and the facts that the log indicates to hold.

The *certification criterion* simply formalizes the contract between the user and the cooperative interface that governs the use of the log. In this chapter, we adopt a certification criterion that accepts a deduction D as *certified* for a log λ iff, for any positive fact A used during the construction of D, the log λ does not indicate that A does not hold in the database. Note that the certification criterion is asymmetric in the sense that it depends only on the positive facts used. This follows because the cooperative interface can always block the derivation of a negative fact $\neg B$ by indicating, in the log, that B holds. Indeed, if this is the case, there will be a proof of B (since the log, together with the user model, indicates that B holds), which suffices to block the derivation of $\neg B$ by negation as finite failure.

The *cooperativeness domain* just defines a class of deductions. We agree that deductions outside the cooperativeness domain need not be simulated, which puts deliberate bounds on the level of cooperativeness required from the interface. In fact, we have to design the interface in such a way that, after it processes each query in a given session, for every deduction from the user model and the current information in the log, if the deduction is in the cooperativeness domain and it is certified for the current log, then its result is correct with respect to the database.

In this chapter, we fix the cooperativeness domain as the set of all derivations of conjunctions of positive facts. Moreover, we assume that the user model is such that any positive fact derivable purely from the model (i.e., without looking at the log) is also derivable from the database. These choices are motivated by what we call the *log initialization problem*, which we now discuss briefly.

Let U be an (unrestricted) user theory, D be a deductive database, and $\mathcal{E}$ be an (unrestricted) cooperativeness domain. Suppose that there is a fact A that follows from U alone by a deduction in $\mathcal{E}$ but not from D. Then, we are in the presence of a misconstrual, which means that the cooperative interface has to inform the user that A does not hold as soon as he starts a session. This becomes even more cumbersome if we recall that the user may derive negative facts by negation as failure. In other words, if we do not restrict U or $\mathcal{E}$ the interface will have to initialize the log, even before the user submits his first query, with a potentially enormous collection of positive facts. However, if $\mathcal{E}$ and U conform to the restrictions we imposed, then the initialization is unnecessary.

We conclude this section with two informal examples that indicate how the interface operates. The first example illustrates how to avoid misconstruals that arise when the user incorrectly invokes negation as finite failure for the lack of information.

Suppose that the user believes that a flight will always depart, if it arrived and it is not raining. This is equivalent to assuming a user model U that contains only one rule:

U.1. Flight x will depart, if x arrived and it is not raining

Consider that the deductive database has this same rule, that flight XY202 arrived and that the airport is closed due to bad weather. That is, let D be the following deductive database:

D.1. Flight x will depart, if x arrived and it is not raining
D.2. Flight XY202 arrived
D.3. It is raining

Suppose now that the user starts the dialogue with the query:

Q. Has flight XY202 arrived?

The answer to Q is therefore YES. That is, at this point the user knows:

A_1. Flight XY202 arrived

If no extra information is passed to the user in the log, after the first query he will know fact A_1, from which he can infer fact A_2:

A_2. Flight XY202 will depart

However, the interface will discover that the user is about to infer fact A_2 wrongly as follows. It will first simulate a deduction R of A_2 from the user model U and A_1. Then, the interface will analyse all steps of R and detect that R cannot be accepted because it requires inferring fact A_3:

A_3. It is not raining

from U and A_1, by negation as finite failure, whereas it is not possible to infer A_3 from the database (since the database in fact includes $D.3$). Hence, the interface will include $D.3$ in the log to avoid the user's misconstrual. Indeed, the user can no longer infer A_2 using the complete information he obtained from the database (that is, A_1 and $D.3$).

The answer combined with the extra information in the log is roughly equivalent to the following English sentence:

Flight XY202 arrived and it is raining.

We stress that the misconstrual we just illustrated was caused by an incorrect use of negation as finite failure and that it could be blocked by including an additional fact in the log. Our next example illustrates a second type of misconstrual that arises when the user has inadequate rules.

Suppose that the user believes that a flight always departs, if it arrived. That is, let the user model now be V:

$V.1$. Flight x will depart, if x arrived

Assume the same deductive database D (including rule $D.1$ exactly as before). Then, the answer to Q remains unchanged, from which the user can again wrongly infer fact A_2. The interface will again detect that A_2 does not follow from the database. The interface cannot block this misconstrual, however, by inserting additional facts in the log because the user's perception of the domain of discourse differs from that captured by the rules of the database. The interface will then act differently and include in the log an indication that A_2 is not deductible from the database.

The user can still infer A_2 from the answer to his query. However, his inference will not be certified for the current log, since the log indicates that A_2 does not hold.

The final answer will then be equivalent to the sentence:

Flight XY202 arrived but it will not depart.

In Section 4, we will formally define the concepts introduced here intuitively. In particular, we will show that, in the context of logic programming, it is conceptually simple to simulate the user's deductions and to detect misconstruals.

3 Logic programming background

In this section we recall some basic concepts of logic programming [Llo87].

An expression of the form $A \leftarrow B_1, \ldots, B_n$ is a *program clause* or simply a *clause* iff A is a positive literal and $B_1, \ldots, B_n$ are literals. An expression of the form $\leftarrow B_1, \ldots, B_n$ is a *normal goal* iff $B_1, \ldots, B_n$ are literals. The literals $B_1, \ldots, B_n$ are called the *body* of the program clause or of the normal goal and the literal A is called the *head* of the program clause. The empty clause $\square$ is also considered to be a normal goal. Note that a normal goal $\leftarrow B_1, \ldots, B_n$ represents the negation of $B_1 \wedge \ldots \wedge B_n$.

A program clause is *allowed* iff every variable that occurs in the clause occurs in a positive literal of its body. A normal goal G is *allowed* if every variable that occurs in G occurs in a positive literal of G.

Let P be a set of program clauses and $\leftarrow Q$ be a normal goal. An *answer substitution* α *for* $\leftarrow Q$ *from* P is a substitution for the variables of $\leftarrow Q$.

If G is a normal goal of the form $\leftarrow L_1, \ldots, L_p$ and C is a program clause of the form $A \leftarrow M_1, \ldots, M_q$, then we say that a normal goal G' is *derived* from G and C using a substitution θ iff θ is a most general unifier (mgu) of L_i and A and G' is the normal goal $\leftarrow (L_1, \ldots, L_{i-1}, M_1, \ldots, M_q, L_{i+1}, \ldots, L_p)\theta$, where L_i is the literal selected from G by the selection function in question.

We now formally define a variation of SLDNF-resolution, called Φ-*SLDNF-resolution*, that is the basis for both our cooperative interface and our model of how the user reasons and how he utilizes the information in the log.

Definition 3.1 Let $\mathcal{R}$ be the set of all triples such that the first element is a finite sequence, with length $n+1$, of normal goals, the second element is a finite sequence, with length n, of substitutions, and the third element is a finite sequence, also with length n, of clauses, for some $n > 0$. A *certification test* is a boolean function whose domain is $\mathcal{R}$.

In the next sequence of definitions, let P be a set of program clauses and G be a non-empty normal goal. Without loss of generality, also let the selection function be that which selects the leftmost literal. We will then refer to the literal selected from a goal G as the first literal of G, and vice-versa. Finally, let Φ be a certification test.

Definition 3.2 A Φ-*SLDNF-derivation from* $P \cup \{G\}$ is a triple S consisting of a sequence $G_0, G_1, \ldots, G_i, \ldots$ of normal goals, a sequence $C_1, \ldots, C_i, \ldots$ of variants of clauses in P or negative literals, and a sequence $\theta_1, \ldots, \theta_i, \ldots$ of mgu's such that $G_0 = G$ and, for each non-empty goal G_i of S, with $i \geq 0$, if G_i is of the form $\leftarrow L_1, \ldots, L_m$ and L_1 is the literal selected from G_i, then:

(i) if L_1 is a positive literal, then G_{i+1} is derived from G_i and C_{i+1} using θ_{i+1};

(ii) if L_1 is a ground negative literal $\neg A$, then there is a finitely failed or uncertified Φ-SLDNF-tree from $P \cup \{\leftarrow A\}$. In this case, G_{i+1}

is $\leftarrow L_2, \ldots, L_m$, the substitution θ_{i+1} is the identity substitution, C_{i+1} is $\neg A$.

Definition 3.3 Let S be a finite Φ-SLDNF-derivation from $P \cup \{G\}$. Suppose that, for some $n \geq 0$, the sequence of goals of S is $G_0, G_1, \ldots, G_n$ and that the sequence of mgu's of S is $\theta_1, \ldots, \theta_n$.

(a) S has *rank* 0 iff only positive literals are selected; otherwise S has *rank* $k+1$ iff the largest rank of a Φ-SLDNF-tree used to cancel a negative literal in S is k.

(b) S is *failed* iff G_n is non-empty and the literal selected from G_n is either a positive literal M and there is no clause in P whose head unifies with M, or a ground negative literal $\neg A$ and there is a certified Φ-SLDNF-refutation from $P \cup \{\leftarrow A\}$.

(c) S is a *Φ-SLDNF-refutation from* $P \cup \{G\}$ iff G_n is the empty goal.

The *answer to G from P computed by S* is the composition $\theta_1 \ldots \theta_n$, restricted to the variables of G.

The Φ-SLDNF-refutation S is *certified* (for Φ) iff $\Phi(S)$=TRUE. Similarly, the Φ-SLDNF-refutation S is *uncertified* (for Φ) iff $\Phi(S)$=FALSE.

Definition 3.4 A *Φ-SLDNF-tree from* $P \cup \{G\}$ is a tree T satisfying the following conditions:

(i) the root is G;

(ii) each node of the tree is a normal goal;

(iii) each branch forms a Φ-SLDNF-derivation from $P \cup \{G\}$.

Assume that T is finite. Then, T has *rank* k iff the largest rank of the Φ-SLDNF-derivation corresponding to a branch of T is k. Moreover, T is *finitely failed or uncertified* iff each branch is a failed Φ-SLDNF-derivation or an uncertified Φ-SLDNF-refutation.

When Φ is the trivial test that always returns TRUE, all refutations are certified. In this case, the above concepts for Φ-SLDNF-resolution coincide with the standard concepts for SLDNF-resolution and we drop the reference to Φ.

In particular, note that the definition of finitely failed or uncertified Φ-SLDNF-trees differs from that of finitely failed SLDNF-trees to the extent that it allows branches that correspond to refutations, as long as they are uncertified. The reader should be aware that this departure from SLDNF-resolution implies that the process of checking for Φ interferes with negation as failure, as the following simple example illustrates.

Example 3.5 Let Φ be the certification test such that $\Phi(S)$=TRUE iff all substitutions in S replace each variable by a ground term. Let $P = \{p(x) \leftarrow q(x,y)\ ,\ q(a,z)\}$. Hence, there is a Φ-SLDNF-refutation R from $P \cup \{\leftarrow \neg p(a)\}$ because there is a finitely failed or uncertified Φ-SLDNF-tree T from $P \cup \{\leftarrow p(a)\}$:

R: 1. $\leftarrow \neg p(a)$
2. $\square$
success

T: $\leftarrow p(a)$
|
$\leftarrow q(a,y)$
|
$\square$
uncertified
(by assumption on Φ)

But there is no (standard) SLDNF-refutation from $P \cup \{\leftarrow \neg p(a)\}$, since the SLDNF-tree T' from $P \cup \{\leftarrow p(a)\}$ has a success branch. Indeed, R' is the only SLDNF-derivation from $P \cup \{\leftarrow \neg p(a)\}$, but R' is failed:

R': 1. $\leftarrow \neg p(a)$
fail

T': $\leftarrow p(a)$
|
$\leftarrow q(a,y)$
|
$\square$
success

We conclude with a simple proposition that states a property of allowed clauses that we will use in the sequel.

Proposition 3.6 *Let P be a set of allowed program clauses and G be an allowed normal goal. If R is a Φ-SLDNF-refutation from $P \cup \{G\}$ then the answer R computes is ground.*

(The proof follows directly from Proposition 15.1 of [Llo87]).

4 The formal model

4.1 Deductive databases and user models

This section formally defines the concepts of deductive database, log, and user model, along with the certification criterion and the cooperativeness domain, while Section 4.2 describes the cooperative interface we propose.

A *deductive database* is a finite set D of allowed program clauses, and a *query* over D is a non-empty allowed normal goal G.

A *log* λ is a set of expressions of the form $success(A)$ or $fail(A)$, where A is a positive ground literal. Intuitively, the cooperative interface will include $success(A)$ (or $fail(A)$) to inform the user that A (or $\neg A$) is deductible from the database.

A *user model for* D is a set U of program clauses such that: (i) each clause is in the language of D; (ii) each clause is allowed; (iii) for any positive fact A, if there is an SLDNF-refutation from $U \cup \{\leftarrow A\}$ then there is no finitely failed SLDNF-tree from $D \cup \{\leftarrow A\}$. The first restriction is just a technical convenience and may be easily lifted, the second one is important for the adequacy of some of our key definitions, as discussed later on, and the reason from the third one is the log initialization problem, already discussed in Section 2.

Let U be a user model and λ be a log. The *user state* induced by U and λ is the set $U[\lambda]$ obtained by adding to U all positive literals A such that $success(A) \in \lambda$.

We then identify user inferences in the presence of a log λ with the SLDNF-derivations from $U[\lambda]$ that do not contradict the information in λ. This is formalized by introducing a certification test $\Phi[\lambda]$ saying that, whenever the user needs to derive a positive fact A in the course of his reasoning, he must check whether the log λ does not indicate that A must be rejected, that is, whether $fail(A)$ is not in λ.

Recall that $\mathcal{R}$ is the set of all triples such that the first element is a finite sequence, with length $n+1$, of normal goals, the second element is a finite sequence, with length n, of substitutions, and the third element is a finite sequence, also with length n, of clauses, for some n.

Definition 4.1 The *certification test for a log* λ is the function $\Phi[\lambda] : \mathcal{R} \mapsto$ {TRUE,FALSE} defined as follows:

> Let $S \in \mathcal{R}$. Assume that $G_0, \ldots, G_n$ is the sequence of goals and $\theta_1, \ldots, \theta_n$ is the sequence of substitutions of S, for some $n \geq 0$. Then, $\Phi[\lambda](S)$=FALSE iff there is $i \in [0, n)$ such that the literal selected from G_i (the first literal by assumption) is a positive literal A and $fail(A\theta_{i+1} \ldots \theta_n) \in \lambda$.
>
> In this case, we also say that $A\theta_{i+1} \ldots \theta_n$ is a $\Phi[\lambda]$*-failure literal* of S and that G_i is a $\Phi[\lambda]$*-failure goal* of S.

Furthermore, we say that S is *uncertified for* λ iff $\Phi[\lambda](S)$=FALSE. Otherwise, we say that S is *certified for* λ.

The certification test for a log λ then formalizes the notion of certification criterion mentioned in Section 2. Note that there is a natural ordering for the $\Phi[\lambda]$-failure literals and the $\Phi[\lambda]$-failure goals of S induced by the position of the goals in the sequence. In particular, we may refer to the last $\Phi[\lambda]$-failure literal and the last $\Phi[\lambda]$-failure goal of S.

Let U be a user model, λ be a log and Q be a query. Then, by the restrictions on user models, logs, and queries, $U[\lambda]$ is a set of allowed program clauses and Q is an allowed normal goal. Suppose that S is a $\Phi[\lambda]$-SLDNF-refutation from $U[\lambda] \cup \{Q\}$. Hence, by Proposition 3.6, if the literal selected from a goal G_i of S is a positive literal A, then $A\theta_{i+1}\ldots\theta_n$ is ground. Therefore, the test $fail(A\theta_{i+1}\ldots\theta_n) \in \lambda$ is well-defined, since λ contains only ground expressions.

Given a log λ and a user model U, the user inferences are then identified with the set of all $\Phi[\lambda]$-SLDNF-refutations from $U[\lambda]$ and a non-empty normal goal. As already discussed in Section 2, we further identify the *cooperativeness domain* with the set of all $\Phi[\lambda]$-SLDNF-derivations from $U[\lambda] \cup \{Q\}$ such that U is a user model, λ is a log, and Q is a non-empty normal goal that contains only positive literals.

The following example formalizes one of the examples given in Section 2 and illustrates the concepts introduced in this section:

Example 4.2 Let U be a user model that contains only one clause:

$U.1.$ $depart(x, f(t)) \leftarrow arrived(x, t)$

Let λ be the following log:

$$\lambda = \{success(arrived(XY202, 10{:}00am),\\ fail(depart(XY202, f(10{:}00am)))\}$$

Then, the current user state $U[\lambda]$ contains the following clauses:

$U.1.$ $depart(x, f(t)) \leftarrow arrived(x, t)$
$U.2.$ $arrived(XY202, 10{:}00am)$

Consider the following sequence R of goals:

$R.1.$ $\leftarrow depart(XY202, f(10{:}00am))$
$R.2.$ $\leftarrow arrived(XY202, 10{:}00am)$
$R.3.$ $\square$

Then, R is a (standard) SLDNF-refutation from $U[\lambda] \cup \{\leftarrow depart(XY202, f(10{:}00am))\}$ (that is, a certified Φ-SLDNF-refutation, where Φ is the test that always returns true). However, R is an uncertified $\Phi[\lambda]$-SLDNF-refutation from $U[\lambda] \cup \{\leftarrow depart(XY202, f(10{:}00am))\}$ because $depart(XY202, f(10{:}00am))$ was selected in $R.1$, but $fail(depart(XY202, f(10{:}00am)))$ is in λ.

4.2 Description of a cooperative interface

In this section, we give a very high-level description of the cooperative interface we propose. The interface depends on a second variation of SLDNF-resolution, based on a different certification test, that checks refutations from the user state against the database.

Definition 4.3 The *certification test for a deductive database D* is the function $\Phi[D] : \mathcal{R} \mapsto \{\text{TRUE, FALSE}\}$ defined as follows:

> Let $S \in \mathcal{R}$. Assume that $G_0, \ldots, G_n$ is the sequence of goals and $\theta_1, \ldots, \theta_n$ is the sequence of substitutions of S, for some $n \geq 0$. Then, $\Phi[D](S)$=FALSE iff there is $i \in [0, n)$ such that:
>
> - either the literal selected from G_i is a positive literal A and there is a finitely failed SLDNF-tree from $D \cup \{\leftarrow A\theta_{i+1} \ldots \theta_n\}$;
> - or the literal selected from G_i is a negative ground literal $\neg B$, and there is an SLDNF-refutation from $D \cup \{\leftarrow B\}$.
>
> In this case, we also say that $A\theta_{i+1} \ldots \theta_n$, in the first case, and $\neg B$, in the second case, is a *$\Phi[D]$-failure literal* of S and that G_i is a *$\Phi[D]$-failure goal* of S.

Furthermore, we say that S is *uncertified for D* iff $\Phi[D](S)$=FALSE.

As for $\Phi[\lambda]$, we may refer to the last $\Phi[D]$-failure literal and the last $\Phi[D]$-failure goal of S.

Let U be a user model, λ be a log, and Q be a query. Then, $U[\lambda]$ is a set of allowed program clauses and Q is an allowed normal goal. Suppose that S is a $\Phi[D]$-SLDNF-refutation from $U[\lambda] \cup \{Q\}$. Again, by Proposition 3.6, if the literal selected from a goal G_i of S is a positive literal A, then $A\theta_{i+1} \ldots \theta_n$ is ground. Therefore, testing if there is a (standard) finitely failed SLDNF-tree from $D \cup \{\leftarrow A\theta_{i+1} \ldots \theta_n\}$ is simplified since the initial goal $\leftarrow A\theta_{i+1} \ldots \theta_n$ is always ground.

If $A_1, \ldots, A_p$ are the positive literals and $\neg B_1, \ldots, \neg B_q$ the negative literals of a normal goal G, define

$$expand(G) = \{success(A_1), \ldots, success(A_p), fail(B_1), \ldots, fail(B_q)\}.$$

A high-level description of the cooperative interface is given in Figure 1. Note that steps 1 and 3a of the procedure are subjected to the usual limitations of logic programming systems, in particular, that which says that it is in general undecidable to determine if a query will fail or not (see also Example 4.6 for further discussions). Moreover, note that, if λ is the current log, the procedure simulates only the $\Phi[D]$-SLDNF-refutations from $U[\lambda]$ starting on a goal $\leftarrow A$ such that A is the head of a clause in U. We will prove in the next section that this suffices to correctly avoid misconstruals in the cooperativeness domain.

---

input: a query $\leftarrow Q$
output: an answer α for $\leftarrow Q$ or $FAIL$.
parameters: a deductive database D, a user model U and a log λ

1. Find an answer substitution α for $\leftarrow Q$ from D;
   if the query fails then return $FAIL$ and stop.
2. Add all expressions in $expand(Q\alpha)$ to λ.
3. While λ changes do:
   (a) Simulate all $\Phi[D]$-SLDNF-refutations
   from $U[\lambda] \cup \{\leftarrow A | A \leftarrow B_1, \ldots, B_m \in U\}$.
   (b) If R is uncertified then:
      i. if the last $\Phi[D]$-failure literal of R is a positive literal A, then add $fail(A)$ to λ;
      ii. if the last $\Phi[D]$-failure literal of R is a negative literal $\neg B$, then add $success(B)$ to λ;
4. Return α.

Figure 1: The cooperative interface - procedure 1

During a session, the user may then pose several queries to the system. Each query is then passed to the cooperative interface, along with the log produced by the processing of the previous query (the log at the beginning of a session is always empty). The behaviour of the system during a session then induces a *cooperative dialog* C, defined as a sequence of triples $(Q_1, \alpha_1, \lambda_1), \ldots, (Q_n, \alpha_n, \lambda_n)$ where, for each $i \in [1, n]$, Q_i is a query, α_i is an answer substitution for Q_i or the expression $FAIL$, and λ_i is a log. Note that, for each $i \in [1, n]$, $\lambda_{i-1} \subseteq \lambda_i$ and $expand(Q_i\alpha_i) \subseteq \lambda_i$, if α_i is not $FAIL$.

We now give two examples that indicate how the interface operates and that formalize the examples given in Section 2.

Example 4.4 Let U be a user model that contains only one clause:

$U.1.$ $\quad depart(x, f(t)) \leftarrow arrived(x, t), \neg rain(f(t))$

Let D be the following deductive database:

$D.1.$ $\quad depart(x, f(t)) \leftarrow arrived(x, t), \neg rain(f(t))$
$D.2.$ $\quad arrived(XY202, 10{:}00am)$
$D.3.$ $\quad rain(f(10{:}00am))$

Suppose that the user starts a new session with the query:

$Q.$ $\quad \leftarrow arrived(XY202, t)$

Recall that the log λ at the beginning of a section is empty by assumption. The interface will compute the following answer substitution for Q:

$$\alpha = \{t/10{:}00am\}$$

and add $expand(Q\alpha)$ to the current log, which then becomes:

$$\lambda = \{success(arrived(XY202, 10{:}00am))\}$$

The user state at this point is the theory:

$$U[\lambda] = U \cup \{arrived(XY202, 10{:}00am)\}$$

from which it is possible to infer $depart(XY202, f(10{:}00am))$. The interface proceeds to simulate refutations. In particular, it will simulate the following uncertified $\Phi[D]$-refutation R from $U[\lambda] \cup \{\leftarrow depart(x, f(t))\}$:

$R.1.$ $\quad \leftarrow depart(x, f(t))$
$R.2.$ $\quad \leftarrow arrived(x, f(t)), \neg rain(f(t))$
$R.3.$ $\quad \leftarrow \neg rain(f(10{:}00am))$
$R.4.$ $\quad \sqcup$

whose $\Phi[D]$-failure literal is $\neg rain(f(10{:}00am))$ because there is a trivial (standard) SLDNF-refutation from $D \cup \{\leftarrow\ rain(f(10{:}00am))\}$. Hence, the interface will include the expression $success(rain(f(10{:}00am)))$ in the log, which becomes:

$$\lambda = \{success(arrived(XY202, 10{:}00am)),\ success(rain(f(10{:}00am)))\}$$

The interface then stops and returns the answer α and, implicitly, the final value of the log λ. The final user state is the theory:

$$U[\lambda] = U \cup \{arrived(XY202, 10{:}00am),\ rain(f(10{:}00am))\}$$

from which it is no longer possible to infer $depart(XY202, f(10{:}00am))$.

Example 4.5 Suppose that the user model now is V:

$V.1.\quad depart(x, f(t)) \leftarrow\ arrived(x, t)$

Assume the same deductive database D and the same query Q as before, which means that the answer substitution α for Q remains unchanged. The log and the user state immediately before the interface begins simulating refutations is:

$$\lambda = \{success(arrived(XY202, 10{:}00am))\}$$

$$\bar{V}[\lambda] = V \cup \{arrived(XY202, 10{:}00am)\}$$

The interface will simulate, among others, the following uncertified $\Phi[D]$-refutation S from $\bar{V}[\lambda] \cup \{\leftarrow\ depart(x, f(t))\}$:

$S.1.$	$\leftarrow\ depart(x, f(t))$	
$S.2.$	$\leftarrow\ arrived(x, t)$	$\theta_1 = \varepsilon$
$S.3.$	$\square$	$\theta_2 = \{x/XY202, t/10{:}00am\}$

whose $\Phi[D]$-failure literal is $(depart(x, f(t)))\theta_1\theta_2$, that is, $depart(XY202, f(10{:}00am))$, because there is a (standard) finitely failed SLDNF-tree from $D \cup \{\leftarrow\ depart(XY202, f(10{:}00am))\}$. Hence, the interface will include the expression $fail(depart(XY202, f(10{:}00am)))$ in the log. The log returned after the query and the final user state will be:

$$\lambda \;=\; \{success(arrived(XY202, 10{:}00am)),\; fail(depart(XY202, f(10{:}00am)))\}$$

$$\bar{V}[\lambda] \;=\; V \cup \{arrived(XY202, 10{:}00am)\}$$

Note that there is a $\Phi[\lambda]$-SLDNF-refutation from $\bar{V}[\lambda] \cup \{\leftarrow depart(XY202, f(10{:}00am))\}$, but it will not be certified for $\Phi[\lambda]$, since λ contains $fail(depart(XY202, f(10{:}00am)))$. This intuitivelly means that the extra information in the log suffices to warn the user that he must reject this (faulty) inference.

We close this section with a third example that illustrates how to compute the failure literal of a refutation easily. The key point is to instrument the clauses of the user model with *belief literals*, which are literals enclosed in square brackets that help trace the literals cancelled in refutations. The standard selection function is also altered to select the leftmost (normal) literal, if there is one, or the leftmost belief literal, if there are only belief literals in the goal.

Note that the implementation of the $\Phi[D]$ certification test is subjected to the usual limitations of logic programming systems.

Example 4.6 Let U, D, and Q be as in Example 4.4. We instrument the only clause in U as follows:

$U.1$ $\quad depart(x, f(t)) \leftarrow arrived(x, t),\ \neg rain(f(t)),\ [\neg rain(f(t))],\ [depart(x, f(t))]$

The refutation R now becomes the sequence:

$R.1.$ $\quad \leftarrow depart(x, f(t))$
$R.2.$ $\quad \leftarrow arrived(x, f(t)),\ \neg rain(f(t)), [\neg rain(f(t))],\ [depart(x, f(t))]$
$R.3.$ $\quad \leftarrow \neg rain(f(10{:}00am)),\ [\neg rain(f(10{:}00am))],\ [depart(XY202, f(10{:}00am))]$
$R.4.$ $\quad \leftarrow [\neg rain(f(10{:}00am))],\ [depart(XY202, f(10{:}00am))]$

The selection of the negative belief literal $[\neg rain(f(10{:}00am))]$ from $R.4$ signals that the interface must try to find a (standard) SLDNF-refutation from $D \cup \{\leftarrow rain(f(10{:}00am))\}$.

Since the search is successful, the $\Phi[D]$-failure literal of the original refutation R is $\neg rain(f(10{:}00am))$.

Now, let V be the user model introduced in Example 4.5. We instrument V with belief literals as follows:

$V.1.$ $\quad depart(x, f(t)) \leftarrow arrived(x, t), [depart(x, f(t))]$

which means that the refutation S becomes:

$S.1.$ $\quad \leftarrow depart(x, f(t))$
$S.2.$ $\quad \leftarrow arrived(x, f(t)), [depart(x, f(t))]$
$S.3.$ $\quad \leftarrow [depart(XY202, f(10{:}00am))]$

This time, the selection of the positive belief literal $[depart(XY202, f(10{:}00am))]$ from $S.3$ signals that the interface must try to find a (standard) finitely failed SLDNF-tree from $D \cup \{\leftarrow depart(XY202, f(10{:}00am))\}$. Since the search is successful, the $\Phi[D]$-failure literal of S is $depart(XY202, f(10{:}00am))$.

5 Theoretical results

5.1 Soundness of the cooperative interface

In this section we prove that the cooperative interface is correct in the sense that, for any log it creates, if a fact F can be obtained from the user model and the log by a deduction in the cooperativeness domain, then we cannot detect using finite failure that F is false in the database. Recall that $U[\lambda]$ denotes the set obtained by adding to a user model U all positive literals A such that $success(A)$ occurs in a log λ.

Definition 5.1 Let U be a user model, D be a deductive database, and $\mathcal{E}$ be a cooperativeness domain. A log λ is *finitely sound for D and U with respect to $\mathcal{E}$* iff, if R is a certified $\Phi[\lambda]$-SLDNF-refutation R in $\mathcal{E}$ from $U[\lambda]$ and a goal $\leftarrow G$, and if α is the answer computed by R for $\leftarrow G$, then there is no finitely failed SLDNF-tree from $D \cup \{\leftarrow G\alpha\}$.

In the next sequence of results, let U be a user model, D be a deductive database, $\leftarrow G$ be a query containing only positive literals, and $\mathcal{D}$ be the cooperativeness domain introduced in Section 4, that is, the set of all refutations starting on a goal containing only positive literals. Also let C be a dialogue produced by Procedure 1, and λ be a log in the dialogue. Note that any $\Phi[\lambda]$-SLDNF-derivation from $U[\lambda] \cup \{\leftarrow G\}$ is then in $\mathcal{D}$, since $\leftarrow G$ contains only positive literals.

To prove the correctness of the interface, we need some auxiliary results. The first one is a direct consequence of the definitions in Section 4 and Procedure 1:

Proposition 5.2 *Let A be a ground positive literal. Then:*

(a) *If* success$(A) \in \lambda$ *then there is an SLDNF-refutation from* $D \cup \{\leftarrow A\}$.

(b) *If* fail$(a) \in \lambda$ *then there is a finitely failed SLDNF-tree from* $D \cup \{\leftarrow A\}$.

The next corollary follows directly from the above proposition and the definition of SLDNF-resolution.

Corollary 5.3 *Let* A *be a ground positive literal. Thus, if* success$(A) \in \lambda$ *then* fail$(A) \notin \lambda$.

The second result establishes a relationship between user's derivations in the presence of a log and the derivations simulated by the interface.

Lemma 5.4

(a) *If* S *is a* $\Phi[\lambda]$*-SLDNF-derivation from* $U[\lambda] \cup \{G\}$ *in* $\mathcal{D}$, *then* S *is also a* $\Phi[D]$*-SLDNF-derivation from* $U[\lambda] \cup \{G\}$.

(b) *If* S *is a failed* $\Phi[\lambda]$*-SLDNF-derivation from* $U[\lambda] \cup \{G\}$ *in* $\mathcal{D}$, *then* S *is also a failed* $\Phi[D]$*-SLDNF-derivation from* $U[\lambda] \cup \{G\}$.

(c) *If* S *is a certified* $\Phi[\lambda]$*-SLDNF-refutation from* $U[\lambda] \cup \{G\}$ *in* $\mathcal{D}$, *then* S *is also a certified* $\Phi[D]$*-SLDNF-refutation from* $U[\lambda] \cup \{G\}$.

(d) *If* S *is an uncertified* $\Phi[\lambda]$*-SLDNF-refutation from* $U[\lambda] \cup \{G\}$ *in* $\mathcal{D}$, *then* S *is also an uncertified* $\Phi[D]$*-SLDNF-refutation from* $U[\lambda] \cup \{G\}$.

(e) *If* N *is a finitely failed or uncertified* $\Phi[\lambda]$*-SLDNF-tree from* $U[\lambda] \cup \{G\}$ *in* $\mathcal{D}$, *then* N *is also a finitely failed or uncertified* $\Phi[D]$*-SLDNF-tree* $U[\lambda] \cup \{G\}$.

PROOF. The proof will be by induction on the rank of SLDNF-derivations, certified or uncertified SLDNF-refutations and finitely failed or uncertified SLDNF-trees. Recall that, since G contains only positive literals, any $\Phi[\lambda]$-SLDNF-derivation from $U[\lambda] \cup \{G\}$ is in $\mathcal{D}$.

Basis: Assume that the rank is 0.

(a) Let S be a $\Phi[\lambda]$-SLDNF-derivation from $U[\lambda] \cup \{G\}$ of rank 0, that is, no negative literal is selected. Since only positive literals are selected in S, the $\Phi[\lambda]$ and $\Phi[D]$ certification tests have no influence on S. Hence, a $\Phi[\lambda]$-derivation of rank 0 is also a $\Phi[D]$-derivation of rank 0.

(b) Let S be a failed $\Phi[\lambda]$-SLDNF-derivation from $U[\lambda] \cup \{G\}$ of rank 0. As in (a), S is trivially a failed $\Phi[D]$-SLDNF-derivation from $U[\lambda] \cup \{G\}$ of rank 0.

(c) Let S be a certified $\Phi[\lambda]$ SLDNF-refutation from $U[\lambda] \cup \{G\}$ of rank 0. By (a), S is also a $\Phi[D]$-SLDNF-derivation from $U[\lambda] \cup \{G\}$. To prove that S is a certified $\Phi[D]$-SLDNF-refutation from $U[\lambda] \cup \{G\}$, we will show that the $\Phi[D]$-certification test succeeds, that is, there are no $\Phi[D]$-failure goals for S.

Assume that S has length n, the sequence of goals is $G_0 = G, \ldots, G_n$, the sequence of variants of clauses in $U[\lambda]$ is $C_1, \ldots, C_n$, and the sequence of mgu's is $\theta_1, \ldots, \theta_n$. Let $i \in [0, n)$. Assume that L_1 is the literal cancelled from G_i. Since S has rank 0, L_1 is a positive literal. Since the $\Phi[\lambda]$-certification test succeeds, we have $fail(L) \notin \lambda$, for $L = L_1\theta_{i+1} \ldots \theta_n$. Assume that A is the head of C_{i+1}. Thus, we may construct from S a $\Phi[D]$-SLDNF-refutation S' from $U[\lambda] \cup \{\leftarrow A\}$, such that S' is simulated in the same iteration that Procedure 1 generates λ, the composition of mgu's is α and $A\alpha = L$. Thus, since $fail(L) \notin \lambda$, by Definition 4.3 and step 3 of Procedure 1, there is no finitely failed SLDNF-tree from $D \cup \{\leftarrow L\}$. Hence, G_i is not a $\Phi[D]$-failure goal.

Therefore, there are no $\Phi[D]$-failure goals for S.

(d) Let S be an uncertified $\Phi[\lambda]$-SLDNF-refutation from $U[\lambda] \cup \{G\}$ of rank 0. By (a), S is also a $\Phi[D]$-SLDNF-derivation from $U[\lambda] \cup \{G\}$. To prove that S is an uncertified $\Phi[D]$-SLDNF-refutation from $U[\lambda] \cup \{G\}$, we will show that the $\Phi[D]$-certification test fails, that is, there is a $\Phi[D]$-failure goal for S.

Assume that S has length n, the sequence of goals is $G_0 = G, \ldots, G_n$ and the sequence of mgu's is $\theta_1, \ldots, \theta_n$. Suppose that G_i is the $\Phi[\lambda]$-failure goal in S, for some $i \in [0, n)$. Since S has rank 0, the literal selected from G_i is a positive literal, say M, and $fail(M\theta_{i+1} \ldots \theta_n) \in \lambda$. By Proposition 5.2, there is a finitely failed SLDNF-tree from $D \cup \{\leftarrow M\theta_{i+1} \ldots \theta_n\}$. Hence, G_i is also a $\Phi[D]$-failure goal in S.

(e) Let N be a finitely failed or uncertified $\Phi[\lambda]$-SLDNF-tree N of rank 0 from $U[\lambda] \cup \{G\}$. By Definitions 3.4 and 4.1, each branch in N is a failed $\Phi[\lambda]$-SLDNF-derivation or an uncertified $\Phi[\lambda]$-SLDNF-refutation, of rank 0. By (b) and (d), N is trivially a finitely failed or uncertified $\Phi[D]$-SLDNF-tree.

Induction step: Let $k > 0$. Suppose that the results hold for all refutations and trees of rank $j < k$.

(a) Let S be a $\Phi[\lambda]$-SLDNF-derivation from $U[\lambda] \cup \{G\}$ of rank k. Assume that S has length n, and that the sequence of goals is $G_0 = G, \ldots, G_n$. We show that S is also a $\Phi[D]$-SLDNF-derivation from $U[\lambda] \cup \{G\}$.

Let $j \in [1, n]$. Consider that L_1 is the literal cancelled in G_{j-1}. If L_1 is a positive literal the proof is the same as for the basis step. Suppose then that L_1 is a ground negative literal $\neg L$. Since $\neg L$ is cancelled in S, it means that there is a finitely failed or uncertified $\Phi[\lambda]$-SLDNF-tree from $U[\lambda] \cup \{\leftarrow L\}$ of rank less than k. By the induction hypothesis, there is also a finitely failed or uncertified $\Phi[D]$-SLDNF-tree from $U[\lambda] \cup \{\leftarrow L\}$.

Then, $\neg L$ can indeed be cancelled in G_{j-1} deriving G_j.

(b) Let S be a finitely failed $\Phi[\lambda]$-SLDNF-derivation from $U[\lambda] \cup \{G\}$ of rank k. By (a), S is also a $\Phi[D]$-SLDNF-derivation from $U[\lambda] \cup \{G\}$. To prove that S is a failed $\Phi[D]$-SLDNF-derivation from $U[\lambda] \cup \{G\}$, we show that the literal selected in the last goal of S cannot be cancelled.

Assume that S has length n and the sequence of goals is $G_0 = G, \ldots, G_n$. Suppose that G_n is a goal of the form $\leftarrow L_1, \ldots, L_m$. If L_1 is a positive literal, the proof is the same as for (b) in the basis step. Suppose then that L_1 is a ground negative literal $\neg L$. Since $\neg L$ is not cancelled in G_n, there is a certified $\Phi[\lambda]$-SLDNF-refutation of rank less than k from $U[\lambda] \cup \{\leftarrow L\}$. Then, by the induction hypothesis, there is also a certified $\Phi[D]$-SLDNF-refutation from $U[\lambda] \cup \{\leftarrow L\}$. Thus, L_1 cannot be cancelled in G_n, that is, S is indeed a failed $\Phi[D]$-SLDNF-derivation from $U[\lambda] \cup \{G\}$.

(c) Let S be a certified $\Phi[\lambda]$-SLDNF-refutation from $U[\lambda] \cup \{G\}$ of rank k. By (a), S is also a $\Phi[D]$-SLDNF-derivation from $U[\lambda] \cup \{G\}$. To prove that S is a certified $\Phi[D]$-SLDNF-refutation from $U[\lambda] \cup \{G\}$, we will show that the $\Phi[D]$-certification test succeeds, that is, there are no $\Phi[D]$-failure goals for S.

Assume that S has length n, the sequence of goals is $G_0 = G, \ldots, G_n$ and the sequence of variants of clauses in $U[\lambda]$ is $C_1, \ldots, C_n$. Let $i \in [0, n)$. Assume that L_1 is the literal cancelled from G_i. If L_1 is a positive literal, the proof is the same as for (c) in the basis step. Suppose then that L_1 is a ground negative literal $\neg L$. Since $\neg L$ is cancelled in S, we have that $success(L) \notin \lambda$. Indeed, if $success(L) \in \lambda$ then, by definition of user state, $L \in U[\lambda]$ and, by Corollary 5.3, $fail(L) \notin L$. Thus, there would be a certified $\Phi[\lambda]$-SLDNF-refutation from $U[\lambda] \cup \{\leftarrow L\}$, which would imply that $\neg L$ could not be cancelled in S. Hence, we conclude that $success(L) \notin \lambda$. Also, since G contains only positive literals, the negative literal $\neg L$ is introduced in S by a variant of a clause in U, say C_q, for some $q \in [1, i]$ with $i > 0$. Assume that A is the head of C_q. We may construct from S a $\Phi[D]$-SLDNF-refutation S' from $U[\lambda] \cup \{\leftarrow A\}$, which is simulated by Procedure 1; in the same iteration it generates λ, and $\neg L$ is cancelled in S'. Thus, since $success(L) \notin \lambda$, by Definition 4.3 and step 3 of Procedure 1, there is no SLDNF-refutation from $D \cup \{\leftarrow L\}$. Hence, G_i is not a $\Phi[D]$-failure goal. Therefore, there are no $\Phi[D]$-failure goals for S.

(d) Let S be an uncertified $\Phi[\lambda]$-SLDNF-refutation from $U[\lambda] \cup \{G\}$ of rank k. By (a), S is also a $\Phi[D]$-SLDNF-derivation from $U[\lambda] \cup \{G\}$. To prove that S is an uncertified $\Phi[D]$-SLDNF-refutation from $U[\lambda] \cup \{G\}$, we will show now that the $\Phi[D]$-certification test fails for S, and the $\Phi[D]$-failure literal is a positive literal.

Assume that S has length n, the sequence of goals is $G_0 = G, \ldots, G_n$ and the sequence of variants of clauses in $U[\lambda]$ is $C_1, \ldots, C_n$. Let G_i be the $\Phi[\lambda]$-failure goal, for some $i \in [0, n)$. Suppose that L_1 is the literal selected from G_i. If L_1 is a positive literal the proof is the same for (d) in the basis step. We now prove that L_1 cannot be a negative literal. By contradiction, suppose that L_1 is ground negative literal $\neg L$. Since $\neg L$ is a $\Phi[D]$-failure literal, there is an SLDNF-refutation from $D \cup \{\leftarrow L\}$. Since G contains only positive literals, there is a variant of a clause in U, say C_q, for some $q \in [1, i]$ with $i > 0$, that introduced the negative literal. Suppose that the head of C_q is A. We may construct from S a $\Phi[D]$-SLDNF-refutation S' from $U[\lambda] \cup \{\leftarrow A\}$ such that $\neg L$ is a $\Phi[D]$-failure literal for S'. Hence, by Definition 4.3 and step 3 of Procedure 1, and since there is an SLDNF-refutation from $D \cup \{\leftarrow L\}$, we have $success(L) \in \lambda$. Thus, $L \in U[\lambda]$ and, by Corollary 5.3, $fail(L) \notin \lambda$. Hence, there is a certified $\Phi[\lambda]$-SLDNF-refutation from $U[\lambda] \cup \{\leftarrow L\}$ and the literal L_1 cannot be cancelled in G_i. Contradiction.

(e) Let N be a finitely failed or uncertified $\Phi[\lambda]$-SLDNF-tree N of rank k from $U[\lambda] \cup \{G\}$. By Definitions 3.4 and 4.1, each branch in N is a failed $\Phi[\lambda]$-SLDNF-derivation or an uncertified $\Phi[\lambda]$-SLDNF-refutation, of rank no greater than k. By (b) and (d), N is trivially a finitely failed or uncertified $\Phi[D]$-SLDNF-tree. ∎

The next auxiliary lemma shows that every answer computed by a certified $\Phi[D]$-SLDNF-refutation does not contradict D.

Lemma 5.5 *Let $\leftarrow Q$ be a query containing positive and negative literals. If R is a certified $\Phi[D]$-SLDNF-refutation from $U[\lambda] \cup \{\leftarrow Q\}$, and if α is the answer computed by R for $\leftarrow Q$, there is no finitely failed SLDNF-tree from $D \cup \{\leftarrow Q\alpha\}$.*

PROOF. Let $\leftarrow Q$ be a query containing positive and negative literals. Let R be a $\Phi[D]$-SLDNF-refutation from $U[\lambda] \cup \{\leftarrow Q\}$, and let α be the answer computed by R. Assume that R has length n, the sequence of goals is $G_0 = \leftarrow Q, \ldots, G_n$ and the sequence of mgu's is $\theta_1, \ldots, \theta_n$. By Proposition 3.6, $Q\alpha$ is ground. Assume that $\leftarrow Q$ is of the form $\leftarrow L_1, \ldots, L_m$. Let $i \in [1, m]$. If $L_i\alpha$ is a positive literal A, then there is a literal A' cancelled in a goal of R, say G_k, for some $k \in [0, n)$, such that $A'\theta_{k+1} \ldots \theta_n = A$. Moreover, by Definition 4.3, since $\Phi[D](R)$=TRUE, there is no finitely failed SLDNF-tree from $D \cup \{\leftarrow A\}$. If $L_i\alpha$ is a negative literal $\neg A$, then $\neg A$ is the literal cancelled from some goal of R and, again by Definition 4.3, there is no SLDNF-refutation from $D \cup \{\leftarrow A\}$, which implies that there is no finitely failed SLDNF-tree from $D \cup \{\leftarrow \neg A\}$. Thus, there is no finitely failed SLDNF-tree from $D \cup \{\leftarrow L_i\alpha\}$, for $1 \leq i \leq m$. Hence, there is no finitely failed SLDNF-tree from $D \cup \{\leftarrow Q\alpha\}$. ∎

We are now ready to state the major result of this section:

Theorem 5.6 (Correctness of the cooperative interface). *Let C be a dialogue produced by Procedure 1. Then, any log λ in C is sound for D and U with respect to the cooperativeness domain $\mathcal{D}$.*

PROOF. Straightforward from Lemmas 5.4(c) and 5.5 ∎

Therefore, we may assert that Procedure 1 correctly avoids all misconstruals that derive conjunctions of positive literals, even though the interface simulates only refutations that start on a goal $\leftarrow A$ such that A is the head of a clause in the user model.

5.2 Other properties of the interface

In the next sequence of results, let U again be a user model, D be a deductive database, $\leftarrow G$ be a query containing only positive literals, and $\mathcal{D}$ be the cooperativeness domain introduced in Section 4, that is, the set of all refutations starting on a goal containing only positive literals. Also, let C be a dialogue produced by Procedure 1 and λ be a log in C.

The next lemma, together with Lemma 5.4, establishes a tight relationship between the user's derivations in the presence of a log and the derivations simulated by the interface.

Lemma 5.7

(a) If S is a $\Phi[D]$-SLDNF-derivation from $U[\lambda] \cup \{G\}$, then S is also a $\Phi[\lambda]$-SLDNF-derivation from $U[\lambda] \cup \{G\}$.

(b) If S is a failed $\Phi[D]$-SLDNF-derivation from $U[\lambda] \cup \{G\}$, then S is also a failed $\Phi[\lambda]$-SLDNF-derivation from $U[\lambda] \cup \{G\}$.

(c) If S is a certified $\Phi[D]$-SLDNF-refutation from $U[\lambda] \cup \{G\}$, then S is also a certified $\Phi[\lambda]$-SLDNF-refutation from $U[\lambda] \cup \{G\}$.

(d) If S is an uncertified $\Phi[D]$-SLDNF-refutation from $U[\lambda] \cup \{G\}$, then S is also an uncertified $\Phi[\lambda]$-SLDNF-refutation from $U[\lambda] \cup \{G\}$.

(e) If N is a finitely failed or uncertified $\Phi[D]$-SLDNF-tree from $U[\lambda] \cup \{G\}$, then N is also a finitely failed or uncertified $\Phi[\lambda]$-SLDNF-tree $U[\lambda] \cup \{G\}$.

PROOF. The proof will be by induction on the ranks of SLDNF-derivations, certified or uncertified SLDNF-refutations, and finitely failed or uncertified SLDNF-trees.

Basis: Assume that the rank is 0.

(a) Let S be a $\Phi[D]$-SLDNF-derivation from $U[\lambda] \cup \{G\}$ of rank 0, that is, no negative literal is selected. Since only positive literals are selected in S, the $\Phi[\lambda]$ and $\Phi[D]$ certification tests have no influence in S. Hence, a $\Phi[D]$-derivation of rank 0 is also a $\Phi[\lambda]$-derivation of rank 0.

(b) Let S be a failed $\Phi[D]$-SLDNF-derivation from $U[\lambda] \cup \{G\}$ of rank 0. As in (a), S is trivially a failed $\Phi[\lambda]$-SLDNF-derivation from $U[\lambda] \cup \{G\}$ of rank 0.

(c) Let S be a certified $\Phi[D]$-SLDNF-refutation from $U[\lambda] \cup \{G\}$ of rank 0. By (a), S is also a $\Phi[\lambda]$-SLDNF-derivation from $U[\lambda] \cup \{G\}$. To prove that S is a certified $\Phi[\lambda]$-SLDNF-refutation from $U[\lambda] \cup \{G\}$, we will show that the $\Phi[\lambda]$-certification test succeeds, that is, there are no $\Phi[\lambda]$-failure goals for S.

Assume that S has length n, the sequence of goals is $G_0 = G, \ldots, G_n$ and the sequence of mgu's is $\theta_1, \ldots, \theta_n$. Let $i \in [0, n)$. Consider that M is the literal cancelled in G_i. Since S has rank 0, M is a positive literal. Since the $\Phi[D]$-certification test succeeds, there is no finitely failed SLDNF-tree from $D \cup \{\leftarrow M\theta_{i+1} \ldots \theta_n\}$. Thus, by Proposition 5.2, $fail(M\theta_{i+1} \ldots \theta_n) \notin \lambda$. Hence, G_i is not a $\Phi[\lambda]$-failure goal. Therefore, there are no $\Phi[\lambda]$-failure goals for S.

(d) Let S be an uncertified $\Phi[D]$-SLDNF-refutation from $U[\lambda] \cup \{G\}$ of rank 0. By (a), S is also a $\Phi[\lambda]$-SLDNF-derivation from $U[\lambda] \cup \{G\}$. To prove that S is an uncertified $\Phi[\lambda]$-SLDNF-refutation from $U[\lambda] \cup \{G\}$, we will show that the $\Phi[\lambda]$-certification test fails, that is, there is a $\Phi[\lambda]$-failure goal for S.

Assume that S has length n, the sequence of goals is $G_0 = G, \ldots, G_n$, the sequence of variants of clauses in $U[\lambda]$ is $C_1, \ldots, C_n$, and the sequence of mgu's is $\theta_1, \ldots, \theta_n$. Let G_i be the $\Phi[D]$-failure goal, for $i \in [0, n)$. Since S has rank 0, the cancelled literal in G_i is a positive literal, say M, and there is a finitely failed SLDNF-tree from $D \cup \{\leftarrow \neg L\}$, such that $M\theta_{i+1} \ldots \theta_n = L$. Assume that A is the head of C_{i+1}. Thus, we may construct from S a $\Phi[D]$-SLDNF-refutation S' from $U[\lambda] \cup \{\leftarrow A\}$, such that S' is simulated by Procedure 1 in the same iteration where the log λ is generated, and the composition of mgu's is α and $A\alpha = L$. Since there is a finitely failed SLDNF-tree from $D \cup \{\leftarrow \neg L\}$, by Definition 4.3 and step 3 of Procedure 1, $fail(L) \in \lambda$. Hence, G_i is also a $\Phi[\lambda]$-failure goal.

(e) Let N be a finitely failed or uncertified $\Phi[D]$-SLDNF-tree N of rank 0 from $U[\lambda] \cup \{G\}$. By Definitions 3.4 and 4.3, each branch in N is a failed $\Phi[D]$-SLDNF-derivation or an uncertified $\Phi[D]$-SLDNF-refutation, of rank 0. By (b) and (d), N is trivially a finitely failed or uncertified $\Phi[\lambda]$-SLDNF-tree.

Induction step: Let $k > 0$. Suppose that the results hold for $j < k$.

(a) Let S be a $\Phi[D]$-SLDNF-derivation from $U[\lambda] \cup \{G\}$ of rank k.

Assume that S has length n and the sequence of goals is $G_0 = G, \ldots, G_n$. We show that S is also a $\Phi[\lambda]$-SLDNF-derivation from $U[\lambda] \cup \{G\}$.

Let $j \in [1, n]$. Suppose that L_1 is the literal cancelled from G_{j-1}. If L_1 is a positive literal the proof is the same as in the basis step. Consider then that the selected literal L_1 is a ground negative literal of the form $\neg L$. Since L_1 is cancelled in S, there is a finitely failed or uncertified $\Phi[D]$-SLDNF-tree of rank less than k from $U[\lambda] \cup \{\leftarrow L_1\}$. By the induction hypothesis, there is also a finitely failed or uncertified $\Phi[\lambda]$-SLDNF-tree from $U[\lambda] \cup \{\leftarrow L_1\}$. Thus, L_1 can indeed be cancelled in S.

(b) Let S be a failed $\Phi[D]$-SLDNF-derivation from $U[\lambda] \cup \{G\}$ of rank k. By (a), S is also a $\Phi[\lambda]$-SLDNF-derivation from $U[\lambda] \cup \{G\}$. To prove that S is a failed $\Phi[\lambda]$-SLDNF-derivation from $U[\lambda] \cup \{G\}$, the literal selected in the last goal of S cannot actually be cancelled.

Assume that S has length n and the sequence of goals is $G_0 = G, \ldots, G_n$. Suppose that G_n is a goal of the form $\leftarrow L_1, \ldots, L_m$. If L_1 is a positive literal, the proof is the same as for (b) in the basis step. Suppose then that L_1 is a ground negative literal $\neg L$. Since $\neg L$ is not cancelled in G_n, there is a certified $\Phi[D]$-SLDNF-refutation of rank less than k from $U[\lambda] \cup \{\leftarrow L\}$. Then, by the induction hypothesis, there is also a certified $\Phi[\lambda]$-SLDNF-refutation from $U[\lambda] \cup \{\leftarrow L\}$. Hence, L_1 cannot be cancelled in G_n, that is, S is indeed a failed $\Phi[\lambda]$-SLDNF-derivation from $U[\lambda] \cup \{G\}$.

(c) Let S be a certified $\Phi[D]$-SLDNF-refutation from $U[\lambda] \cup \{G\}$ of rank k. By (a), S is also a $\Phi[\lambda]$-SLDNF-derivation from $U[\lambda] \cup \{G\}$. The proof that S is a certified $\Phi[\lambda]$-SLDNF-refutation from $U[\lambda] \cup \{G\}$ is the same as for (c) in the basis step.

(d) Let S be an uncertified $\Phi[D]$-SLDNF-refutation from $U[\lambda] \cup \{G\}$ of rank k. By (a), S is also a $\Phi[\lambda]$-SLDNF-derivation from $U[\lambda] \cup \{G\}$. To prove that S is an uncertified $\Phi[\lambda]$-SLDNF-refutation from $U[\lambda] \cup \{G\}$, we will show that the $\Phi[\lambda]$-certification test fails and the $\Phi[\lambda]$-failure literal is a positive literal.

Assume that S has length n, the sequence of goals is $G_0 = G, \ldots, G_n$ and the sequence of variants of clauses in $U[\lambda]$ is $C_1, \ldots, C_n$. Let G_i be the $\Phi[D]$-failure goal, for $i \in [0, n)$. Suppose that L_1 is the literal cancelled from G_i. If L_1 is a positive literal, the proof is the same as for the basis step. We have to show that L_1 cannot be a negative literal. By contradiction, suppose that L_1 is a ground literal $\neg L$. Since $\neg L$ is a $\Phi[D]$-failure literal, there is an SLDNF-refutation from $D \cup \{\leftarrow L\}$. Since G contains only positive literals, there is a variant, say C_q, of a clause in U which introduces the negative literal, for some $q \in [1, i]$ with $i > 0$. Suppose that the head of C_q is A. We may construct from S a $\Phi[D]$-SLDNF-refutation from $U[\lambda] \cup \{\leftarrow A\}$, whose $\Phi[D]$-failure literal is $\neg L$. Hence, by Definition 4.3 and step 3 of Procedure 1, since there is an SLDNF-refutation from $D \cup \{\leftarrow L\}$, we have $success(L) \in \lambda$. Thus, $L \in U[\lambda]$ and there is a certified $\Phi[D]$-refutation from $U[\lambda] \cup \{\leftarrow L\}$. Then, L_1 cannot be cancelled in G_i. Hence, G_i is the last goal of S. Contradiction.

(e) Let N be a finitely failed or uncertified $\Phi[D]$-SLDNF-tree N of rank k from $U[\lambda] \cup \{G\}$. By Definitions 3.4 and 4.3, each branch in N is a failed $\Phi[D]$-SLDNF-derivation or an uncertified $\Phi[D]$-SLDNF-refutation of rank no greater than k. By (b) and (d), N is trivially a finitely failed or uncertified $\Phi[\lambda]$-SLDNF-tree. ∎

6 Conclusions

In this chapter we first described a model for the user's inferences capturing the intuition that, whenever the user needs to derive a positive fact A in his inference, he must check whether the current log does not indicate that A must be rejected. Then, we presented a cooperative interface that is responsible for all the inferences from the deductive database that are necessary to answer the user's queries and to compute what additional information to include in the log to avoid misconstruals. Therefore, we may view the interface as summarizing, for the user, the information in the deductive database and passing it in the log. Finally, we proved that the cooperative interface is correct, in the sense that any log produced during a dialog contains enough information to avoid misconstruals.

We are now experimenting with cooperativeness domains that limit the derivations that the interface must simulate to those satisfying a certain complexity constraint (a simple example would be to limit the length of the derivation). We are also testing the idea of limiting the domain by capturing in advance the goal(s) that the user wants to achieve [AP80]. In the context of Project NICE, we also explored a simpler approach, based on request modification rules compiled from explicit patterns of user inferences [HCF91a].

References

[AP80] J. F. Allen and C. R. Perrault. Analyzing intentions in utterances. *Artificial Intelligence*, 15(3):143–178, 1980.

[BJ86] L. Bolc and M. Jarke, editors. *Cooperative Interfaces to Information Systems.* Springer-Verlag, Berlin, 1986.

[CCL90] W. Chu, Q. Chen, and R. C. Lee. Cooperative query answering via type abstraction hierachy. In *International Working Conference on Cooperating Knowledge Based Systems*, Univ. Keele, England, 1990.

[CD89] F. Cuppens and R. Demolombe. Cooperative answering: a methodology to provide intelligent access to databases. In L. Kerschberg, editor, *2nd International Conference on Expert Database Systems*, pages 621–643. Benjamin/Cummings, 1989.

[CF90] M. A. Casanova and A. L. Furtado. An information system environment based on plan generation. In *International Working Conference on Cooperating Knowledge Based Systems*, Univ. Keele, England, 1990.

[HCF91a] A. S. Hemerly, M. A. Casanova, and A. L. Furtado. Cooperative behaviour through request modification. In *10th International Conference on the Entity-Relationship Approach*, San Mateo, CA, USA, 1991.

[HCF91b] A. S. Hemerly, M. A. Casanova, and A. L. Furtado. Exploiting user models to avoid misconstruals. In *1st International Workshop on Nonstandard Queries and Answers Approach*, Tolouse, France, 1991.

[Kap82] S. J. Kaplan. Cooperative responses from a portable natural language query. *Artificial Intelligence*, 19(2):165–187, 1982.

[KW89] A. Kobsa and W. Wahlster, editors. *User Models in Dialog Systems*. Springer-Verlag, Berlin, 1989.

[Llo87] J. W. Lloyd. *Foundations of Logic Programming*. Springer-Verlag, Berlin, 1987.

[Mot84] A. Motro. Query generalization: a technique for handling query failure. In *1st International Workshop on Expert Database Systems*, pages 314–325, 1984.

[Qui89] A. Quilici. Detecting and responding to plan-oriented misconceptions. In A. Kobsa and W. Wahlster, editors, *User Models in Dialog Systems*, chapter 5. Springer-Verlag, Berlin, 1989.

[Sat87] T. Sato. On Consistency of First Order Logic Programs. Technical Report TR-87-12, Electrotechnical Laboratory, Ibaraki, Japan, 1987.

[Web86] B. L. Webber. Questions, answers and responses: interacting with knowledge base systems. In M. L. Brodie and J. Mylopoulos, editors, *On Knowledge Base Management Systems*. Springer-Verlag, Berlin, 1986.

4

On using logic to represent belief

Rolf T. Nossum

1 Introduction

The overall goal of this chapter is to convey knowledge of some techniques for representing and reasoning about intentional concepts in non-classical logics. Such logics are of central importance in representing and reasoning about belief and knowledge, intention and obligation, planning and acting, and other concepts. Philosophers aptly call them logics of Practical Reasoning.

These logics are gaining wide acceptance as representational vehicles for advanced applications in databases, artificial intelligence, intelligent tutoring, and other fields.

The discussion will be centred around the intentional concept of belief, and some logics are examined with respect to their capability to capture features of that concept.

The chapter is structured as follows. In the next section, some commonsense notions of belief are noted. The degree to which modal logics of belief approximate these commonsense notions will be taken as a measure of their relative goodness. In logic, belief is typically represented as some kind of relation between an actor and a proposition about the actor's environment, and some fundamental misgivings about this perspective are mentioned.

In the subsequent section, classical logic is presented, and its relative inadequacy to represent belief is pointed out.

Next, a basic modal-logical language with possible-world structures is introduced, and the axioms and rules for KD45 are given. KD45 is a logical system much better equipped to handle belief than classical propositional logic. It retains, however, many problematic features as a belief logic, and some of them are reviewed.

Then the logics of general awareness and the logic of local reasoning from [2] are reviewed, and the ways in which they improve upon KD45 are noted.

The structures used to equip this succession of more and more expressive logics with semantics are successive generalizations of each other, leading from a basic propositional semantics through relational modal semantics to minimal modal semantics.

Towards the end of the chapter, Lindenbaum's lemma is given, and the technique of maximal consistent sets is used to prove completeness of an axiomatization from [7] for a combined logic of local reasoning and general awareness. This gives a taste of an important technique for theoretical work in this area.

2 Commonsense notions of belief

Our running example is belief about states of affairs in the world. For instance

Sten believes that Chambery is a town in France

is a belief in this sense. We review some commonsense properties of the concept of belief:

Belief statements are not invariant under substitution of equals:

From: Pierre believes that the king of Norway is a monarch
And: Harald = the king of Norway

We may not conclude:

Pierre believes that Harald is a monarch

Belief is not in general closed under implication:

From: Trixie believes that P
And: P implies Q

We may not conclude:

Trixie believes that Q

(e.g. if Trixie is a robot unaware that P implies Q)

Beliefs interact causally with other intentional states, as in

Sten wants to go to France
And: Sten believes that in order to go to France, he needs a visa

Therefore,

Sten wants to get a visa.

It is only fair to note that the concept of belief alluded to here is folk-psychological, i.e. it is not founded on scientific evidence. A sceptic might remark, 'They could hardly have sent a spaceship to Venus on Folk Astronomy, or have eradicated smallpox on Folk Medicine'. Why should one expect progress in practical reasoning to be based on Folk Psychology?

The author takes no dogmatic stand on this issue, but finds it equally fair to note that belief and other generalizations from everyday experience are communicated among people in the form of relations between agents (e.g. believers) and logical sentences or propositions expressed by logical sentences. The fact that this is useful in everyday life suggests that research along these lines will lead to improvements in the state-of-the-art of computer-based systems, as well as stimulation and challenges for cognitive scientists and theorists of mind.

According to whether mental states (such as belief) are represented by relations between an agent and a proposition, or between an agent and a sentence expressing such a proposition, formal models of mental states are sometimes grouped into Representational and Syntactic theories of mind, respectively.

Representational theories of mind explain mental states as relations between agents and the contents (or meaning, or truth conditions) of sentences. For example, belief statements are explained as relations between believers and the contents of believed sentences (i.e. not the sentences themselves).

There is an important criticism that applies to representational theories of mind. Take belief:

By appeal to *a priori* meaning of sentences, a standard of normality or convention is assumed of the believer. This imposes limits on cognitive theorizing which make it intractable to characterize beliefs of, e.g. young children, brain damaged people, or the mentally ill. It is therefore contentious whether there can be developmental, clinical, or comparative representational theories of mind. Stich [8] elaborates eloquently on this.

Syntactic theories of mind, on the other hand, treat mental states as relations between agents and sentences, or syntactic tokens. Interactions between mental states are interpreted in terms of formal or syntactic properties of these tokens. Once more it is worth while to note some misgivings. Take belief again:

Suppose Pierre (a native of France) believes that the sun is shining, and that Sten (a Norwegian) also believes the sun is shining. It is not very plausible to think that the words 'le soleil brille'

are literally inscribed somewhere in one brain, and

'solen skinner'

in the other. Psychological plausibility dictates that the sentence must be similarly encoded in the two brains. For instance, awareness of the sun is routinely acquired by children before they learn either French or Norwegian language. So some encoding has to be provided for that maps the believed sentence into neuron excitations or whatever. On this view then, belief seems to entail some mapping from sentences to encodings in the brain, but that lands us in a representational theory of mind where these very encodings are the contents or meanings of sentences.

3 Classical semantics

We shall now define a formal language of propositions, and an apparatus for interpreting propositions as true or false. Let us begin with a set of names or symbols for the items or individuals that propositions are to be about:

$$\{Chambery, Harald, the\ king\ of\ Norway, Sten, Pierre, \ldots\}$$

In a given set of circumstances, these names will denote fixed items or individuals under discussion. The technically minded reader should regard them as constant symbols, not variables, and will recognize the language we are about to define as a set of ground formulas.

In addition to the set of names, we need some relation symbols of the form $rel(arg_1, \ldots, arg_n)$ where $n \geq 0$. All of the arguments will be constant symbols. Some relations will have infix syntax, in particular the equality relation.

Finally, we use the logical connectives $\neg$, $\vee$, $\wedge$, $\rightarrow$, and $\leftrightarrow$.

We can now define formulas as either:

1. primitive: $p, q, true, false, the\ sun\ is\ shining, \ldots$, or

2. relational: $rel(arg_1, \ldots, arg_n)$, $Harald = the\ king\ of\ Norway$, *I believe (today) is (Monday)*,
$(Jack)\ loves\ (Jill)$, ..., or

3. compound: $\neg P, P \wedge Q$, where P, Q are formulas.

We take $P \vee Q$ to abbreviate $\neg((\neg P) \wedge (\neg Q))$, $P \rightarrow Q$ to abbreviate $\neg P \vee Q$, and $P \leftrightarrow Q$ to abbreviate $(P \rightarrow Q) \wedge (Q \rightarrow P)$. So we can build complicated formulas from primitive ones.

In order to find out if complicated formulas are true or not, the following semantical structure M is used: $M = (S, \sigma, \pi, R)$ where S is a non-empty set, called the set of worlds, σ assigns an item or an individual to each name or symbol at each world, and π assigns the value true or false to each primitive formula at each world. R is a set of relations which for each relation symbol (*I believe* (...) *is* (...), etc.) and at each world says whether the attached arguments (*today*, *Monday*) are related or not.

The relation corresponding to the equality symbol is required to be an equivalence relation for each world, and had we chosen an only slightly more complex system of names and individuals, we would have called for congruence relations at this point.

A world can thus be viewed as a set of circumstances, determining which items and individuals are denoted by which names and symbols (e.g. who is the present king of Norway), and which basic things are true and which are false (sometimes the sun is shining, sometimes not).

This kind of structure is a convenient means of assigning truth values to formulas. We define a relation $\models$ where $M, s \models P$ is read as 'M satisfies P in s' for $s \in S$ as follows:

$M, s \models P$ where P is primitive, iff $\pi(P, s) = true$
$M, s \models rel(arg_1, \ldots, arg_n)$ iff $R(rel, \sigma(arg_1, s), \ldots, \sigma(arg_n, s), s) = true$
$M, s \models \neg P$ iff not $M, s \models P$
$M, s \models P \wedge Q$ iff $M, s \models P$ and $M, s \models Q$

We say a formula P is valid in the structure M, in symbols $M \models P$, if $M, s \models P$ for all $s \in S$, and that P is simply valid, or $\models P$, if P is valid in every structure. P is said to be satisfiable if it is true at some world in some structure, i.e. $M, s \models P$ for some M and s.

This logic, unfortunately, provides only a very poor encoding of intentional attitudes such as belief, knowledge, agency, obligation, and related concepts.

For instance, the formula

$$I\ believe\ (today)\ is\ (today)$$

is true in all circumstances that we need consider. Nevertheless, it is conceivable, such as during a pleasant holiday excursion in a remote location, that

$$today{=}Monday$$

although it may not be the case that

I believe (today) is (Monday).

However, in the above semantical regime,

I believe (today) is (Monday)

is entailed by

I believe (today) is (today)

and

$$today{=}Monday$$

together. Thus we see that this logic is uncomfortably strict for our purposes.

4 Relational modal semantics

When construed as relations between agents and propositions, beliefs can be represented in so-called modal systems of logic in a suitable way. Kanger [5] gave the semantical framework now popularly known as possible-world semantics, and inaccurately attributed to Kripke [4]. Makinson [6] discovered how to simplify proofs of completeness of axiomatizations of modal systems by the use of maximal consistent sets.

We proceed to review some modal systems of logic that are used to model variants of belief.

4.1 Modal logic and a simple belief model

We define a simple modal language and review an interpretation of it.

Instead of the relational formulas of classical propositional logic we now admit: $\Box P$, where P is a formula, and take $\diamond P$ to abbreviate $\neg\Box\neg P$.

Hintikka [3] studied interpretations of this kind of language where $\Box P$ was interpreted as the belief by some agent α that P is true. With this interpretation in mind, it is convenient to represent $\Box P$ as $B_\alpha P$.

A possible-world structure for this language is a tuple $M = (S, \pi, R_\alpha)$ where S is a non-empty set, π is an assignment of truth values to primitive formulas for each element in S, with $\pi(true, s) = true$ and $\pi(false, s) = false$, and R_α is a serial, transitive, and euclidian binary relation on S.

S is thought of as the set of possible worlds, or states of affairs that could obtain. R relates each world to one or more (because of seriality) worlds that α conceives as possible in those states of affairs.

The truth conditions for 'M satisfies P in s' for $s \in S$ are now defined as follows:

$M, s \models P$ where P is primitive, iff $\pi(P, s) = true$ $M, s \models \neg P$ iff not $M, s \models P$
$M, s \models P \wedge Q$ iff $M, s \models P$ and $M, s \models Q$
$M, s \models B_\alpha P$ iff $M, t \models P$ for all t such that $sR_\alpha t$

This notion of belief is also often called KD45, which is an acronym composed of conventional indices of some axioms that characterize properties of it.

4.2 KD45

The following axiomatization is sound and complete for possible-world structures of belief: axiom schemas:

- P, whenever P is an instance of a propositional tautology.
- K: $B_\alpha P \wedge B_\alpha(P \rightarrow Q) \rightarrow B_\alpha Q$.
- D: $B_\alpha P \rightarrow \neg B_\alpha \neg P$.
- 4: $B_\alpha P \rightarrow B_\alpha B_\alpha P$.
- 5: $\neg B_\alpha P \rightarrow B_\alpha \neg B_\alpha P$.

Rules of inference:

$$RN : \frac{P}{B_\alpha P}$$

$$MP : \frac{P, P \rightarrow Q}{Q}$$

KD45 reveals some dubious features of Hintikka models of belief, which are loosely characterized as ascribing omniscience to the believer α.

For instance, RN means that α believes every valid formula, which is at best an approximation.

K means that α reasons according to modus ponens, in other words α's beliefs are closed under believed implication. This is at least not true of everybody.

D, 4, and 5 specify consistency in α's beliefs, and some introspective capability.

What is really troublesome is the fact [1] that RN and K together entail the inference rule:

$$RM : \frac{P \rightarrow Q}{B_\alpha P \rightarrow B_\alpha Q}$$

which means that α's beliefs are closed under valid implication. This is patently untrue of everyone, humans and machines alike.

We shall review some attempts to remedy the problems of omniscience within the modal-logical framework. Specifically, Fagin and Halpern [2] have proposed several logics of belief that attempt to solve the problem of logical omniscience. We shall review two of them, the logic of General Awareness and the logic of Local Reasoning. In the interest of simplicity, we limit the presentation to the essential features of each logic, in particular we shall omit their implicit-belief notions, and deal only with single-believer systems.

4.3 A logic of general awareness

This logic is designed so as to avoid closure of belief under valid implication. A separate notion of 'awareness' is introduced, and used as a filter that limits the believer's capacity of implication chains.

The notion of awareness that is intended is quite general, and meant to encompass a wide variety of interpretations. The phrase 'α is aware of P' could mean different things in different applications, such as:

'α can figure out the truth of P'
'α knows that P is a formula'
'α can figure out the truth of P within time T'

The language of General Awareness is the same as for Hintikka-style belief, but with an additional modality which we denote A_α. The phrase 'α is aware of P' is then written $A_\alpha P$. Formal interpretation is via possible-world structures, and we define a possible-world structure for General Awareness as a tuple $M = (S, \pi, W_\alpha, R_\alpha)$, where S, π, and R_α are as before, and W_α is a mapping from S to sets of formulas (not just primitive ones). Truth of formulas at possible worlds is now defined as follows:

$M, s \models P$ where P is primitive, iff $\pi(P, s) = \mathit{true}$
$M, s \models \neg P$ iff not $M, s \models P$
$M, s \models P \wedge Q$ iff $M, s \models P$ and $M, s \models Q$
$M, s \models A_\alpha P$ iff $P \in W_\alpha(s)$
$M, s \models B_\alpha P$ iff $P \in W_\alpha(s)$ and $M, t \models P$ for all t such that $sR_\alpha t$

This logic obeys neither K nor RN for , and therefore lacks some of the problems of logical omniscience.

However,

$$B_\alpha P \wedge B_\alpha(P \to Q) \wedge A_\alpha Q \to B_\alpha Q$$

is valid, and the logic is closed under the rule

$$\frac{P}{A_\alpha P \to B_\alpha P}$$

and if awareness is constrained in the following way:

$$\text{if } sR_\alpha t \text{ then } W_\alpha(s) = W_\alpha(t)$$

then we also get analogues of axioms 4 and 5:

$$B_\alpha P \wedge A_\alpha B_\alpha P \rightarrow B_\alpha B_\alpha P$$

and

$$\neg B_\alpha P \wedge A_\alpha(\neg B_\alpha P) \rightarrow B_\alpha \neg B_\alpha P$$

Moreover, α does not hold contradictory beliefs in this logic:

$$\neg(B_\alpha P \wedge B_\alpha \neg P)$$

5 Minimal modal semantics

5.1 A logic of local reasoning

The logic of General Awareness is very flexible through variation of the awareness concept, but cannot model agents whose beliefs are contradictory. Fagin and Halpern [2] also give a logic of belief which accomodates this possibility, built on the assumption that beliefs come in non-interacting clusters. An agent is thus modelled as a cluster or society of minds, each with its own set of beliefs which may contradict those of the others. $B_\alpha P$ is now interpreted as 'α believes P in some frame of mind'.

The language for Local Reasoning is the same as the one for Hintikka-style belief, and we define possible-world structures for Local Reasoning as tuples $M = (S, \pi, C_\alpha)$ with S and π as before, and C_α a mapping from possible worlds to non-empty sets of non-empty sets of possible worlds. Thus $C_\alpha(s)$ is a non-empty set of non-empty subsets of S. Truth of formulas at possible worlds is now defined as follows:

$M, s \models P$ where P is primitive, iff $\pi(P, s) = true$
$M, s \models \neg P$ iff not $M, s \models P$
$M, s \models P \wedge Q$ iff $M, s \models P$ and $M, s \models Q$
$M, s \models B_\alpha P$ iff there is some $T \in C_\alpha(s)$ such that $M, t \models P$ for all $t \in T$

This logic also lacks K, this time because in one frame of mind α may believe P, in another $P \rightarrow Q$, while putting them together to conclude Q in neither one. Furthermore, this logic captures agents who may hold contradictory beliefs;

$$B_\alpha P \wedge B_\alpha \neg P$$

is satisfiable since in one frame of mind agent α may believe P and in another $\neg P$. But

$$B_\alpha(P \wedge \neg P)$$

is not satisfiable, because in one and the same frame of mind α reasons as in KD45.

5.2 Lindenbaum's lemma and an exercise in completeness

Makinson [6] showed how to apply Lindenbaum's lemma to proving completeness of axiomatizations of modal systems. We review the lemma and apply it to proving completeness of an axiomatization of a logic of General Awareness and Local Reasoning.

Let us call a formula P consistent with respect to an axiomatization if $\neg P$ is not provable from it. A set Γ of formulas is called consistent if it is finite and the conjunction of all its members is consistent, otherwise it is called consistent if every finite subset of it is consistent. Γ is called maximal if it is consistent and has only inconsistent proper extensions.

Maximal sets of formulas have interesting properties, and we state below the ones we need for this exercise. See [1] for more.

Suppose Γ is maximal with respect to an axiomatization containing MP and the propositional tautologies. Then the following properties hold:

If A is provable, then $A \in \Gamma$
$\neg A \in \Gamma$ iff $A \notin \Gamma$
$A \wedge B \in \Gamma$ iff both $A \in \Gamma$ and $B \in \Gamma$

5.3 Lindenbaum's lemma

The following theorem is known as Lindenbaum's lemma: *Suppose that Γ is consistent. Then there exists a maximal Δ such that $\Gamma \subseteq \Delta$.*

PROOF. With consistent Γ, let us construct an extension Δ that we can prove is maximal. Supposing an enumeration $A_1, A_2, A_3, \ldots$ of all sentences in the modal language, we inductively define a sequence of sets $\Delta_0, \Delta_1, \Delta_2, \ldots$ and Δ as follows:

$$\Delta_0 = \Gamma$$
$$\Delta_n = \Delta_{n-1} \cup \{A_n\} \text{ if } \Delta_{n-1} \cup \{A_n\} \text{ is consistent,}$$

$$\Delta_n = \Delta_{n-1} \text{ otherwise.}$$
$$\Delta = \textstyle\bigcup_{i=0}^{\infty} \Delta_i$$

Since $\Delta_i \subseteq \Delta$, in particular $\Gamma \subseteq \Delta$. Also, observe that $\Delta_i \subseteq \Delta_j$ whenever $0 \leq i \leq j$, and that $A_i \in \Delta_i$ whenever $A_i \in \Delta$. Finally, we need to know that for every finite subset Δ' of Δ, $\Delta' \subseteq \Delta_i$ for some i. This is obvious if Δ' is empty, otherwise consider the $A_n \in \Delta'$ which has the highest index n. Then $\Delta' \subseteq \Delta_n$.

By compactness, the consistency of Δ follows from that of every finite subset. But suppose that Δ' is a finite subset of Δ. Then $\Delta' \subseteq \Delta_i$ for some i, but Δ_i is consistent by virtue of its construction, and then Δ' is consistent also. So Δ must be consistent.

To show that Δ has no consistent proper extension, suppose that $\Delta \cup \{A\}$ is consistent for some sentence A. Since A occurs in the enumeration of sentences, this amounts to the consistency of $\Delta \cup \{A_n\}$ for some n. Since $\Delta_{n-1} \subseteq \Delta$, also $\Delta_{n-1} \cup \{A_n\} \subseteq \Delta \cup \{A_n\}$, so $\Delta_{n-1} \cup \{A_n\}$ must be consistent. But then $A = A_n \in \Delta_n \subseteq \Delta$ by construction, so $A \in \Delta$ follows.

This completes the proof of Lindenbaum's lemma. ■

5.4 An exercise in completeness

Nossum [7] gave the following axiomatization of a combined logic of General Awareness and Local Reasoning, but without the syntactic awareness modality. Awareness figures prominently in the semantics, however. We review the completeness proof, which uses Lindenbaum's lemma.

The language remains the same as for Hintikka-style belief.

A possible-world structure for General Awareness and Local Reasoning is a tuple $M = (S, \pi, W_\alpha, C_\alpha)$ and we define $\models$ as follows:

$M, s \models P$ where P is primitive, iff $\pi(P, s) = true$
$M, s \models \neg P$ iff not $M, s \models P$
$M, s \models P \wedge Q$ iff $M, s \models P$ and $M, s \models Q$
$M, s \models B_\alpha P$ iff $P \in W_\alpha(s)$ and there is some $T \in C_\alpha(s)$ such that $M, t \models P$ for all $t \in T$

The following axioms and rules are sound and complete for the combined logic of General Awareness and Local Reasoning:

- Axioms:

  P, whenever P is an instance of a propositional tautology.

- Rules of inference:

$$RP: \frac{\neg P}{\neg B_\alpha P}$$

$$MP: \frac{P, P \to Q}{Q}$$

Soundness of this axiomatization is immediate, but completeness is proved by an application of Lindenbaum's lemma.To prove that every valid formula is provable, we can prove equivalently that every consistent formula is satisfiable.

Suppose, then, that P is consistent, i.e. $\neg P$ is not provable. We construct a possible-world structure for General Awareness and Local Reasoning which satisfies P:

Let $M = (S, \pi, W_\alpha, C_\alpha)$ where:

$S =$ the set of maximal sets of consistent formulas
$\pi(R, s)$ iff $R \in s$
$W_\alpha(s) = \{R | B_\alpha R \in s\}$
$C_\alpha(s) = \{U | U = \{u | R \in u \in S\} \textit{ for some } R\}$

We prove the more general result that

$$M, s \models P \text{ iff } P \in s$$

by induction on the structure of P. This suffices because every consistent formula is contained in some maximal consistent set. Recall the properties stated earlier about maximal consistent sets.

- P is primitive: the result follows directly from the definition.

- P is $\neg Q$: if Q is not consistent, then P is provable, so $M, s \models P$ by soundness and every member of S contains P. Otherwise Q is consistent, and for all s, $Q \in s$ iff not $\neg Q \in s$. But by induction $M, s \models Q$ iff $Q \in s$, so $M, s \models P$ iff $P \in s$ follows.

- P is $Q \wedge R$: since P is consistent, so are Q and R, and by induction $M, s \models Q$ iff $Q \in s$ and $M, s \models R$ iff $R \in s$. But since $P \in s$ iff $Q \in s$ and $R \in s$, this is precisely what we need.

- P is $B_\alpha Q$: then Q must be consistent by RP. Then by induction $M, s \models Q$ iff $Q \in s$. Now, by definition, $M, s \models P$ iff $Q \in \{F | B_\alpha F \in s\}$ and $M, t \models Q$ for all $t \in T$ for some $T \in \{U | U = \{u | R \in u\} \textit{ for some } R\}$, in other words, iff $B_\alpha Q \in s$ and $M, t \models Q$ for all $t \in T$ for some $T \in \{U | U = \{u | R \in u\} \textit{ for some } R\}$. But, the first condition is just $P \in s$, and we may take $\{u | Q \in u\}$ for T, so the second condition is met. We therefore obtain $M, s \models P$ iff $P \in s$ as required.

This is the end of the proof of completeness.

6 Conclusion

We have illustrated classical propositional logic, and relational and minimal modal logic, by considering applications of them to represent belief. We observed that these logics are increasingly good for this purpose, but that none of them are perfect.

We saw that the semantical structures underlying these three logics are successive generalizations of each other.

Finally, we carried out a proof of completeness in a logic of the minimal-modal kind using maximal consistent sets, thereby getting to know a common technique for working in this logical territory.

References

[1] B. F. Chellas. *Modal Logic.* Cambridge Univ. Press, 1980.

[2] R. Fagin and J. Y. Halpern. Belief, awareness, and limited reasoning, *Artificial Intelligence Journal*, **34**, 39–76, 1988.

[3] J. Hintikka. *Knowledge and Belief*, Cornell Univ. Press, 1962

[4] S. Kripke. Semantical analysis of Modal Logic I, normal propositional calculi. *Zeitschrift fur mathematische Logik und Grundlagen der Mathematik*,**9**, 67–69, 1963.

[5] S. Kanger. *Provability in Logic*, Stockholm Studies in Philosophy, Vol. 1, Almqvist och Wiksell, 1957.

[6] D. Makinson. On some completeness theorems in modal logic, *Zeitschrift fur mathematische Logik und Grundlagen der Mathematik*, **12**, 379–384 1966.

[7] R. T. Nossum. Belief without omniscience. In *Proceedings SCAI Conf., Tampere*, 1989.

[8] S. Stich. *From Folk Psychology to Cognitive Science*, MIT Press, 1983.

5

Deriving answers to safety queries

Robert Demolombe and Andrew Jones

Abstract

In addition to asking questions concerning the actual content of the database, a user may also wish to query the reliability of the messages it contains. We argue that, in reasoning about the reliability of the information in his database (or its 'Safety', as we choose to call it), the database administrator will need to consider the source, or sources, which sent in the signals containing this information. In attempting to answer 'Safety queries', therefore, the administrator will need to be able to consider not only what is believed or known to be the case, but also the signalling acts which various agents have performed when supplying input. Here we show how some tools from applied modal logic—specifically, the logic of action, and logics of belief and knowledge—may be used to represent reasoning about Safety. We supply both a general formal analysis of the concepts involved, and a simplified formalization suitable for implementation. This is a preliminary report on work in progress, and so we conclude with a list of problems that might be investigated within this framework.

1 Introduction

Let's imagine a person asking the following query in a travel agency:

What are the flights from Toulouse to London today?

If the employee of the travel agency obtains the answer by querying a database it can happen that he provides an answer which is a list of flight numbers obtained from the database, and the following complementary information:

A_1: *I can guarantee the departure times are correct only for the flights by Air France, because time tables for the other companies have not been updated recently.*

A_2: *It may be that there are other flights, since I do not have time tables for all the companies.*

Answers A_1 and A_2 inform the person about the validity of the direct answer, and about its completeness. Provision of these kinds of answers requires, first, keeping in mind a clear distinction between a description of the world as stored in a database and a correct description of the world, and, second, having information (meta-information) about the validity and completeness of the former description.

In our example the employee of the travel agency knows that the information in the database about the flights by Air France is correct, and he also knows that the information is complete only for some companies. Notice that this employee knows this meta-information but he does not necessarily know the information which is in the database about these flights.

These notions of validity and completeness were first introduced by A.Motro in [5, 6]; they are illustrated by Figure 1. In this diagram we have a description of the world stored in a database, called DB, and a correct description of the world, called W, in exactly the same language. We see that the extension of the predicate P in DB is not Valid, while the extension of the predicate Q is not Complete.

DB:	P(a) P(b) P(c)	Q(c) Q(d)
W :	P(a) P(b)	Q(c) Q(d) Q(e)

Figure 1: Mapping between the description of the world stored in the database, and the correct description of the world.

The words 'Valid' and 'Complete' refer here to the correspondence between two descriptions of the world, in the same language, that don't necessarily represent the same information, while, usually, in Logic, they refer to the correspondence between the proof theoretic and model theoretic representations of the same information.

To avoid any confusion, in the following we will use the word 'Safety' instead of 'Validity'. We have not introduced another word for 'Completeness' because in this chapter we concentrate only on Safety.

A substantial difference in our approach with respect to Motro, who deals with standard databases, is that we consider a more general kind of information than sets of facts. Moreover, we adopt an axiomatic approach instead of a semantic approach. We now mean by 'database' any kind of first-order theory. This means that DB and W are two first-order theories defined on the same language. In this context some part of the description of the world represented by p(x) is said to be Safe iff we have:

$$\text{For every x (DB} \vdash \text{p(x) implies W} \vdash \text{p(x))}$$

Another important difference is that we do not necessarily assign the same status to the information which is explicitly stored in the database (the DB axioms), and the information derived from the database (the DB theorems).

Let's consider, for example, the database:

$$\text{DB} = \{ \forall x(r(x) \leftrightarrow p(x) \land q(x)),\ p(a),\ q(a),\ r(a)\}$$

In DB the fact r(a) has two occurrences: an explicit one and a derived one. It is our claim that, from the point of view of Safety, these two occurrences do not necessarily have the same status. As a consequence we consider that r(a) may be Safe in DB_1 and not Safe in DB_2:

$$DB_1 = \{r(a)\} \qquad DB_2 = \{\forall x(r(x) \leftrightarrow p(x) \land q(x)),\ p(a),\ q(a)\}$$

Furthermore, from the point of view of Safety, we do not consider the following theories DB_1' and DB_2' to be equivalent databases:

$$DB_1' = \{p(a) \land q(a)\} \qquad DB_2' = \{p(a),\ q(a)\}$$

The reason for making this distinction is illustrated by the next example. Let's consider a scenario where the information inserted in the database comes from several sensors. Imagine that there are sensors sending meteorological information which are of three different types. Sensors of type s_1 measure the light intensity, and, depending on a given threshold they can send the information to DB that it is cloudy. Sensors of type s_2 detect whether the water is frozen, and they transmit the information that the weather is cold. Sensors of type s_3 determine whether it is snowing and, if it is, they send the information that it is cloudy and it is cold. If there are sensors in different places: l, m, n, ... the information transmitted to DB by the sensors of types s_1, s_2, and s_3, located in l, are represented by messages of the form: 'cloudy(l)', 'cold(l)', 'cloudy(l) and cold(l)', respectively. The administrator of the database may know, for example, that the information sent by the sensors of types s_2 and s_3 in l is correct, because these sensors have been recently controlled, while the sensor of type s_1 in that place is not reliable (see Figure 2).

From this meta-information one can infer that if DB 'believes' that cloudy(l) $\land$ cold(l) holds, because it received the message 'cloudy(l) and cold(l)' from s_3, then cloudy(l) $\land$ cold(l) is true in the world. However, if DB 'believes' that cloudy(l) $\land$ cold(l) holds because it received the message

Sensor s_1(not reliable): ⟶ “cloudy(l)’

Sensor s_2(reliable): ⟶ “cold(l)’

Sensor s_3(reliable): ⟶ “cloudy(l) and cold(l)’

Figure 2: Messages sent by reliable, or not reliable, sensors in place l.

‘cloudy(l)’ from s_1, and the message ‘cold(l)’ from s_2, then cloudy(l)$\wedge$cold(l) is not necessarily true, because s_1 is not reliable.

This scenario shows that the reliability of a sentence which is explicitly stored in DB depends on the source of the information. Therefore, it is very important to keep trace of this source. For sentences derived from DB the reliability depends on the reliability of the sentences used in the derivation. For this reason a formalization of such a scenario needs to make a clear distinction between, on the one hand, the representation of the performed actions of inserting sentences[1] in the DB and, on the other hand, the world ‘believed’ by the DB. A very simple way to make this distinction, which is no more than a trick, is to assume that sentences explicitly stored in DB come only from insertion actions (i.e. a sentence resulting from a derivation is never stored in DB). Then explicitly stored sentences can be interpreted as a trace of the insertion actions. In this approach the link between sentences, operations of insertion, and the corresponding sources of information is implicitly represented by assuming that all the sentences of a given form are inserted by a given source. For example, it can be assumed that all sentences of the form: cloudy(x), are inserted by sensors of type s_1. Under this assumption if cloudy(l) is present in DB this means that the operation of inserting cloudy(l) has been performed, and that the source of the information was the sensor s_1.

On the basis of this simple scenario we can highlight other important aspects concerning meta-information representing Safety. First, it is clear that it is not necessarily the same agent who both inserts the information in DB, and makes claims of a meta-informational kind about Safety. Second, the administrator who is the agent asserting which kind of information is Safe does not necessarily know if this information is true or not at a given time. He only knows that if this information has been inserted in DB, then it is true in the world. For example if the administrator knows that all the sensors of the type s_2 are reliable, then his meta-information can be expressed by: ‘the administrator guarantees that if information of the

[1]Notice that in the presented scenario sensors might transmit signals, or messages, which are not logical sentences and must be transformed (interpreted) into logical sentences.

form: cold(x), has been inserted in DB, then this information is true'.[2] Notice that this meta-information clearly has a conditional form.

2 Tentative formalization

We have seen that the concept of Safety is closely related to the reliability of the sources of information. For this reason we have adopted the general framework of signalling acts, in order to obtain an explicit representation of the different types of agents involved in the process of information storage and retrieval. In our approach the DB is considered as a means for communication. Some agents, called 'information sources', which may be users or sensors, ensure that messages are stored in DB. These messages can be read by another agent, namely the DB management system, called the 'system' for short, who knows the meaning of every stored message. The system is able to derive the consequences of the information read in DB in order to compute answers to standard queries. There is another agent, called DB administrator, who plays a special role in the communication process. He is the person who knows information about source reliability. This meta-information, called Safety information, is stored by the administrator in a meta-database MDB, and it can be read by the system to compute answers to Safety queries.

Agents, called 'standard users', send queries and Safety queries to the system and receive corresponding answers (see Figure 3). As a matter of simplification, since it is not the purpose of this chapter to investigate communication between the system and standard users, these will be ignored in the following, and we shall concentrate on system reasoning about DB and MDB content.

We mention in passing that we think of transmission of messages to DB in much the same way that D.K. Lewis described elementary signalling acts in [4].

As a first step, a general formalization is presented that can also be used to investigate issues other than computing answers to Safety queries, such as database updates, or other issues related to database security. As a second step, the formalism is simplified and specialized for the context of Safety queries.

[2] As a matter of simplification we do not consider deletions. Of course a Safe sentence is no more guaranteed to be true after the operation of deleting this sentence has been performed.

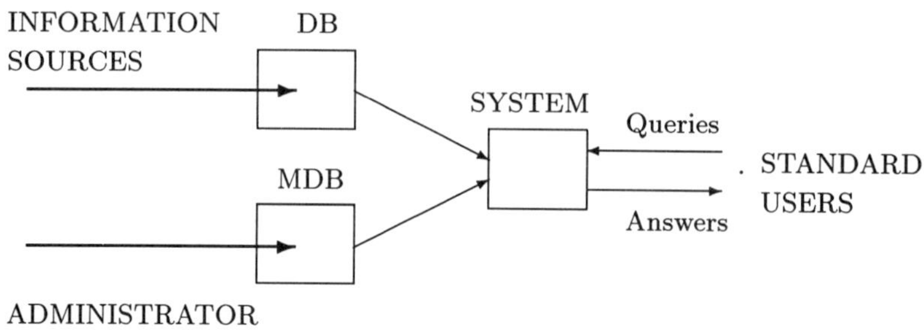

Figure 3: The information flow between the different categories of agents.

2.1 General formalization

An action modality E is introduced to represent transmission of messages to the DB. Wffs of the form $E_a p$ will be read 'the agent a brings it about that p', where p is a sentence about messages that are stored in DB. In the case where p is an atomic formula, it is of the form: In.DB(m), and its intended meaning is 'the message m is stored in DB'.

Our present inclination is to assign E the logic of a weak classical (and non-normal) system of modal logic [3] (in the sense of B.F. Chellas in [1]). Since the result of a signalling act could equally well be represented by any sentence expressing the same proposition, E will be closed under logical equivalence:

$$\text{(RE)} \ \frac{p_1 \leftrightarrow p_2}{E_a p_1 \leftrightarrow E_a p_2}$$

and it will be a 'success' operator, in the sense that all instances of the schema (ET) are assumed true:

$$\text{(ET)} \quad E_a p \rightarrow p$$

It is important to note that acceptance of (ET) does not imply that all signalling acts are reliable.

Since we take tautologies to be outside the scope of anyone's agency, we accept the schema (¬N):

$$\text{(E}\neg\text{N)} \quad \neg E_a \top \qquad \text{(where } \top \text{ is any tautology)}$$

We reject the distibution principle (Em):

[3]Various modal-logical treatments of the action operator exist in the literature, e.g. [7], [2].

$$\text{(Em)} \quad E_a(p_1 \wedge p_2) \rightarrow (E_a p_1 \wedge E_a p_2)$$

since it can readily be shown that one cannot consistently accept (Em) together with both (RE) and (E¬N), unless one assumes that there are no true sentences of the form $E_a p$. Indeed, since we have $\vdash p \leftrightarrow p \wedge \top$, from (RE) we have $\vdash E_a p \leftrightarrow E_a(p \wedge \top)$. So, from the assumption $E_a p$ we can infer $E_a(p \wedge \top)$, and if (Em) is accepted we have $E_a(\top)$, which contradicts the axiom (E¬N).

A case can be made for accepting the converse principle, (Ec):

$$\text{(Ec)} \quad (E_a p_1 \wedge E_a p_2) \rightarrow E_a(p_1 \wedge p_2)$$

(See Elgesem, [2] for a discussion of this). We indicate below the effect that adoption of (Ec) would have on our characterization of the Safety concept.

We leave the question as to the specific nature of the act performed entirely open, except to say that it will be transmission of a message, in some form or other, to the DB.[4] But we must nevertheless find a way of representing how the result of each signalling act (the messages stored in DB) is interpreted by the system.

In a general approach we can consider that messages have no structure, and that they might be just strings of characters, or strings of bits. In that case the meaning of each message m_i is represented by an axiom (S_i) of the form:

$$(S_i) \quad K_s(E_a p_i \rightarrow B_a q_i)$$

If p_i is the sentence: In.DB(m_i), axiom (S_i) can be rephrased as 'the system knows that if agent a brings it about that the message m_i is stored in DB, then a believes q_i'. Formulas of the form $E_a p_i \rightarrow B_a q_i$ define the meaning assigned to signalling acts by agent a. It is assumed here that agent a is known by s to be sincere; were he to be merely believed (perhaps mistakenly) to be sincere, K_s would be replaced by B_s in the axioms (S_i). The axioms (S_i) express the idea that the system knows in which way agent a interprets signalling acts, which means that it is assumed that there is no risk of misunderstanding between agent a and the system. In a more elaborate version of the theory, we would drop this assumption, and leave open the possibility both of a's insincerity, and s's awareness of insincerity; but we do not develop this complication here.

The messages stored in DB may have many different forms. If, for example, m_i is the string of characters 'cloudy(l)' then the system believes that it is cloudy in l, i.e. the sentence q_i is: cloudy(l), and the system believes that cloudy(l) holds. In another situation we might have '314116'

[4]See footnote 1.

instead of the string of characters 'cloudy(l)', and the system might be the only agent able to uncode '314116'. Notice that the meaning of a message is not necessarily an atomic formula, for example the message '27186' might be interpreted by the system as: $\mathrm{cloudy(l)} \wedge \mathrm{cold(l)}$.

In most of the existing databases the autonaming convention is adopted. That is, sentences are represented by strings of characters that are the sentences themselves. In this situation if 'q' is the message interpreted by the system by the sentence q, instead of a set of axioms (S_i) the meaning of the messages above is represented by the unique axiom schema:

$$\text{(S)} \quad K_s(E_a(\mathrm{In.DB}('q')) \to B_a q)$$

For simplicity the core modality K is defined by:

$$K_a q \stackrel{\text{def}}{=} (B_a q) \wedge q$$

and the modality B will be assigned a logic of type KD45.

We have assumed that the system is observing the DB, and that he is informed of every signalling act performed by information-transmitting sources. More technically, the system has complete knowledge of the DB content, and who stored the messages in DB. This assumption is formally represented by the axiom schema:

$$\text{(OBS)} \quad E_a p \to K_s E_a p$$

It may also be necessary for the system to collate the beliefs of the various agents who have inserted messages into DB, and to draw conclusions from this collection of beliefs. Where a is any agent, we thus introduce:

$$\text{(BEL)} \ K_s B_a q \to K_s B q$$

where 'K_sBq' is read 'the system knows that it is believed that q'. Thus, for instance, if s knows that a believes that q, and also knows that b believes that if q then r, then the conclusion may be drawn that s knows that it is believed that r.

The concept of Safety is defined by:

$$\mathrm{Safe}(a, p, q) \stackrel{\text{def}}{=} K_{adm}(E_a p \to q)$$

where 'q' is the meaning of the signalling act '$E_a p$'.

Sentences of the form Safe(a,p,q) can be read 'the agent a is reliable when he performs an action whose result is p, and whose meaning is q'. The formal definition of Safe(a,p,q) means that the administrator, called 'adm', knows that if agent a brings it about that p then q is true.

If the autonaming convention is accepted the definition of Safe takes the form:

$$\mathrm{Safe(a, q)} \stackrel{\mathrm{def}}{=} \mathrm{K_{adm}(E_a(In.DB('q')) \rightarrow q)}$$

The axiom schema (SAF) expresses that all the safety information is known by the system, or, in more technical terms, the system knows the content of the meta-database MDB:

$$\text{(SAF)} \quad \mathrm{K_{adm}(E_a p \rightarrow q) \rightarrow K_s(E_a p \rightarrow q)}$$

A simple example may be used to illustrate how the system can derive answers to queries and Safety queries; consider a situation in which the contents of DB and MDB are formally represented by the following set (T) of sentences:

(1) $\mathrm{E_a p_1}$
(2) $\mathrm{E_b p_2}$
(3) $\mathrm{Safe(a, p_1, q)}$
(S_1) $\mathrm{K_s(E_a p_1 \rightarrow B_a q)}$
(S_2) $\mathrm{K_s(E_b p_2 \rightarrow B_b(q \rightarrow r))}$

The standard query: q? is formally represented by: $\mathrm{K_sBq}$? It is read: 'does the system know from DB content that it is believed that q ?'. The answer is 'yes' if the logic allows the derivation from (T) of: $\mathrm{K_sBq}$.

The Safety query: q? is formally represented by: $\mathrm{K_sq}$? It is read: 'does the system know from DB content that q?'. The answer is 'yes' if the logic allows the derivation from (T) of: $\mathrm{K_sq}$.

The derivation below shows that, in this case, the answer to both queries is affirmative (lines (7) and (10)):

(1)	$\mathrm{E_a p_1}$	
(4)	$\mathrm{K_s E_a p_1}$	(1),(OBS), (MP)
(5)	$\mathrm{K_s(E_a p_1 \rightarrow B_a q)}$	(S_1)
(6)	$\mathrm{K_s B_a q}$	(4),(5),(modal logical schema K)
(7)	$\mathrm{K_s Bq}$	(6), (BEL), (MP)
(3)	$\mathrm{K_{adm}(E_a p_1 \rightarrow q)}$	(by definition from (3))
(8)	$\mathrm{K_s(E_a p_1 \rightarrow q)}$	(3), (SAF), (MP)
(9)	$\mathrm{K_s q}$	(4), (8), (K)

The next derivation shows that for the standard query: r? the answer is affirmative; but the answer to the Safety query: r? is not affirmative, since $\mathrm{K_sr}$ cannot be derived.

(2)	$E_b p_2$	
(11)	$K_s E_b p_2$	(2),(OBS), (MP)
(12)	$K_s(E_b p_2 \rightarrow B_b(q \rightarrow r))$	(S_2)
(13)	$K_s B_b(q \rightarrow r)$	(11),(12),(K)
(14)	$K_s B(q \rightarrow r)$	(13), (BEL), (MP)
(15)	$K_s(Bq \rightarrow Br)$	(by application of schema K to the belief operator, and by closure of the epistemic operator under logical consequence)
(16)	$K_s Br$	(7), (15), (K)

Before moving on to the presentation of a simpler approach, we conclude this section by noting the main effect that adoption of the principle (Ec) would have, in regard to our characterization of Safety. Suppose that

(17) $\mathrm{Safe}(a, p_1 \wedge p_2, q)$; by definition this means:

(18) $K_{adm}(E_a(p_1 \wedge p_2) \rightarrow q)$

If now (Ec) is adopted as an axiom, then it will follow by elementary properties of the epistemic logic that:

(19) $K_{adm}((E_a p_1 \wedge E_a p_2) \rightarrow E_a(p_1 \wedge p_2))$; then, from (18) and (19), we obtain:

(20) $K_{adm}((E_a p_1 \wedge E_a p_2) \rightarrow q)$

because the epistemic operator is closed under logical consequence. By way of illustration, consider now the following simple example of signalling: suppose that '$E_a p_1$' denotes a's act of raising his right arm to a horizontal position, and that the governing signalling conventions assign this act the meaning 'q_1: food supplies are needed'; suppose that '$E_a p_2$' denotes a's act of raising his left arms to a horizontal position, and that the same signalling conventions assign this act the meaning 'q_2: medical supplies are needed'. Then the act denoted by '$E_a(p_1 \wedge p_2)$' is a's act of raising both his right and left arm to a horizontal position; suppose that the signalling convention assigns this act the meaning 'q'. Now it seems that, at least for examples of this sort, the principle (Ec) is intuitively correct; but then it is also apparent that acceptance of (Ec) will make it imperative that the signalling conventions should themselves be required to be 'well-ordered', in the sense that whatever 'q' is, it must be a logical consequence of '$q_1 \wedge q_2$'. But if the assignments are well-ordered, then it would seem perfectly justifiable for adm to draw the conclusion that 'q', on the basis of observing '$E_a p_1 \wedge E_a p_2$' (assuming (18) and (19)). And note also that adm's inference here would not need to assume that the the two acts '$E_a p_1$' and '$E_a p_2$', considered individually, were both Safe; the point is that their joint performance entails the performance of an act ('$E_a(p_1 \wedge p_2)$') which is Safe. It is clear that a good deal more needs to be said about such matters, concerning the interplay of the organization of the signalling system, the definition of Safety, and the properties of the underlying logics. We aim to pursue these issues in more detail in future work.

2.2 Simplified formalization

The formalization we have presented in the previous section was designed to provide a general framework for understanding the notion of Safety. In this section a simplified formalization that is suitable for a simple implementation will be presented.

A first simplification is to represent only the result of signalling acts, and the agents who performed such acts. In technical terms, instead of E_a(In.DB(m)), whose meaning is ' agent a brings it about that the message m is stored in DB', we represent only the result of the action: In.DB(a,m), whose meaning is 'the message m is in DB, and it has been stored by agent a'. As a consequence the inference rule (RE), and the axiom schemas (ET) and (E¬N), are no longer needed.

A second simplification is to assume that all the information known by the administrator is also known by the system. This leads one to ignore the distinction between the administrator and the system. A consequence of these simplifications is that in the deductions that allow the derivation of answers to standard queries and safety queries, all the consequences are within the scope of the operator K_s. For this reason K_s can be omitted, and it will be implicitly assumed that deductions are deductions made by the system.

A technical consequence of this simplification is that we do not need axioms SAF and OBS, and the definition of Safe(a,p,q) can be replaced by:

$$\text{In.MDB(a, m, q)} \stackrel{\text{def}}{=} \text{In.DB(a, m)} \rightarrow \text{q}$$

where In.MDB(a,m,q) means 'if the message m is stored in DB, and its meaning is q, and it has been stored by agent a, then q holds'.

This new definition reflects two important features of Safety information. The first one is that, in general, Safety depends on the information sources. The second one is that Safety information basically has a conditional form. Roughly speaking this conditional form can be expressed by: 'if agent a says q, then reasoning about the reliability of his message can proceed'.

The axioms (S_i) defining the meaning of the messages m_i take the form:

$$(\text{S}_\text{i}) \quad \text{In.DB(a, m}_\text{i}) \rightarrow \text{B}_\text{a}\text{q}_\text{i}$$

and the axiom schema (BEL) is now simplified into:

$$(\text{BEL}) \quad \text{B}_\text{a}\text{q} \rightarrow \text{Bq}$$

If we accept the autonaming convention, we have the simpler definition of Safety:

$$\text{In.MDB}(a, 'q') \stackrel{\text{def}}{=} \text{In.DB}(a, 'q') \rightarrow q$$

and the axiom schema:

$$\text{(S)} \quad \text{In.DB}(a, 'q') \rightarrow Bq$$

Here we do not need the axiom (BEL) because the texts of the messages define their meanings.

The formalism could be still further simplified to take into account examples similar to the example about a travel agency presented at the beginning of the chapter, where Safety is independent of information sources, and depends only on the type of information. In such situations we just have to remove the name of the agents in DB and in MDB.

The example presented in the previous section is represented in the latter formalization by:

(1) $\text{In.DB}(a, 'q')$
(2) $\text{In.DB}(b, 'q \rightarrow r')$
(3) $\text{In.MDB}(a, 'q')$

The standard query q? is now represented by Bq?, and the Safety query q? is represented by q?

In our example we can derive, by the following deduction, the answer 'yes' to the standard query q?, and to the Safety query q?

(1) $\text{In.DB}(a, 'q')$	
(4) Bq	(1),(S)
(3') $\text{In.DB}(a, 'q') \rightarrow q$	by definition of Safety
(5) q	(1), (3'), (MP)

The next deduction shows how we derive the answer 'yes' for the standard query r?; as before we cannot derive an affirmative answer to the Safety query r?

(2) $\text{In.DB}(b, 'q \rightarrow r')$	
(6) $B(q \rightarrow r)$	(2),(S)
(7) Br	(4), (6), (K)

This example shows that this simplified formalization could easily be implemented with a deductive data base management system, with small changes. For the representation of the information the only changes would be to add the information source to every piece of stored information, and to extend the database with a meta-database of similar structure. For the derivation of answers to Safety queries, we can easily see that an answer can be guaranteed to be Safe if and only if there exists at least one derivation, where all axioms used are Safe, i.e. are both in DB and in MDB.

Indeed, from In.MDB(a,'q') and In.DB(a,'q') we can infer that q is true, and consequences of true sentences are true sentences. Then to answer Safety queries we just need to propagate via modus ponens the meta-information about the truth of sentences from antecedents to consequents.

Notice that the meta-information about Safety represented by sentences of the form In.MDB(a,'q') cannot be propagated via modus ponens. Indeed, from In.MDB(a,'q') and In.MDB(a,'$q \rightarrow r$') we cannot infer In.MDB(a,'r'), because In.DB(a,'q') and In.MDB(a,'$q \rightarrow r$') does not imply In.DB(a,'r').

In formal terms we have:

In.MDB(a,'q') and In.DB(a,'q') implies q,
In.MDB(a,'$q \rightarrow r$') and In.DB(a,'$q \rightarrow r$') implies $q \rightarrow r$,
q and $q \rightarrow r$ implies r.

However we also have:

In.MDB(a,'q') and In.MDB(a, '$q \rightarrow r$') does not imply In.MDB(a,'r').

A specific example may be used to illustrate these points. Consider again meteorological information of the same type as was used in the introduction. Imagine that there are three sensors of types s_1, s_2, and s_3, both in Oslo and London, that are called, respectively, O_1, O_2, O_3 and L_1, L_2, and L_3. Let's assume that only L_1, O_2, and O_3 are reliable. The content of the meta database is represented in the simplified formalism by:

In.MDB(L_1, cloudy(London))
In.MDB(O_2, cold(Oslo))
In.MDB(O_3, cloudy(Oslo) $\wedge$ cold(Oslo))

Let's consider a particular state of the database represented by:

In.DB(L_1, cloudy(London))
In.DB(O_2, cold(London))
In.DB(O_3, cloudy(Oslo) $\wedge$ cold(Oslo))
In.DB(L_1, cold(Oslo))

In that context the answer to the standard query: cloudy(x) $\wedge$ cold(x)? is: {Oslo, London}, but the answer to the safety query: cloudy(x)$\wedge$cold(x)? is: {Oslo}. London is not in the second answer because the only information inserted by the sensor O_2 in Oslo that is guaranteed to be true is cold(Oslo). So the information cold(London) is not guaranteed to be true, and cloudy(London) $\wedge$ cold(London) is also not guaranteed to be true, though cloudy(London) is known to be true. Notice that if cloudy(Oslo) and cold(Oslo) had been independently inserted in the database by O_1 and O_2, that is, if we had In.DB(O_1, cloudy(Oslo)) and In.DB(O_2, cold(Oslo)) instead of In.DB(O_3, cloudy(Oslo) $\wedge$ cold(Oslo)), then it would not have been possible to infer that cloudy(Oslo) $\wedge$ cold(Oslo) is known to be true.

The answer to the standard query: cold(x)? is: {Oslo,London}, and the answer to the safety query cold(x)? is: {Oslo}. Indeed, London is not in the answer to the safety query for the same reason as we mentioned for the previous query, and Oslo is in the answer because cold(Oslo) is a consequence of the information cloudy(Oslo) $\wedge$ cold(Oslo), which is known to be true.

Finally, the answer to the standard query cloudy(x)? is: {Oslo, London}, and the answer to the safety query cloudy(x)? is also {Oslo,London}. Oslo is in the answer to that query for the same reason that it is in the answer to the safety query cold(x)?.

This illustration shows that intuition can easily lead to wrong conclusions even in the case of a not very complex example. This is because reasoning about the safety of an answer is not governed by the same rules as reasoning about standard answers.

3 Conclusion

We have presented a specific Logic for reasoning about Safety information. It is defined in terms of the modal operators E, B, and K, that have been investigated extensively in the literature. Semantic and axiomatic characterizations of operators of these types, together with proofs of soundness and completeness, can be found in text books on Modal Logic, for example in [1]. Several assumptions that are implictly accepted in the field of data and knowledge bases are explictly represented in this Logic by appropriate axioms. In the perspective of possible implementations a simplified version of the Logic has also been presented. We have shown that signalling act theory will be of relevance in clarifying the notions of Safety query, and of reliable information source. This general framework can also be used, with small changes, for many other problems to be investigated in the future. Some of them are briefly sketched below.

Inconsistent databases. It may happen, for example in the case of distributed databases that are managed independently, that different databases contain inconsistent data. To describe this situation each database can be considered as an agent, and the fact that two databases, say a and b, contain messages whose meanings are q and $\neg$q, can be represented by the assumptions:

(1) $E_a p_1$

(2) $E_b p_2$

(3) $K_s(E_a p_1 \rightarrow B_a q)$
(4) $K_s(E_b p_2 \rightarrow B_b \neg q)$

In this case, to avoid the formal contradiction Bq and ¬Bq we must, of course, remove the axiom schema (BEL), but we could alternatively express the idea that it is believed in DB_1 that q, and believed in DB_2 that ¬q.

Encrypted data. For security reasons the database content may be encrypted in such a way that even if agents other than the system know the database content, only some of them are able to decipher its content. In this situation we can represent the idea that an agent u is able to decipher the messages stored by agent a by adopting the assumption:

$$K_u(E_a p \rightarrow B_a q)$$

We can also represent the idea that another agent v is *not* able to decipher these messages by adopting the assumption:

$$\neg K_v(E_a p \rightarrow B_a q)$$

To represent the idea that agents u and v can know the DB content (not its meaning) assumptions similar to (OBS) have to be added for each of them:

$$E_a p \rightarrow K_u E_a p$$
$$E_a p \rightarrow K_v E_a p$$

These axioms can be used to reason about what an agent is or is not able to know, on the basis of DB.

In the same context the idea that different agents encrypt data in different ways can easily be represented. For example, the following assumptions state that the system knows that agents a and b use two different messages to express the same information q:

$$K_s(E_a p_1 \rightarrow Bq)$$
$$K_s(E_b p_2 \rightarrow Bq)$$

In this formalism we can also represent situations where the system has only partial knowledge about the meaning of some messages. For example, the system may know that, when agent a brings it about that p, a believes either q or r. This is expressed by:

$$K_s(E_a p \rightarrow (B_a q \vee B_a r))$$

Updates. Data and knowledge base updates may lead to inconsistencies. In these situations, if we want to restore consistency, there are many different approaches. In most of the approaches presented in the literature there are, in general, several different possibilities for restoring consistency, and additional information is needed to select one of them, or to restrict the set of all the possibilities. We would like to point out that the formalism we have presented could well be appropriate for what Gärdenfors, in [3] calls: the Foundations Theory, where some beliefs play the role of justifications for other beliefs. In our case justifications would be the information stored in DB, and Safety information might be used to select justifications that have to be removed to restore consistency. It is worth noting that this formalism can provide a logical framework to reason both about 'reliable justifications', and updates. Indeed, updates can be represented by axioms of the form:

(1) $\mathrm{E_a(In.DB('q'))}$
(2) $\mathrm{E_a(In.DB('\neg q'))}$
(3) $\mathrm{E_a(\neg In.DB('q'))}$

where (1) and (2) represent the insertion of q or ¬q by agent a, and (3) represents the deletion of q.

Acknowledgement

This work has been partially suported by the CEC, in the context of the Basic Research Action, MEDLAR. Andrew Jones thanks the UK Science and Engineering Research Council for support during the academic year 1990-91, and the Région Rhône-Alpes for support during the academic year 1991-92.

References

[1] B. F. Chellas. *Modal Logic: An introduction.* Cambridge University Press, 1988.

[2] D. Elgesem. *Action Theory and Modal Logic.* PhD thesis, University of Oslo, Department of Philosophy, 1992.

[3] P. Gärdenfors. The dynamics of belief systems: foundations vs. coherence theories. *Revue Internationale de Philosophie*, **44**(172), 1990.

[4] D. K. Lewis. *Convention.* Harvard University Press, 1969.

[5] A. Motro. Completeness information and its application to query processing. In *Proceedings 12th International Conference on Very Large Data Bases*, 1986.

[6] A. Motro. Integrity = validity + completeness. *ACM TODS*, **14**(4), 1989.

[7] I. Porn. Action theory and social science. Some formal models. *Synthese Library*, **120**, D. Reidel Publishing Co., Dordrecht, Holland, 1977.

6

Abductive reasoning in three-valued logic for knowledge bases

Philippe Mathieu and Jean-Paul Delahaye

Abstract

In this chapter we study the case of monotonic rule-based systems which use a forward chaining algorithm to make deductions and a query algorithm to compute queries to be asked of the user in order to draw closer to the expected goal (as Guru [11], IS [12] or Nexpert [18]). Unfortunately, in many systems the query algorithm is not consistent with the deduction algorithm. Queries asked by these systems are often useless. We show that computing a query for these systems is equivalent to abductive reasoning in three-valued logic and we propose a formalization of useful queries for expert systems. We give two definitions of intelligent queries and two levels on which to compute them: the logical level which aims at computing a list of intelligent queries, and the heuristic level which aims at choosing which query on that list it will ask of the user. The following are three examples:

If b then a	If b then a	If b and c then a
If c then b	If c then a	If d then a
If d then b	If d then b	If e then b
If e then not c	If b then e	not c
If f then d	If b then not e	

If we run a mixed chaining on the first example with goal a then almost all the commercial expert systems will ask the query 'Is e true?'. Unfortunately, e does not help the system to draw closer to the expected goal because e gives not c and then nothing is deduced. In this case, there is just one useful query, which is 'Is f true?'.

In the same way we can see that the only useful query in the second example is c (d is useless since 'yes' to this query leads to a contradiction) and in the third example only d is useful (c is useless).

1 Formalism

1.1 External representation

Definition 1.1 A literal is an atomic formula or a negated atomic formula. We denote by *Lit* the finite or infinite set of literals. A rule is a propositional formula of the form $L_1, \ldots, L_n \rightarrow L$ with $n > 0$ and $L, L_1, \ldots, L_n \in Lit$. A *knowledge base* is a set of rules. A *working memory* (WM) is a set of literals.

Let p and q be two literals, we note $p \prec q$ and we say that p strictly depends on q iff there is a rule with q in its premises and p as conclusion (for example $q \rightarrow p$). We note $<$ the transitive closure of $\prec$. $p < q$ means that p depends on q. We say that a knowledge base is *without cycle* iff there is no literal p for which $p < p$. We say that a literal is a *basic literal* iff there is no literal q for which $p < q$.

To simplify the problem in this chapter, we only work on knowledge bases without cycles. The formalism used here is an elementary one; it can easily be extended. Allowing only conjunctions in rule conditions and only one literal in rule conclusions is not restrictive. With this formalism we can easily represent the rules usually used in many expert systems. For example, conjunction in the rule conclusion or the connectors and, or, not in the rule condition can easily be represented by transforming rule methods as in distributivity laws, De Morgan's laws, and double negation laws, (see [3], for example).

The working memory (WM), also called the extensional knowledge base, contains the literals known at the beginning of a session. Forward chaining will complete this memory by adding new facts obtained by deduction.

1.2 Internal representation

The system used here can ask queries of the user. Of course the user can answer *'I don't know'* to a query, as in many expert systems. We choose to represent each literal of the working memory by a triplet (Name,Meta-value,Value). Name is the name of the atom used, its Meta-value can be Known if the atom has a value (Value at True or False) or Undefined if the user has answered *'I don't know'* to the query (Value is then empty). An Unknown atom is not explicitly present in the working memory, it is its absence which feels like the Unknown value and meta-value.

First of all, an atom is Unknown. It can become Known (True or False) if the user tells it to the system or if the system infers it. It can also become Undefined if the user answers *'I don't know'* to a query on that atom (that meta-value helps the system to ask just one time each query).

The working memory is according to the *not-contradiction principle:*

two opposite literals cannot both be in WM. If this were the case, a contradiction would be detected. It is not according to the *excluded middle principle:* an atom is not always True or False. It can be Unknown. This is the reason why we will work in three-valued logic.

2 Deduction system

The general system used in this chapter is mixed chaining, often used in expert systems because it allows the search to centre on a given goal and allows the system to ask queries of the user during the deduction [5]. It is the relevance of these queries which leads the user to qualify a given expert system as *'intelligent'*. Thus it is imperative to compute these queries correctly.

Mixed chaining uses a forward chaining algorithm to deduce new facts and a backward chaining algorithm to compute queries to ask of the user. To ensure a friendly user interface *we assume that the expected goal is an atom* and the system tries to deduce a value for this atom. At the end of the session the expected atom is True, False, or Unknown if it has not been proved either True or False. Of course, as we ask queries of the user, we suppose that some atoms are askable and some are not. These considerations are very classical and have been used many times (for example in [12], [5], [11], [18] or recently in [10]). To simplify the problem we will assume that only basic facts are askable in all our examples. We can specify the working of this mixed chaining in the following algorithm:

Mixed chaining algorithm (Ato)

```
Saturate the knowledge base with forward chaining (Section 3).

While Ato is unknown (neither true nor false) and
        no contradiction has been detected and
        a query can be asked of the user.
                Ask this query.
                add the answer to the working memory.
                saturate with forward chaining.
End_while

Case  - Ato is true in the working memory: write 'Ato true'
      - Ato is false in the working memory: write 'Ato false'
      - else write 'I cannot deduce any value on Ato'
end_case
```

Remark: in this algorithm, the computation of queries is always made after a step of saturation by forward chaining.

3 How forward chaining works?

Our forward chaining infers literals (classical approach). A literal L (either positive or negative) is added to the working memory iff there is a rule which has L as its conclusion and all its premises in the working memory.

Forward chaining algorithm by saturation: Sat.

```
While there exist rules with their conclusions not in WM and
        all the literals of their condition part present in WM
                Search for the first of these rules.
                If the conclusion of this rule is consistent
                with all the literals in WM then
                        add the conclusion in WM.
                else
                        return 'inconsistent knowledge base'
                        Stop
                End_If
End_While
```

We can see that an atom is not always True or False. It can be Unknown. We have shown in [6] that this forward chaining is sound and complete with respect to the three-valued logic defined by these connectives:

$\wedge$	T	F	U
T	T	F	U
F	F	F	F
U	U	F	U

$\vee$	T	F	U
T	T	T	T
F	T	F	U
U	T	U	U

$\rightarrow$	T	F	U
T	T	F	F
F	T	T	T
U	T	T	T

$\neg$	T	F	U
	F	T	U

The logical meaning of the implication we consider is: $A \rightarrow B$ is false when A is true and B is not, $A \rightarrow B$ is true in the other cases (as in two-valued logic). With this logic, the set of three-valued models is stable by intersection and we will see that it is very useful to characterize the set of literals computed by forward chaining. More details and justifications for this connective can be found in [6][7].

Let us denote a knowledge base by Kb, by $Cons_B(Kb)$ (respectively $Cons_T$) the two-valued (respectively three-valued) consequence literals of

Kb, and by $Sat(Kb)$ the output of the saturating operation by forward chaining on Kb.

Proposition 3.1 ([6]).

- *For a set of rules without negation (Horn clauses) the set of two-valued models is stable for intersection. Thus it has a minimal two-valued model denoted by* $\mathbf{mm_B(Kb)}$. *We also obtain the equality*

$$Cons_B(Kb) = mm_B(Kb) = Sat(Kb) \cap Ato(Kb)$$

- *For a set of rules with negations, the set of three-valued models is stable for intersection. Thus it has a minimal three-valued model denoted by* $\mathbf{mm_T(Kb)}$. *We also obtain the equality*

$$Cons_T(Kb) = mm_T(Kb) = Sat(Kb) \cap Lit(Kb)$$

We can see that forward chaining computes a minimal threevalued model (and not a two-valued one) for knowledge bases with negations. Conversely, for the two–valued logic we can easily compute in three-valued logic with polynomial time algorithms as forward chaining. We have proposed in other papers a method for solving the two-valued incompleteness of forward chaining (w.r.t. classical two-valued logic) for knowledge bases with negations [15][16][17], but this is not the aim of this chapter.

4 Semantics of useful queries

To compute a useful query it is obvious that the query algorithm must be consistent with the deduction algorithm. In our case, it must be consistent with the forward chaining. *It is unfortunately not the case for all the commercial expert systems tested* (test the examples of the abstract with yours !).

Since we work in literals, the query algorithm will compute a literal. To have a friendly user interface we consider that *we will only ask of the user the value of the atom used in the literal computed* by the query algorithm (i.e. we ask 'is a True?' and not 'is $\neg a$ True ?')

Of course, the system must deduce the expected goal in a minimum number of queries. First of all we must define a useful query. To do this we introduce two notions: the relevant queries and the intelligent queries.

If a formula F has a formula G for a three-valued consequence we note that $F \models_T G$.

Definition 4.1 ([17]). Let Kb be a knowledge base, L a conjunction of basic unknown literals, and x a literal; we say that L is an *intelligent query list* w.r.t. x iff:

- $Kb \cup L$ is consistent;
- $Kb \cup L \models_T x \vee \neg x$ ($L \rightarrow x$ or $L \rightarrow \neg x$ is a three-valued consequence of Kb);
- There is no intelligent query list L' w.r.t. x such that L' subsumes L.

As we have shown that forward chaining computes three-valued consequences of literals we could give a more pragmatic definition: L is an intelligent query list w.r.t. x iff $x \in Sat(Kb \cup L)$ and there is no subset L' of L for which we have $x \in Sat(Kb \cup L')$.

Definition 4.2 ([17]). Let x and q be two literals, q is an *intelligent query* w.r.t. x iff there exists an intelligent query list w.r.t. x which contains q.

Unfortunately, the computation of intelligent queries is an algorithmically complex problem (In Section 7 we show that it is an NP-complete problem). This is why we introduce a weaker definition.

Definition 4.3 ([17]). Let Kb be a knowledge base, L a conjunction of basic unknown literals, and x a literal; we say that L is a *relevant query list* w.r.t. x iff there exists a subset R of Kb for which:

- $R \cup L$ is consistent;
- $R \cup L \models_T x \vee \neg x$ ($L \rightarrow x$ or $L \rightarrow \neg x$ is a three-valued consequence of R);
- there is no relevant query list L' w.r.t. x such that L' subsumes L.

In the same way as for intelligent queries we could give a more pragmatic definition: L is a relevant query list w.r.t. x iff there exists a subset R of Kb for which we have $x \in Sat(R \cup L)$ and there is no subset L' of L for which we have $x \in Sat(R \cup L')$.

Definition 4.4 ([17]). Let x and q be two literals; q is a *relevant query* w.r.t. x iff there exists a relevant query list w.r.t. x which contains q.

These definitions are in fact the three-valued version of similar two-valued notions of [8] called conditional answers or called minimal supports in [19]. We can see that computing a query for expert systems is equivalent to abductive reasoning in three-valued logic (with our connectives). Thus we can see the computation of relevant queries as a weak abductive strategy and the computation of intelligent queries as a strong abductive strategy.

Intuitively, when we compute a relevant query we work on one part of the knowledge base only. This subset R of Kb could be called a *deductive cone* associated to the expected goal.

Of course, an intelligent query is a relevant one. To prove it, we just have to take $R = Kb$. Conversely it is not true that a relevant query is an intelligent one, as we can see in examples 4.5 and 4.6.

Example 4.5

				WM=∅ goal: a
r1	b,c	→	a	b is a relevant query (consider R={r1}) but not
r2	c	→	a	an intelligent one. c is an intelligent query
				(thus relevant).

Example 4.6

				WM=∅ goal: a
r1	b	→	a	b is a relevant query (consider R={r1}) but not
r2	c	→	a	an intelligent one because the 'yes' answer leads
r3	b	→	x	to a contradiction. c is an intelligent query
r4	b	→	¬x	(thus relevant).

Of course, computing an intelligent query is more difficult than computing a relevant query. This is the reason why we propose the two definitions. To have a useful query we must compute a relevant or intelligent query and ask the value of this query to the user. This is what we call *the logical level.* But we often have many relevant or intelligent query lists, thus we must choose which list we will use, and in this one, which literal we will ask of the user. This is what we call *the heuristic level.*

5 The logical level

The aim of the logical level is to compute a list of literals (relevant or intelligent query list) for which we could deduce the expected goal with a forward chaining by adding the query list to the working memory.

Note that most of expert systems do not satisfy to this logical level, as can be seen in the examples proposed in the abstract

The first idea that we will explore is to use a backward chaining with backtracking in this way:

Naive_query_algorithm(Ato). Consider the expected goal as the initial goal. If there exists a rule (choice point) with this atom in the conclusion (either positively or negatively) then take one of the atoms used in the condition part of this rule (choice point), and consider it as the new goal. If we obtain an atom which does not belong to WM and which is askable, ask the user about it, else go back to the last choice point. If all the choice points have been studied, the goal cannot be deduced.

Example 5.1

r1	c	→	¬a	WM=∅ goal: a
r2	¬e	→	a	a depends on atoms c and e, c depends on the atom d and e depends on f. The atoms
r3	¬d	→	c	d and f are unknown and are basic facts so we
r4	f	→	¬e	ask the user about one of them.

This algorithm simply consists of searching a leaf in the dependence graph of the atoms of the knowledge base. It is correct for knowledge bases without negations (This is the reason why it is often used) but unfortunately it is not only inefficient but also incorrect in the case of knowledge bases with negations.

5.1 Working on literals

This naive algorithm considers all the rules which have the expected atom in their conclusion (either in positive or negative form). (The idea is: if the atom appears in a rule conclusion then this rule will produce interesting queries about it.) Unfortunately, if we apply this kind of reasoning to a knowledge base with negations we obtain useless queries, as in the following example:

Example 5.2

r1	¬b	→	a	WM=∅ goal: a
r2	c	→	b	It is obvious that the only useful query is e.
r3	d	→	¬c	The query d, found by the naive algorithm is
r4	e	→	¬b	neither intelligent nor relevant.

By definition, only forward chaining can add literals to the working memory. Forward chaining works on literals, thus it is obvious that the computation of a query cannot be performed by chaining from atoms to atoms but, rather, from literals to literals. The initial goal must then be a literal. We will call this sort of algorithm a single tentative algorithm [14].

Definition 5.3 We call each algorithm which works in the following way a *single tentative algorithm*:

The initial goal is a literal and the query algorithm tries to compute a query by chaining from literals to literals. If it is not able to find a query then the goal is considered not deducible (it does not mean that this negation is True but only that this literal cannot be deduced by a query).

This sort of algorithm is in fact very natural because it is the direct extension of the algorithms used for knowledge bases without negation (for knowledge bases without negation the two-valued and the three-valued consequences are identical, which is why many algorithms which are incorrect with negation become correct without negation).

When we defined the mixed-chaining algorithm we said that it was more useful for the user to have an atom as the initial goal. The system must try to deduce the value of this atom. Thus the single tentative algorithm cannot be used alone. Thus we add a new level to this algorithm to allow the user to have an atom as the initial goal and to obtain its value. We will call this algorithm a double tentative algorithm [14].

Definition 5.4 We call each algorithm which works in the following way a *double tentative algorithm*: The initial goal is an atom and the query algorithm tries to deduce the value of this atom. If it is not able to deduce that this atom is True or False then this atom is Unknown.

To make this deduction, the system can use three sorts of methods: trying to deduce True, and if it cannot, trying to deduce False; trying to deduce False, and if it cannot, trying to deduce True. The third method consists on trying True and False simultaneously. In this case the queries which are able to deduce True and the queries which are able to deduce False are shuffled. This is the best way to optimize the choice of query to ask of the user when many queries are possible (it is not very interesting in fact to optimize the truth and only afterwards to optimize the falsehood. The best query must be chosen from the queries which allow deduction of truth and falsehood simultaneously).

Many methods can be chosen to implement this point according to the heuristics used. We propose two of them. Let us denote x as the atom asked by the user as the initial goal.

- Compute all the queries which allow deduction of x, compute all the queries which allow deduction of $\neg x$ and concatenate them. We have explicitly a higher level up to the *single tentative algorithm.*

- Add two rules of the form $x \to goal$ and $\neg x \to goal$ where *goal* is a fictitious goal used as the initial goal. Thus we use a *single tentative algorithm* directly on a fictitious goal.

These two methods are equivalent. In an implementation it is often easier to use the first one, but when we work on examples by hand, it is easier to use the second one, which can easily be represented by a dependence tree.

b,c → a
d → ¬a
e → b
f → b

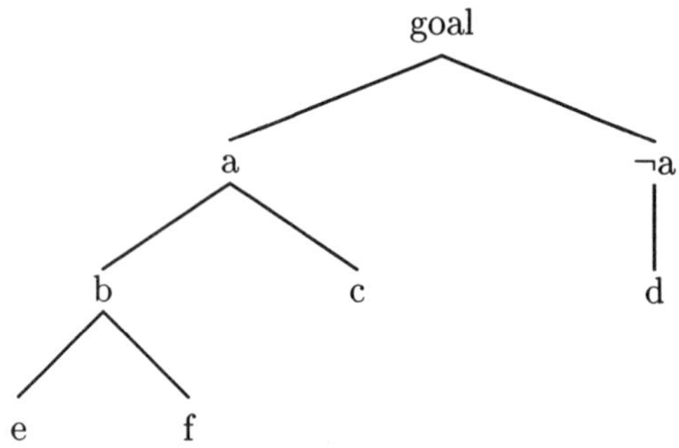

Take care. If x is the initial goal, even if we are interested in the rules which have both x and $\neg x$ in conclusion, we do not repeat this procedure recursively. Indeed, if we do not do so, we risk computing useless or stupid queries as in example 5.2. It is because of the confusion between *single tentative* and *double tentative algorithms* that there are many systems which chain from atoms to atoms. The initial goal being (for practical considerations) an atom, the system must be interested in the rules which use this atom in their conclusion. Designers of such systems often think (unfortunately, as we can see in example 5.2) that this process must be recursive. This is not the case! After the first step we must chain from literals to literals.

5.2 Consistency with the working memory

During the computation of a query we develop a literal as soon as a rule has this literal in its conclusion. Unfortunately, this literal may already be inconsistent with the working memory. In this case the query obtained will not be useful because forward chaining will later detect an inconsistency and the expected goal will not be deduced.

Example 5.5

Rules	

`r1 b → a`
`r2 c → b`
`r3 d → a`
	`WM={¬b}` Goal: `a`
	`d` is the only intelligent query at this time. The query `c` is not relevant because `b` is already false.

All the problems are not so simple. In many cases we need several queries to deduce the expected goal. If we only chain from literals to literals we may compute a query which will be useless because one of the other queries required is inconsistent with the working memory.

Example 5.6

r1	b	→	a	WM={¬d} Goal: a
r2	c, d	→	b	e and f are intelligent queries at this time. c
r3	e, f	→	b	is not relevant because d is already false.

The only way to solve this problem is to develop not only a literal but a list of literals which are able to deduce the goal, and to verify at each step that all the literals of that list are consistent with the working memory. Our algorithm will not compute a query as in the preceding algorithms but a list of queries. To draw closer to our definitions of intelligent and relevant queries we will develop each list of facts with a breadth first strategy (knowledge bases are usually not very deep) to detect inconsistencies as soon as possible.

5.3 Consistency of the future deduction

An algorithm that is consistent with the preceding points appears to compute a relevant list of queries, but in fact other problems are also present. The consistency of the future deduction is one of them. In fact, forward chaining can add two opposite literals to the working memory during the same saturating operation as in the following examples. In that case, the query list is useless because it will not deduce the expected goal.

Example 5.7

r1	b, c	→	a	WM=∅ goal: a
r2	d	→	b	The only intelligent query list is (x,y,z)
r3	¬b	→	c	and not (d,e), which will give a contra-
r4	e	→	¬b	diction on b by forward chaining.(d,e) is
r5	x,y,z	→	a	neither an intelligent query list nor a relevant one.

Example 5.8

r1	b	→	a	WM=∅ goal: a
r2	c	→	b	The only intelligent query list is (x,y) and
r3	c	→	d	not (c), which will give a contradiction on
r4	c	→	¬d	d. Nevertheless (c) is a relevant query
r5	x, y	→	b	list because with R=r1,r2 our definition is satisfied.

In example 5.7 the facts that give the contradiction are computed during the computation of the query list. In example 5.8 the contradiction comes from rules, that are never used during the computation of the query list.

We will now define two levels for verifying the consistency of the future deduction.

Complete verification

The only way to solve a problem such as example 5.8 is to run a fictitious forward chaining by considering all the literals of the computed query list to be known and verifying that the expected goal will be deduced. This forward chaining is like the usual one except that it cannot add new facts in WM but in a temporary working memory used solely for this verification. The temporary working memory is simpler than WM because it has to treat only known facts. It does not need meta-values. A fact is then satisfied if it is either present in WM or present in the temporary working memory.

This verification, which is very expensive in computation time, may be used by the expert during the development of the knowledge base and then inhibited during normal use to speed up deductions.

This verification is not necessary for computing a relevant query list but it is indispensable for computing an intelligent query list.

Partial verification of the deduction cone

As we have said before, the deductive cone is the set of rules used by the backward chaining algorithm to compute the relevant query list. We propose to verify at each development of a list that the new list is consistent both with its ancestors and with itself. Thus at each development we must store all the ancestors of the current list. This verification is able to solve many problems, as in example 5.7. We will see later that this verification is very useful for knowledge bases with symbolic facts because it allows one to cut useless branches very quickly. Of course, this verification is necessary for the computation of a relevant query list.

5.4 Computing minimal query lists

When we develop a list of facts with a breadth first strategy by chaining from literals to literals and verifying at each development the consistency of that list with the working memory, we are sure to obtain queries which will be useful to obtain the goal by forward chaining. Unfortunately, some facts of the query list computed can make the same deduction many times. In this case we do not obtain a minimal query list and thus we are not fulfilling our intentions entirely.

Example 5.9

r1	b, c	→	a	WM=∅ goal: a
r2	d	→	b	The query lists (x,y) and (y,x) are not relevant ones because they are subsumed by other query lists. The only two intelligent query lists in this example are (x) and (y).
r3	e	→	d	
r4	e	→	c	
r5	x	→	e	
r6	y	→	e	

To obtain a minimal query list we must verify at each development of a list that no literal is already developed. To do this we have to verify that there is no literal already present in the ancestors of the list. If a literal is already present in the ancestor list or in the current list we delete it from the current list. This deletion is correct because our knowledge bases have no cycles. In example 5.9 the literal e is present in the ancestor list. We are sure that all the literals which allow deduction of e are present in the current list because e has been developed before and there is no cycle. Thus e can be deleted from the current list during the development.

6 Resulting algorithms

The first algorithm proposed allows computation of a relevant query list consistent with the definition of Section 4. It takes care of all the points studied in Section 5. The second computes an intelligent query list. It has been built on the first one.

6.1 The computation of a relevant query

The initial set of literals incorporates the expected goal.

While one of the literals of the current list is unknown and not askable there exists at least a rule with this literal in conclusion. Choose one of these rules (choice point). Replace this literal in the current list by the premises of the rule chosen while deleting all the literals already present in WM and in the current list. If one of the literals is not consistent with WM or is not consistent with the ancestor list, stop and go back to the last choice point. If one of the literals is already present in the ancestor list delete that literal from the current list. If there is no rule with this literal as conclusion, go back to the last choice point.

Relevant_query_list algorithm

```
We call x the atom asked by the user
```

Add two rules of the form $x \to goal$ and $\neg x \to goal$
The initial list *List* and the ancestor list *Anc* are equal to (*goal*)

```
Computing_relevant_query_list(List,Anc)
   While there exists a literal in List which is not askable
      For all the literals in List
         If there is a rule with that literal as conclusion
            Choose this rule.  (choice point)
            Substitute that literal in List by the premises of
            the rule chosen while deleting literals already
            present in the working memory.

            If one of the literals of List is not consistent
            with WM or is not consistent with Anc
               Go back to the last choice point.
            End_if

            If one of the literals of List is already present
            in Anc or in List.
               Delete this literal
            End_if
         Else
            Go back to the last choice point.
         End_if
      End_for
   End_while

   Let us call L the new obtained list.
   Add L to Anc giving A.
   computing_relevant_query_list(L,A).
   End_computing_relevant_query_list
```

Theorem 6.1 *The relevant_query_list algorithm computes a relevant query list.*

PROOF. See [17]. ∎

It is important to note that our forward chaining cannot loop because if a literal appears in its ancestor list it is deleted. Unfortunately, the computed query for knowledge bases with cycles is not correct. This is why we have assumed at the beginning that our knowledge bases were without cycles. It is in fact very easy to verify during a compilation session that a knowledge base does not contain cycles. In the next example we can see a case of incompleteness for a cyclic knowledge base.

Example 6.2

r1	b, c	→	a	WM=∅ goal: a There is a cycle on b (b depends on itself). One of the lists computed is (e). Unfortunately this list is not complete. The only intelligent list is of course (d,e).
r2	b	→	b	
r3	d	→	b	
r4	e	→	c	

6.2 The computation of an intelligent query list

To obtain an intelligent query list we must compute all the relevant lists and then verify for each of them that it will not give a contradiction on the full knowledge base with forward chaining (section 5.3). If one of the relevant query lists gives a contradiction we delete it. At the end, we also delete all the query lists included in other lists to be consistent with the subsumption point of the definition.

Intelligent_query_list algorithm

```
We call x the atom asked by the user
Add two rules of the form x → goal and ¬x → goal
The initial list List and the ancestor list Anc are
equal to (goal)

   Compute the set E of all the lists L for which
      L=computing_relevant_query_list(List,Anc)
      and for which goal ∈ Sat(Kb ∪ L)
   End.

   Delete all the subsumed lists from E.
```

Theorem 6.3 *The intelligent_query_list algorithm computes an intelligent query list.*

PROOF. See [17]. ∎

7 Complexity

After having defined these algorithms it is interesting to know if the problem of computing a relevant or intelligent query is a difficult (in the sense of time complexity) problem. It is both a good and a bad thing to see that the relevant query problem is an NP-complete problem. Good because it shows that this problem is not a trivial, but rather a fundamental one, bad because there is no longer any hope (unless P=NP) of obtaining efficient algorithms to solve that problem in the general case.

To prove that the relevant query problem is an NP-complete problem we must show first that a non-deterministic Turing machine solves it in polynomial time. Then we must show that this problem is a generic one, which means that it can solve other NP-complete problems by a polynomial reduction [2].

Theorem 7.1 *Computing a relevant query list is an NP-complete problem.*

PROOF.

1. For a given goal it is easy to see that a non-deterministic Turing machine will solve this problem in linear time if there is a solution. The Turing machine will choose the best rule to use each time, so the problem will be solved in n steps if n is the length of the tallest branch of the knowledge base.

2. To prove that this problem is a generic one, we will show that if we can solve the relevant query problem then we can solve the satisfiability problem by a polynomial transformation. Let us take a set of m clauses for which we want to know if it is satisfiable. Let it be of the form

$$\begin{array}{c} x_{1,1} \vee x_{1,2} \vee \ldots \vee x_{1,n_1} \\ x_{2,1} \vee x_{2,2} \vee \ldots \vee x_{2,n_2} \\ \vdots \\ x_{m,1} \vee x_{m,2} \vee \ldots \vee x_{m,n_m} \end{array}$$

   For each clause of the form $x_{i,1} \vee x_{i,2} \vee \ldots \vee x_{i,n_i}$ write n_i rules of the form $x_{i,j} \rightarrow y_i$ for $j = 1 \ldots n_i$. Then write a rule of the form $y_1, \ldots, y_m \rightarrow z$. By construction, any relevant query list is a model of the set of clauses. The size of the associated knowledge base is obviously ($n * m$ rules where n is the average of the premises of each clause) polynomial in the size of the set of clauses.

The relevant query list problem is then an NP-complete problem. ∎

Example 7.2

a∨b	will be transformed to	a	→	y_1
a∨¬b		b	→	y_1
c∨¬a		a	→	y_2
¬c∨¬a		¬b	→	y_2
		c	→	y_3
		¬a	→	y_3
		¬c	→	y_4
		¬a	→	y_4
		y_1, y_2, y_3, y_4	→	z

With the goal z we cannot compute a list of relevant queries, thus the set of clauses is inconsistent.

Example 7.3

a∨b	will be transformed to	a	→	y_1
a∨¬c		b	→	y_1
c∨¬b		a	→	y_2
¬c∨¬a		¬c	→	y_2
		c	→	y_3
		¬b	→	y_3
		¬c	→	y_4
		¬a	→	y_4
		y_1, y_2, y_3, y_4	→	z

With the goal z we can compute the relevant query list (a,¬b,¬c) which is also a model of the initial set of clauses.

We have seen before that an intelligent query is a relevant one, thus computing an intelligent query is also an NP-complete problem.

8 The heuristic level

We are now able to compute a list of relevant or intelligent queries. We must now choose which list we will use if there are many of them and which literal of that list we will use to ask the query. There are two different approaches: choosing one list during the backward step or computing all the lists and then choose the list which seems more interesting.

8.1 Partial calculus of query lists

Heuristics proposed in this part do not need to compute all the lists before choosing the best one. Thus they have the advantage of working more quickly. It is also easy for the expert to follow the reasoning by hand (choices are less difficult to understand). Realization of programs is easier. It will not be the case for the other methods. We note that by convention, we will always ask the query on the first literal of the list.

8.1.1 Priority number on rules

This is the most frequently used heuristic in expert systems. If many rules have the same conclusion, the expert gives a priority number to each of them. The system will first examine the rule which has the higher (or lower) priority number. This method is often used because it gives the expert an easier way of controlling deductions.

Of course, systems which examine rules in the writing order of the knowledge base or which first examine the rules with the smallest premiss use the same kind of heuristic. Other frequently used variants are also here. We will indicate them: choosing the rules which use facts more recently obtained, choosing the rules with most conclusions, choosing the rules with most premises.

8.1.2 Rules which have fewer unknown premises

The heuristics presented earlier are static. Other variants are theoretically identical except that they are dynamic. The choice is not always the same for all the deductions. The best of these heuristics is the choice of rules which have fewer unknown premises. It supposes that the fewer the unknown premises there are in a rule, the more chance we have of obtaining the expected goal quickly. It often gives good results but it is still an heuristic !

Example 8.1

				`WM={f}` Goal: `a`
`r1`	`b`	→	`a`	Between the lists `(c,d)` and `(e)`, the list `(e)`
`r2`	`c,d`	→	`b`	is chosen instead of `(c,d)` because it contains
`r3`	`e,f`	→	`b`	only one unknown literal and `(c,d)` contains
				two.

8.2 Complete calculus of query lists

In Section 7, no comparison between the different possible query lists was made. Unfortunately it is often interesting to choose one list instead of another one by following precise ideas. This leads us to propose a method which gives order to the different lists, and also gives order to the different literals of the chosen list.

8.2.1 Choosing the smallest query list

If we suppose that all the facts have the same probability of becoming True or False, by choosing the smallest list we have more chance of obtaining the expected goal. Thus we can ask, for example, about the first literal of that list.

8.2.2 Choosing the atom most often present in all the query lists

When many lists are possible, an atom can be present in many of them. Thus it gives more information than the others because if it is false it will allow simultaneous deletion of many query lists.

Example 8.2

`r1`	`b`	$\rightarrow$	`a`	WM=$\emptyset$ Goal: `a`
`r2`	`c`	$\rightarrow$	`a`	The query lists obtained are `(d,x)` and `(e,x)`.
`r3`	`d,x`	$\rightarrow$	`b`	Asking `x` first seems more interesting than ask-
`r4`	`e,x`	$\rightarrow$	`c`	ing `d` or `e`

Of course this heuristic can also be used with the previous one. If an atom is frequently present we choose this one or else we choose the smallest query list.

8.2.3 Satisfiability coefficients

Until now we have assumed that all the askable facts have the same probability to become True or False. But in many cases we have more chances of obtaining one answer than another one to the query about a fact.

We have proposed a method in [17] which associates a satisfiability coefficient at each literal, which corresponds to the chance to satisfy this literal with a query about it. These coefficients are given by the expert with the knowledge base. To be consistent with the probability theory our coefficients are reals between 0 and 1 (like a percentage). If x is an atom the sum of the coefficients of x and $\neg x$ must be less than 1. The coefficient of the answer *'I don't know'* is then the complement to 1 of the sum of the coefficients of x and $\neg x$. We compute a value for each query list. We choose the list with the best value and we then choose the literal which has the biggest coefficient.

8.2.4 Cumulative method

As we can see, all these points (the smallest query list, the atom most often present, and the satisfiability coefficients) are necessary for a good heuristic. Thus we propose to generalize all these points in a cumulative method. First of all, we will compute for each literal x a weight which takes care of the length of the minimal list which contains it, the number of lists which contain it, and the satisfiability coefficients. Thus we compute a value to the associated atom which takes care of the weight of the literal and its opposite form. In [17] we propose to compute this value in the following way: we denote by $l(X)$ the length of the shortest list which contains the literal X, by $nb(X)$ the number of lists which contain X, and by $c(X)$ the satisfiability coefficient of X. First we compute for each literal X

$$p(X) = c(X)^{\frac{l(X)}{nb(X)}}$$

We then compute for each atom X

$$n(X) = p(X) + p(\neg X) - p(X).p(\neg X)$$

The query is then asked about the atom X which has the greatest value $n(X)$.

9 Symbolic facts

We will now discuss knowledge bases which use not only boolean facts but also symbolic facts and we will see that the previous algorithms are also necessary for these bases. Symbolic facts are often used in expert systems because they allow the expert to reduce the number of rules of the knowledge base and to obtain not only the answers True or False but also a symbolic answer. Even if this knowledge base does not contain any negation, the computation of relevant or intelligent queries is necessary to obtain a correct computation.

Example 9.1

r1	b='3'	$\rightarrow$	a	WM=$\emptyset$ Goal: a
r2	x	$\rightarrow$	b='1'	The first query computed by many expert systems is x. Of course the
r3	y	$\rightarrow$	b='2'	only interesting one is z. all the
r4	z	$\rightarrow$	b='3'	systems tested ask them !)

What is the sense of this knowledge base? We will return to a boolean problem which we are now able to solve. First of all we can rewrite all the facts of the form $x =$'v' with a boolean fact of the form x_v, but it is not sufficient. We can see that if b is equal to '1' it cannot be equal to '2' or '3'. Let us denote by $Def(x)$ the set of symbolic values that a fact x can take. For each symbolic fact x of the knowledge base and for each couple of values $v1$ and $v2$ of $Def(x)$ we write a rule of the form $x\_v1 \rightarrow \neg x\_v2$.

Example 9.2

r1	b='3' →	a	will be transformed to	b_3	→	a
r2	x →	b='1'		x	→	b_1
r3	y →	b='2'		y	→	b_2
r4	z →	b='3'		z	→	b_3
				b_1	→	¬ b_2
				b_1	→	¬ b_3
				b_2	→	¬ b_1
				b_2	→	¬ b_3
				b_3	→	¬ b_1
				b_3	→	¬ b_2

On the transformed knowledge base we can see that negations have been introduced. This is the reason why classical expert systems are unable to solve these problems. The computed intelligent query list in this example must be `(z)` as it is on the transformed knowledge base. We can see that our three-valued logic is also able to give a good semantic to study this type of knowledge bases.

In [17] we have proposed extensions of the two queries algorithms proposed here which are able to compute relevant and intelligent queries for knowledge bases with symbolic facts, symbolic variables as in the following examples, and also meta-values as in [12] or [18].

Example 9.3

r1	b=c →	a	b<>'1', b<>'2'	→	a
r2	x1 →	b='1'	d	→	b=c
r3	y1 →	b='2'	e	→	c='1'
r4	x2 →	c='2'	f	→	c='2'
r5	y2 →	c='3'	g	→	c='3'

In the first example with the goal `a`, the only intelligent query list is `(y1, x2)`. Neither `x1` nor `y2` should be asked to the user. In the second example with the goal `a`, the only intelligent query list is `(d, g)`. Neither `e` nor `f` should be asked of the user.

10 Conclusion

First of all we have presented a particular three-valued logic which is able to characterize exactly the set of literals computed by forward chaining algorithms. Then we have shown that actual expert systems based on mixed chaining ask queries which are not consistent with the deduction algorithm used. We have defined two sorts of queries based on our logic and two levels of computation to compute them. We have also proposed two algorithms to compute these queries. We have shown that the problem of computing a relevant query list for knowledge bases with negations is not a trivial problem. It is in fact in the class of NP-complete problems. Finally, we have extended this formalism to symbolic facts and meta-values. All these query algorithms have been implemented in the BIVOUAC system developed at the LIFL (UA CNRS 369) which contains logical tools for knowledge bases with negations.

All this research can easily be extended to deductive databases. This provides us with more intelligent systems for knowledge bases, based on a well-defined three-valued semantic.

References

[1] F. Bancilhon and R. Ramakrishnan. An amateur's introduction to recursive query processing strategies. *Proceedings ACM SIGMOD Conference.* 1986, pp. 16–52.

[2] S. Cook. The complexity of theorem proving procedure. *Third ACM Symposium on Theory of Computing*, 1971.

[3] C. L. Chang and R. C. T. Lee. *Symbolic Logic and Mechanical Theorem Proving.* Academic Press, 1973.

[4] M. O. Cordier. Les systèmes experts. *La Recherche*, 151, 60–70. Janvier 1984.

[5] J. P. Delahaye. *Systèmes experts: Organisation et programmation des bases de connaissances en calcul propositionnel.* Ed Eyrolles, Paris 1987.

[6] J. P. Delahaye. Chaînage avant et calculs de modèles en logique bivaluée et trivaluée. *7èmes Journées Internationales sur les Systèmes Experts et leurs Applications.* Avignon 1987.

[7] J. P. Delahaye and V. Thibau. Programming in three-valued logic, *TCS*, **78**, 189–216, 1991.

[8] R. Demolombe. *A Strategy for the Computation of Conditional Answers.* Internal Report ONERA/CERT, IRIT Toulouse.

[9] R. Demolombe and L. Farinas Del Cerro. *An Inference Rule for Hypothesis Generation.* Internal Report ONERA/CERT, IRIT Toulouse.

[10] P. Frot. *Trois systèmes experts en Turbo-Pascal.* Collection Utile, Sybex 1990.

[11] Guru 3.0 MDBS Inc. *Reference Manual*, 1987.

[12] Intelligence service II. GSI-TECSI. *User manual*, 1986.

[13] K. Inoue. Linear resolution for consequence finding. *Artificial Intelligence*, **56**, 301–353, 1992.

[14] P. Mathieu. *The Computation of Useful Queries for Expert Systems* (in French). Internal Report IT 185 LIFL, 1990.

[15] P. Mathieu and J. P. Delahaye. The logical compilation of knowledge bases. *JELIA 90, Amsterdam.* Lecture Note in Artificial Intelligence 478, pp. 386–398, Springer Verlag.

[16] P. Mathieu and J. P. Delahaye. For which Bases Chaining is Sufficient. *COGNITIVA 90*, Madrid, 699–702.

[17] P. Mathieu. The Use of Three-valued Logic in Expert Systems. PhD thesis, Université de Lille 1, Janvier 1991 (In French).

[18] Nexpert Object. Neuron Data Inc. *Reference Manual*, 1991.

[19] R. Reiter and J. De Kleer. Foundations of assumption-based truth maintenance system. *AAAI Conference*, 1987.

[20] J. D. Ullman. *Principles of Database and Knowledge-Base Systems. Vol I & II*, Computer Science Press, 1989.

7

Labelled abduction and relevance reasoning

Dov Gabbay, Ruth Kempson, and Jeremy Pitt

Abstract

The aim of this chapter is to explore modelling a more non-standard interaction between a human and a database. We try to equip the database with the capability of understanding queries in natural language and answering them in a more 'intelligent' manner than by mere yes/no factual answers. This capability of the database requires (at least) two components. First the database must possess a front-end logic module which can parse the natural language input I and translate it into a query (or update) Q_I in its own (logical) query language. Second, and in fact more difficult, it must cope with the logical patterns of human query and answer, which is logically more (non-monotonic) commonsense than ordinary query languages.

In this chapter, we first address the preliminary parsing and translation component. We present an approach to utterance interpretation which takes as input sequences of natural language words and builds linked labelled databases as output, and also involves additional abductive choices which are made on-line and captured through the labelling algebra. We describe the outlines of the formal model we are developing, and provide an experimental implementation of the on-line construction of linked labelled databases and interpretation relative to a context. We then turn to discussion of the second component, and consider in detail the formal properties of the abduction principles required to equip a database with the 'commonsense' faculties required to participate in question-answering and dialogues.

1 Introduction

The aim of this chapter is to explore modelling a more non-standard interaction between a human and a database. We try to equip the database with the capability of understanding queries in natural language and answering them in a more 'intelligent' manner than by mere yes/no factual answers. This capability of the database requires (at least) two components. First the database must possess a front-end logic module which can parse the natural language input I and translate it into a query (or update) Q_I in its own (logical) query language. Second, and in fact more difficult, it must cope with the logical patterns of human query and answer, which is logically more (non-monotonic) commonsense than ordinary query languages.

To exemplify informally the problems we seek to address, we will first consider what needs to be added to the process of answering a database query in a way that reflects human reasoning in response to natural language input. Take, to begin with, the following extract from a simple Prolog-like database Δ_1, which, let us assume, can be accessed via some machine much like a cash dispenser:

$$\Delta_1 : \quad \begin{array}{|l|}\hline \mathit{Holiday}(x,y) \ \mathit{if} \ \mathit{Available}(y) \wedge \mathit{Afford}(x,y) \\ \mathit{Afford}(x,y) \ \mathit{if} \ \mathit{Cost}(y,z) \wedge \mathit{Credit}(x,z) \\ \mathit{Credit}(x,y) \ \mathit{if} \ \mathit{Card\_limit}(x,z) \wedge y \leq z \\ \mathit{Sunnyplace}(a_i), i = 1 \ldots 3 \\ \mathit{Cost}(a_1, 200) \\ \mathit{Cost}(a_2, 250) \\ \mathit{Cost}(a_3, 700) \\ \mathit{Sunnyplace}(b) \\ \mathit{Cost}(b, 500) \\ \hline \end{array}$$

A customer accesses the database by inserting his visa card into the slot and typing the query (*holiday*, a_1, a_2, a_3). The database can automatically obtain from the visa card his name x_0, and other credit details, and asks itself the queries:

$$?\mathit{Holiday}(x_0, a_i), i = 1, 2, 3,$$

An ordinary non-intelligent database will simply check if each query succeeds and output the details if it does and output fail if not. A more intelligent database might output an explanation in case of failure, such as:

You can't have a_1 because it is not available

or:

You can't have a_3 because you cannot get credit

An even more intelligent database may recognize, for example, that none of the a_i are available but they are all sunny places and b is a sunny place within the nearest price range. So using a metaprogram of 'interest', 'view', etc., it might ask the user (in whatever way it 'communicates'):

Would you like (holiday, b)?

and output the details. We are sure that many chapters in this volume address many of the issues related to the above capabilities.

Ultimately, though, we would like the human to ask in natural language rather than type the 'agreed' form of input (e.g. (holiday, a)) and, furthermore, reply naturally to a computer query. This might transcend simple 'yes' and 'no' answers: for example, a 'natural' form of response to the computer-generated query above might be:

b is expensive.

The computer should understand the English and deduce (as a human would) that the answer to the query is 'no', *and* that any holiday costing more than $500 is not a candidate. Ideally, we would like to imbue the intelligent database with the same faculty, so that it could now reply:

There are no cheaper holidays

to which a possible form of response might be:

OK, I will take it.

which includes anaphora, *it* referring to b, and withdrawal of the previous denial of b as a suitable holiday.

There are a number of hidden problems here, but essentially we need to spell out two processes: one the reasoning underlying the parsing process, including the interpretation of anaphoric expressions, the access of related information, etc.; and the other the reasoning underlying question–answer dialogues, which may involve indirect answers, negotiation requiring changes in beliefs, plans, and goals, and so on.

In the first process, the process of *utterance interpretation*, there are two reasoning problems. Firstly there is the reasoning that the hearer engages in to establish the form and content which the utterance directly expresses, and secondly there is the reasoning required for the construal of pronouns, adverbs of tense, etc. How these are construed depends on what is already established in the discourse, in some sense that needs to be explained. Moreover, as the array of examples (1)–(5) shows, this phenomenon ranges from deciding on the value of a pronominal, through deciding on how to fix the proposition expressed in a flow of time, to reconstructing an entire structure on the basis of some fragment provided:

(1) *John came in. He had failed.*
(2) *Every student worried he had failed.*
(3) *If he had failed, John would be at home by now.*
(4) *John had failed. Bill too.*
(5) *If he had failed, John would be at home by now. Bill too.*

The second process, how a speaker intends, and can rely on, the hearer to retrieve considerably more from some utterance than merely what its words can be taken to express in the context, is clearly displayed in the use of an indirect answer. For example, consider the responses of two dinner party guests to their host's question on arrival:

(6)	HOST	*Do you like Spaghetti Bolognese?*
(7)	GUEST 1	*I'm Italian.*
(8)	GUEST 2	*I'm vegetarian.*

The result of the two guests hearing (6) above leads them to deduce that dinner is Spaghetti Bolognese, although this is not explicitly stated. For the host hearing the indirect reply (7), he (or she) should retrieve the 'common knowledge' that all Italians like pasta, and therefore deduce the answer 'yes', but on hearing (8) he should retrieve the 'common knowledge' that all vegetarians do *not* eat meat, and hence deduce the answer 'no'.

There is a general pattern to this variety of effects in natural language processing. Given some string of words as input, hearers systematically add to the information that these words provide in an active process of structure-building and inference-drawing. If, then, we wish to model dialogue successfully, we have to reconstruct the reasoning that underpins this enrichment process in a maximally general way, applying it both to the decisions involved in establishing what a sentence expresses, and what additional information to draw from it.

This is the task of this chapter. We adopt the general Labelled Deductive Systems (LDS) framework of [4], and use it to model the dynamic process of utterance interpretation whereby some database is created, and describe how the resulting database is then used in the more general process of on-line reasoning. In Section 2 we describe the formal framework underpinning our model of utterance interpretation, and in Section 3 we describe a prototype implementation of the parsing process in a restricted context. Section 4 considers more general reasoning processes, in particular abductive reasoning, involved in question-answering and dialogue processing in general. The parsing system is intended to be embedded within such reasoning processes, to provide a database with an intelligent capability allowing it to participate in question-answering and dialogues.

2 The formal framework

In this section, we briefly introduce the framework of Labelled Deductive Systems, and abductive mechanisms within this framework (Sections 2.1 and 2.2 respectively). In Section 2.3 we consider the general problem of parsing requiring two types of abductive reasoning for interpretation and inferential effect, and in Section 2.4 we combine LDS with these ideas on parsing to develop a formal model of utterance interpretation.

2.1 Labelled deductive systems

Labelled deductive systems provide a uniform algorithmic characterization of a wide variety of logics. An LDS is a triple $<\mathbf{L}, \Gamma, \mathcal{M}>$, where:

(i) $\mathbf{L}$ is a logical language (connectives and well-formed formulas).

(ii) Γ is an algebra of labels, with some operations over the labels.

(iii) $\mathcal{M}$ is a discipline of labelling formulas of the logic $\mathbf{L}$ with elements from the algebra of labels Γ, together with deduction rules and agreed ways of propagating the labels *via* the application of the deduction rules.

The basic data item in LDS is the *labelled formula* $\alpha : P$, where $\alpha \in \Gamma$ is the label and $P \in \mathbf{L}$ is the formula. The role of the label is to provide additional information about the formula which is not of the same declarative nature as the formula itself; for example, α could represent the 'degree of reliability' of the formula P, or the 'time' at which P was true, or the 'source' of the information represented by P. A collection of data items, i.e. a database, is no longer just a 'set of assumptions', but can have a much more general structure, e.g. multisets, lists, partially-ordered sets, etc.

However, the algorithmic rules still define the notion of a consequence relation, but now between labelled formulas, i.e.:

$$\alpha_1 : P_1, \ldots, \alpha_n : P_n \vdash \beta : Q$$

We will be particularly interested in the computation of this consequence relation, which takes the general form:

prove $\{\alpha_1 : P_1, \ldots, \alpha_n : P_n\} \vdash \beta : Q$

$\delta :$ $\vdots$

exit $\beta = \ldots$

i.e. we want to prove, from a given sequence of labelled formulas, a formula Q, and in doing so we want to compute the label of the formula (β) and the label of the proof (or database) itself (δ).

The way the inference rules are used in such computations (the box above represents the application of inference rules used in a computation) is more or less uniform to all systems. For example, for the language with implication, the rules are predetermined in their structure for all logics, with only some fixed and agreed room for variations. The →–elimination rule (i.e. modus ponens) has the form:

$$\frac{\alpha : P \quad \beta : P \to Q}{\alpha + \beta : Q} \; [\to \text{-E}]$$

where +, a binary function symbol, is an operation over the algebra of labels. The →–introduction rule has the form:

$\alpha : P$	*assume*
$\vdots$	
$\alpha + \beta : Q$	*show*

exit $\beta : P \to Q$

which intuitively may be read as stating: to show $\beta : P \to Q$ start a subcomputation (again represented by the box), assume $\alpha : P$, and show $\gamma : Q$, with α, β, and γ satisfying the equation $\gamma = \alpha + \beta$.

The methodology of LDS has provided a general framework for the formalization of many aspects of practical reasoning [2], including those where the reasoning involved in planning, co-operative problem solving, etc. is often manifest in natural language dialogues. However, it is not just the mechanisms that drive intelligent dialogues, but also natural language phenomena themselves (syntax, semantics, and pragmatics), that are amenable to analysis by LDS. In Section 2.3 we discuss applying LDS to the parsing process itself.

2.2 Labelled abductive mechanisms

The basic *deductive* apparatus of LDS is a precise system of rules allowing one to show (or fail to show) whether $\Delta \vdash \Gamma$, for Δ a data structure and Γ a goal structure. Most useful among the goal structures is the unit structure of the form $t : G$. Thus for the purpose of explaining what abduction is going to be in our framework, we assume that the notion of:

$$\Delta \vdash t : G$$

is precisely (algorithmically) defined, thus yielding a particular LDS system **L**. We now explain schematically how abduction principles fit into this framework. Consider a database Δ, containing $\alpha : X$ inside it, which we write as $\Delta[\alpha : X]$. Somewhere in the structure Δ, α is a label variable and X is a propositional variable standing for a wff. For any particular choice of X, say $X = A$ and $\alpha = \alpha_0$, $\Delta[\alpha_0 : A]$ is a proper database.

Suppose we want to prove a goal $t : G$. Then for some (maybe no) wffs A_i and labels α_i we may have:

$$\Delta[\alpha_i : A_i] \vdash t : G$$

A principle of abduction:

$$Abduce(\alpha : X)$$

is a computation (algorithm) that can choose one or more of the $\alpha_i : A_i$ above. Of course for different t and G we obtain different α_i and A_i.

The importance of the above point of view is:

1. Databases can take abductive principles as part of their data, slotted in at the right places.
2. The abductive principle is relative to the computation procedure and the rest of the database. Thus when new data is put in, the abductive principle changes.

A fuller account of abduction in LDS can be found in [5].

2.3 Utterance interpretation: the Parsing Problem

We take as our background the informal insights of Relevance Theory [17] and their view of the psychological process of inference. Interpreting signals presented in a dialogue is taken to involve providing the essential preliminary for any such process to take place: i.e. by building a well-formed structure in some inference system. This structure is then used to derive further inferences using additional information chosen on the basis of the signal. The hearer's task is thus two-fold. She has to decode the signal with whatever her knowledge of words of her language provides (and as we have already seen, there is the additional problem that the intrinsic 'content' of natural language signals characteristically underdetermines any such assigned 'interpretation'); and she has to enrich that information by making additional choices. Both these tasks are carried out with a certain goal in mind, which is to derive extra inferential effect, i.e.:

1. establish a vehicle for inference Δ_k from the sequence of words;
2. combine Δ_k with some other information Δ_j to yield extra inferential effect Δ_m:

$$\Delta_k, \Delta_j \vdash \Delta_m$$

The *principle of relevance* at the heart of Relevance Theory is that these tasks are constrained to provide cognitively the best possible outcome—a set of inferential effects sufficiently rich to offset whatever cognitive effort is involved in making these additional choices Δ_j. Cognitive effort is always to be balanced by inferential benefit, which will, in general, mean using whatever information is most easily available to make these choices. Although we refer to this principle on occasion within this chapter, its formalization is not our primary concern. At this point we wish to set out a logical framework within which the study of such choices can be made.

Thus we reconstruct these tasks by natural deduction within the LDS framework. The overall goal is to achieve non-trivial inferences in some proof domain. The subgoal is to build a database capable of establishing the requisite well-formed inference structure to constitute the major premise in such a domain. These goals are achieved by taking the words in sequence, constructing a database from them, and using abduction to make additional choices whenever the information presented is insufficient. We wish to use this approach to model not only the extra information that the hearer accesses to yield indirect implications but also the extra information that the hearer accesses in resolving anaphora and temporal relations. The former involves abduction of whole premises of a relatively familiar sort. For the latter, we shall require a concept of *structural abduction*, for which we develop the idea that *abduction principles are data.*

For example, consider the following database and query:

a_1 $\quad A$
a_2 $\quad A \to (B \to S)$
a_3 $\quad B$
$\dots$ $\quad \dots$
a_4 $\quad X$, abduce on structure to find X
a_5 $\quad B \to D$
The goal is $?S + D$.

By writing $S + D$ for the goal we are saying that we want to partition the database, which is a list of assumptions, into two parts; the first part must prove S and the second part must prove D. This is done in resource logics, where one pays attention to the question of which part of the database proves what.

Such considerations arise in many areas for example in what is known as *parsing as deduction* [13]. As an example, consider the parsing problem presented by the natural language sequence: *Mary hit John. He cried.* The way this can be analysed is by assuming that each word is assigned a wff of some resource logic, corresponding to its type (i.e. the Curry–Howard interpretation of formulas as types), with a label which corresponds to the lexical item itself. Here we use logical types defined inductively from basic types e (entities) and t (truth values) and the rule *if A and B are types then $A \to B$ is a type.*

Assignment is done at the lexical level. Thus a proper noun n is assigned $n : e$, an intransitive verb v_1 is assigned $v_1 : e \to t$, and a transitive verb v_2 is assigned $v_2 : e \to (e \to t)$. These assignments are commonly used in computational linguistics and in categorial grammar (see e.g. [10]), and give us straightforward data—the building blocks of the database. The pronoun *he*, on the other hand, is assigned an abduction principle. Our problem then becomes:

Data
1. *Mary:* e
2. *hit:* $e \to (e \to t)$
3. *John:* e
4. *he:* Abduce on structure: Take the first literal up the list.
5. *cried:* $e \to t$.

Query
Prove $?S$ *or* $?S + S$ *or* $?S + S + S \ldots$ *etc.*

We are thus saying that anaphora resolution makes use of structural abduction, and that a database can either display data items or give us pointers to where to obtain them. Thus a labelled database can look like:

n_1:	data m
$\vdots$	$\vdots$
n_k:	get datum from ...
$\vdots$	$\vdots$

From the logical point of view we are using the following principle:

- Abduction principles can serve as items of data in one database Δ_0, being a pointer to another database Δ_1 where some computation is carried out jointly involving both databases and the result is the abduced data item in Δ_0.

2.4 Language and reasoning

With this simple and highly idealized example, we none the less have the basis of our approach to natural language processing, which involves building structured databases by deduction over declarative units made up of a word as label and a formula, making additional abductive choices as necessary. The result of this goal-driven parsing task is a predicate logic formula which can then perform a role in more general inference tasks. Furthermore, we want all decisions made at each stage of database building or inference drawing to be driven by the need to achieve the goal of deriving inferential effects relative to some constraint of 'minimal effort'.

The natural language input itself provides the trigger to this process of interpretation. Some words provide the premises themselves, some provide procedures which determine where further requisite information may be found, while others dictate the form of the goal to be achieved. The common property that words share is that they provide procedures for the hearer to follow, which, if followed, are intended to guarantee the right choice of well-formed output. That is, the hearer will recover the information that the speaker intended her to—modelled in our approach by a predicate logic formula derived as the conclusion of some linked labelled database.

With these informal ideas to hand, we can now set out our model of the parsing process. The model we are developing (called L&R (Language and Reasoning), see also [7]) merges aspects of grammar, parsing, and interpretation, and consists of:

(i) *a lexicon,* in which each word of the language is associated with declarative and procedural information; more specifically a triple <*labels, formulas, instructions*>, where the labels and formulas are declarative information and the instructions are procedural

$$< \underbrace{\textit{labels, formulas,}}_{\textit{declarative}} \overbrace{\textit{instructions}}^{\textit{procedural}} >$$

(ii) *a logic,* which is an LDS, and so defines *declarative units*, each of which is a pair consisting of a label and a formula; and *linked labelled databases*, where a database is an ordered collection of declarative units and can be linked by shared variables;

(iii) *an algorithm,* which, given a linked database and a triple as input, constructs a new linked database by adding the declarative unit specified by the triple; the result is computed by the interaction of the instructions specified by the triple, the inference rules of the logic, and the algebra of the labels.

Parsing a sentence in L&R is a matter of proving that a well-formed linked database of the form $\alpha : t$ results from a given input sequence of words, which are lexically analysed into triples. This linked database also constitutes a representation of the meaning of that input. It is also used in 'abductive enrichment': the choice of additional databases as premises which, when combined, yield inferential effect.

We exemplify the building of the initial database by considering the steps involved in interpreting the utterance *'John likes Mary, who he admires'*. A natural deduction proof of parsing/interpreting this utterance in the L&R model is shown in Figure 1, and the following description is best read with reference to this diagram.

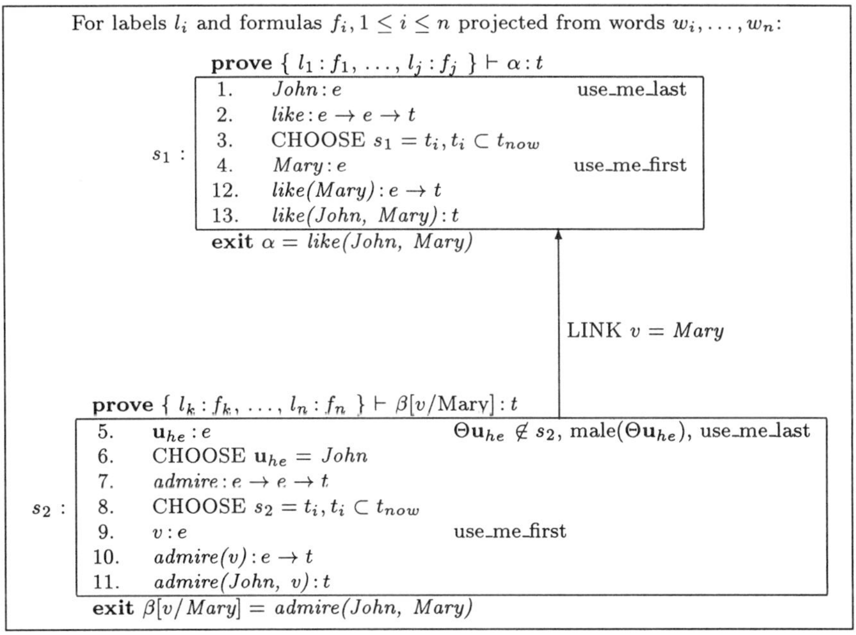

Figure 1: Utterance interpretation in the L&R model.

The goal is to prove that a formula $\alpha : t$ follows from a given sequence of assumptions. The proof itself is a labelled database, the sequence of assumptions is the labels and formulas of the words in the utterance, which also provide instructions for manipulating these data items.

The words *John* and *Mary* each provide a pair comprising a label (the word itself) and a formula (e). These are simply inserted in the database s_1 at steps 1 and 4, and are used as minor premises in the chain of reasoning involved in the interpretation. The verbs *like* and *admire* constitute the major premises in their respective databases, and also carry instructions about the labelling of the database itself (steps 3 and 8) and putting side-conditions on the proof steps (e.g. 'use_me_last' and 'use_me_first' in steps 1, 4, 5, and 9, which respectively dictate that $John : e$ is used last in some chain of premises leading to $\alpha : t$, and, conversely, $Mary : e$ is used first). The side-conditions are used in the modelling of subject and object relations, and (here) the database label indicates that the temporal flow against which the database is constructed includes the time of evaluation.

Unlike standard analyses in terms of some higher-type specification (e.g. [9]) the word *who* is modelled directly as projecting the procedural instruction that a new database (here s_2) should be built but with a more specific goal, i.e. that the label of the formula t should be linked to the current database through a shared label (v). Finally, *he* provides a data item similar to *John* and *Mary*, although the label is a meta-variable: the word also comes with instructions on how to identify the expression that instantiates the meta-variable in step 6.

The goal specification of s_2 and the lexical (type) specification of *admire* dictate that $v: e$ is assumed in step 9. The remaining steps 10, 11, 12, and 13 are then applications of modus ponens as in Section 2.1, with the '+' operator on labels being function–argument applications. The resultant linked labelled databases are as shown in Figure 1. It then remains to complete the mapping from a sequence of English words on to some predicate logic formula, for details of which see [7].

Many of the details presented in the proof configuration displayed in Figure 1 require detailed linguistic justification, see [7]. In particular, there is no account here of quantification. We simply presume that noun phrases project a premise of the form $\alpha : e$, with *who* not projecting a premise into the database but a goal specification on its outcome. We are concerned merely to demonstrate how, from a set of lexical specifications and assumptions of natural deduction set within an LDS framework, we can model the parsing process as a process which simultaneously provides a recognition device and an interpretation builder. Note in particular that the parsing process is not a trivial decoding of some signal. Essential steps of reasoning are involved at every step of the way.

3 An experimental implementation

This section describes a prototype implementation of the formal model described in Section 2.4. Section 3.1 discusses the implementation of a parser for the model, Section 3.2 describes a restricted context (a blocks world), and Section 3.3 describes how the parsing process can be embedded in such a context to provide an implementation of utterance interpretation relative to a context. We should stress that the significance of this particular application lies not in the implementation itself, but, rather, in the way in which deductive systems constructed for logical purposes can be applied equally in natural language parsing, natural language interpretation, and planning tasks.

3.1 L&R parsing

Although the algorithm for constructing sentence-meanings is intended to be *procedural*, our experimental implementation has used our own externalized knowledge of grammar rules, although the *combinatorial* information specified in such rules is ignored completely. The implementation is based on an adaptation of the so-called *shift-reduce* LR parsing algorithm [1], but the shift-reduce actions are used merely as a guide for the L&R algorithm. Indeed, we could rationalize our implementation by saying that the shift-reduce information, determined from the grammar rules, is like associating with each word instructions such as 'if you've seen input X, and Y is the next lookahead, then do procedure P', for the appropriate combinations of X, Y, and P.

Pitt [14] describes a parser-generator, which given a grammar specification automatically generates a Prolog LR parser for the language described by the grammar. The parser-generator constructs the LR parsing tables containing the shift-reduce information, and compiles each grammar rule into a Prolog clause, i.e. it turns the specification into a type of logic grammar (see Definite Clause Grammars [12]). The tables and the logic grammar are passed as supplements to the LR shell to form a complete LR parser for the language.

The parser-generator and parser shell are also used in our experimental implementation of L&R for a subset of English $\mathcal{E}$, where $\mathcal{E}$ is a mapping from a set of words W to <*labels, formulas, instructions*> triples, supplemented by a set of terminal categories Σ and a set of grammar rules P. The implementation comprises three modules:

(i) a language specification which includes:

- for each word $w \in W$ a predicate ς, where $\varsigma = \sigma(l : f)$ such that $\sigma \in \Sigma$ is the word's 'traditional' terminal category, and l and f are respectively the word's labels and formulas specified in the L&R lexicon;
- for each terminal category $\sigma \in \Sigma$ a Prolog clause $\sigma(X)$:- ...;
- for each grammar rule $p \in P$ a Prolog clause A_p :- ...;

where the bodies of the clauses $\sigma(X)$:- ... and A_p :- ... implement the instructions associated with the words (also as specified in the L&R lexicon);

(ii) a theorem prover for the logic, which applies inference rules to the data items in the linked labelled databases, such that it uses all the assumed data items in order, respects the side-conditions on the data items, and succeeds if the 'last' data item is of type t;

(iii) an adaptation of the LR parsing algorithm (hence L&R parsing), such that for every move the following pseudo-code is executed, for i and j parser states, σ the functor of the 'lookahead predicate' ς and p a grammar rule:

$$\textbf{if } action(\ i, \sigma\ ) = shift\ j \textbf{ then } call(\ \varsigma\ ) \textbf{ end};$$
$$\textbf{if } action(\ i, \sigma\ ) = reduce\ \ p \textbf{ then } call(\ A_p\ ) \textbf{ end};$$

The interaction of the three modules implements the L&R algorithm.

To show this, we consider a parse of *John likes Mary, who he admires.* The implementation maintains a pointer to the current position in the current database. The lexical specifications of words contain, *inter alia*, instructions to insert the data items as assumptions at the appropriate position in the current database, and/or to put side-conditions (e.g. use_me_last) on data items. Pronouns come with the instruction to CHOOSE their antecedents. In particular, the instructions associated with relative markers, such as *who*, start a new database, link this new database to the old ('parent') database, and mark the link with the last data item of type e assumed in the parent database.

We also have the following instructions associated with the grammar rules, such that:

(i) reducing *via* the empty rule for noun phrases causes an assumption $v\colon e$ to be inserted in the current database, whereupon variable v is instantiated (LINK) to whatever marked the link between this database and its parent;

(ii) reducing to a sentence invokes the theorem prover, which tries to close the current database and exit with a formula $\alpha : t$;

(iii) reducing to a relative clause causes the pointer to be moved back to the parent database.

This process is illustrated by the automated proof/parse/interpretation shown in Figure 2.

3.2 Imperative sentences in the blocks world

We now work towards an account of language parsing in context to yield a full array of inferential effects. First we develop a 'blocks world', such as is described by [8], so that it can interface with our L&R parsing mechanism. Secondly, we address the problem of the additional reasoning principles required to establish the full import of some utterances as processed in context. Finally, we consider an example where the separate strands of parsing and planning can be brought together.

Essentially, the blocks world of Genesereth and Nilsson comprises:

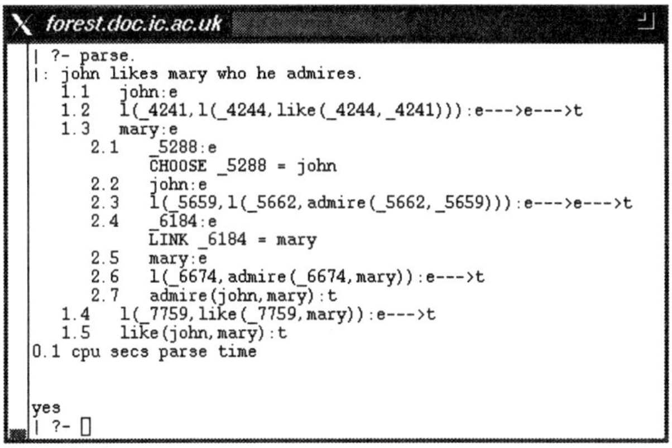

Figure 2: Automated analysis of *John likes Mary, who he admires.*

(i) a description of the *objects* in the world, their *properties* and the *relations* between them: the objects include three blocks and a table, blocks may be clear, and each block may be on another block or the table;

(ii) a description of the permissible *actions*, which are to either stack or unstack a block, and the pre- and post-conditions on each action; these are, for any blocks x and y:

Pre-conditions

To stack x on y:	*To unstack x from y:*
x must be clear,	*x must be clear,*
x must be on the table,	*x must be on y,*
y must be clear,	*x and y are different.*
x and y are different.	

Post-conditions

After stacking x on block y:	*After unstacking x from y:*
x is on y.	*x is on the table.*
	y is clear

(iii) a description of the *axioms* which the blocks must satisfy. In this case:

every block is either on the table or on another block,
every block is either clear or has another block on it,

To describe this 'world', there are, in effect, three languages involved:

1. the database language containing the predicates $on(x, y)$ and $clear(x)$;

2. the imperative (Input) command language with the predicates (actions) $stack(x, y)$;

3. the mixed metalanguage with the connectives '$\wedge$' for 'and' and '$\Rightarrow$' for 'pre-condition and action imply post-condition'.

The state of the blocks world can be represented by an extensional database comprising formulas of a sorted logic, with sorts $BLOCKS = \{b1, b2, b3\}$ and $TABLE = \{table\}$, and predicates *on* and *clear*. The database can be labelled by a label representing a 'time point': performing an action then changes the state of the database (i.e. the representation of the world) and advances the time point.

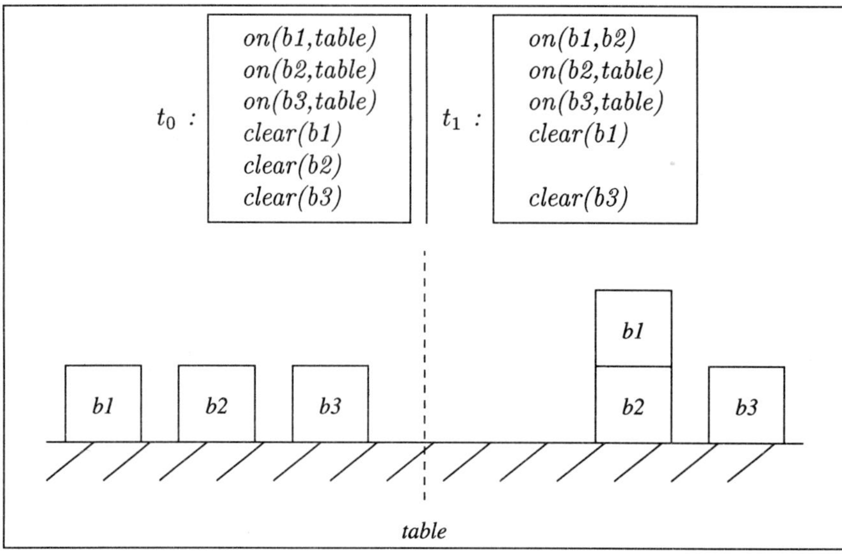

Figure 3: Initial State and State after *stack(b1,b2)*.

The situation is illustrated by Figure 3, which shows the database in its initial state, ready to respond to commands, and its state after executing a command to stack a block. t_0 labels all data true at the initial situation and t_1 the data true after the action. We also have:

$$t_0 < t_1,$$

and if we query the system with:

$$?on(b1, x)$$

we obtain two answers, with different labels, indicating where the answer was obtained in the database, namely:

$$\begin{array}{l} \vdash t_0 : on(b1, table) \\ \vdash t_1 : on(b1, b2) \end{array}$$

The reply to the user is determined by the system as the answer proved with the 'stronger' label, i.e. *on*(b1, b2).

Call the deductive system governing the planning consideration LDS_1. This system involves proving where the blocks are after which action. The system accepts commands in logical form $stack(x, y)$; it does not accept commands in English. If the command does come in English, which we can represent as *stack x on y*, it needs to be parsed into the LDS_1 language. This is done in a parsing logic LDS_0. The schema of Figure 4 illustrates this.

English Input:

stack $b1$ on $b2$. move it on to the table

↓

Parsing Logic LDS_0

↓

stack($b1, b2$); move($b1, table$)

Planning Logic LDS_1

Figure 4: Schema for parsing and planning with LDS.

The following database Δ_2 illustrates processing the database update in LDS_0. Notice that the abduction principle in LDS_0 also uses inferential effect in LDS_1. Intuitively we are trying to abduce on who 'it' refers to. If we choose 'it' to be a block which is already on the table, it makes no sense to move it on to the table. Thus the command when applied to the database will produce no change. The abduction principle gives preference to abduced formulas which give some effect.

Δ_2 :

stack:	$e \to (e \to t)$	$?S + S$
b1:	e	
b2:	e	
move:	$e \to (e \to t)$	
it:	use abduction. First use structural abduction to obtain the first e higher in the list, then use inferential abduction to try and obtain maximal inferential effects in LDS_1.	
table:	e	

3.3 Implementing the blocks world

This blocks world can be implemented in Prolog, to provide a module which can be integrated with the L&R parser, comprising:

(i) an (extensional) database representing the state of the world;

(ii) procedures for executing the actions stack and unstack, and changing the state;

(iii) procedure for ensuring that the new state satisfies the axioms.

To ensure that the labelled database satisfies the blocks world axioms, we have exploited a theorem proving technique called the *consistency method*, developed for checking integrity in *deductive* databases [16]. For our purposes, a deductive database Δ is defined as a finite set of horn clauses of the form:

$$A \leftarrow L_1 \wedge \ldots \wedge L_n, n \geq 0$$

where A is an atom and each $L_i, 0 \leq i \leq n$, is a literal (i.e. a negated or un-negated atom). If $n = 0$ then the rule is called a *fact*. Integrity constraints $\mathcal{I}$ are a set of closed first-order formulas which Δ must satisfy, and have the form of a *denial*:

$$\leftarrow L_1 \wedge \ldots \wedge L_n, n \geq 1$$

where each L_i is a literal as before. Suppose we now have a transaction T, which in our case will involve either the addition or deletion of a fact to produce an updated database Δ_T. The consistency method uses forward reasoning to ensure that $\Delta_T \cup \mathcal{I}$ is consistent (cf. STRIPS-style systems [3] and its descendants).

Considering again the blocks world, the initial information state of the blocks world, encoded as an extensional labelled database, is then as shown in the left-hand side of Figure 3. In (iii) we have the following (implicitly universally quantified) integrity constraints:

$$\mathcal{I} = \{ \leftarrow on(X,table) \wedge on(X,Y), \quad \leftarrow clear(X) \wedge on(Y,X) \}$$

The operation of the system incorporating the L&R parser and the blocks world module is as follows. The user enters a command, which is interpreted by the L&R parser to produce a labelled database representing its meaning. This logical expression is then executed by the blocks world module: its pre-conditions are verified as satisfiable, and the post-condition is treated as a transaction with which to update the database. The axioms are then checked, and, if necessary, the appropriate action is taken to restore integrity.

For example, in the initial state (0), from the user command *'stack block1 on block2'*, the L&R parser deduces the labelled database:

prove $\{\ldots\} \vdash \alpha : t$

0 : [$\vdots$
 stack(me,b1,b2) : t]

exit $\alpha =$ *stack(me,b1,b2)*

(Note that here we have specified discourse referents lexically, i.e. *block1* and *block2* are treated as proper nouns referring to *b1* and *b2* respectively; similarly the system infers that the missing subject of the command is it (*me*). More rigorous treatments are possible, see e.g. [15].)

The label α is executed as a command, and the pre-conditions (in the initial state) are satisfied, so the database is updated with the transaction *on(b1,b2)*. Using the consistency method, the system detects violation of both integrity constraints, and infers that (one way) to restore integrity is to withdraw the facts *on(b1,table)* and *clear(b2)*. These, then, are the contextual implications of the command, which although no longer true in the current' state, are left as facts in a database labelled by the 'previous' time point, thus:

0 : [*clear(b1)*
 clear(b2)
 clear(b3)
 on(b1,table)
 on(b2,table)
 on(b3,table)] $\xrightarrow{stack(b1,b2)}$ 1 : [*clear(b1)*
 clear(b3)
 on(b1,b2)
 on(b2,table)
 on(b3,table)]

0 : [*clear(b2)*
 on(b1,table)]

As a result, we also have a facility for 'historical' queries, and for retracting moves.

From this state, the user command *'move it on to the table'* returns the system to the same configuration as in state 0, only now labelled by 2. This is because taking the meaning of *it* to be either *b2* or *b3* gives no inferential effects, whereas $it = b1$ does.

4 Unexpected answers to yes–no questions

Our picture of dialogue, though emerging, is as yet incomplete. We have a parsing process which takes English input and delivers a predicate logic formula as the label to a conclusion in some labelled database. We have a means of capturing how this resulting formula is embedded in an update mechanism expressed in a predicate logic notation. This was only part of the interpretation problem as we face it in natural dialogue. We also have to consider the array of indirect inferential effects that utterances may give rise to before they are ever used to revise one's beliefs (or not) in some system of updating. In this latter task, we face free manipulation of abductive choices. In many cases, the participants in a dialogue reply to sentences and answer queries with deliberate indirectness. The effect is always the same: the hearer obtains more information than she would by a direct answer. The paradigm case of such indirectness is the case of the indirect reply to a yes–no question. We approach this problem by considering the nature of queries in general, setting aside the parsing problem itself for the time being.

4.1 'First principles'

Given a set of wffs Δ, taken as assumptions, and a formula or query Q, we can pose the logical question $\Delta ? Q$. The meaning of this question is: Does Q follow from Δ in the logic we are dealing with, i.e. is $\Delta \vdash Q$ true? There are three possibilities:

1. $\Delta \vdash Q$ holds;

2. $\Delta \vdash \sim Q$ holds;

3. Neither $\Delta \vdash Q$ nor $\Delta \vdash \sim Q$ hold.

We do not adopt any additional conventions such as $\Delta \nvdash Q$ implies $\Delta \vdash \sim Q$, where Q is atomic (i.e. the closed-world assumption). We thus want a definite proof of the negation $\sim Q$ in all cases. We denote by $\Delta ?! Q = 1$ the situation where the database is logically consistent and is able to prove either Q or $\sim Q$. In other words $\Delta ?! Q = 1$ means that the database Δ decides the truth of Q in a definite way.

The situation we are going to study arises when there is an exchange of information between an asker A and a responder R. At the outset of the exchange, A has a set of assumptions Δ_A: so too does R, i.e. Δ_R. Note that Δ_A may include A's beliefs about the content of Δ_R, and vice versa.

Suppose now that A asks R the query Q. If Δ_A were sufficient to prove or disprove Q then we can assume that A could have figured out Q for himself (unless, of course, he wanted to find out if R knew that Q). However, we will begin by assuming that $\Delta_A?!Q \neq 1$.

R should now respond by supplying some new information B to be added to Δ_A to enable $\Delta_A \cup \{B\}?!Q = 1$. The answer could be:

- $B = Q$ (i.e. 'yes'), in which case $\Delta_A \cup \{Q\}?!Q = 1$;
- $B = {\sim}Q$, (i.e. 'no'), in which case $\Delta_A \cup \{{\sim}Q\}?!Q = 1$;
- some B such that $\Delta_A \cup \{B\}?!Q = 1$;
- some B such that $\Delta_A \cup \{B\}?!Q \neq 1$.

In the first three cases things are fine for A. The situation becomes more interesting when the new data B is still insufficient for A to (logically) determine an answer to Q.

R may have her own reasons for not answering directly and saying Q or ${\sim}Q$. Perhaps she wants to forestall any future questions. Perhaps she wants to give the reason for Q (or for ${\sim}Q$), namely B. For whatever reason, and assuming that R is trying to be co-operative rather than evasive, A expects the answer B to logically decide the query Q, i.e. for $\Delta_A \cup \{B\}?!Q = 1$ but nevertheless finds this not to be the case. At this point we invoke what we call *the Rule of Relevant Assumptions*; and require that further data B' should be abduced such that $\Delta_A \cup \{B, B'\}?!Q = 1$. We assume by relevance that R gives A the minimal input B which allows him to decide the query Q. To find B' we need to know and use the computation procedure we have for $\vdash$.

We call the relevance-theoretic principle which allows us to find the enrichment B' *The Rule of Relevant Assumptions (RRA): the principle of consistent least enrichment relative to a proof procedure for* $\vdash$, whereby:

1. Given a proof procedure for finding answers to queries of the form $\Delta?Q$, then if Δ is a partial database and we ask a query $\Delta?Q$ and we obtain the input B, then we try to prove Q from $\Delta \cup \{B\}$ and assume that any information $B_1, B_2, \ldots$ required for the success of the proof was intended to be added to Δ along with the input B. $\Delta \cup \{B, B_1, B_2, \ldots\}$ must emerge as consistent. When we are talking about proof or deduction, we do not necessarily restrict ourselves to monotonic deduction. The deduction rules used in trying to prove $\Delta \cup$

$\{B\} \vdash Q$ may be defeasible or non-monotonic. These rules correspond better to commonsense reasoning. The nature of the logic involved is as yet unspecified by us.

2. If there are several ways of adding $\{B_i\}$ leading to success, we choose the one which involves the least deductive effort for some inferential effect. (These notions will be made precise in later work: they require specification of links between databases so that we can describe, for example, some concept of closeness between a pair of databases.)

We note that the process of finding the necessary B_i requires a given proof procedure for the logic licensing the addition of such assumptions to the database. Thus for different proof procedures we may obtain different B_i. We also note that the asker A may get his enriched database $\Delta_A \cup \{B, B_i\}$ wrong, in which case further interaction would be required to clarify the matter.

4.2 An example

Suppose we have a database Δ for an asker A and his query Q to a responder R. Δ could contain the fact that A has apples, and Q could be 'would you like [to eat] an apple?' Here we assume that success in the parsing process is achieved and we have some outcome to be evaluated against the database, i.e.:

$$\begin{aligned} \Delta &\ni \exists x[\text{Apple}(x)] \\ Q &= \exists x[\text{Apple}(x) \wedge \text{Eat}(x)] \end{aligned}$$

The answer that A obtains from the responder R may be 'yes' (Q) or 'no' ($\sim Q$), or A may obtain another answer B which allows A to conclude Q or $\sim Q$ (e.g. 'I'm not hungry'). Consider instead the answer: B = 'I don't eat South African apples.' Our proposed formal mechanism for parsing must bring the content of the sentence out, i.e.:

$$B = \forall x[\text{SA}(x) \wedge \text{Apple}(x) \rightarrow \sim \text{Eat}(x)]$$

A has asked on the basis of Δ whether Q and obtained the answer B. We can therefore assume by the principle of relevance that $\Delta \cup \{B\}?!Q = 1$, i.e. the extra input information B is expected to (logically) decide the question Q. However, adding B to Δ does not decide Q in this case. Now A can invoke the principle of consistent least enrichment and try to abduce some further data B' such that $\Delta \cup \{B, B'\}?!Q = 1$.

We will now examine one way to compute the enrichment of Δ with some B' to give the desired effect. In this case, we will use as the RRA for this $\vdash$ the (propositional) abduction algorithm given by [6], which we have also implemented in Prolog, whereby:

1. $\text{Abduce}(\Delta, Q) = \top$ if $\Delta ?Q = 1$.
2. $\text{Abduce}(\Delta, q) = q$, for q atomic such that q is not the head of any clause in Δ.
3. $\text{Abduce}(\Delta, Q_1 \wedge Q_2) = \text{Abduce}(\Delta, Q_1) \wedge \text{Abduce}(\Delta, Q_2)$.
4. $\text{Abduce}(\Delta, A_1 \to (A_2 \to \ldots (A_n \to q)\ldots)) = A_1 \to (A_2 \to \ldots (A_n \to \text{Abduce}(\Delta \cup \{A_1, A_2, \ldots A_n\}, q))\ldots)$.
5. Let q be atomic and let $B^j = B_1^j \to (B_2^j \to \ldots (B_{n_j}^j \to q)\ldots)$ for $j = 1, \ldots, m$ be all clauses in Δ with head q. Then $\text{Abduce}(\Delta, q) = \bigvee_{j=1}^{m} \bigwedge_{i=1}^{n_j} \text{Abduce}(\Delta, B_i^j)$.

If we introduce skolem constants and herbrand constants so that we are dealing only with propositional variables, put Δ in clausal form, and rewrite $\sim p$ as $p \to \bot$, we can apply this abduction algorithm to the example. We also focus on the relevant parts of Δ, i.e. $\exists x[\text{Apple}(x)]$.

We want to know whether the answer to $\Delta \cup \{B\}?Q$ is yes or no. We therefore try to prove both Q and $\sim Q$, abducing any further assumptions along the way. We have:

1.	a	(i.e. Δ skolemized)
2.	$a \to (sa \to (e \to \bot))$	(i.e. B herbrandized in clausal form)

We want to prove $Q = a \wedge e$ and $\sim Q = (a \wedge e) \to \bot$. We will examine each in turn.

For Q we have:

$$\begin{aligned}\text{Abduce}(\Delta, a \wedge e) &= \text{Abduce}(\Delta, a) \wedge \text{Abduce}(\Delta, e)\\ &= \top \wedge \text{Abduce}(\Delta, e)\\ &= \text{Abduce}(\Delta, e)\end{aligned}$$

To compute $\text{Abduce}(\Delta, e)$ we have two policies. Firstly, if we don't unify e with $\bot$, then the result of $\text{Abduce}(\Delta, e) = e$. Since we are assuming that the RRA yields some new information B' and $Q \vdash e$ anyway, we ignore this result.

Secondly, we do let e unify with $\bot$. Then the algorithm gives:

$$\begin{aligned}\text{Abduce}(\Delta, e) &= \text{Abduce}(\Delta, a) \wedge \text{Abduce}(\Delta, sa) \wedge \text{Abduce}(\Delta, e)\\ &= sa \wedge \text{Abduce}(\Delta, e)\end{aligned}$$

We therefore need to solve the following 'equations' for the unknown $x = \text{Abduce}(\Delta, e)$:

$\Delta \cup \{x\} \vdash e$

$x = sa \wedge x$

x is minimal in satisfying the two previous properties

The only solution is $x = sa \wedge e$. This, however, will yield an inconsistent database when added to Δ. Therefore, the RRA 'fails' for Q.

For $\sim Q$ we have:

$$\begin{aligned} \text{Abduce}(\Delta, (a \wedge e) \rightarrow \bot) &= (a \wedge e) \rightarrow \text{Abduce}(\Delta \cup \{a, e\}, \bot) \\ &= (a \wedge e) \rightarrow sa \end{aligned}$$

Since, in effect, this came from the herbrandized query $\text{Apple}(c) \wedge \text{Eat}(c) \rightarrow \bot$ (from $\forall y[\text{Apple}(y) \wedge \text{Eat}(y) \rightarrow \bot]$, itself rewritten from $\sim \exists y[\text{Apple}(y) \wedge \text{Eat}(y)]$, i.e. $\sim Q$), we unherbrandize to give:

$$B' = \forall x[\text{Apple}(x) \wedge \text{Eat}(x) \rightarrow \text{SA}(x)]$$

which is added to A's database Δ and so yields an answer to $\sim Q$. We now have $\Delta \cup \{B, B'\}?!Q = 1$, as required.

It should be noted that although adding B' is the minimal information enrichment for success (using an implicit ordering relation such that $p \leq q \rightarrow p \rightarrow q$), it does cost in deductive effort. This additional cost must be offset by some additional inferential effect for A, the details of which are not necessarily accessible to R. In this case, one natural such additional conclusion is that R is telling A that she believes that all the apples he has to eat are South African (and is inviting A to refute that belief before she will eat one of his apples). There may also be other conclusions in respect of other fruit that R wouldn't eat for the same reason or, more vaguely, of R's political beliefs. A is encouraged to derive inferences in either of these directions given R's indirect mode of expression, but the only inference he is forced to make is that which induces an answer to his question in one step (this in itself is a reflection of the cognitive cost intrinsic to relevance).

Note that the need to add B' arose directly from the proof procedure involved. We 'hit' on the need to succeed with B' and we decided to add. Different proof procedures may give slightly different results, especially when considerations such as cost of deduction are involved. But given the question as input, no further enrichment (such as 'If the apples are Polish, R might not eat them either') is even attempted until it is established whether the indicated enrichment itself yields a definitive answer.

4.3 An extended dialogue

There are many issues to clarify here, but this provides an indication of how we think such abduction resolution should be addressed. We now turn to the analysis of an extended dialogue, in which indirect answers play a prominent part. The example shows a continuing temporal interaction which can lead to different enrichments as time progresses. Furthermore, the process of utterance interpretation in the dialogue will be embedded within an overall planning framework, in which the participants have certain desired outcomes in mind and plan what they say with these outcomes in mind, but during the course of the conversation have to renegotiate the source of conflicts between these outcomes as they become manifest in the discourse scenario.

Consider a situation in which a customer wants to hire a car 'today', and has a fair idea of the type of car she wants. She approaches a salesman who, understandably, wants to maximize his income by hiring and selling the biggest and most expensive cars. The following dialogue, let us suppose, ensues between the customer C and the salesman S:

C:	*I want to hire a car.*	(1)
S:	*When for?*	(2)
C:	*Today.*	(3)
S:	*Would you like to hire this Sierra?*	(4)
C:	*I don't drive big cars.*	(5)
S:	*The small cars are reserved for members only.*	(6)
C:	*Can I join?*	(7)
S:	*It will take a week to process the papers.*	(8a)
	Would you like to reconsider?	(8b)
C:	*Big cars are not easy for me to drive. I can't control them.*	(9)
S:	*But the Sierra has power-assisted steering!*	(10)
C:	*So?*	(11)
S:	*Power-assisted steering makes a car easy to control.*	(12)

The dialogue is one which requires successive steps of abduction, both 'inferential' and 'structural'. We will analyse this dialogue closely to try to bring this out, using formal notation quite loosely. We are assuming, *inter alia*, a logic with sorts, modal operators of wants and belief, that agents have goals and plans, temporal labels on formulas which we can reason with, etc. Because of the complexity of, and interaction between these phenomena, we will gloss over many details, but aim for the exposition to establish the principles involved.

At step (1) the customer C sets out her goal, the hiring of a car. At step (2) the salesman, S, seeks to pinpoint this at some particular point in the temporal flow, and at step (3), C provides S with this information. From the salesman's point of view, we have (in our assumed logic):

$$\begin{array}{rcl} G_S & = & W_S W_C \exists x_{car}[\text{hire}(C, x_{car}) \wedge \text{profitable}(x_{car})] \\ \Delta_S & \ni & t_{now} : W_C \exists x_{car}[\text{hire}(C, x_{car})] \end{array}$$

i.e. his goal G_S is to hire out a car 'profitably', and from (1) and (3) he has added to his database Δ_S the customer's goal.

From now on, the conversation is a successive attempt by each speaker to push the conversation towards satisfaction of his or her own ends—S

to hire out an expensive car, C to hire a small car. We see immediately the point of indirect answers in dialogue. S offers (4). Rather than reply 'no', C provides an indirect answer (5) which is intended to be pre-emptive. She is maximizing to S the relevance of her utterance, since the indirect answer, albeit *a priori* more costly (cognitively), obviates a whole series of similar questions.

This pattern of question and answer is similar to that discussed in Section 4.2, and it is instructive to observe the effect of applying the RRA in this case.

First we assume that in Δ_S there is the 'common knowledge' that if someone can't drive a car then they won't hire it, and that there is some correlation between the size of a car and its profitability. So we now have:

$$\begin{array}{rcl} G_S & = & W_S W_C \exists x_{car}[\text{hire}(C, x_{car}) \wedge \text{profitable}(x_{car})] \\ \Delta_S & \ni & t_{now} : W_C \exists x_{car}[\text{hire}(C, x_{car})] \\ & & \forall x_{car}[\sim \text{drive}(C, x_{car}) \rightarrow \sim \text{hire}(C, x_{car})] \\ & & \forall x_{car}[\text{big}(x_{car}) \leftrightarrow \text{profitable}(x_{car})] \\ & & B_C \forall x_{car}[\text{big}(x_{car}) \rightarrow \sim \text{drive}(C, x_{car})] \\ Q & = & W_C \text{hire}(C, \text{Sierra}_{car}) \end{array}$$

Informally, the abduction algorithm of Section 4.2 gives Abduce$(\Delta_S, Q) = Q$, which is ignored. However, Abduce$(\Delta_S, \sim Q) = B_C\text{big}(\text{Sierra}_{car})$, which is enough to prove $\sim Q$. This is then added to Δ_S.

At this point the salesman should be able to detect a refinement of the customer's goal, i.e.:

$$t_{now} : W_C \exists x_{car}[\text{hire}(C, x_{car}) \wedge \text{small}(x_{car})]$$

and that there is a conflict between the salesman's goal and the customer's goal, caused by the customer's beliefs. Rather than relaxing his own goal, (6) is an attempt by the salesman to revise the customer's belief so that she will revise her own goal and, in turn, communicate this to him.

So he tells her that the set of cars in which she is interested are for members only. In processing (6), C has to abduce *structurally* the existence of some association (A_{assoc}, say) to which these members belong. Making this step, she asks (7), requiring her hearer, S, in turn to abduce structurally the second argument of the relation 'join' as being this same association. In our model, we expect that S's 'parsing database' may look something like:

⋮	
prove $\{\mathrm{I}\!:\!e, \mathrm{join}\!:\!e \to e \to t\} \vdash \gamma\!:\!t$	
n:	$\mathrm{I}\!:\!e$ — abduce: set $I = C$
$n+1$:	$\mathrm{join}\!:\!e \to e \to t$
$n+2$:	abduce: $?\!:\!e$ is required to exit
$n+3$:	abduce on structure: set $? = A_{assoc}$ as right sort for second argument of join
exit $\gamma = \mathrm{join}(C,\ A_{assoc})$	
⋮	

We would also expect, in context, that S can work out the implication of (7), namely that if C joins this association, then she will become a member (and so eligible to hire small cars).

S, presuming C able to reason that joining an association involves filling out, sending off, and processing application papers, replies *indirectly* with (8a). She is required to abduce, again structurally, that the papers so indicated are the papers relevant to her application of this presumed association, and that if she wants to join then the papers need to be processed before she becomes a member. Furthermore, the indirect answer requires 'inferential' abductive reasoning on the customer's part. So we have:

$$\begin{aligned}
\Delta_C &\ni \forall x_{car}\forall t[t : \mathrm{member}(C, A_{assoc}) \to t : (\mathrm{hire}(C, x_{car}) \wedge \mathrm{small}(x_{car}))]\\
Q &= [t_1 \leq t_2] : \exists t_1, t_2[t_1 : \mathrm{join}(C, A_{assoc}) \to t_2 : \mathrm{member}(C, A_{assoc})]\\
B &= [t_3 \leq t_4, t_4 = t_5 - 1\mathrm{week}] : \exists t_3, t_4, t_5[t_3 : \mathrm{join}(C, A_{assoc}) \to\\
&\qquad t_4 : \mathrm{process(papers)} \to t_5 : \mathrm{member}(C, A_{assoc})]
\end{aligned}$$

Applying the abduction algorithm of Section 4.2 to an intuitively skolemized and herbrandized version of the above, and assuming the ability to propagate temporal constraints (i.e. labels of the form $[t_1 \leq t_2]$), we obtain:

$$\begin{aligned}
&\mathrm{Abduce}(\Delta, [t_1 \leq t_2] : t_1 : \mathrm{join} \to t_2 : \mathrm{member})\\
&= [t_1 \leq t_2] : t_1 : \mathrm{join} \to \mathrm{Abduce}(\Delta \cup \{t_1 : \mathrm{join}\}, t_2 : \mathrm{member})\\
&= [t_1 \leq t_2, t_2 = t_5, t_3 \leq t_4, t_4 = t_5 - 1\mathrm{week}] : t_1 : \mathrm{join} \to\\
&\qquad \bigwedge(\mathrm{Abduce}(\Delta\cup\{t_1 : \mathrm{join}\}, t_3 : \mathrm{join}), \mathrm{Abduce}(\Delta\cup\{t_1 : \mathrm{join}\}, t_4 : \mathrm{process}))\\
&= [t_1 \leq t_2, t_2 = t_5, t_3 \leq t_4, t_4 = t_5 - 1\mathrm{week}, t_1 = t_3] : t_1 : \mathrm{join} \to\\
&\qquad (\top \wedge t_4 : \mathrm{process})\\
&= [t_1 \leq t_4] : t_1 : \mathrm{join} \to t_4 : \mathrm{process}
\end{aligned}$$

Although the RRA has succeeded, C is also able to reason that by adding this to the database and asking herself $\Delta_C?t_{now} : \mathrm{join}(C, A_{assoc})$ she can conclude:

$$\forall x_{car}[[t_{now} \leq t - 1\text{week}] : t : (\text{hire}(C, x_{car}) \wedge \text{small}(x_{car}))]$$

but the time constraint on when she can hire a small car, requiring this time t to be greater than t_{now} by at least one week, renders this conclusion inconsistent with her goal.

This, according to relevance, is what the salesman intends her to abduce, and since he knows that C cannot reconcile her goal with the given information he continues with (8b). With this question, he reminds her of the first steps in their negotiation (indeed we posit that the lexical content of reconsider forces her to set up as its second argument some step in the 'consideration' so far to hand). In (9) C now provides the reason for her earlier judgment (5) and in so doing gives S the information he needs to subvert her belief and to fulfil his own goal. He responds with (10). The keyword here is *but*. We intend the procedural specification of *but* to be formulated so that it instigates a search for a set of premises that derive inconsistency at some level of inference—the inference to be derived from the second conjunct to replace the inference to be derived from the first. Since in (9) it is the customer's assertion that big cars are not safe, which is the reason for her belief of (5), it is this assertion that S will want her to retract. Accordingly he utters (10) requiring her to recover premises that combine with this to replace the inference from C's utterance (9).

Despite recognizing this, the customer refuses to provide the requisite premise herself. However, the word *so* invites the salesman to build just this premise for her. We can specify *so* to be an anaphoric expression precisely for this purpose. S duly provides C with the premise needed. The customer now has to reason (non-monotonically) from (12) to the point where she can relax her goal and inform the salesman that she is prepared to hire a big car, presuming it has power-assisted steering.

This example displays all the phenomena we have so far investigated—the general parsing problem, the manipulation of abduction principles both structural and inferential, the use of words as procedural instructions dictating the flow of inference, the embedding of all such reasoning tasks in an overall cooperative reasoning enterprise which constitutes the dialogue itself. However, we are still far from formally modelling and implementing every aspect of this.

5 Conclusions

Our aim in this chapter has been to explore a more non-standard interaction between a human and a database, and in particular the prerequisites for equipping the database with the 'intelligence' to participate 'rationally' in natural language question-answering and dialogue. We observed that (at least) two components were necessary: a front-end module to parse natural language statements/queries and a second module for reasoning with the result of parsing. In Sections 3 and 4, respectively, we described our experimental implementation of the first module and discussed (some of) the reasoning requirements of the second module. Our proposals have synthesized aspects of abductive reasoning and relevance theory in the framework of Labelled Deductive Systems, used not only to bring together aspects of the parsing and interpretation processes, but also to provide a general framework for reasoning about the implicit content of communicative acts.

Due to the breadth and complexity of the phenomena we have investigated and are attempting to model, many of the details are omitted in this chapter, and some remain to be addressed in depth. Work remaining to be done includes:

- formalization of the trade off between inferential effect vs. deductive effort;
- integration of the parsing system with first-order abduction algorithms, set in a general knowledge representation framework;
- interaction of the results of abductive reasoning with algorithms used to provide co-operative answering from computerized databases;
- development and integration of abduction algorithm(s) for the first-order case, and exploration of the space of different algorithms combined with different $\vdash$.
- further analysis of, and integration of reasoning methods for, other 'commonsense' intuitions about time, permission, beliefs, wants, etc. (see [11]).

We remain some way from our stated aim of 'intelligent databases', nevertheless we believe that the LDS framework provides a requisite foundation within which the heterogeneous reasoning activities involved in utterance interpretation can be set out, linked, and absorbed into a single composite reasoning system.

Acknowledgements

We would like to thank two anonymous reviewers and, in particular, Robert Demolombe for their useful suggestions and comments on an earlier version of this chapter.

Professor Dov Gabbay is a Senior Research Fellow, UK Science and Engineering Research Council. Dr Jermey Pitt was supported by the UK

Economic and Social Science Resarch Council under grant ESRC R-000-23-2069.

References

[1] A. Aho and S. Johnson. LR parsing. *Computing Surveys*, **6**(2):99–124, 1974.

[2] J. Cunningham, D. Gabbay, and H.-J. Ohlbach. Towards the MEDLAR framework. In *Esprit '91: Proceedings of the Annual Esprit Conference*, pp. 822–841. Kluwer/CEC DGXIII, 1991.

[3] R. Fikes and N. Nilsson. STRIPS: A new approach to the application of theorem proving to problem solving. *Artificial Intelligence*, **3**(4):251–288, 1971.

[4] D. Gabbay. *Labelled Deductive Systems*, Part I. *Technical Report* CIS-Bericht-90-22, Centrum für Informations und Sprachverarbeitung, Universität München, 1990.

[5] D. Gabbay. Abduction in labelled deductive systems: a conceptual abstract. In R. Kruse and P. Siegel, editors, *Proceedings of the European Conference on Symbolic and Quantitative Approaches for Uncertainty*, volume 548 of *LNCS*. Springer Verlag, 1991.

[6] D. Gabbay. What is a logical system. In D. Gabbay and F. Guenthner, editors, *What is a Logical system.* Oxford University Press, to appear.

[7] D. Gabbay and R. Kempson. Natural language content: a proof-theoretic perspective. In *Proceedings of the 8th Amsterdam Colloquium on Formal Semantics*, 1992.

[8] M. Genesereth and N. Nilsson. *Logical Foundations of Artificial Intelligence.* Morgan Kaufmann, 1987.

[9] G. Morrill. Grammar and logical types. In *Proceedings of the 7th Amsterdam Colloquium on Formal Semantics*, 1990.

[10] R. Oehrle, E. Bach, and D. Wheeler (editors). *Categorial Grammars and Natural Language Structures.* Reidel, 1988.

[11] H.-J. Ohlbach and I. Pratt. Sample dialogues. Medlar II PPR 1, Deliverable I.1.1; CEC Esprit Basic Research Action Medlar II (Esprit 6471), 1993.

[12] F. Pereira and D. Warren. Definite clause grammars for language analysis. *Artificial Intelligence*, **13**:231–278, 1980.

[13] F. Pereira and D. Warren. Parsing as deduction. In *Proceedings of the 21st Annual Meeting of the Association for Computational Linguistics*, Cambridge, MA, 1983.

[14] J. Pitt. *Compositional Grammars and Natural Language Processing.* PhD thesis, Department of Computing, Imperial College of Science Technology and Medicine, 1991.

[15] J. Pitt, J. Cunningham, and K. Van den Bergh. An automated reasoning approach to natural language understanding. *Discipline Filosofiche (Analitika)*, 2, 1992.

[16] F. Sadri and R. Kowalski. An application of general purpose theorem proving to database integrity. In J. Minker, editor, *Proceedings of the Workshop on Foundations of Deductive Databases and Logic Programming.* Morgan Kaufmann, 1987.

[17] D. Sperber and D. Wilson. *Relevance: Communication and Cognition.* Blackwell, 1986.

8

Hypothetical reasoning with intuitionistic logic

Anthony J. Bonner

Abstract

This chapter addresses a limitation of most deductive database systems: they cannot reason hypothetically. Although they reason effectively about the world as it is, they are poor at tasks such as planning and design, where one must explore the consequences of hypothetical actions and possibilities. To address this limitation, this chapter presents a logic-programming language in which a user can create hypotheses and draw inferences from them. Two types of hypothetical operations are considered: the *insertion* of tuples into a database, and the *creation* of new constant symbols. These two operations are interesting, not only because they extend the capabilities of database systems, but also because they fit neatly into a well-established logical framework, namely *intuitionistic logic.* This chapter presents the proof theory for the logic, outlines its intuitionistic model theory, and summarizes results on its complexity and on its ability to express database queries. Our results establish a strong link between two previously unrelated, but well-developed areas: intuitionistic logic and computational complexity. This, in turn, leads to a strong link with classical second-order logic. Furthermore, unlike many expressibility results in the literature, our results do not depend on the artificial assumption that the data domain is linearly ordered.

1 Introduction

Researchers from several areas have recognized the need for computer systems that reason hypothetically. Decision support systems (DSS) are a good example, especially in domains such as financial planning where many 'what if' scenarios must be considered [35, 44]. A typical example is an analyst who must predict a company's deficit for the forthcoming year assuming that employee salaries are increased by a given percentage. Or he might want a table of deficit predictions for a number of hypothetical salary increases [55]. Similar problems occur in computer aided design (CAD). Here, one must evaluate the effect on the overall design of local design alternatives and of various external factors [25, 47]. For example, an engineer may need to know how much the price of an automobile would increase if supplier X raised his prices by Y percent [25]. The number of hypothetical scenarios multiplies quickly when several factors are varied simultaneously, such as prices, interest rates, tax rates, etc. One may also need to consider variations in more complex factors, such as government regulations, company policy, tax laws, etc.

The database community has addressed some of these needs by developing systems that integrate query processing with hypothetical updates. Such systems allow a user to pose queries not only to the real database, but also to hypothetical databases. Hypothetical databases are derived from a real database by a series of hypothetical assumptions, or updates. Early work in this area was done by Stonebraker, who showed that hypothetical databases can be efficiently implemented by slight extensions to conventional database mechanisms [51, 50]. He pointed out that hypothetical databases are useful for debugging purposes, for generating test data, and for carrying out a variety of simulations. He also argued that 'there are advantages to making hypothetical databases central to the operation of a database management system' [50].

The logic-programming community has taken these ideas one step further, integrating hypothetical updates not just with query processing, but with logical inference as well. Since the premise of a logical rule is just a query, several researchers have developed *hypothetical rules*, in which the premise can query not only a real database, but hypothetical databases as well. Vieille *et al.*, for instance, have developed a deductive database along these lines [55], and Warren and Manchanda have used hypothetical rules to reason about database updates [56, 37]. In [42], Miller shows that hypothetical insertions can structure the runtime environment of logic programs, resulting in programs that are more elegant, more efficient, and easier to maintain. In [43], he develops a theory of lexical scoping based on the hypothetical creation of constant symbols during inference.

These logical systems are well-suited to solving problems in Artificial Intelligence, especially problems that involve reasoning about alternative courses of action. For example, an AI program may need to infer that *if* the pawn took the knight, *then* the rook would be threatened. The program may also have to consider sequences of possible moves, exploring hypothetical possibilities to great depth. Hypothetical inference has also extended the capabilities of expert systems. Gabbay and Reyle, for instance, have reported a need to augment Prolog with hypothetical rules in order to encode the British Nationality Act, because the act contains rules such as,

'You are eligible for citizenship if your father *would* be eligible *if* he were still alive.' [27] And McCarty, also motivated by legal applications, has developed a wide class of hypothetical rules for computer-based consultation systems, especially systems for reasoning about corporate tax law and estate tax law [39, 41, 46].

Theoretical work on hypothetical inference has also been carried out, largely by the logic-programming community. Most of this work focuses on the hypothetical insertion of atoms into a database. These updates, it turns out, fit neatly into a well-known logical system, *intuitionistic logic* [24]. Most of this work has been semantic, first showing that hypothetical insertion is indeed intuitionistic, and then casting the semantics in terms of a least fixpoint theory, in the logic-programming tradition. Gabbay first showed that hypothetical insertion is intuitionistic [26]. Working independently, McCarty and Miller extended this result to operations that create new constant symbols during inference, and they developed fixpoint semantics based on intuitionistic logic [39, 42]. Earlier, Statman showed that intuitionistic logic is PSPACE-complete in the propositional case [48]. Several researchers have also investigated the the semantics of negation-as-failure for hypothetical insertions [26, 15, 32, 30, 31, 23]. We discuss this work in Section 6.

This chapter adds to the picture by summarizing some of our own results on hypothetical inference. Our work has considered a variety of hypothetical operations, including insertion, deletion, and bulk updates [12, 11, 16, 13, 14, 15, 10, 8]. This chapter, however, focuses on two specific operations: (i) adding formulas to a database hypothetically ('insertion'), and (ii) creating new constant symbols hypothetically ('creation'). The ability to create new constants is achieved *without* using function symbols. In fact, because of its importance to database systems, the entire chapter focuses on the function-free case. Since the language has an *infinite* set of constant symbols, however, it may be possible to generalize our development to include function symbols, in which case the Herbrand universe would be infinite.

The operations of hypothetical insertion and creation promise new capabilities and applications for deductive databases and logic-programming systems. For example, in testing a circuit design, we might ask, '*If* input X is high at time t, *will* output Y be high at time $t + \Delta$?' This simple hypothetical query can be represented by the formula $high(X, t) \rightarrow high(Y, t + \Delta)$. We might also want to know whether this query is true for *any* time t, not just for a specific time. This would be the case if we wanted a guarantee that the circuit will always behave in a certain way. The query then becomes universally quantified and has the following logical form:

$$\forall_t[high(X, t) \rightarrow high(Y, t + \Delta)]$$

Notice that this formula is a *query*, not a rule. It is very different from the queries normally found in the deductive-database and logic-programming literature, since it contains an implication and is universally quantified. Numerous examples of such queries can be constructed, including sophisticated rulebases in which such queries appear in the premises of rules. Such rules are called *embedded implications* [39]. As we shall see, the implication sign in queries and rule bodies corresponds to hypothetical insertion, and the universal quantifier corresponds to the hypothetical creation of new constant symbols. It is in this way that the two operations of insertion and creation fit neatly into a logical, first-order framework.

In addition to applications, these two operations have important practical and theoretical properties. For instance, since they can be handled entirely within first-order intuitionistic logic, they have a well-established semantics. In addition, they have an efficient Prolog-style inference procedure, one based on resolution and unification, in the logic-programming tradition [40]. Lastly, these hypothetical operations have important complexity-theoretic properties. For instance, as we show in Section 7, they characterize the database queries in many well-known complexity classes, such as NP, PSPACE, *re*, and the polynomial-time hierarchy. One outcome of this chapter, then, is to develop a strong link between two previously unrelated, but well-established areas: intuitionistic logic and computational complexity. As a corollary, Section 7.3 links intuitionistic logic and classical second-order logic.

2 Introductory examples

This section gives several examples of hypothetical queries and rules. The examples are centred on a deductive database that describes university policy. In these examples, the atomic formula $take(s, c)$ intuitively means that student s has taken course c, and $grad(s)$ means that s is eligible for graduation.

Conceptually, the deductive database has two parts, extensional and intensional. The extensional part consists of atomic facts, such as $take(tony, cs250)$; and the intensional part consists of rules, such as

$$grad(s) \leftarrow take(s, his101),\ take(s, eng201).$$

Formally, the deductive database is a set, R, of rules and facts, and the notation $R \vdash \phi$ means that formula ϕ can be inferred from the rules and facts in R.[1] In the examples, each query is described in three ways: (i)

[1] Later, when we study complexity, we will need to distinguish more carefully between rules and facts. We will then adopt the notation $R + DB \vdash \phi$, where R denotes a set of rules, and DB denotes a database of atomic facts. Until then, however, there is no need to be so discriminating, so we shall simply assume that R contains both rules and facts.

informally in English, (ii) formally at the meta-level, and (iii) formally at the object-level.

Example 2.1 Consider the query, 'If Tony took $cs452$, would he be eligible to graduate?' That is, if $take(tony, cs452)$ were added to the database, could we infer $grad(tony)$? This query can be formalized at the meta-level as follows:

$$R + take(tony, cs452) \vdash grad(tony) \qquad (1)$$

At the object level, the expression $grad(tony) \leftarrow take(tony, cs452)$ represents this query. That is, $R \vdash grad(tony) \leftarrow take(tony, cs452)$ iff meta-level condition (1) is satisfied.

Example 2.2 'Retrieve those students who could graduate if they took one more course.' That is, at the meta-level, we want those s for which the following statement is true for some c:

$$R + take(s, c) \vdash grad(s)$$

The expression $\exists_c[grad(s) \leftarrow take(s, c)]$ represents this query at the object-level. That is, for each value of s, the statement $R \vdash \exists_c[grad(s) \leftarrow take(s, c)]$ is true iff the meta-level condition is satisfied.

Queries such as these can be used in the premises of rules. Such rules turn the query language into a logic for building rulebases.

Example 2.3 Consider the following university policy:

> 'A student qualifies for a degree in *math and physics* if he is within one course of a degree in *math* and within one course of a degree in *physics*.'

This policy can be represented as two rules:

$$within1(s, d) \leftarrow \exists_c[grad(s, d) \leftarrow take(s, c)].$$
$$grad(s, mathphys) \leftarrow within1(s, math),\ within1(s, phys).$$

Here, $grad(s, d)$ means that student s is eligible for a degree in discipline d, and $within1(s, d)$ means that s is within one course of a degree in d. Note that the premise of the first rule is a query similar to the one in Example 2.2.

In [8], it is shown that the university policy in Example 2.3 cannot be expressed in Datalog or in any query language based on classical logic. Hypothetical rules thus increase the capabilities of deductive database systems. The next two examples demonstrate the use of universal quantification in queries and rule bodies.

Example 2.4 'Retrieve those departments for which any student can graduate by taking just one course.' That is, at the meta-level, we want those departments d such that

$$\forall_s \exists_c \; [R + take(s,c) \vdash grad(s,d)]$$

Or, using the notation of the previous example, we want those departments d for which any student is within one course of graduation. That is,

$$\forall_s \; [R \vdash within1(s,d)] \qquad (2)$$

At the object level, this query is represented by the expression

$$\forall_s \; within1(s,d).$$

That is, for each value of d, the statement

$$R \vdash \forall_s \; within1(s,d)$$

is true iff condition (2) is satisfied.

Example 2.5 The following rule defines a department to be 'easy' if any student can obtain a degree from the department by taking history 100 and English 100.

$$easy(d) \leftarrow \forall_s[grad(s,d) \leftarrow take(s, his100), take(s, eng100)]$$

The last two examples illustrate a subtle point about our use of universal quantification: quantification occurs not just over those students currently mentioned in the database, but over all *possible* students, including those who *might* enroll in the future. In Example 2.4, for instance, we are asking if a hypothetical student (who might have taken no courses) can graduate by taking just one course. The fact that every student in the database may have already taken several courses is irrelevant. For this reason, the idea of hypothetical objects is central to our interpretation of universal quantification, and this is what gives it an intuitionistic semantics, as we shall see in Section 4. Proof theoretically, the creation of hypothetical objects means creating new constant symbols to represent them. The next section describes an inference system that does exactly this.

3 Proof theory

This section describes a proof theory for hypothetical inference, one based on a generalization of Horn rules called *embedded implications*. Embedded implications are first-order formulas that can hypothetically insert formulas into a database, and can hypothetically create new constant symbols. Such systems have been developed by several researchers [27, 39, 42, 11, 16, 38]. This section defines a simplified version of these systems, one that retains many of the essential properties of the more elaborate systems while admitting a clean theoretical analysis. One notable feature of this system is that it allows universal quantifiers in rule bodies. In the logic programming context, such rules were first treated by McCarty. In [39], McCarty develops an intuitionistic fixpoint semantics for embedded implications, and in [40], he describes a practical, tableau proof procedure. Such rules have also been extensively investigated by Miller. In [42], Miller develops an intuitionistic fixpoint semantics for embedded implications, and in [43], he develops an interpreter for them.

The language of our logic includes three infinite, enumerable sets: a set of variables $x, y, z, \ldots$; a set of constant symbols $a, b, c, \ldots$; and a set of predicate symbols $A, B, C, \ldots$. Note that the language, as defined here, does not include function symbols.

Definition 3.1 (Embedded implications).

1. An atomic formula is an embedded implication.
2. If A is atomic and if $\phi_1, ..., \phi_k$ are embedded implications, then $A \leftarrow \phi_1, ..., \phi_k$ is also an embedded implication.
3. If $\phi(x)$ is an embedded implication, then $\forall_x \phi(x)$ is also an embedded implication.

Embedded implications thus include formulas of the form A, $A \leftarrow B$, $A \leftarrow (B \leftarrow C)$, $A \leftarrow (B \leftarrow (C \leftarrow D)$, etc. They also include formulas with embedded universal quantifiers, such as $A \leftarrow \forall_x B(x)$ and $A \leftarrow \forall_x [B(x) \leftarrow C(x), D(x)]$. They do not, however, include formulas with explicit disjunction or existential quantification.

This chapter is concerned primarily with embedded implications that are *closed*, i.e., that have no free variables. A set of closed embedded implications is called a *hypothetical deductive database*, or simply a *rulebase*. In a rulebase, universal quantifiers at the top level may be implicit and need not be written. Thus, the following set:

$$\{ A(x) \leftarrow B(x), \qquad C \leftarrow \forall_x (D(x,y) \leftarrow E(x,y)) \}$$

is an abbreviation for the following rulebase:

$$\{ \forall_x [A(x) \leftarrow B(x)], \qquad \forall_y [C \leftarrow \forall_x (D(x,y) \leftarrow E(x,y))] \}$$

Definition 3.2 (Hypothetical inference). The five items below define an inference system for closed embedded implications. The first item specifies axioms, and the other four items specify rules of inference. Here, R is a hypothetical deductive database, ϕ and each ϕ_i are closed embedded implications, and $\phi(x)$ is an embedded implication whose only free variable is x. b is a constant symbol.

1. $R \vdash \phi$ if $\phi \in R$.
2. $R \vdash \phi(b)$ if $R \vdash \forall_x \phi(x)$.
3. $R \vdash \phi$ if $R \vdash \phi \leftarrow \phi_1 ... \phi_n$ and $R \vdash \phi_i$ for each i (modus ponens).
4. $R \vdash \phi \leftarrow \phi_1, ..., \phi_k$ if $R + \{\phi_1, ..., \phi_k\} \vdash \phi$.
5. $R \vdash \forall_x \phi(x)$ if $R \vdash \phi(b)$ provided b is new, i.e., does not appear in R or $\phi(x)$.

This inference system derives expressions of the form $R \vdash \phi$, where both R and ϕ are closed. When this system is used for query processing, ϕ represents a yes/no query. That is, given ϕ and R, the system returns 'yes' iff $R \vdash \phi$ can be derived. In databases and logic programming, it is common to ask queries that return a set of tuples as answers. Such queries can be defined using embedded implications with free variables [11, 16, 10, 27, 28, 40]. We address this issue in Section 7, where we discuss database queries in general. Until then, however, we shall assume that a query is a closed formula. Indeed, as far as the above inference system is concerned, a query (or goal) is *always* a closed formula.

Notice that the first three items in Definition 3.2 form an inference system for definite Horn logic (e.g., Prolog and Datalog). The last two rules extend this to an inference system for hypothetical reasoning by formalizing two hypothetical operations: insertion and creation. Like all inference systems, this one can be run in either a top–down (backward) or a bottom–up (forward) mode. When run top–down, the fourth rule inserts formulas $\phi_1 \ldots \phi_k$ into the database, and the fifth rule creates a new constant symbol, b. Although these two operations might seem procedural, the inference system provides a simple, logical semantics, since the order in which the rules are applied is unimportant. Moreover, the next section provides that other essential ingredient of logical systems, a model theory.

Inference rule 5, above, is somewhat unusual in that it creates new constant symbols during inference. It therefore deserves some discussion. Since the constant symbol b is new, it does not appear in any of the rules, and so is not given any special treatment by them. That is, if $R \vdash \phi(b)$ is derivable when b is new, then it will be derivable for any b. Intuitively, this is why we can replace the universal quantifier in rule 5 by a single constant symbol. Alternatively, we can view b as a kind of skolem constant. That is, if R were interpreted according to classical semantics,[2] then we could reason as follows, where $\vdash_c$ denotes classical inference:

	$R \vdash_c \forall_x \phi(x)$	
iff	$R \wedge \neg\forall_x \phi(x)$	is unsatisfiable.
iff	$R \wedge \exists_x \neg\phi(x)$	is unsatisfiable.
iff	$R \wedge \neg\phi(b)$	is unsatisfiable, where b is a skolem constant (i.e., b is new).
iff	$R \vdash_c \phi(b)$	

Notice that b is a skolem *constant*, not a skolem function. This is always the case, since, according to Definition 3.2, both R and $\forall_x \phi(x)$ are closed. Rule 5 is therefore a sound rule of classical logic. It is also a sound rule of intuitionistic logic.[3] Normally, skolemization is a preprocessing phase prior to resolution. This is not necessary, however, and in the inference system of Definition 3.2, 'skolemization' is effectively integrated into the inference process. This kind of runtime skolemization is central to the tableau proof procedure developed in [40], and to the interpreter presented in [43]. Runtime skolemization is treated in a more general setting by Gabbay and Reyle in [28]. Because Gabbay's language includes existential quantifiers, his analogue of rule 5 uses skolem functions, not just skolem constants.

The rest of this section gives examples illustrating the basic properties of the inference system above. These examples use the following lemma, which is an immediate consequence of inference rules 1, 2, and 3. This lemma is useful when the topmost universal quantifiers in a rulebase are implicit, e.g., when we write $A(x,y) \leftarrow B(x,y)$ instead of $\forall_x\forall_y[A(x,y) \leftarrow B(x,y)]$.

Lemma 3.3 *Let $\phi \leftarrow \phi_1 ... \phi_n$ be a rule in R, and let θ be a substitution such that $\phi\theta$ and each $\phi_i\theta$ are closed. If $R \vdash \phi_i\theta$ for each i, then $R \vdash \phi\theta$.*

3.1 Examples of inference

The examples below view hypothetical inference as a top-down process that starts from the goal, as in Prolog. The first example illustrates the basic idea.

Example 3.4 (Propositional inference). Suppose that R consists of the following three rules:

[2] In fact, when R consists entirely of Horn rules, the inference system of Definition 3.2 is classical, i.e., it is sound and complete with respect to classical model theory.

[3] The proof is an adaptation of a proof given in [24, Chapter 5] on the correctness of Beth Tableaux, which also create new constant symbols.

$$A \leftarrow (B \leftarrow D).$$
$$B \leftarrow C.$$
$$C \leftarrow D.$$

Then $R \vdash A$. This can be proved by a straightforward, top–down argument:

	$R \vdash A$	
if	$R \vdash B \leftarrow D$	by Lemma 3.3, using the rule $A \leftarrow (B \leftarrow D)$.
if	$R + D \vdash B$	by inference rule 4
if	$R + D \vdash C$	by Lemma 3.3, using the rule $B \leftarrow C$.
if	$R + D \vdash D$	by Lemma 3.3, using the rule $C \leftarrow D$.

But the last line is trivially true, by inference rule 1.

The next two examples show how simple, hypothetical updates can be cascaded to produce more complex, hypothetical transactions. The first example is propositional. The second example extends the idea to recursive, predicate inference.

Example 3.5 (Cascaded hypotheticals). Suppose R consists of rules defining a predicate A_n plus the following n rules:

$$\begin{array}{l} A_0 \leftarrow (A_1 \leftarrow B_1) \\ A_1 \leftarrow (A_2 \leftarrow B_2) \\ \quad \cdots \\ A_{n-1} \leftarrow (A_n \leftarrow B_n) \end{array}$$

Then $R \vdash A_0$ *if* $R + B_1 + B_2 + \ldots + B_n \vdash A_n$. This can be proved in a top–down fashion as follows:

$$\begin{array}{ll} & R \vdash A_0 \\ \textit{if} & R \vdash A_1 \leftarrow B_1 \\ \textit{if} & R + B_1 \vdash A_1 \\ \textit{if} & R + B_1 \vdash A_2 \leftarrow B_2 \\ \textit{if} & R + B_1 + B_2 \vdash A_2 \\ & \quad \cdots \\ \textit{if} & R + B_1 + B_2 + \ldots + B_n \vdash A_n \end{array}$$

Example 3.6 (Recursion). Suppose R contains the following rule and atomic formulas:

$$A(x) \leftarrow NEXT(x,y),\ [A(y) \leftarrow B(y)].$$
$$NEXT(c_0, c_1),\ \ NEXT(c_1, c_2)\ \ldots\ NEXT(c_{n-1}, c_n)$$

Then, for $0 \leq i \leq n$,

$$R \vdash A(c_0) \quad \textit{if} \quad R + B(c_1) + B(c_2) + \ldots + B(c_n) \ \vdash\ A(c_n) \qquad (3)$$

To prove this statement, first note that $R \vdash NEXT(c_{i-1}, c_i)$, and in fact, $R + S \vdash NEXT(c_{i-1}, c_i)$ for any set of formulas S. Hence,

$$\begin{array}{ll} & R + S \ \vdash\ A(c_{i-1}) \\ \textit{if} & R + S \ \vdash\ NEXT(c_{i-1}, c_i) \quad \text{and} \quad R + S \ \vdash\ A(c_i) \leftarrow B(c_i) \\ \textit{if} & R + S \ \vdash\ A(c_i) \leftarrow B(c_i) \\ \textit{if} & R + S + B(c_i) \ \vdash\ A(c_i) \end{array}$$

Thus, to prove $A(c_{i-i})$, we can add $B(c_i)$ to the database and then try to prove $A(c_i)$. Carrying out this process recursively leads to statement (3). That is,

$$\begin{array}{ll} & R \ \vdash\ A(c_0) \\ \textit{if} & R + B(c_1) \ \vdash\ A(c_1) \\ \textit{if} & R + B(c_1) + B(c_2) \ \vdash\ A(c_2) \\ & \ldots \\ \textit{if} & R + B(c_1) + B(c_2) + \ldots + B(c_n) \ \vdash\ A(c_n) \end{array}$$

The next example extends Example 3.4 to include universal quantification in a rule premise. The quantifier is dealt with by creating a new, hypothetical constant symbol during inference.

Example 3.7 (Creating new constants). Suppose R consists of the following rules:

$$\begin{array}{l} A \leftarrow \forall_x [B(x) \leftarrow D(x)] \\ B(x) \leftarrow C(x) \\ C(x) \leftarrow D(x) \end{array}$$

Then $R \vdash A$, as the following top down argument shows:

	$R \vdash A$	
if	$R \vdash \forall_x[B(x) \leftarrow D(x)]$	by lemma 3.3.
if	$R \vdash B(c) \leftarrow D(c)$	where c is new, by inference rule 5.
if	$R + D(c) \vdash B(c)$	by inference rule 4.
if	$R + D(c) \vdash C(c)$	by lemma 3.3, using the rule $B(x) \leftarrow C(x)$.
if	$R + D(c) \vdash D(c)$	by lemma 3.3, using the rule $C(x) \leftarrow D(x)$.

But the last line is trivially true, by inference rule 1.

In this example, the constant symbol c is created during inference, when inference rule 5 is invoked in a top–down mode. The ability to create constants in this way is crucial to the inference system, and it is the basis of the Prolog-style proof procedure developed in [40]. In [16], this ability is used to simulate the computations of arbitrary Turing machines. Without the ability to create new constant symbols, it is only possible to simulate Turing machines that use a polynomial amount of space, i.e., PSPACE-machines (see Section 5). The next example uses recursive rules to generate an unbounded number of new constant symbols and to build a counter of unbounded range.

Example 3.8 (Unbounded counters). Suppose R contains the following rule:

$$B(x) \leftarrow \forall_y[B(y) \leftarrow NEXT(x,y)]$$

Then, for any $n \geq 0$,

$$\begin{array}{ll} & R \vdash B(c_0) \\ \textit{if} & R + NEXT(c_0, c_1) + NEXT(c_1, c_2) + \ldots \\ & \quad +NEXT(c_{n-1}, c_n) \;\vdash\; B(c_n) \end{array} \tag{4}$$

where $c_1, ..., c_n$ are new and distinct constant symbols. To see this, first suppose that S is a set of formulas that mentions the constants $c_0....c_{i-1}$, but not c_i. Then,

$$\begin{array}{ll} & R + S \vdash B(c_{i-1}) \\ \textit{if} & R + S \vdash \forall_y[B(y) \leftarrow NEXT(c_{i-1}, y)] \\ \textit{if} & R + S \vdash B(c_i) \leftarrow NEXT(c_{i-1}, c_i) \\ \textit{if} & R + S + NEXT(c_{i-1}, c_i) \vdash B(c_i) \end{array}$$

Thus, to prove $B(c_{i-1})$, we can create a new constant symbol, c_i, add $NEXT(c_{i-1}, c_i)$ to the database, and then try to prove $B(c_i)$. Carrying out this process recursively leads to statement (4). That is,

$$\begin{array}{ll} & R \vdash B(c_0) \\ \textit{if} & R + NEXT(c_0, c_1) \vdash B(c_1) \\ \textit{if} & R + NEXT(c_0, c_1) + NEXT(c_1, c_2) \vdash B(c_2) \\ & \ldots \\ \textit{if} & R + NEXT(c_0, c_1) + NEXT(c_1, c_2) + \ldots \\ & +NEXT(c_{n-1}, c_n) \vdash B(c_n) \end{array}$$

4 Model theory

The inference system of Definition 3.2 is not classical. That is, it is not sound and complete with respect to classical model theory. This might seem surprising, since each of the five inference rules *is* classical. Indeed, the first three are familiar classical inference rules, the fourth is the deduction theorem, and the fifth was shown to correspond to classical skolemization. Thus, the entire inference system is classically sound, so every inference is a classical theorem. However, the system is not classically complete. That is, there are some classical theorems that it cannot (and should not!) prove.

To see this, consider a deductive database R consisting of the following three rules:

$$A \leftarrow (B \leftarrow C) \qquad D \leftarrow A \qquad D \leftarrow C$$

If these rules are interpreted classically, then $R \models_c D$. To see this, note that from the classical definition of implication, the first rule can be expanded in terms of disjunction and negation to give $(A \vee \neg B) \wedge (A \vee C)$. Furthermore, the last two rules can be combined to give $D \leftarrow (A \vee C)$. Thus $R \models_c D$. However, the expression $R \vdash D$ cannot be derived from inference rules in Definition 3.2. In particular, there are only two lines of top–down inference, both of which fail. First,

$$\begin{array}{ll} & R \vdash D \\ \textit{if} & R \vdash C \end{array}$$

which fails, since there are no rules for inferring C. Second,

$$\begin{array}{ll} & R \vdash D \\ \textit{if} & R \vdash A \\ \textit{if} & R \vdash B \leftarrow C \\ \textit{if} & R + C \vdash B \end{array}$$

which fails, since there are no rules for inferring B. Our inference system is therefore not complete with respect to classical semantics. That is, hypothetical inference is not classical.

Instead, hypothetical inference is intuitionistic. That is, the inference system of Definition 3.2 is sound and complete with respect to intuitionistic model theory, and therefore forms a fragment of intuitionistic logic. (It is not full intuitionistic logic since embedded implications do not include disjunction or negation.) The intuitionistic nature of embedded implications was first established by Gabbay [26]. Working independently, McCarty and Miller extended this work to include rules with universal quantifiers in their premises [39, 42]. The work of McCarty also includes formulas with negations in rule heads. Recently, a greatly simplified proof of soundness and completeness was developed by Bonner, first for the propositional case [8], and then for the full predicate case [16]. The proof is not based on the fixpoint constructions of logic programming, but on the canonical-model constructions of Modal logic [22].

The rest of this section outlines intuitionistic model-theory, specializing the presentation for the special case of embedded implications. Note that the syntax of the logic is first-order, but its model theory is modal, i.e., it is based on a set of possible worlds. A complete development of intuitionistic logic can be found in [24, 36].

Definition 4.1 (Structures). An intuitionistic structure is a triple $M = \langle S, \leq, \pi \rangle$, where

- S is a non-empty set,
- $\leq$ is a transitive, reflexive relation on S,
- π is a mapping from elements of S to sets of ground atomic formulas,
- for any two elements s_1 and s_2 in S, if $s_1 \leq s_2$ then $\pi(s_1) \subseteq \pi(s_2)$.

The elements of S are called the substates of M.

In a complete development of intuitionistic model theory, each substate may have its own distinct domain of constant symbols. We have assumed here, however, that the domain of each substate is equal to the universe of all constant symbols. In [16], we show that for embedded implications, these are the only kind of structures that one needs to consider. We use these simplified structures since they simplify the theoretical development.

Truth in an intuitionistic structure M is defined relative to its substates. Thus, one can ask whether a formula ψ is true at a particular substate s of M, written $s, M \models \psi$. The following definition makes this idea precise.

Definition 4.2 (Satisfaction). Suppose M is an intuitionistic structure and s is a substate of M. Then,

$s, M \models A$	iff	$A \in \pi(s)$ when A is atomic.
$s, M \models \psi_1 \wedge \psi_2$	iff	$s, M \models \psi_1$ and $s, M \models \psi_2$.
$s, M \models \forall_x \psi(x)$	iff	$r, M \models \psi(b)$ for all $r \geq s$, and all constant symbols b.
$s, M \models \psi_2 \leftarrow \psi_1$	iff	$r, M \models \psi_1$ *implies* $r, M \models \psi_2$ for all $r \geq s$.

Note that unlike classical logic, intuitionistic implication is not defined in terms of disjunction and negation. Rather, it has an independent semantic definition. In effect, intuitionistic implication is a binary modal operator. An intuitive interpretation may be found in [36] and [24].

Definition 4.3 (Models). $M \models \psi$ iff $s, M \models \psi$ for all substates s of M. If $M \models \psi$, then M is a *model* of ψ.

Definition 4.4 (Validity). A formula ψ is valid iff $M \models \psi$ for all intuitionistic structures M.

Definition 4.5 (Entailment). Suppose ψ_1 and ψ_2 are formulas. Then $\psi_1 \models \psi_2$ iff the formula $\psi_2 \leftarrow \psi_1$ is valid.

The following theorem is a central result of [16]:

Theorem 4.6 (Soundness and completeness). *If ϕ is an embedded implication, and R is a set of embedded implications, then $R \models \phi$ iff $R \vdash \phi$.*

5 Data complexity

This section establishes the data complexity of embedded implications. To do this, we formally divide a deductive database into two parts: (i) a set of embedded implications, R, called the rulebase, and (ii) a set of ground atomic formulas, DB, called the database. Derivations thus have the form $R + DB \vdash \psi$. Informally, the *data complexity* of this system is the complexity of inference when the rulebase is fixed and the database varies (acts as input). More formal definitions are given in [19, 54, 12]. We first show that inference with embedded implications is semi-decidable, and, more specifically, that its data complexity is complete for *re*. We then show that the data complexity can be reduced—first to PSPACE, and then to NP— by imposing natural restrictions on the syntax of the rulebase.

Theorem 5.1 *The data complexity of embedded implications is complete for re.*

To prove completeness, we use embedded implications to encode the computations of an arbitrary Turing machine. The main step is to generate new constant symbols during inference, and to use them to construct a counter, as in Example 3.8. The counter provides a way of keeping track of computation time and tape position. Since embedded implications can generate an unbounded number of new constant symbols, we can construct a counter of unbounded range, and thereby use as much time and tape as the Turing machine needs. A detailed proof is given in [16].

The computational power of embedded implications thus comes from their ability to generate new constant symbols during inference. This ability, in turn, comes from the presence of universal quantifiers in rule bodies, as in the rule $A(x) \leftarrow \forall_y B(x,y)$. By banning such quantifiers, we can eliminate the creation of new constants and thus reduce the complexity of inference considerably. To do this, we simply ignore item 3 in Definition 3.1. Note that in the resulting rules, all variables are free. As in Horn logic, such variables are assumed to be universally quantified at the top level. Thus, a rule such as $A(x) \leftarrow [B(x,y) \leftarrow C(x,y)]$ is taken to mean $\forall_x \forall_y A(x) \leftarrow [B(x,y) \leftarrow C(x,y)]$.

Theorem 5.2 (No new constants). *If universal quantifiers are not used in rule bodies, then the data complexity of embedded implications is complete for PSPACE.*

Detailed proofs of this theorem are given in [12] and [11]. Briefly, inference can be viewed as a top–down search through an and/or proof tree of polynomial depth. Because of the depth bound, the search can be carried out in polynomial space, which establishes the complexity upper bound. In addition, because it is an and/or tree, the search can be highly complex. In fact, the search can simulate the computations of an arbitrary Alternating PTIME machine. This establishes the complexity lower bound, since APTIME = PSPACE [21].

By imposing another syntactic restriction, called *linearity*, we can reduce the complexity of inference again, from PSPACE to NP. When a rulebase is linear, a proof tree has very few 'and' nodes; so inference is simplified, becoming largely a process of searching an or-tree. Such searches can be done in non-deterministic polynomial time.

Informally, a rule is linear iff recursion occurs through only *one* premise. In Horn-clause logic, 'linear rules play an important role because, (i) there is a belief that most "real life" recursive rules are linear, and (ii) algorithms have been developed to handle them efficiently' [6]. A precise definition of linear recursion for embedded implications is given in [12, 10]. The following example illustrates the idea.

Example 5.3

A linear rulebase	A non-linear rulebase
$A \leftarrow (B \leftarrow D_1),\ (G \leftarrow D_2)$	$A \leftarrow (B \leftarrow D_1),\ (C \leftarrow D_2)$
$B \leftarrow (C \leftarrow E_1),\ (H \leftarrow E_2)$	$B \leftarrow (C \leftarrow E_1),\ (A \leftarrow E_2)$
$C \leftarrow (A \leftarrow F_1),\ (K \leftarrow F_2)$	$C \leftarrow (A \leftarrow F_1),\ (B \leftarrow F_2)$

The following theorem is the main result about linear embedded implications. Detailed proofs are given in [12, 10].

Theorem 5.4 (Linear recursion). *If universal quantifiers are not used in rule bodies, and if recursion is linear, then the data complexity of embedded implications is complete for NP.*

6 Negation as failure

This section extends embedded implications by allowing negated premises. Thus, rules of the form $A \leftarrow \neg(B \leftarrow C)$ are now allowed. Operationally, the expression $\neg(B \leftarrow C)$ is interpreted as the failure to prove $B \leftarrow C$. Thus, A is inferred if $B \leftarrow C$ cannot be inferred. This semantics is similar to the semantics of negation as commonly defined in Horn logic programming [5].

Example 6.1 The rules below are part of a rulebase that defines a student's eligibility for financial aid.[4] Intuitively, a student s is eligible for a stipend if he is a near-graduate but not a graduate. On the other hand, if he is neither a graduate nor a near-graduate, then he is eligible for a fellowship.

$$\begin{aligned}
&stipend(s) \leftarrow admitted(s),\ near_grad(s),\ \neg grad(s).\\
&fellowship(s) \leftarrow admitted(s),\ \neg near_grad(s),\ \neg grad(s).\\
&near_grad(s) \leftarrow [grad(s) \leftarrow take(s,c)]
\end{aligned}$$

In applying the rule for $near\_grad(s)$, we ask if the student s is within one course of graduation. That is, is there some course c such that, if $take(s,c)$ were assumed to be true, then $grad(s)$ would also be true? The student is eligible for a fellowship only if this hypothetical test fails. Conversely, he is eligible for a stipend only if it succeeds. Note that this hypothetical test is vacuously true if $grad(s)$ is true (as long as there exists a course somewhere in the database!). But we do not want to give a stipend to a student who has already graduated, so we include the test $\neg grad(s)$ in the

[4]This example, taken from [15], is an improvement by McCarty on an example originally due to Bonner [11].

rule for *stipend*(s). This means that a stipend is available only to those students who need *exactly* one course to graduate.

A major difficulty with negation-as-failure is that it is not always well-defined. This is true both for Horn rules and for embedded implications. For instance, given the two rules $A \leftarrow \neg B$ and $B \leftarrow \neg A$, it is unclear whether A is to be inferred, or B, or both, or neither. Numerous approaches to this problem have been proposed. One approach has been to identify classes of Horn rulebases in which such problems do not arise. Perhaps the best known of these classes is the *stratified rulebases*. These rulebases are layered, and within each layer, a negated premise refers only to rules found in the layers below [4]. In this way, recursion never occurs through a negated premise, so the semantics of negation is always well-defined. Another approach has been to allow limited recursion through negation. This approach generalizes the notion of stratification to *local stratification* [45]. Intuitively, a rulebase is locally stratified if its ground instantiation is stratified (with possibly infinitely many strata). Locally stratified rulebases are perhaps the largest class of logic programs for which the semantics of negation is uncontroversial. A third approach to negation-as-failure attempts to define semantics for arbitrary Horn programs with negation. There have been numerous attempts here too. Perhaps the best known are the well-founded semantics [53, 52] and the stable model semantics [29]. Although, these semantics offer different interpretations of recursion through negation, they are equivalent when rulebases are stratified or locally stratified.

Several researchers have extended these ideas to embedded implications with negation. For instance, [15, 11, 12] develop a semantics of stratified rulebases, including a proof theory and model theory. Examples 6.1, 7.1, and 7.2 show stratified rulebases and describe their semantics informally. In the special case in which all the embedded implications are Horn, this semantics is equivalent to that of [4]. As in Horn logic, stratified rulebases act as a kind of benchmark in the semantics of negation. One reason is that most natural examples of negation are stratified. Another is that the semantics of non-stratified rulebases is likely to remain unsettled for some time. In addition, stratified embedded implications have important complexity-theoretic properties, as shown in Section 7.

Recently, there have been several proposals for a semantics of non-stratified embedded implications [32, 30, 31, 23]. Following [42], these proposals each define a model as a mapping from a set of logic programs to a set of values. These proposals are therefore not model theories in the traditional sense, since they only consider models of a certain syntactic form. (By contrast, [15] takes the traditional position that a model is a mapping from *any* set to a set of first-order semantic structures.) In [32], Harland develops a semantics in which predicates are labelled as 'completely defined' or 'incompletely defined'. Unfortunately, restrictions on the labelling preclude many stratified programs, such as those in Examples 7.1 and 7.2. They also preclude the rulebases used to achieve the expressibility results of Section 7. This point is discussed at greater length in [15]. In [31], Olivetti and Terracini present a three-valued modal semantics for the propositional case, and in [30], Giordano and Olivetti develop a three-valued fixpoint semantics for the predicate case. In both cases, the semantics is of finite failure in arbitrary rulebases. [30] also develops a top–down SLD-style proof procedure. Under a syntactic restriction call *allowedness*, this procedure is sound and avoids floundering. Unfortunately, this restriction seems to preclude many stratified programs, such as those in Examples 6.1, 6.2, and 7.2. Finally, in [23], Dung proposes a stable model semantics that allows arbitrary rulebases, stratified or unstratified, though no proof theory is presented.

None of the expressibility results in Section 7 depends on recursion through negation. For the purpose of this chapter, then, we need only consider stratified rulebases. As described above, [15, 11, 12] extend the notion of stratification from Horn programs to embedded implications. The main new idea is that in defining strata, hypothetical assumptions can be ignored. For example, in the rule $A \leftarrow (B \leftarrow C)$, the atom C may be defined in any stratum, including strata that are *above* the strata in which A and B are defined. By contrast, the atom B must be defined in the same stratum as A or in lower strata, exactly as with stratified Horn rulebases. Intuitively, the atom B is 'executed' in order to prove A, while the atom C is 'assumed'. This is why C does not affect the stratification; i.e., since C is not 'executed', it cannot lead to recursion through negation.

Example 6.2 The following rulebase is stratified and has three strata, R_0, R_1, and R_2:

$$R_2 \quad \left\{ \begin{array}{l} A_2(x) \leftarrow B(x,y),\ [A_2(y) \leftarrow D(y)]. \\ A_2(x) \leftarrow C(x,y),\ \neg A_1(y). \end{array} \right.$$

$$R_1 \quad \left\{ \begin{array}{l} A_1(x) \leftarrow B(x,y),\ [A_1(y) \leftarrow D(y)]. \\ A_1(x) \leftarrow C(x,y),\ \neg A_0(y). \end{array} \right.$$

$$R_0 \quad \left\{ \begin{array}{l} A_0(x) \leftarrow B(x,y),\ [A_0(y) \leftarrow D(y)]. \\ A_0(x) \leftarrow C(x,y). \end{array} \right.$$

As originally pointed out by Gabbay [26], negation-as-failure displays curious paradoxes when extended from Horn rules to embedded implications. This is true even for very simple, non-recursive rulebases. In fact, if implicational queries are allowed, then these paradoxes arise even for *Horn* rules. The next example shows, for instance, that for stratified Horn rules, implication is not transitive. Other apparent paradoxes, including a failure of modus ponens, are described in [15].

Example 6.3 Suppose that R consists of the following two rules:

$$A \leftarrow B, \sim C.$$
$$B \leftarrow C.$$

Then $R \vdash A \leftarrow B$ and $R \vdash B \leftarrow C$, but $R \nvdash A \leftarrow C$. Each of these points is straightforward to prove. For instance, to infer $A \leftarrow C$ from R, we would have to add C to the rulebase and then infer A; that is, we would have to derive the expression $R + C \vdash A$. However, once C is added to the rulebase, the first rule is permanently blocked, so there is no way to derive A. Thus, $R + C \nvdash A$. Hence $R \nvdash A \leftarrow C$.

These paradoxes are not difficult to resolve, and as the examples in this chapter suggest, they do not affect the practice of logic programming. As first pointed out in [15], embedded implications really have two distinct kinds of implication—a distinction that one naturally makes when writing logic programs. In the rule $A \leftarrow (B \leftarrow C)$, for instance, the outer implication and the inner implication are of a different kind. As noted above, the outer implication means that B is *executed*, in order to prove A, while the inner implication means that C is *assumed*. The paradoxes arise from an attempt to treat these two kinds of implication as one and the same thing. Even the inference system of Definition 3.2 distinguishes these two kinds of implication: inference rule 3 deals with 'execution', and inference rule 4 deals with 'assumption'. It should not be surprising, then, that these two types of implication have different semantics. Indeed, the real surprise is that this difference does not make itself apparent until the proof theory is augmented with negation-as-failure. In the rest of this chapter, we distinguish implicitly between these two kinds of implication. Thorough developments of them can be found in [12] and in [15]. Reference [12] develops a relatively simple semantics, while [15] develops a more complex semantics, but one that is much closer to intuitionistic model theory. These works address the paradoxes due to hypothetical insertion. Additional paradoxes arise, however, when universal quantifiers are allowed in rule bodies. For instance, it is possible that a rulebase may entail $\forall_x A(x)$, and yet it may *not* entail $A(b)$ for any constant, b. Such issues have received little attention in the literature, and we address them in [7].

7 Expressibility

This section studies the impact of negation-as-failure on the ability of embedded implications to express database queries. We first show that with negation, embedded implications are expressively complete, i.e., that they can express *any* computable database query. We then focus on the syntactic restrictions of Section 5 and the impact that negation has on them. We show, for instance, that if new constants are not created during inference, then the logic is expressively complete for PSPACE, so that it can express *any* database query computable in polynomial space. Based on this result, we develop an *exact* characterization of the queries in PSPACE in terms of embedded implications. If we add the additional restriction that recursion is linear, then negation has a subtle and interesting effect on the logic. In this case, the complexity and expressibility depend on the number of strata in the rulebase: with each additional strata, the complexity and expressibility climb one level in the polynomial-time hierarchy. As a corollary, we conclude that stratified linear rulebases express exactly the second-order definable queries.

Unlike other results in the literature [33, 54, 20], the results in this section do *not* assume that the data domain is linearly ordered. The assumption of ordered domains is a technical device that is often used to achieve expressibility results, but it is not an intrinsic feature of databases [1]. Embedded implications do not need this artificial assumption, since they can generate a linear order on the domain hypothetically. Thus, the results of this section are for arbitrary databases, ordered or not. These results characterize the queries in well-known complexity classes based on ordinary Turing machines. In particular, our results are unrelated to the relational complexity classes introduced in [1], which are based on so-called relational Turing machines. Although relational Turing machines capture many of the important features of database programming, they are less expressive than ordinary Turing machines. For instance, the query $EVEN$ discussed below is in the complexity class P, but is not in the relational version of P. As we shall see, this query is expressible in embedded implications, although it is not expressible in many other relational query languages.

Before continuing, we must define what it means to express a database query using embedded implications. Complete definitions are given in [11, 12, 16]. Here, we summarize the main ideas. Formally, a database query is a mapping that takes a database as input and returns a set of ground tuples as output [18]. We can use embedded implications with free variables to define such mappings. Some care is required, though, since the inference system of Definition 3.2 is defined only for embedded implications that are closed, i.e., that have no free variables. This presents no conceptual difficulties however, since we can focus on ground instantiations of the free variables. Formally, let $\phi(x_1, ..., x_k)$ be an embedded implication with free variables $x_1, ..., x_k$. Also, given a rulebase, R, and a database, DB, let $dom(DB)$ be the set of constant symbols in $R + DB$. Together, R and

$\phi(x_1, ..., x_k)$ define a database query. When applied to database DB, the answer to this query is the following set of tuples:

$$\{ \langle c_1, ..., c_k \rangle \mid c_i \in dom(DB) \quad and \quad R + DB \vdash \phi(c_1, ..., c_k) \}$$

The inferences in this definition are all well defined since each $\phi(c_1, ..., c_k)$ is closed. Furthermore, if $dom(DB)$ has n elements, then there are exactly n^k ground instances of $\phi(x_1, ..., x_k)$. Thus, computing the answer to a query requires checking n^k inferences. This adds only a polynomial factor to the complexity bounds established in Section 5. Thus, the bounds are the same for yes/no queries and for queries that return tuples as answers. Moreover, in practice, it is not necessary to actually check n^k ground inferences, since unification-based proof procedures exist for embedded implications with free variables. One of the first such procedures was developed by McCarty [40] for the negation-free case. Having defined what it means to express queries with embedded implications, the rest of this section characterizes the exact sets of queries that can be expressed.

As shown in Section 5, without negation-as-failure, embedded implications can simulate arbitrary Turing machines. Nevertheless, there are some simple, low-complexity queries that they cannot express. This is because the negation-free logic is *monotonic*: As the database expands, the answer to a query also expands. This behaviour is typical of many logical inference systems, such as Datalog, Horn logic, full classical logic, and modal logics. Such systems cannot express non-monotonic queries, such as relational algebra queries involving complementation. Retrieving those students 'who are *not* eligible to graduate' is an example of a non-monotonic query. Even with enormous computational power, monotonic query languages cannot express this simple query, simply because it is non-monotonic.

As another example, consider the query $EVEN$, which determines the parity of a database relation D: $EVEN$ returns *true* if D has an even number of entries, and *false* otherwise. $EVEN$ is non-monotonic since as entries are added to D, the value of $EVEN$ 'flips back and forth' between *true* and *false*; i.e., once $EVEN$ becomes true, it does not remain true, as a monotonic query would. Without negation, our hypothetical logic is monotonic and cannot express the query $EVEN$. To be precise, there is no set of (negation-free) embedded implications, R, that makes the following statement true for *every* database, DB:

$R + DB \vdash EVEN$ *iff* DB has an even number of entries of the form $D(x)$.

where $EVEN$ is a 0-ary predicate symbol. Again, this is true not just of embedded implications, but of all monotonic logics.

Augmenting a logic with negation-as-failure gives it the power to express non-monotonic queries. Often, however, this increased power is still limited. For instance, Datalog with negation-as-failure still cannot express *EVEN* [19]. In such cases, a logic is often augmented with other devices, to guarantee expressive completeness. One typical device is to assume that the data domain is linearly ordered [33, 54, 20]. Datalog, for instance, is expressively complete for PTIME if augmented with *both* negation-as-failure and a linear order. Embedded implications do not need to make this latter assumption, however, since they can generate a linear order for themselves, and insert it into the database hypothetically [12, 11]. Indeed, negation-as-failure is the only device needed to achieve expressive completeness for embedded implications. Furthermore, negation-as-failure is a natural extension to the logic, since any practical logic-programming system must have it.

7.1 Examples

This section gives two examples of the expressiveness of embedded implications augmented with negation-as-failure. The first example shows how to express *EVEN*. The second example shows a simple encoding of an NP-complete problem.

The rulebase in Example 7.1 expresses *EVEN*. To understand this rulebase, we view its operation as top–down. From this perspective, the first two rules select and mark elements one-by-one from the database relation D. As elements are marked, query processing 'flips back and forth' between the two subqueries *EVEN* and *ODD* until all the elements in D are marked. In effect, these subqueries ask for the parity of the unmarked tuples in D. Thus, when there are no unmarked tuples left, the parity is even. The third and fourth rules handle this situation, terminating the recursion. Note that a tuple x is 'marked' by hypothetically adding the formula $MARK(x)$ to the database. The fifth rule uses this fact to select an unmarked tuple from D.

Example 7.1 Suppose R is the following collection of rules:

$$
\begin{aligned}
&EVEN \leftarrow SELECT(x), [ODD \leftarrow MARK(x)].\\
&ODD \leftarrow SELECT(x), [EVEN \leftarrow MARK(x)].\\
&EVEN \leftarrow \neg SOMELEFT.\\
&SOMELEFT \leftarrow SELECT(x).\\
&SELECT(x) \leftarrow D(x), \neg MARK(x).
\end{aligned}
$$

Then $R + DB \vdash EVEN$ *iff* DB contains an even number of entries of the form $D(x)$.

With negation-as-failure, it is possible to write simple hypothetical rule bases that solve complex problems. The next example illustrates this by showing how to find a Hamiltonian path in a directed graph. Since this is an NP-complete problem, the example provides a simple demonstration of why the data complexity of hypothetical reasoning is not in P (assuming that P $\neq$ NP).

Example 7.2 Suppose that DB is a database representing a directed graph. That is, $NODE(a) \in DB$ iff a is a node in the graph, and $EDGE(a, b) \in DB$ iff there is an edge in the graph from a to b. Suppose also that R is the following collection of rules:

$$
\begin{array}{l}
YES \leftarrow SELECT(x), [PATH(x) \leftarrow MARK(x)] \\
PATH(x) \leftarrow EDGE(x, y), NODE(y), [PATH(y) \leftarrow MARK(y)] \\
PATH(x) \leftarrow \neg SOMELEFT. \\
SOMELEFT \leftarrow SELECT(x). \\
SELECT(x) \leftarrow NODE(x), \neg MARK(x).
\end{array}
$$

Then $R + DB \vdash YES$ iff the graph represented by DB has a directed Hamiltonian path.

To understand the rulebase in Example 7.2, we view its operation as top–down. From this perspective, the rulebase tries to construct a Hamiltonian path one node at a time. The first rule selects a node x at which the path is to begin. The second rule is then applied repeatedly, selecting a node y connected to the last node in the path by a single edge. Each time a node is selected, it is marked so that it will not be selected again. In this way, no node is selected twice. The third and fourth rules say that a Hamiltonian path has been found when there are no unmarked nodes left in the graph, that is, when every node has been visited exactly once. Note that each node selection is non-deterministic, so, in effect, the rulebase searches the graph for all possible Hamiltonian paths.

7.2 Expressive Completeness

Negation-as-failure increases the expressibility of embedded implications. In fact, with negation, they are expressively complete, and can therefore express any computable generic query. In database theory, the ability to express generic queries is the normal measure of expressiveness for database query languages [2, 3, 18, 19, 33, 34].

Genericity captures the idea that constant symbols are uninterpreted, i.e., that they have no innate meaning. To make this idea more precise, consider the effect on a query of renaming the constant symbols in the database. If a query is generic, then this should have no effect other than to rename the constants in the output of the query. As a special case, the output of a yes/no query should not be affected at all. Thus, the query $EVEN$ in Example 7.1 is generic, since its output is not affected by a renaming of the constant symbols in the database. Likewise, the query in Example 7.2 is generic. More precise definitions of genericity are given in [18, 12]. The following theorem is our first result about the ability of embedded implications to express generic queries.

Theorem 7.3 *Stratified embedded implications are expressively complete; that is, they express all the generic queries in re.*

Although they express all the generic queries in re, stratified embedded implications can also express queries that are *not* in re. For example, suppose the rulebase R defines a query $A(x)$ that is complete for re. Then the query $\neg A(x)$ is complete for $co\text{-}re$, and thus is not in re. Thus, negation-as-failure increases the data complexity of embedded implications. In fact, by using multiple strata, it provides enough power to express queries at any level in the arithmetic hierarchy. It would be interesting, however, to provide an exact, logical characterization of the generic queries in re. To this end, [16] presents simple syntactic restrictions that do precisely this. Any query satisfying these restriction is guaranteed to be in re, and all queries in re can be expressed by a rulebase satisfying these restrictions.

Section 5 showed that under certain syntactic restrictions, the data complexity of embedded implications is PSPACE complete. Unlike re, however, PSPACE is closed under complementation; that is, PSPACE = coPSPACE. Thus, if $A(x)$ is a PSPACE-complete query, then so is $\neg A(x)$. For this reason, negation-as-failure does not increase the complexity of these restricted embedded implications. It does, however, increase their expressiveness, since with negation, they can express non-monotonic queries. In fact, the following result shows that negation-as-failure increases their expressiveness as much as possible.

Theorem 7.4 *Under the following restrictions, embedded implications are expressively complete for PSPACE, that is, they express all the generic queries in PSPACE:*

1. *The rulebase is stratified.*
2. *Universal quantifiers do not appear in rule bodies.*

Although the rulebases in Theorem 7.4 can express every generic query in PSPACE, they can also express some non-generic queries. Non-genericity is caused by constant symbols in a rulebase, which cause the rulebase to give special treatment to some elements of the data domain. For example, a rulebase consisting of the single rule $A \leftarrow B(c)$ will infer A iff $B(c)$ is in the database. Since renaming c in the database will stop the inference of A, this rulebase defines a non-generic query. On the other hand, if the rulebase were $A \leftarrow B(x)$, where x is a variable, then a renaming of the database would not affect the inference of A at all. In this case, the rulebase defines a generic query. In general, queries defined by constant-free rulebases are guaranteed to be generic. In fact, such rulebases provide an exact characterization of the generic queries in PSPACE.

Theorem 7.5 *Under the following restrictions, embedded implications express exactly the generic queries in PSPACE:*

1. *The rulebase is stratified.*
2. *Universal quantifiers do not appear in rule bodies.*
3. *The rulebase contains no constant symbols.*

Theorem 7.5 is particularly interesting because it establishes a strong link between an important complexity class, polynomial space, and a well-known logic, intuitionistic logic. Other database query languages have been developed that are expressively complete for PSPACE [17, 19, 2, 3], but the language of stratified embedded implications is the only one based on a model theoretic semantics, and the only one to have a Prolog-style proof procedure, one based on resolution and unification in the logic-programming tradition [40]. Furthermore, unlike other languages, our results on PSPACE can be extended, as shown below, to include the polynomial-time hierarchy and its various levels, thereby linking intuitionistic logic to other important complexity classes.

7.3 The polynomial-time hierarchy

Section 5 showed that if embedded implications do not create new constant symbols, then the complexity of inference decreases from *re* to PSPACE. In addition, if recursion is linear, then complexity decreases again, from PSPACE to NP. Since NP is not closed under complementation (i.e., NP $\neq$ coNP), it should not be surprising that negation-as-failure effects the data complexity of these linear rulebases. For instance, if $A(x)$ is an NP-complete query, then $\neg A(x)$ is a coNP-complete query. In general, the data complexity will correspond to some level in the polynomial-time hierarchy, depending on the number and type of strata in the rulebase. This result eventually leads to a characterization of the second-order definable queries in terms of (first-order) embedded implications.

The polynomial-time hierarchy is a sequence of complexity classes between P and PSPACE. It is based on the idea of an oracle Turing machine and can be defined recursively as follows [49]:

- $\Sigma_0^{\mathrm{P}} = \Delta_0^{\mathrm{P}} = \mathrm{P}$.
- $\Delta_{k+1}^{\mathrm{P}} = \mathrm{P}^{\Sigma_k^{\mathrm{P}}}$ = those languages accepted in deterministic polynomial time by an oracle machine whose oracle is a language in Σ_k^{P}.

- $\Sigma_{k+1}^{\mathrm{P}} = \mathrm{NP}^{\Sigma_k^{\mathrm{P}}}$ = those languages accepted in non-deterministic polynomial time by an oracle machine whose oracle is a language in Σ_k^{P}.

- $\mathrm{PHIER} = \cup_k \Sigma_k^{\mathrm{P}} = \cup_k \Delta_k^{\mathrm{P}}$.

Note that $\Delta_1^{\mathrm{P}} = \mathrm{P}^{\mathrm{P}} = \mathrm{P}$. Likewise, $\Sigma_1^{\mathrm{P}} = \mathrm{NP}^{\mathrm{P}} = \mathrm{NP}$. It is well known that $\mathrm{P} \subseteq \Delta_k^{\mathrm{P}} \subseteq \Sigma_k^{\mathrm{P}} \subseteq \Delta_{k+1}^{\mathrm{P}} \subseteq \mathrm{PHIER} \subseteq \mathrm{PSPACE}$.[5] This section provides several results linking the polynomial-time hierarchy to embedded implications. The simplest one to state is the following.

Theorem 7.6 *Under the following restrictions, the data complexity of embedded implications is complete for Σ_k^{P}, for $k \geq 1$:*

1. *The rulebase has k strata.*
2. *Recursion is linear.*
3. *Universal quantifiers do not appear in rule bodies.*

It turns out, however, that additional strata can often be added to a rulebase with only a small cost in complexity, as long as the new strata contain only Horn rules (with possibly negated premises). We say that such strata are *Horn*. Other strata will be called *hypothetical*. A hypothetical stratum thus contains at least one rule with an implication in its rule body, e.g., $A \leftarrow (B \leftarrow C)$. The rulebase in Example 7.1 has one Horn stratum (the last two rules) and one hypothetical stratum (the first three rules). The following theorem shows that if a rulebase has k hypothetical strata, then no matter how many Horn strata are inserted into it, the data complexity will not exceed $\Delta_{k+1}^{\mathrm{P}}$.

Theorem 7.7 *Under the following restrictions, the data complexity of embedded implications is complete for $\Delta_{k+1}^{\mathrm{P}}$, for $k \geq 0$:*

1. *The rulebase has k hypothetical strata.*
2. *Recursion is linear.*
3. *Universal quantifiers do not appear in rule bodies.*

As discussed at the beginning of Section 7, it does not follow from these complexity results that stratified linear rulebases are expressively complete. That is, although their data complexity may be complete for some class, there may still be many queries in that class that they cannot express. This is in fact the case for the rulebases described in Theorems 7.6 and 7.7. They do not appear to be expressively complete for Σ_k^{P} or Δ_k^{P} respectively. Technically, we can obtain expressive completeness for Σ_k^{P} by assuming that the top stratum of the rulebase is hypothetical, as in Examples 7.1

[5] Although considered likely, it is an open question as to whether any of these containments are strict.

and 7.2. This result leads to a characterization of the queries in Σ_k^{P} [12]. It also leads to an elegant characterization of the entire polynomial-time hierarchy.

Theorem 7.8 *Under the following restrictions, embedded implications express exactly the generic queries in PHIER:*

1. *The rulebase is stratified.*
2. *Recursion is linear.*
3. *Universal quantifiers do not appear in rule bodies.*
4. *The rulebase contains no constant symbols.*

This corollary immediately gives rise to a characterization of the second-order definable queries, since Immerman has shown that the generic queries in PHIER are precisely the queries definable in second-order logic [34]. This gives us an alternative characterization of the queries expressed by linear embedded implications. It also gives the interesting result that the second-order queries can be characterized by a first-order logic.

Corollary 7.9 *The rulebases described in Theorem 7.8 express exactly the second-order definable queries.*

Acknowledgements

The work of Thorne McCarty on the intuitionistic semantics of embedded implications was the original stimulus for this work; and discussions with Tomasz Imielinski were invaluable in giving the work a database perspective. Many of the results relating to the creation of new constant symbols were developed in collaboration with Thorne McCarty and Kumar Vadaparty [16]. They also provided useful comments on the present chapter. Thanks go to Eric Allender for answering all my questions about computational complexity, and to Ashok Chandra for providing valuable comments. Jan Chomicki and Ron van der Meyden also provided useful feedback during the development of the work presented herein. The anonymous reviewers of this chapter also provided valuable references.

References

[1] S. Abiteboul, M.Y. Vardi, and V. Vianu. Fixpoint logics, relational machines, and computational complexity. In *Proceedings of the Seventh Annual Structure in Complexity Theory Conference*, pp. 156–168, Boston, MA, June 22–25 1992. IEEE Computer Society Press.

[2] S. Abiteboul and V. Vianu. A transaction language complete for database update specification. In *Proceedings of the ACM Symposium on the Principles of Database Systems (PODS)*, pp. 260–268, 1987. Published in expanded form as Rapports de Recherche no. 715, INRIA, 78153 Le Chesnay Cedex, France.

[3] S. Abiteboul and V. Vianu. *Datalog Extensions for Database Queries and Updates.* Technical Report 900, Institut National de Recherche en Informatique et en Automatique (INRIA), Le Chesnay Cedex, France, 1988.

[4] K.R. Apt, H.A. Blair, and A. Walker. Towards a theory of declarative knowledge. In Jack Minker, editor, *Foundations of Deductive Databases and Logic Programming*, chapter 2, pp. 89–148. Morgan Kaufmann, 1988.

[5] K. R. Apt and M. H. Van Emden. Contributions to the theory of logic programming. *Journal of the ACM*, **29**(3):841–862, 1982.

[6] F. Bancilhon and R. Ramakrishnan. An amateur's introduction to recursive query processing strategies. In *Proceedings of the ACM SIGMOD International Conference on Management of Data*, pp. 16–52, Washington, D.C., May 28–30 1986.

[7] A. J. Bonner. Adding Negation-as-Failure to Intuitionistic Logic Programming: Part II. In preparation.

[8] A. J. Bonner. A logic for hypothetical reasoning. In *Proceedings of the Seventh National Conference on Artificial Intelligence*, Saint Paul, Minnesota, August 21–26 1988. Published in expanded form as Technical Report TR-DCS-230, Department of Computer Science, Rutgers University, New Brunswick, NJ 08903.

[9] A. J. Bonner. Hypothetical datalog: complexity and expressibility. In *Proceedings of the International Conference on Database Theory (ICDT)*, pp. 144–160, Bruges, Belgium, August 31–September 2 1988. Springer-Verlag. Published as volume 326 of *Lecture Notes in Computer Science.*

[10] A. J. Bonner. Hypothetical datalog: negation and linear recursion. In *Proceedings of the ACM Symposium on the Principles of Database Systems (PODS)*, pp. 286–300, Philadelphia, PA, March 29–31 1989.

[11] A. J. Bonner. Hypothetical datalog: complexity and expressibility. *Theoretical Computer Science (TCS)*, **76**:3–51, 1990. Special issue on the Second International Conference on Database Theory (ICDT). An expanded version of [9].

[12] A. J. Bonner. *Hypothetical Reasoning in Deductive Databases.* PhD thesis, Department of Computer Science, Rutgers University, New Brunswick, NJ 08903, USA, October 1991. Published as Rutgers Technical Report DCS-TR-283.

[13] A. J. Bonner. The complexity of reusing and modifying rulebases. In *Proceedings of the ACM Symposium on the Principles of Database Systems (PODS)*, pp. 316–330, San Diego, CA, June 2–4 1992.

[14] A. J. Bonner and T. Imielinski. The reuse and modification of rulebases by predicate substitution. In *Proceedings of the International Conference on Extending Database Technology (EDBT)*, pp. 437–451, Venice, Italy, March 26–30 1990. Springer-Verlag. Published as volume 416 of *Lecture Notes in Computer Science.*

[15] A. J. Bonner and L. T. McCarty. Adding negation-as-failure to intuitionistic logic programming. In *Proceedings of the North American Conference on Logic Programming (NACLP)*, pp. 681–703, Austin, Texas, October 29–November 1 1990. MIT Press.

[16] A. J. Bonner, L. T. McCarty, and K. Vadaparty. Expressing database queries with intuitionistic logic. In *Proceedings of the North American Conference on Logic Programming (NACLP)*, pp. 831–850, Cleveland, Ohio, October 16–20 1989. MIT Press.

[17] A.K. Chandra. Theory of database queries. In *Proceedings of the ACM Symposium on the Principles of Database Systems (PODS)*, pp. 1–9, Austin, Texas, March 1988.

[18] A. K. Chandra and D. Harel. Computable queries for relational databases. *Journal of Computer and System Sciences (JCSS)*, **21**(2):156–178, 1980.

[19] A. K. Chandra and D. Harel. Structure and complexity of relational queries. *Journal of Computer and System Sciences (JCSS)*, **25**(1):99–128, 1982.

[20] A. K. Chandra and D. Harel. Horn clause queries and generlizations. *Journal of Logic Programming (JLP)*, **2**(1):1–15, 1985.

[21] A. K. Chandra, D. Kozen, and L. J. Stockmeyer. Alternation. *Journal of the ACM*, **28**:114–133, 1981.

[22] B. F. Chellas. *Modal Logic: An Introduction.* Cambridge University Press, 1980.

[23] P. M. Dung. Declarative semantics of hypothetical logic programming with negation as failure. In *Proceedings of the Third International Workshop on Extensions of Logic Programming*, pp. 45–58, Bologna, Italy, February 1992. Springer-Verlag. Published as volume 660 of *Lecture Notes in Artificial Intelligence*, 1993.

[24] M. C. Fitting. *Intuitionistic Logic, Model Theory and Forcing*. North-Holland, 1969.

[25] The Committee for Advanced DBMS function. Third-generation database system manifesto. *SIGMOD Record*, **19**(3):31–44, September 1990. Also published as Memorandum No. UCB/ERL M90/28, Electronics Research Laboratory, College of Engineering, University of California, Berkeley.

[26] D. M. Gabbay. N-Prolog: an extension of Prolog with hypothetical implications. II. Logical foundations and negation as failure. *Journal of Logic Programming (JLP)*, **2**(4):251–283, 1985.

[27] D. M. Gabbay and U. Reyle. N-Prolog: an extension of Prolog with hypothetical implications. I. *Journal of Logic Programming (JLP)*, **1**(4):319–355, 1984.

[28] D. M. Gabbay and U. Reyle. Computation with run time skolemization. *Journal of Applied Non-Classical Logics*, **3**:93–134, 1993.

[29] M. Gelfond and V. Lifschitz. The stable model semantics for logic programming. In *Proceedings of the Fifth Logic Programming Symposium*, pp. 1070–1080. MIT Press, 1988.

[30] L. Giordano and N. Olivetti. Negation as failure in intuitionistic logic programming. In *Proceedings of the Joint International Conference and Symposium on Logic Programming (JICSLP)*, pp. 431–445, Washington, D.C., 1992. MIT Press.

[31] N. Olivetti and L. Terracini. N-Prolog and equivalence of logic programs (Part 1). *Logic, Language and Information*, **1**(4):253–340, 1992.

[32] J. Harland. A Kripke-like model for negation as failure. In *Proceedings of the North American Conference on Logic Programming (NACLP)*, pp. 626–642, Cleveland, Ohio, October 1989. MIT Press.

[33] N. Immerman. Relational queries computable in polynomial time. In *Proceedings of the ACM Symposium on Theory of Computing (STOC)*, pp. 147–152, 1982.

[34] N. Immerman. Languages that capture complexity classes. *SIAM Journal of Computing*, **16**(4):760–778, 1987.

[35] R. H. Sprague Jr. and H. J. Watson, editors. *Decisions Support Systems: Putting Theory into Practice.* Prentice Hall, Englewood Cliffs, NJ, 1989.

[36] S. Kripke. Semantical analysis of intuitionistic logic. I. In J.N. Crossley and M.A.E. Dummett, editors, *Formal Systems and Recursive Functions*, pp. 92–130. North Holland, Amsterdam, 1965.

[37] S. Manchanda and D.S. Warren. A logic-based language for database updates. In Jack Minker, editor, *Foundations of Deductive Databases and Logic Programming*, chapter 10, pp. 363–394. Morgan Kaufmann, 1988.

[38] S. Manchanda. *A Dynamic Logic Programming Language for Relational Updates.* PhD thesis, Department of Computer Science, State University of New York at Stony Brook, Stony Brook, New York, December 1987. Also published as Technical Report TR 88-2, Department of Computer Science, The University of Arizona, Tuscon, Arizona 85721, January, 1988.

[39] L. T. McCarty. Clausal intuitionistic logic. I. Fixed-point semantics. *Journal of Logic Programming (JLP)*, **5**(1):1–31, 1988.

[40] L. T. McCarty. Clausal intuitionistic logic. II. Tableau proof procedures. *Journal of Logic Programming (JLP)*, **5**(2):93–132, 1988.

[41] L. T. McCarty. A language for legal discourse. I. Basic features. In *Proceedings of the Second International Conference on Artificial Intelligence and Law*, pp. 180–189. ACM Press, June 1989.

[42] D. Miller. A logical analysis of modules in logic programming. *Journal of Logic Programming (JLP)*, **6**:79–108, 1989.

[43] D. Miller. Lexical scoping as universal quantification. In G. Levi and M. Martelli, editors, *Logic Programming: Proceedings of the Sixth International Conference*, pp. 268–283, Cambridge, MA, 1989. MIT Press.

[44] R. L. Olson and R. H. Sprague Jr. Financial planning in action. In R.H. Sprague Jr and H.J. Watson, editors, *Decisions Support Systems: Putting Theory into Practice*, pp. 373–381. Prentice Hall, Englewood Cliffs, NJ, 1989.

[45] T. Przymusinski. On the declarative semantics of deductive databases and logic programs. In Jack Minker, editor, *Foundations of Deductive Databases and Logic Programming*, chapter 5, pp. 193–216. Morgan Kaufmann, 1988.

[46] D. A. Schlobohm and L. T. McCarty. EPS-II: estate planning with prototypes. In *Proceedings of the Second International Conference on Artificial Intelligence and Law*, pp. 1–10. ACM Press, June 1989.

[47] Editor: A.P. Seth. Database research at Bellcore. *SIGMOD Record*, **19**(3):45–52, September 1990.

[48] R. Statman. Intuitionistic propositional logic is polynomial-space complete. *Theoretical Computer Science (TCS)*, **9**(1):67–72, 1979.

[49] L. J. Stockmeyer. The polynomial time hierarchy. *Theoretical Computer Science (TCS)*, **3**(1):1–22, 1976.

[50] M. Stonebraker. Hypothetical databases as views. In *Proceedings of the ACM SIGMOD International Conference on Management of Data*, pp. 224–229, 1981.

[51] M. Stonebraker and K. Keller. Embedding expert knowledge and hypothetical databases into a data base system. In *Proceedings of the ACM SIGMOD International Conference on Management of Data*, pp. 58–66, Santa Monica, CA, 1980.

[52] A. Van Gelder, K. A. Ross, and J. S. Schlipf. Unfounded sets and well-founded semantics for general logic programs. In *Proceedings of the ACM Symposium on the Principles of Database Systems (PODS)*, pp. 221–230, March 1988.

[53] A. Van Gelder, K.A. Ross, and J.S. Schlipf. The well-founded semantics for general logic programs. *Journal of the ACM*, **38**:620–650, 1991.

[54] M. Vardi. The complexity of relational query languages. In *Proceedings of the ACM Symposium on Theory of Computing (STOC)*, pp. 137–146, 1982.

[55] L. Vieille, P. Bayer, V. Kuchenhoff, and A. Lefebvre. EKS-V1, a short overview. Presented at the AAAI-90 Workshop on Knowledge Base Management Systems, July 1990, Boston, USA.

[56] D. S. Warren. Database updates in pure Prolog. In *Proceedings of the International Conference on Fifth Generation Computer Systems*, pp. 244–253, 1984.

9

A modal analysis of subjunctive queries

Craig Boutilier

1 Introduction

An important and well-studied problem in philosophical logic, artificial intelligence, and database systems is that of modelling theory change or belief revision. That is, given a knowledge base *KB*, we want to characterize semantically the knowledge base that results after learning a new fact α. However, the question of how to revise *KB* is important not just in the case of changing information, but also when we want to investigate questions of the form 'What if A were true?' A subjunctive conditional $A > B$ is one of the form[1] 'If A were the case then B would be true.' Subjunctives have been widely studied in philosophy and it is generally accepted that (some variant of) the *Ramsey test* is adequate for evaluating the truth of such conditionals:

> First add the antecedent (hypothetically) to your stock of beliefs; second make whatever adjustments are required to maintain consistency (without modifying the hypothetical belief in the antecedent); finally, consider whether or not the consequent is true. [29, p.44]

The connection to belief revision is quite clearly spelled out in this formulation of the Ramsey test: to evaluate a subjunctive conditional $A > B$, we revise our beliefs to include A and see if B is believed. If we take *KB* to represent some initial state of knowledge, a characterization of subjunctive reasoning must include an account of how to revise *KB* with new information.

In this chapter, we will develop a family of logics for belief revision using a conditional connective $\stackrel{\text{KB}}{\longrightarrow}$, where $A \stackrel{\text{KB}}{\longrightarrow} B$ is interpreted roughly as 'If *KB* were revised by A, then B would be believed'. The connective

[1] At least, in 'deep structure'.

will not be primitive however; instead it is defined in terms of two unary modal operators, which refer to truth at accessible and *inaccessible* worlds. We will then use this logic to develop a framework in which subjunctive queries of a knowledge base can be answered, and show that it improves on existing subjunctive logics and systems in several crucial respects. Finally, we provide a semantic characterization of integrity constraints within the bimodal logic that is suitable for this type of subjunctive reasoning. Proofs of all results may be found in [3; 8], but we include proofs of the main representation results in the Appendix.

1.1 Revision and the AGM postulates

Recently, work on the logic of theory change has been adopted by the AI community for use in the task of belief revision. By far the most influential approach to revision has been that of Alchourrón, Gärdenfors, and Makinson [1], which we refer to as the AGM theory of revision. The exposition of Gärdenfors [14] is particularly detailed. Most of this work assumes belief sets to be modelled as deductively closed sets of sentences, and for concreteness we will assume that the underlying logic of beliefs is CPL, although nothing critical hinges on this decision. We let $\models$ and Cn denote propositional entailment and consequence respectively. We will use K to denote arbitrary belief sets, and if $K = Cn(KB)$ for some finite set of sentences KB, we say that K is *finitely specified* by KB.[2]

Revising a belief set K is required when new information is learned and must be accommodated. If $K \not\models \neg A$, learning A is relatively unproblematic as the new belief set $Cn(KB \cup \{A\})$ seems adequate for modelling this change in theory. This process is known as *expansion*. More troublesome is the revision of K by A when $K \models \neg A$. Simply adding A to the belief set will result in an inconsistent theory. Some beliefs must be given up before the new fact can be accommodated. Typically, there are a multitude of choices for changing a theory K in order to accept new information. The problem lies in choosing which beliefs to give up as, in general, there are no logical grounds for choosing which of these alternative revisions is acceptable [30], the issue depending largely on context. Fortunately, there are some logical criteria for reducing this space of possibilities.

The main criterion for discarding some revisions in deference to others is that of *minimal change*. Informational economy dictates that as few beliefs as possible from K be discarded to facilitate belief in A [14], where by 'few' we intend that, as far as possible, the informational content of K

[2] In this case, we will often refer to the revision of K as the revision of its base set KB; and since this should cause no confusion, we will also refer to the sentence formed by conjoining its members as KB. Typically, it will only be finitely specifiable theories with which we concern ourselves.

be kept intact. While pragmatic considerations will often enter into these deliberations, the main emphasis of the work of Alchourrón, Gärdenfors, and Makinson is in logically delimiting the scope of acceptable revisions. To this end, the AGM postulates, given below, are assumed to hold for any reasonable notion of revision [14]. We use K^*_A to denote the belief set that results from the revision of K by A.[3]

(R1) K^*_A is a belief set.

(R2) $A \in K^*_A$.

(R3) $K^*_A \subseteq K^+_A$.

(R4) If $\neg A \notin K$ then $K^+_A \subseteq K^*_A$.

(R5) $K^*_A = Cn(\bot)$ iff $\models \neg A$.

(R6) If $\models A \equiv B$ then $K^*_A = K^*_B$.

(R7) $K^*_{A \wedge B} \subseteq (K^*_A)^+_B$.

(R8) If $\neg B \notin K^*_A$ then $(K^*_A)^+_B \subseteq K^*_{A \wedge B}$.

Of particular interest are (R3) and (R4), which taken together assert that if A is consistent with K then K^*_A should merely be the expansion of K by A. This seems to reflect our intuitions about informational economy, that beliefs should not be given up gratuitously.

Some other models of belief revision have been proposed that capture essentially the same ideas as the AGM model. For instance, Grove [19] has proposed a *system of spheres* model for revision[4] that captures a number of intuitions regarding revision. He shows that his model determines precisely the same revision functions as the AGM postulates. Still other approaches to revision have also used representations of belief sets that don't allow arbitrary theories, but only those representable by a sentence in some language. Katsuno and Mendelzon [23] define a sentential connective for revision where $A \circ B$ is intended to represent the theory resulting from revising A by B. They also show that the revision of KB by A coincides with imposing a total preorder on interpretations (such that all KB-worlds are minimal) and considering the models of A minimal in this ordering to represent the revised state of affairs. In a sense, this corresponds to Grove's [19] system of sphere representation.

[3] K^+_A denotes expansion, and $\bot$ denotes falsity. The postulates are taken from Gärdenfors [14].

[4] This model is similar to Lewis's [25] system of spheres model for counterfactual conditionals which we will examine presently.

Recently, a distinction has been made between the revision of a knowledge base and the *update* of a knowledge base [31; 32; 22; 16]. Winslett [31] presented the *possible models approach* to update, which is similar to revision except that each *KB*-world is 'updated separately'. Rather than considering the A-worlds closest to the *set* of *KB*-worlds, update represents the revised state as those A-worlds closest to *each* (individually) *KB*-world. Update seems more appropriate than revision for reasoning about a *KB* being revised to reflect a changing world rather than the beliefs about a fixed situation, and is distinguished from revision by a lack of adherence to (R4). Katsuno and Mendelzon [22] have proposed a general definition of update and provided postulates that capture arbitrary partial orderings on worlds while respecting the intuition that each world be considered separately when updating. Grahne [16] has axiomatized a logic for updates in which the notion is related to subjunctive implication.

1.2 Revision and subjunctive conditionals

A number of people have argued that counterfactual and subjunctive conditionals have an important role to play in AI, logic programming and database theory. Bonner [2] has proposed a logic for hypothetical reasoning in which logic programs or deductive databases are augmented with *embedded implications* of the form

$$A \leftarrow (B \leftarrow C).$$

Roughly, such an implication is read as 'If adding C to the database causes B to be true, then A is true.' The embedded rule $(B \leftarrow C)$ acts like a subjunctive premise 'If C were true, then B would be', from which one can infer A. Bonner provides an interesting intuitionistic semantics and proof procedure for logic programs with this feature.

Ginsberg [15] has identified a number of areas in AI in which counterfactuals may play an important role in the semantic analysis of various tasks. For instance, in a planning domain a robot may ask of a state of belief

'If I removed the cup from my hand could I pick up the spoon?'

If this counterfactual $A > B$ is true, it suggests a natural regression of goals: in order to accomplish B the robot should take steps to ensure the truth of A.

Ginsberg proposes a system for reasoning about counterfactuals based on the ideas of Lewis [25]. Given some *KB*, to determine the counterfactual consequences of A we consider those maximal subsets of *KB* consistent with A and add A to these. Notice, if A is consistent with *KB* then only one such subset (KB itself) exists and $A > B$ is true iff $A \supset B$ is entailed by KB, coinciding with our intuitions about consistent revision. However, Ginsberg's model of counterfactual reasoning suffers from sensitivity to the syntactic structure of KB.

Jackson [21] considers the problems with Ginsberg's approach and presents a model-theoretic system BERYL that addresses these difficulties. When revising K by A, as in Winslett's possible models approach to update, those worlds that satisfy A and differ minimally (with respect to set inclusion of atoms) from some world in $\|K\|$ are models of the revised state of affairs.[5] To satisfy the postulate of consistent revision (R4) (which distinguishes BERYL from the possible models approach) Jackson, in a somewhat *ad hoc* fashion, requires that $\|K_A^*\| = \|K\| \cap \|A\|$ whenever A is consistent with K. This would seem to void either the claim that set inclusion of atoms reflects some notion of comparative similarity or that BERYL respects this notion.

These systems both take very seriously the idea that counterfactuals are intimately tied to belief revision. However, this connection had not gone unappreciated by the revision community. Gärdenfors [14] provides an explicit postulate for revision and conditional reasoning based on the Ramsey test. If we assume that conditionals can be part of our belief sets then a concise statement of the Ramsey test is

(RT) $A > B \in K$ iff $B \in K_A^*$.

Gärdenfors also describes a formal semantics for conditionals in terms of *belief revision systems*. By imposing certain constraints on these models, in the form of a weakened version of postulates (R1) through (R8), and using (RT) to evaluate conditionals, Gärdenfors comes up with a conditional logic based on a revision 'style' semantics that corresponds exactly to Lewis's [25] counterfactual logic VC. We note, however, that all eight postulates are not respected in Gärdenfors's revision systems because they lead to a form of *triviality* [13; 14; 27]. In particular, the crucial postulate (R4) must be abandoned. In [6; 8] we examine the approach to subjunctives that we present here with respect to triviality, concluding that the negative result is avoided in the most reasonable way possible.

2 Modal logics with inaccessibility

Consider the problem of belief revision in the case where some new fact A must be reconciled with a theory or belief set K such that $K \models \neg A$. In order to accommodate this new fact certain beliefs in K must be given up before A is accepted because inconsistency must be avoided. The maxim

[5] $\|\alpha\|$ denotes the set of worlds or valuations that satisfy α.

of informational economy dictates that as 'few' beliefs as possible be given up, where by 'few' we mean that information loss should be kept to a minimum. There are very few logical constraints on what counts as an acceptable revision, or what form minimal loss of information should take. For this reason, AGM revision allows one to consider arbitrary maximal subsets of K consistent with A in the course of these deliberations and order these so that 'preferred' subsets give up the least information.

A key observation of Grove [19] and Katsuno and Mendelzon [23] is that such an ordering of subsets can be viewed as an ordering on possible worlds reflecting a preference on states of affairs that an agent would accept as epistemically possible if change in belief required it. We take this observation as a starting point for our Kripkean possible worlds semantics for belief revision. In this section we present a family of modal logics that we will later use to model revision.

2.1 Logics CT4O and CT4O*

Our semantics will be based on structures consisting of a set of possible worlds W and a binary accessibility relation R over W. Implicit in any such structure for revision will be some theory of interest K intended as the object of revision. We return momentarily to the problem of specifying K within the structure. The interpretation of R is as follows: wRv iff v is at least as *plausible* a state of affairs as w, given that K represents our state of belief. As usual, v is *more plausible* than w iff wRv but not vRw. Plausibility is a pragmatic measure that reflects the degree to which one would accept w as a possible state of affairs given that belief in K may have to be given up. If v is more plausible than w, loosely speaking, v is 'more consistent' with our beliefs than w, and is a preferable alternative world to adopt. This view may be based on some notion of *comparative similarity*, for instance as described by Lewis [25] and Stalnaker [30].

The minimal requirements on relation R are quite straightforward. Clearly, R should be reflexive for any world is as plausible as itself. Furthermore, R must be transitive if it is to be interpreted as an ordering. Such reflexive, transitive models will be dubbed CT4O-models. Other requirements on R are a bit harder to defend, but will be explored in the next section.

Our bimodal language $\mathbf{L}_B$ will be formed from a denumerable set $\mathbf{P}$ of propositional variables, together with the connectives $\neg$, $\supset$, $\Box$, and $\overleftarrow{\Box}$. The connectives $\wedge$, $\vee$, and $\equiv$ are defined in terms of these in the usual way. We denote by $\mathbf{L}_{CPL}$ the propositional sublanguage of $\mathbf{L}_B$.

Definition 2.1 A *CT4O-model* is a triple $M = \langle W, R, \varphi \rangle$, where W is a set (of possible worlds), R is a reflexive, transitive binary relation on W

(the accessibility relation), and φ maps $\mathbf{P}$ into 2^W ($\varphi(A)$ is the set of worlds where A is true).

Definition 2.2 Let $M = \langle W, R, \varphi \rangle$ be a CT4O-model, with $w \in W$. The truth of a formula α at w in M (where $M \models_w \alpha$ means α is true at w) is defined inductively as:

1. $M \models_w \alpha$ iff $w \in \varphi(\alpha)$ for atomic sentence α.
2. $M \models_w \neg\alpha$ iff $M \not\models_w \alpha$.
3. $M \models_w \alpha \supset \beta$ iff $M \models_w \beta$ or $M \not\models_w \alpha$.
4. $M \models_w \Box\alpha$ iff for each v such that wRv, $M \models_v \alpha$.
5. $M \models_w \overleftarrow{\Box}\alpha$ iff for each v such that not wRv, $M \models_v \alpha$.

It is important to note that, unlike most bimodal logics used in knowledge representation, the second modality does not carry with it additional semantic baggage. The semantic structures we use to capture the truth of such modal sentences are of the standard Kripkean variety used for a single modality. The extra connective merely increases the expressive power of our language, and allows us to impose much stronger constraints on the form of our intended structures (as we will see below).

We now define several new connectives as follows: $\Diamond\alpha \equiv_{\text{df}} \neg\Box\neg\alpha$; $\overleftarrow{\Diamond}\alpha \equiv_{\text{df}} \neg\overleftarrow{\Box}\neg\alpha$; $\overleftrightarrow{\Box}\alpha \equiv_{\text{df}} \Box\alpha \wedge \overleftarrow{\Box}\alpha$; and $\overleftrightarrow{\Diamond}\alpha \equiv_{\text{df}} \Diamond\alpha \vee \overleftarrow{\Diamond}\alpha$ It is easy to verify that these connectives have the following truth conditions: $\Diamond\alpha$ ($\overleftarrow{\Diamond}\alpha$) is true iff α holds at some accessible (inaccessible) world; $\overleftrightarrow{\Box}\alpha$ ($\overleftrightarrow{\Diamond}\alpha$) is true iff α holds at all worlds (some world) whether accessible or inaccessible. Validity is defined in a straightforward manner as truth at all worlds in all models; α is valid is denoted $\models_{CT4O} \alpha$.

The logic associated with this semantics is CT4O. Completeness is proved using a technique of Humberstone [20].

Definition 2.3 The conditional logic CT4O is the smallest $S \subseteq \mathbf{L}_B$ such that S contains CPL and the following axiom schemata, and is closed under the following rules of inference:

K $\Box(A \supset B) \supset (\Box A \supset \Box B)$.

K′ $\overleftarrow{\Box}(A \supset B) \supset (\overleftarrow{\Box}A \supset \overleftarrow{\Box}B)$.

T $\Box A \supset A$.

4 $\Box A \supset \Box\Box A$.

H $\overleftrightarrow{\Diamond}(\Box A \wedge \overleftarrow{\Box} B) \supset \overleftrightarrow{\Box}(A \vee B)$.

Nes From A infer $\overleftrightarrow{\Box} A$.

MP From $A \supset B$ and A infer B.

As usual, a sentence α is *provable* in CT4O (written $\vdash_{CT4O} \alpha$) iff $\alpha \in$ CO.

Theorem 2.4 $\vdash_{CT4O} \alpha$ *iff* $\models_{CT4O} \alpha$.

In the context of revision, we often want to ensure that all logically possible worlds are taken into consideration. No matter how implausible some situation is, if it is logically consistent it has *some* degree of plausibility. For this purpose we introduce the logic CT4O*, which is based on the class of CT4O-models in which all propositional valuations are represented. The additional axiom schema, of course, depends on satisfiability, and is taken from Levesque [24].

Definition 2.5 CT4O* is the smallest extension of CT4O closed under all rules of CT4O and containing the following axioms:

NB $\overleftarrow{\Box}\alpha \supset \neg \Box \alpha$ for all falsifiable propositional α.[6]

Definition 2.6 A *CT4O*-model* is any $M = \langle W, R, \varphi \rangle$, such that M is a CT4O-model and

$\{f : f \text{ maps } \mathbf{P} \text{ into } \{0,1\}\} \subseteq \{w^* : w \in W\}$.[7]

Theorem 2.7 $\vdash_{CT4O*} \alpha$ *iff* $\models_{CT4O*} \alpha$.

We will investigate only briefly CT4O and CT4O* and the properties they induce on revision functions. We will be more interested in the following extensions of these logics.

2.2 Logics CO and CO*

A very natural condition on our ordering of plausibility of worlds is that of *connectedness*: for any two worlds v, w, either vRw or wRv. Thus, any two worlds are comparable in our ordering. If neither is more plausible than the other, then they are equally plausible. This reflects the view adopted by Grove [19] and Katsuno and Mendelzon [23] that imposing a total preorder on worlds is suitable for modelling revision. A CO-model is a connected CT4O-model, and has a structure like that shown in Figure 1. Each large circle represents a *cluster*[8] of mutually accessible worlds (having

---

[6] Alternatively, we could use $\overleftrightarrow{\Diamond}\alpha$ for all satisfiable α.

[7] For all $w \in W$, w^* is defined as the map from $\mathbf{P}$ into $\{0,1\}$ such that $w^*(A) = 1$ iff $w \in \varphi(A)$; in other words, w^* is the valuation associated with w.

[8] A cluster in a model is a *maximal* set of worlds $C \subseteq W$ such that wRv for each $w, v \in C$ (that is, no extension of C enjoys this property).

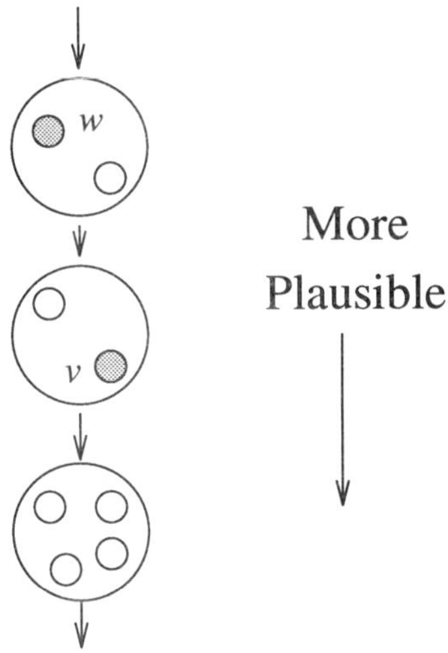

Figure 1: A CO-model.

equal degree of plausibility), while clusters lower in the diagram contain worlds that are more plausible than those higher in the diagram, the arrows indicating the accessibility relation. In the diagram we have wRv but not vRw, so v is more plausible than w. A CO*-model is simply a CO-model in which all logically possible worlds are represented.

Definition 2.8 A *CO-model* is a CT4O-model $M = \langle W, R, \varphi\rangle$ where R is a connected relation.

Definition 2.9 The conditional logic CO is the smallest $S \subseteq \mathbf{L}_B$ such that S contains CPL and the following axiom schemata, and is closed under the following rules of inference:

K $\Box(A \supset B) \supset (\Box A \supset \Box B)$.

K′ $\overleftarrow{\Box}(A \supset B) \supset (\overleftarrow{\Box} A \supset \overleftarrow{\Box} B)$.

4 $\Box A \supset \Box\Box A$.

S $A \supset \overleftarrow{\Box}\Diamond A$.

H $\overleftrightarrow{\Diamond}(\Box A \wedge \overleftarrow{\Box} B) \supset \overleftrightarrow{\Box}(A \vee B)$.

Nes From A infer $\overleftrightarrow{\Box} A$.

MP From $A \supset B$ and A infer B.

Theorem 2.10 $\vdash_{CO} \alpha$ *iff* $\models_{CO} \alpha$.

Definition 2.11 A *CT4O*-model* is any $M = \langle W, R, \varphi \rangle$, such that M is a CT4O-model and
$\{f : f \text{ maps } \mathbf{P} \text{ into } \{0,1\}\} \subseteq \{w^* : w \in W\}$.

Theorem 2.12 $\vdash_{CO*} \alpha$ *iff* $\models_{CO*} \alpha$.

We now introduce some notation. For a fixed model M, usually clear from context, we use $\|\alpha\|$ to denote the set of worlds in M that satisfy α. Such worlds are called α-worlds. If K is a set of sentences, $\|K\|$ denotes the set of worlds satisfying each element of K. In a slight abuse of notation, we use $\|\neg K\|$ to denote those worlds that fail to satisfy K, or falsify *some* element of K. The elements of these sets are called K-worlds and $\neg K$-worlds, respectively.

3 A conditional approach to revision

3.1 K-revision models

In this section, we will concentrate on CO and CO*-models for belief revision to keep the presentation simple. Near the end we will discuss the generalization afforded by the move to CT4O-models.

Given a belief set K, we can use a CO-model to represent the degrees of plausibility adopted by an agent for various situations. However, arbitrary CO-models are inappropriate. We should insist that those worlds consistent with K be *most* plausible. Given that K is the state of belief of the agent, certainly every K-world is more plausible than any world falsifying some belief in K. Furthermore, we should not distinguish one K-world as being more plausible than another, for this would indicate that some additional knowledge, *not represented in the state of belief* K, distinguished the two. Thus, in a model suitable for modelling the revision of K, we insist that all K-worlds be equally plausible, and that these are more plausible than any $\neg K$-world.

Definition 3.1 A *revision model for theory* K is any structure $M = \langle W, R, \varphi \rangle$ such that

(a) R is reflexive, transitive, and connected on W;

(b) $M \models_w \alpha$ for all $\alpha \in K$ iff w is R-minimal in M.

Figure 2 illustrates a K-revision model.

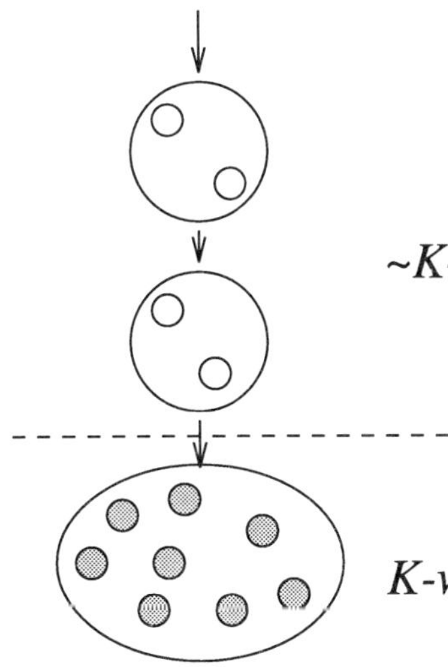

Figure 2: A K-revision model.

If our belief set K is finitely specifiable by some sentence KB, that is, if $K = Cn(KB)$, then such a constraint can be expressed in our language. To ensure that *only* KB-worlds are minimal in R (or most plausible), we can simply assert $KB \supset \Box KB$. To see this, notice that a KB-world cannot see a $\neg KB$-world in a model satisfying this sentence, so $\neg KB$-worlds cannot be minimal. To ensure that *all* KB-worlds are equally plausible, we simply insist that $KB \supset \overleftarrow{\Box}\neg KB$ hold. To see this, imagine that some KB-world w is not R-minimal. Then there must be some minimal KB-world v such that vRw fails; but then v violates $KB \supset \overleftarrow{\Box}\neg KB$. Making some simplifying assumptions, these conditions combine to give us

$$\overleftrightarrow{\Box}(KB \supset (\Box KB \wedge \overleftarrow{\Box}\neg KB)).^9 \tag{1}$$

We will abbreviate sentence (1) as $O(KB)$ and intend it to mean we 'only know' KB. The reason for this nomenclature will become apparent later.

Theorem 3.2 *Let K be finitely specified by KB and $M = \langle W, R, \varphi\rangle$ be a CO-model such that $M \models O(KB)$. Then M is a revision model for K.*

[9] We use $\overleftrightarrow{\Box}$ in front of this formula α so that the truth of α at all worlds in structure M can be expressed as $M \models_w \alpha$ for any w. We could equivalently ask $M \models \alpha$ when α has no $\overleftrightarrow{\Box}$, but find the former notation more convenient.

We will refer to such models more simply as K-revision models. In case $K = Cn(KB)$, a revision model for KB is taken to mean a revision model for K.

As expressed in the AGM revision postulates, in particular (R5), it is usually the case that we want to allow revision by any satisfiable sentence to result in a consistent belief set. In other words, we rule out no logically possible worlds in the course of our deliberations. This intuition is captured by insisting that revision models have among their set of worlds all propositional valuations. In other words, they should be CO*-models. We refer to this class of revision models as 'full'.

Definition 3.3 A *full revision model* for K is any revision model that is also a CO*-model.

Naturally, any CO*-model satisfying $O(KB)$ is a full revision model for KB.

3.2 A conditional for revision

The class of CO-models is adequate for revision satisfying the minimal requirements on the plausibility relation. The question remains: how do we express the revision of K by A within the modal logic? The intuition is that when revising by A we should consider the most plausible worlds at which A is satisfied to represent the revised state of affairs. It is precisely these worlds that represent the minimal change or loss of information in our belief set, that we are most willing to adopt if we accept A. One problem with this characterization of the revised belief set is the assumption that such minimal or most plausible A-worlds exist. Fortunately, we can define an approach to revision without this constraint.

By adopting a different perspective on belief revision in which conditionals are the key, we can ignore this *Limit Assumption* [25; 29]. It is often the case that when revising a belief set, we are not interested so much in characterizing the entire new belief state as in certain consequences of the revised theory. In other words, we are interested in facts of the sort 'If I revised my beliefs to include A then I would believe B'. Indeed, we typically cannot (or do not want to) specify the entire belief set that results from revision since it will often be too large, even for a finite KB, or will contain many facts that aren't of interest.

We will use a conditional connective $\xrightarrow{\text{KB}}$ to represent these statements and read $A \xrightarrow{\text{KB}} B$ as 'B is a consequence of revising (an implicit theory K or KB) by A.' In the case where some set of minimal A-worlds exists, clearly such an assertion is true iff B is true at every such world. However, if such a set does not exist, for instance if every A-world has some A-world more plausible than itself, we can still tell if $A \xrightarrow{\text{KB}} B$ is true.

Recall that CO-models consist of a totally ordered set of clusters of (mutually accessible) possible worlds. Hence, a revision model has the cluster $\|K\|$ as a minimum. In the case where A is inconsistent with K, clearly $A \xrightarrow{\text{KB}} B$ is true exactly when the formula

$$\overleftarrow{\Diamond}(A \wedge \Box(A \supset B))$$

is true at any $w \in \|K\|$. This formula says there is some world satisfying A such that $A \supset B$ is true at all more plausible worlds. Since the ordering on W is total, this ensures that any 'minimal' A-world satisfies B. However, if there is an A-world in $\|K\|$, this is unsatisfactory, as the operator $\overleftarrow{\Diamond}$ refers only to possibility at inaccessible worlds (hence, not to any K-worlds). In such a circumstance $A \xrightarrow{\text{KB}} B$ is true when

$$\Diamond(A \wedge \Box(A \supset B))$$

holds at any $w \in \|K\|$. This is so because $\Box(A \supset B)$ means that $K \models A \supset B$. Therefore, the most plausible A worlds, those in $\|K\|$, satisfy B. Disjoining the two, we arrive at

$$\overleftrightarrow{\Diamond}(A \wedge \Box(A \supset B)).$$

We can drop the restriction that $A \xrightarrow{\text{KB}} B$ be evaluated at some $w \in \|K\|$, since if it holds at some $w \in W$ it holds at all worlds. This sentence does not account for impossible antecedents, in which case we should expect the conditional to be vacuously true; that is, revising by impossible A entails every sentence B. Finally, the definition of the *revision conditional* $A \xrightarrow{\text{KB}} B$ in $\mathbf{L}_B$ is given as

$$A \xrightarrow{\text{KB}} B \equiv_{\text{df}} \overleftrightarrow{\Box}\neg A \vee \overleftrightarrow{\Diamond}(A \wedge \Box(A \supset B)).$$

Figure 3 illustrates the truth conditions for $A \xrightarrow{\text{KB}} B$ in the case where there is a set of most plausible A-worlds and $\neg A$ is in the belief set K. Since B holds at each of the most plausible A-worlds (the shaded region), $A \xrightarrow{\text{KB}} B$ is true. Notice that $A \wedge \Box(A \supset B)$ holds at each world in this region.

3.3 Properties of revision

3.3.1 Representation results

The connective $\xrightarrow{\text{KB}}$ does not characterize revision in the manner of a function $*$. Rather than asserting that a belief set K^*_A results when we revise by

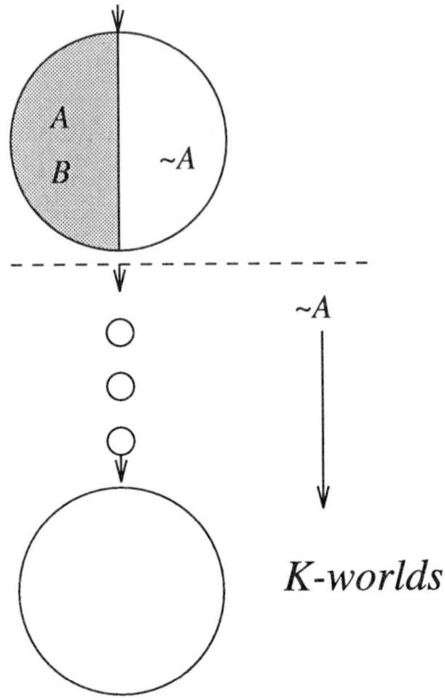

Figure 3: Truth conditions for the conditional.

A, the sentence $A \stackrel{\text{KB}}{\longrightarrow} B$ makes a weaker assertion, that B will be believed when we revise by A, or $B \in K^*_A$. While this seems to make a comparison to the AGM model difficult, we can in fact use $\stackrel{\text{KB}}{\longrightarrow}$ to define a revision function.

Definition 3.4 Let M be a revision model for K. The *revision function determined by M* is denoted $*^{\text{M}}$ and is defined for each $A \in \mathbf{L}_{CPL}$ by

$$K_A^{*^{\text{M}}} = \{B \in \mathbf{L}_{CPL} : M \models A \stackrel{\text{KB}}{\longrightarrow} B\}.$$

Some derived theorems and rules of inference for the logic CO will shed some light on the nature of the connective $\stackrel{\text{KB}}{\longrightarrow}$ and on the induced revision functions $(*^{\text{M}})$.[10]

RCM From $B \supset C$ infer $(A \stackrel{\text{KB}}{\longrightarrow} B) \supset (A \stackrel{\text{KB}}{\longrightarrow} C)$

ID $A \stackrel{\text{KB}}{\longrightarrow} A$

KC $(A \stackrel{\text{KB}}{\longrightarrow} B) \supset (KB \wedge A \supset B)$

[10]Where KB is mentioned we assume $O(KB)$ to be a premise.

CK $\overleftrightarrow{\Diamond}(KB \wedge A) \supset ((KB \wedge A \supset B) \supset (A \stackrel{\text{KB}}{\longrightarrow} B))$

Cons $\overleftrightarrow{\Box}\neg A \equiv (A \stackrel{\text{KB}}{\longrightarrow} \perp)$

LLE From $A \equiv B$ infer $(A \stackrel{\text{KB}}{\longrightarrow} C) \supset (B \stackrel{\text{KB}}{\longrightarrow} C)$

KCI $(A \wedge B \stackrel{\text{KB}}{\longrightarrow} C) \supset (A \stackrel{\text{KB}}{\longrightarrow} (B \supset C))$

CKI $\neg(A \stackrel{\text{KB}}{\longrightarrow} \neg B) \supset ((A \stackrel{\text{KB}}{\longrightarrow} (B \supset C)) \supset (A \wedge B \stackrel{\text{KB}}{\longrightarrow} C))$

These theorems ensure that $*^{\text{M}}$ behaves in a reasonable manner. In fact, these correspond precisely to the eight AGM postulates, which can be expressed at the object level in our logic. Given this, it should be clear that any full revision model determines a revision function that satisfies the AGM postulates. We can also show that any AGM revision function can be represented by a CO* revision model. (Proofs of these results can be found in the appendix.)

Theorem 3.5 *Let M be a full revision model and $*^{\text{M}}$ the revision function determined by M. Then $*^{\text{M}}$ satisfies postulates (R1) through (R8).*

Theorem 3.6 *Let $*$ be a revision function satisfying postulates (R1) through (R8). Then for any theory K there exists a full revision model M for K such that $K_A^* = K_A^{*^{\text{M}}}$ for all A.*

In other words, the class of revision functions determined by revision models is exactly the class of AGM revision functions. Hence, the modal logic CO* is an appropriate calculus for reasoning about belief revision. In fact, CO*, together with the defined connective $\stackrel{\text{KB}}{\longrightarrow}$, appears to be the first sound and complete logical axiomatization of AGM revision. We note here that while the revision function determined by a specific revision model (as per Theorem 3.5) is unique, the converse is not true. For a specified revision function $*$ and theory K, there may be a number of K-revision models that determine $*$ as applied to K (as per Theorem 3.6).

3.3.2 Partial order revision

The logic CT4O* is a weaker version of CO* in which clusters of equally plausible worlds need not be totally ordered, but merely partially ordered. Thus, we can have worlds with incomparable degrees of plausibility. This provides us with a generalization of the AGM theory of revision known as *preorder revision* (see the proposal of Katsuno and Mendelzon [23]). When dealing with CO-models, simply asserting $O(KB)$ was enough to ensure that we had a K-revision model, where K-worlds were most plausible. However, the fact that CO-models are connected made the task easier. Since CT4O-models can have 'disconnected' fragments (if we consider the graph induced by accessibility R), simply ensuring that the set of K-worlds forms a minimal cluster is inadequate. Some disconnected fragment of the model may possess a minimal cluster of $\neg K$-worlds, even though $O(KB)$ is satisfied. For this reason, we insist that preorder revision models be *cohesive.*[11] Intuitively, this ensures that each $\neg K$-world is less plausible than the cluster of K-worlds, even though $\neg K$-worlds may be incomparable among themselves.

Definition 3.7 A *preorder revision model for theory* K is any structure $M = \langle W, R, \varphi\rangle$ such that R is reflexive, transitive, and cohesive on W and $w \in W$ is R-minimal in M iff $M \models_w \alpha$ for all $\alpha \in K$.

Cohesiveness for a KB-revision model can be captured by asserting $\overleftrightarrow{\Box} \Diamond KB$. This ensures that *every* world can see the minimal cluster of KB-worlds.

Theorem 3.8 *Let K be finitely specified by KB and $M = \langle W, R, \varphi\rangle$ be a CT4O-model such that $M \models O(KB)$ and $M \models \overleftrightarrow{\Box} \Diamond KB$. Then M is a preorder revision model for K.*

The *full preorder revision models* are simply CT4O*-models that satisfy these conditions. The conditional connective $\stackrel{\mathrm{KB}}{\longrightarrow}$ also requires a different definition in CT4O, for once again we cannot exploit the connectedness of R a with CO. To take into account the different possible paths in the model we use the following definition (see [3; 8] for further details):

$$A \stackrel{\mathrm{KB}}{\longrightarrow} B \equiv_{\mathrm{df}} \overleftrightarrow{\Box}(\Box\neg A \vee \Diamond(A \wedge \Box(A \supset B))).$$

It is easy to verify that this is equivalent to the earlier definition in the logic CO; but in the weaker logic CT4O, this stronger definition is required to capture the set of most plausible A-worlds (which can now be distributed among incomparable clusters).

Using the same definition of revised belief set $K_A^{*^{\mathrm{M}}}$ for a preorder revision model M, we can show that $*^{\mathrm{M}}$ satisfies the first seven AGM postulates.

Theorem 3.9 *Let M be a full preorder revision model and $*^{\mathrm{M}}$ the revision function determined by M. Then $*^{\mathrm{M}}$ satisfies postulates (R1) through (R7).*

3.3.3 Relative revision

The behaviour of this semantic model for revision is rather interesting when we consider general K-revision (or preorder revision) models, rather than their 'full' counterparts. When revising K by A in the context of full

[11] That is, the underlying graph of accessibility is connected. For each pair of worlds w, v, there is a path from w to v through the relation $(R \cup R^{-1})$.

revision, the resulting belief set will clearly be non-trivial whenever A is propositionally satisfiable. This is due to the fact that there must be *some* world in the revision model satisfying A.

When using arbitrary CO-models to represent revision of K by A, this need not be the case. It may be that A is logically satisfiable, yet there are no A-worlds in the model. Since $\overleftrightarrow{\Box}\neg A$ holds in such a model, $A \xrightarrow{\text{KB}} B$ is true for all B and the belief set $K_A^{*^{\text{M}}}$ is the inconsistent theory $Cn(\bot)$. Clearly, this violates postulate (R5), which insists that revision by a logically consistent sentence result in a consistent belief set. The use of arbitrary revision models therefore weakens the AGM theory. This weakening corresponds precisely to 'relativizing' the notion of satisfiability and validity to the space of logical possibilities represented by the revision model in question.

Let us say that a sentence A is *satisfiable relative to model M* just when there is some A-world in M. In other words, $M \models \overleftrightarrow{\Diamond} A$. Relative validity of A naturally corresponds to $M \models \overleftrightarrow{\Box} A$. We can then define a notion of consequence with respect to this model by applying these notions in the standard way. For example, A entails B *relative* to M ($A \models_M B$) just when each A-world in M satisfies B (that is, $M \models \overleftrightarrow{\Box}(A \supset B)$). The notion of expansion is changed by these considerations as well, for K_A^+ now becomes the set of sentences B such that $K \models_M A \supset B$ relative to M. If $K \models_M \neg A$ then K_A^+ is still identical to $Cn(\bot)$, but when A is consistent with K, K_A^+ reflects the stronger notion of entailment induced by M, rather than simply $Cn(K \cup \{A\})$.

Given these notions of relative satisfiability and entailment, it is easy to verify that arbitrary CO-models capture the AGM postulates if the relative notions replace logical satisfiability and entailment in the specification of the postulates. For example, any (non-full) K-revision model satisfies the relative form of (R5):

$$K_A^* = Cn(\bot) \quad \text{iff} \quad M \models \overleftrightarrow{\Box}\neg A.$$

Therefore, we can think of CO (and CT4O) as logics that generalize AGM revision to reflect a specific set of possibilities, rather than considering any logically consistent state of affairs to be achievable. This has implications on our representation of integrity constraints in Section 5.

3.3.4 Reasoning about revision

In general, reasoning about the process of revising an objective *KB* with the modal logic CO* requires one to assert as a background theory the sentence $O(KB)$. This background theory enforces the restriction that all states of affairs consistent with our objective knowledge are minimal in our ordering of plausibility, that we prefer to 'hang on to these beliefs' if possible. This background induces the logical constraints required of belief revision but specifies little else.

Example 3.10 Consider theory $O(KB)$ where $KB = \{\mathtt{bird}, \mathtt{fly}, \mathtt{bird} \supset \mathtt{fly}, \mathtt{penguin} \supset \neg\mathtt{fly}\}$. If we want to ask about revision of KB by $\mathtt{green}$, we can show

$$O(KB) \vdash_{CO*} \mathtt{green} \xrightarrow{\text{KB}} \alpha \quad \text{iff} \quad KB \cup \{\mathtt{green}\} \vdash \alpha$$

for any proposition α, since $\mathtt{green}$ is consistent with KB. However, if we ask

$$O(KB) \vdash_{CO*} \mathtt{penguin} \xrightarrow{\text{KB}} \alpha$$

very little is derivable as $\mathtt{penguin}$ is inconsistent with KB. In general, this will only hold for those α that are logical consequences of $\mathtt{penguin}$.

This example illustrates the extreme generality of the AGM postulates and our approach to revision. From the context of KB (in particular, the suggestively labelled atomic propositions), it seems that we ought to be able to derive more than $\mathtt{penguin}$ when we revise by it, but this is a matter of pragmatics. These contextual difficulties are resolved by introducing as premises conditional sentences constraining the revision process. In fact, most of our information might be of this form. Asserting $\mathtt{penguin} \xrightarrow{\text{KB}} \neg\mathtt{fly}$ ensures that $\mathtt{penguin} \supset \neg\mathtt{fly}$ is not given up.

Example 3.11 Let KB be as before and let S be the set of additional premises containing

$$\mathtt{bird} \xrightarrow{\text{KB}} \mathtt{fly}, \ \mathtt{penguin} \xrightarrow{\text{KB}} \neg\mathtt{fly}, \ \mathtt{penguin} \xrightarrow{\text{KB}} \mathtt{bird}.$$

From $S \cup \{O(KB)\}$ we can derive in CO* both $\mathtt{penguin} \xrightarrow{\text{KB}} \neg\mathtt{fly}$ and $\mathtt{penguin} \wedge \mathtt{bird} \xrightarrow{\text{KB}} \neg\mathtt{fly}$.

Some further theorems derivable in CO are given below.

And $(A \xrightarrow{\text{KB}} B) \wedge (A \xrightarrow{\text{KB}} C) \supset (A \xrightarrow{\text{KB}} B \wedge C)$

Or $(A \xrightarrow{\text{KB}} C) \wedge (B \xrightarrow{\text{KB}} C) \supset (A \vee B \xrightarrow{\text{KB}} C)$

RT $(A \xrightarrow{\text{KB}} B) \supset ((A \wedge B \xrightarrow{\text{KB}} C) \supset (A \xrightarrow{\text{KB}} C))$

CM $(A \xrightarrow{\text{KB}} B) \wedge (A \xrightarrow{\text{KB}} C) \supset (A \wedge B \xrightarrow{\text{KB}} C)$

RM $(A \xrightarrow{\text{KB}} C) \wedge \neg(A \wedge B \xrightarrow{\text{KB}} C) \supset A \xrightarrow{\text{KB}} \neg B$

As well, revision by A need not result in the belief of B or $\neg B$, hence $\xrightarrow{\text{KB}}$ fails to satisfy CEM, the *Conditional Law of Excluded Middle* [29]; for in general the set

$$\{\neg(A \xrightarrow{\text{KB}} B), \neg(A \xrightarrow{\text{KB}} \neg B)\}$$

is consistent. However, if revision by A results in belief B, it cannot also result in $\neg B$ (for consistent A), since $\overleftrightarrow{\Diamond} A \supset ((A \xrightarrow{\text{KB}} B) \supset \neg(A \xrightarrow{\text{KB}} \neg B))$ is valid.

Example 3.12 Let S be the set of premises

$$\{\texttt{bird} \xrightarrow{\text{KB}} \texttt{fly},\ \texttt{penguin} \xrightarrow{\text{KB}} \texttt{bird},\ \texttt{emu} \xrightarrow{\text{KB}} \texttt{bird},\ \texttt{penguin} \xrightarrow{\text{KB}} \neg\texttt{fly},\ quad\texttt{emu} \xrightarrow{\text{KB}} \neg\texttt{fly}\}.$$

We can show that $\texttt{penguin} \vee \texttt{emu} \xrightarrow{\text{KB}} \texttt{bird} \wedge \neg\texttt{fly}$ is derivable from S, as well as $\texttt{bird} \xrightarrow{\text{KB}} \neg\texttt{penguin}$ and $\texttt{bird} \xrightarrow{\text{KB}} \neg\texttt{emu}$.

Our approach has a number of advantages over the traditional view of revision. First, it implies no commitment to the Limit Assumption, in contrast to, for example, Grove [19] and Katsuno and Mendelzon [23], while still adhering to the AGM postulates (see the next section). Second, it provides a logical axiomatization of revision and expresses the requisite concepts in well-understood modal terms. Finally, because the bimodal language is so expressive, it allows us to logically specify intensional constraints (including integrity constraints) that are not readily amenable to analysis in the AGM framework. We return to this final point in the next section.

3.3.5 The limit assumption

Our approach to revision makes no assumption about the existence of minimal A-worlds, which Grove [19] claims forms an integral part of any model of revision. As Lewis [25] emphasizes, there is no justification for such an assumption other than convenience. Consider a KB that contains the proposition 'I am 6 feet tall.' Revising by $A =$ 'I am over 7 feet tall' would allow one to evaluate Lewis's classic counterfactual 'If I were over 7 feet tall I would play basketball.' However, it doesn't seem that there should exist a most plausible A-world, merely an infinite sequence of more and more plausible A-worlds approaching the limit world where 'I am 7 feet tall' is true. Our model allows one to assume the truth of the counterfactual $A \xrightarrow{\text{KB}} B$ if the consequent B ('I play basketball') is strictly implied (i.e., if $\Box(A \supset B)$ holds) at any world in this sequence of A worlds. In this respect, we take Lewis's semantics to heart.

Models of revision that rely on the the Limit Assumption (e.g., [19; 23]) would also make $A \xrightarrow{\text{KB}} B$ true, but for the wrong reasons. It holds vacuously since there are no minimal A-worlds. Of course, $A \stackrel{\text{KB}}{\longrightarrow} \neg B$ is true in this case too, which is strongly counterintuitive. How can this be reconciled with Theorems 3.5 and 3.6, which show that our notion of revision is equivalent to the AGM version, including those that make the Limit Assumption?

In fact, this points to another advantage of the modal approach, namely increased expressive power. We can easily state that worlds of decreasing height (ht), down to my actual height of 6 feet, are more plausible using:[12]

$$\overleftrightarrow{\Box}\forall y > 6[y < x \supset (\mathtt{ht(Me)} = x \equiv \overleftarrow{\Box}\mathtt{ht(Me)} \neq y)]. \tag{2}$$

Not only can we constrain the revision process directly, but also indirectly using such *intensional constraints.* Of course, there must be some AGM operator that has $\beta \in K^*_\alpha$ exactly when our model satisfies $\alpha \stackrel{\text{KB}}{\longrightarrow} \beta$, including $B \in K^*_A$ (the basketball counterfactual). But models making the Limit Assumption do not reflect the same structure as our CO*-model. They cannot express nor represent the constraint relating plausibility to height. In order to ensure $B \in K^*_A$ they must violate sentence (2). The modal language also improves on AGM revision in general, where such a constraint can only be expressed by some infinite set of conditions $\beta \in K^*_\alpha$. In [3; 8] we examine the Limit Assumption and intensional constraints in more detail. In particular, we show how constraints on the entrenchment and plausibility of sentences and beliefs can be expressed at the object level.

4 A framework for subjunctive queries

Let *KB* be, as usual, a set of beliefs representing our knowledge of the world. We also expect there to be some conditional beliefs among these that constrain the manner in which we are willing to revise our (objective) beliefs. These take the form $\alpha \stackrel{\text{KB}}{\longrightarrow} \beta$ (or $\alpha > \beta$), and will be referred to as *subjunctive premises.* By a *subjunctive query* we intend something of the form 'If A were true, would B hold?' In other words, is $A \stackrel{\text{KB}}{\longrightarrow} B$ a consequence of our beliefs and subjunctive premises?

Given the connection between Lewis's logic VC and belief revision (see Section 1.2), and assuming the Ramsey test is an appropriate truth test for subjunctives, it would appear that VC is exactly the logical calculus required for formulating subjunctive queries. However, we have misrepresented the Gärdenfors result to a certain degree; in fact, his semantics does not account for the postulate of consistent revision (R4). It is excluded because it results in *triviality* and, together with the other postulates, is

[12]We assume the obvious first-order extension of CO-models, a partial theory of $<$ over (say) the rationals, and so on.

far too strong to be of use.[13] Because (R4) is unaccounted for in VC, it is inadequate for the representation of certain subjunctive queries.

Example 4.1 Suppose $KB = \{B\}$, a belief set consisting of a single propositional letter. If we were to ask 'If A then B?', intuitively we would expect the answer YES, when A is some distinct atomic proposition. With no constraints (such as $A > \neg B$), the postulate of consistent revision should hold sway and revising by A should result in $KB' = \{A, B\}$. Hence, $A > B$ should be true of KB. Similarly, $\neg(A > C)$ should also be true of KB for any distinct atom C.

In VC there is no mechanism for drawing these types of conclusions. At most one could hope to assert B as a premise and derive $A > B$ or $\neg(A > C)$, but neither of

$$B \vdash_{VC} A > B \quad \text{or} \quad B \vdash_{VC} \neg(A > C)$$

is true, nor should they be. It *should* be the case, if A is *consistent with our beliefs*, that $A > B$ holds; but merely asserting B doesn't carry this force. In a sense, when B is a premise we mean 'B is believed', but this does not preclude the possibility of A, or $\neg A$, or C, or anything else being believed. When $KB = \{B\}$ we intend something stronger, namely that 'B is *all* that is believed.' Because B is the only sentence in KB, we convey the added information that, say, neither A nor $\neg A$ is believed. In Levesque's [24] terminology, we *only know* KB.

To only know some sentence is to both know (or believe) A and to know nothing more than A. To know A is to restrict one's set of epistemic possibilities to those states of affairs where A is true. If some $\neg A$-world were considered possible an agent could not be said to know A, for the possibility of $\neg A$ has not been ruled out. To know nothing more than A is to include all possible A-worlds among one's set of epistemic possibilities. Adding knowledge to a belief set is just restricting one's set of epistemic possibilities to exclude worlds where these new beliefs fail, so if some A-world were excluded from consideration, intuitively an agent would have some knowledge other than A that ruled out this world.

In our logic CO* we have precisely the mechanism for stating that we only know a KB. We consider the set of minimal worlds to represent our knowledge of the actual world. Exactly those possible worlds consistent with our beliefs KB are minimal in any KB-revision model; this is precisely what the sentence $O(KB)$ asserts. It says that KB is believed (since only KB-worlds are minimal) and that KB is all that is believed (since all KB-worlds are minimal).

[13] The triviality result of Gärdenfors [13; 14] has attracted much attention in the literature [27; 12; 16; 18]. We discuss the implications of triviality (or lack thereof) on our approach in [6; 8].

Returning to the query $A \xrightarrow{\text{KB}} B$, we take this analysis to mean that $B \vdash_{CO*} A \xrightarrow{\text{KB}} B$ is not the proper formulation of the query. This derivation is not valid (just as it is not in VC). Our analysis suggests that we ought to ask whether $A \xrightarrow{\text{KB}} B$ holds if we only know B. In fact, both

$$O(B) \vdash_{CO*} A \xrightarrow{\text{KB}} B \quad \text{and} \quad O(B) \vdash_{CO*} \neg(A \xrightarrow{\text{KB}} C)$$

are legitimate derivations.

This leads to an obvious framework for subjunctive query answering, given a set of beliefs. Our knowledge of the world is divided into two components, a set KB of *objective* or propositional facts or beliefs, and a set S of subjunctive conditionals acting as premises, or constraints on the manner in which we revise our beliefs. To ask a subjunctive query Q of the form $\alpha \xrightarrow{\text{KB}} \beta$ is to ask whether β would be true if we believed α, given that our *only* current beliefs about the world are represented by KB, and that our deliberations of revision are constrained by subjunctive premises S. The expected answers `YES`, `NO`, and `UNK` (unknown) to Q are characterized as follows:

$$ASK(Q) = \begin{cases} \texttt{YES} & \text{if } \{O(KB)\} \cup S \models_{CO*} Q \\ \texttt{NO} & \text{if } \{O(KB)\} \cup S \models_{CO*} \neg Q \\ \texttt{UNK} & \text{otherwise} \end{cases}$$

Objective queries about the actual state of affairs (or, more precisely, our beliefs) can be phrased as $\top \xrightarrow{\text{KB}} \beta$ where β is the objective query of interest. It's easy to see that

$$ASK(Q) = \texttt{YES} \quad \text{iff} \quad \vdash_{CO*} KB \supset \beta$$

The ability to express that *only* a certain set of sentences is believed allows us to give a purely logical characterization of subjunctive queries of a knowledge base. The logic VC seems adequate for reasoning from subjunctive premises and for deriving new conditionals, but it cannot account for the influence of factual information on the truth of conditionals in a completely satisfying manner; for it lacks the expressive power to enforce compliance with postulate (R4). The approaches of Ginsberg and Jackson take VC to be the underlying counterfactual logic. Indeed, their approaches (under certain assumptions) satisfy the Lewis axioms. However, they recognize that the ability to only know a knowledge base is crucial for revision and subjunctive reasoning, an expressive task not achievable in VC. Therein lies the motivation for their extra-logical characterizations, and the underlying idea that KB is representable as a set of sentences or a set of possible worlds from which we construct new sets in the course of revision. CO* can be viewed as a logic in which one can capture just this process (though important distinctions exist as described in Section 1.2).

5 Integrity constraints

Often it is the case that only certain states of knowledge, certain belief sets, are permissible. The concept of *integrity constraints*, widely studied in database theory, is a way to capture just such conditions. For a database (or in our case, a belief set) to be considered a valid representation of the world, it must satisfy these integrity constraints. For instance, we may not consider feasible any belief set in which certain commonsense laws of physics are violated; or a database in which there exists some student with an unknown student number may be prohibited.

This apparently straightforward concept actually has several distinct interpretations. Reiter [26] surveys those and proposes the definition we favour, which essentially asserts that an integrity constraint C should be entailed by KB. The distinguishing characteristic of Reiter's definition is that integrity constraints can be phrased using a modal knowledge operator, which refers to 'what is known by the database'. This connective is given a semantics, and satisfaction of an integrity constraint is defined using an implicit appeal to the concept of only knowing. Typically, constraint C will contain operators referring to the knowledge contained in KB (see Reiter [26]). For our purposes, since we do not intend to give a full account of what a knowledge base knows, we will assume that constraints are propositional and that KB satisfies C just when KB entails C. We assume in what follows that all constraints are satisfiable.

As emphasized by Fagin, Ullman, and Vardi [11] and Winslett [32], integrity constraints are particularly important when updating a database. Any *new* database (or belief set) should satisfy these constraints, therefore any reasonable model of update or revision must explicitly account for integrity constraints.

Example 5.1 Let the constraint C, that a department has only one chair, be expressed as

$$\texttt{chair(x,d)} \wedge \texttt{chair(y,d)} \supset \texttt{x=y} \tag{3}$$

Suppose we want to update KB with `chair(Ken,DCS)`$\vee$`chair(Maria,DCS)`. If this is consistent with KB, the constraint (3) can be placed in KB and will ensure that exactly one of Ken or Maria is the chair of Computer Science (assuming Unique Names). Suppose, on the contrary, that

$$KB = \{\texttt{chair(Derek,DCS)}\}$$

so the new fact is inconsistent. The constraint can no longer be enforced in the updated KB', for nothing about C says it must be true in the revised state of affairs.

This example demonstrates the need for integrity constraints to be expressed intensionally. They refer not only to the actual world, but to *all (preferred) ways in which we view the world.*

We can ensure that a revised belief set or database satisfies a constraint C by asserting $\overleftrightarrow{\Box}C$ as a premise in our background theory (on the same level as $O(KB)$). This has the effect of ensuring *any* possible worlds ever considered satisfy C (see Section 3.3.3). This tack has two disadvantages. First, it takes us from the realm of CO*, and requires the logic CO. Thus we lose the uniformity of our models and require a proper subset of the axiom schemata corresponding to CO* (and perhaps lose a more uniform proof procedure). Second, it may be too strong an assertion in many applications. Such a statement will force any revision of KB by a fact F inconsistent with C to result in the inconsistent belief set $Cn(\bot)$. In certain (maybe most) circumstances, we can imagine that the violation of a constraint C ought not force us into inconsistency. If F is consistent with C, certainly C should remain true after revision. But if $F \vdash \neg C$, and we *really* want to adopt F, then we may simply want to admit that C was incorrect rather than being forced into inconsistency.

Instead of abolishing $\neg C$-worlds outright, we'd like to say that all C-worlds are 'preferred' to any world violating the constraint. Such a condition is expressible as $\overleftrightarrow{\Box}(C \supset \Box C)$. To see this, imagine that some $\neg C$-world v is more plausible than some C-world w. Then wRv and $M \not\models_w C \supset \Box C$. Of course, we are often concerned with a set of constraints $C = \{C_1, \cdots, C_n\}$. A set of sentences of the form

$$\overleftrightarrow{\Box}(C_1 \supset \Box C_1), \cdots, \overleftrightarrow{\Box}(C_n \supset \Box C_n)$$

will be CO*-inconsistent if any C_i, C_j are pairwise contingent, since it is impossible to satisfy the condition, for some $w \models C_i \wedge \neg C_j$ and $v \models \neg C_i \wedge C_j$, that v is more plausible than w and w is more plausible than v. In the case of a set of C multiple constraints, we use C to denote their conjunction

$$\overleftrightarrow{\Box}(C \supset \Box C) \quad \text{where} \quad C = \bigwedge_{i \le n} C_i.$$

We now define a revision model with integrity constraints.

Definition 5.2 M is a *revision model for K with weak integrity constraints $C_1, \cdots, C_n$* iff M is a revision model for K and $M \models \overleftrightarrow{\Box}(C \supset \Box C)$ where C is the conjunction of the constraints. We will often say that M is a revision model with constraints C where C is understood to be either the set or conjunction of the individual constraints. The singleton set $\{\overleftrightarrow{\Box}(C \supset \Box C)\}$ will be denoted WIC.

Theorem 5.3 *Let M be a revision model for K with weak integrity constraints C. Then $K_A^{*^M} \models C$ for all A consistent with C.*

Thus we validate the definition of integrity constraint. If a sentence A is consistent with C it must be the case that revising by A results in a belief set that satisfies C. Of course, this requires that the original belief set must also satisfy the integrity constraints.

Corollary 5.4 *Let M be a revision model for K with weak integrity constraints C. Then $K \models C$.*

Corollary 5.5 *If $KB \not\models C$ then $\{O(KB)\} \cup WIC$ is CO*-inconsistent.*

These corollaries state that if KB does not entail constraints C, it can have no revision model satisfying WIC. That is, if the initial KB violates C we cannot postulate a model in which KB satisfies C no matter how it is revised. Our concern is not with the (traditional) question of when KB satisfies C, but instead with the question of when KB will satisfy C after arbitrary revisions.

In order to get off the ground, we assume that the original KB in our examples satisfy C (i.e. $KB \models C$). The simplest way to do this is to 'throw in' the constraints, assuming they are part of KB. Otherwise $O(KB)$ will require that $\neg C$-worlds be among those considered to model the actual world. Often, integrity constraints and objective knowledge are kept separately. In our examples, we will always consider KB to include as an objective fact any constraint C,[14] although we may not explicitly write C as a member of KB.

Example 5.6 Let $KB = \{\texttt{chair(Derek,DCS)}\}$ and $C = \{\texttt{chair(x,d)} \wedge \texttt{chair(y,d)} \supset \texttt{x=y}\}$. Suppose we want to update KB with `chair(Ken,DCS)` $\vee$ `chair(Maria,DCS)`. Then from $\{O(KB)\} \cup WIC$ we can derive in CO*

$$\texttt{chair(Ken,DCS)} \vee \texttt{chair(Maria,DCS)} \xrightarrow{KB} \texttt{chair(Ken,DCS)} \equiv \neg\texttt{chair(Maria,DCS)}.$$

This definition of integrity constraint has the unappealing quality of being unable to ensure that as many constraints as possible be satisfied. For instance, if some update A violates some C_i of C, then revision by A is not guaranteed to satisfy other constraints. Only worlds that satisfy *all* constraints in C are preferred. For this reason we included the qualifier 'weak' in the definition. In general, we want other members of C to be satisfied even though a certain C_i may be violated. In order to ensure more reasonable behaviour on the part of integrity constraints, we'd like to insist that as many of them as possible be satisfied. This can be accomplished by asserting that worlds in which a certain subset of constraints $C = \{C_1, \cdots, C_n\}$ is violated are preferred to any world in which a larger

[14] Although, from previous examples we have seen that this is not *sufficient* for C to be considered an integrity constraint.

subset of these is violated, (by preferred worlds we refer to those that are more plausible). Let $S_1, S_2, \ldots, S_{2^n}$ be an enumeration of the subsets of C. We will use S_i and $\overline{S_i}$ to denote the sentences

$$S_i = \bigwedge\{C_j : C_j \in S_i\}$$

$$\overline{S_i} = \bigwedge\{\neg C_j : C_j \notin S_i\}.$$

We can think of $S_i \wedge \overline{S_i}$ as stating that some state of affairs satisfies exactly the subset of constraints in S_i. Suppose $w \models S_i \wedge \overline{S_i}$. To say that w is preferred to any world that violates strictly more constraints is to assert that, for every $S_j \subset S_i$,

$$\overleftrightarrow{\Box}((S_i \wedge \overline{S_i}) \supset \Box\neg\overline{S_j}).$$

To see this, suppose this sentence is violated. Then for some such w there is a world v that is at least as plausible as w at which $\overline{S_j}$ holds. This means some superset, $C - S_j$, of the constraints violated at w, $C - S_i$, is violated at v, yet v is equally or more plausible. We can state this more concisely, without quantifying over all subsets of S_i as follows:

$$\overleftrightarrow{\Box}((S_i \wedge \overline{S_i}) \supset \Box(\overline{S_i} \supset S_i)).$$

The (*strong*) *integrity constraints* determined by C are specified by the set

$$IC = \{\overleftrightarrow{\Box}((S_i \wedge \overline{S_i}) \supset \Box(\overline{S_i} \supset S_i)) : i \leq 2^n\}.$$

Definition 5.7 M is a *revision model for K with* (*strong*) *integrity constraints C* iff M is a revision model for K and $M \models IC$.

Theorem 5.8 *Let M be a revision model for K with strong integrity constraints C. Let $\mathcal{S}$ be the collection of maximal subsets $S_i \subseteq C$ such that S_i is consistent with A. For some $S \subseteq \mathcal{S}$, it is the case that $K_A^{*M} \models \bigvee S$.*

Example 5.9 Let $KB = \{$`chair(Derek,DCS)`$\}$ and $C = \{C_1, C_2\}$, where

$C_1 =$ `chair(x,d)` $\wedge$ `chair(y,d)` $\supset$ `x=y`
and $C_2 =$ `chair(x,DCS)` $\equiv$ `teachnocourse(x)`.

C_2 is intended to constrain the database such that only the chair of Computer Science teaches no courses. From $\{O(KB)\} \cup WIC$ we can derive in CO* neither

`chair(Ken,DCS)` $\wedge$ `chair(Maria,DCS)` $\xrightarrow{\text{KB}}$ `teachnocourse(Ken)` nor

$$\texttt{chair(Ken,DCS)} \wedge \texttt{chair(Maria,DCS)} \xrightarrow{\text{KB}} \texttt{teachnocourse(Maria)}.$$

From $\{O(KB)\} \cup IC$ we can derive both sentences.

The specification of integrity constraints as the set IC seems much more reasonable, but gives equal weight to each constraint in C. Fagin, Ullman, and Vardi [11] have argued that sentences in a database can have different priorities and that updates should respect these priorities by 'hanging on to' sentences of higher priority whenever possible during the course of revision. For instance, as we have argued throughout, sentences with more information content should be retained in a belief set if it is possible to give up those with less information content.

Consider the previous examples where constraints assert that a department has one chair and that the chair of Computer Science is the only person without a course to teach. It can be the case that certain information cannot satisfy both of the constraints, but could satisfy either one singly—for example, when we learn that Maria is the chair and Ken has no course load. It may also be that we prefer to violate the constraint that a non-chair faculty member teaches no course in deference to the fact that Computer Science has only one chair; it seems more plausible that Ken has cut a special deal than that he is another chair.

Suppose that the set $C = \{C_1, \cdots, C_n\}$ is now an *ordered* set of integrity constraints with C_i having higher priority than C_j whenever $i < j$. So we prefer C_i when a conflict arises with C_j. Expressing the fact that C_1 is preferred at all costs is merely asserting that C_1 is a weak integrity constraint, so $\overleftrightarrow{\Box}(C_1 \supset \Box C_1)$ should be satisfied. Since C_2 has the next highest priority, it should be satisfied where possible unless this entails the violation of C_1. This means that any world that satisfies C_2 and C_1 is preferred to any world that does not. In other words, $\overleftrightarrow{\Box}((C_1 \wedge C_2) \supset \Box(C_1 \wedge C_2))$. In conjunction with the first sentence, this implies that any preferred world that violates C_2 will satisfy C_1. Let P_i denote the conjunction of the i highest priority integrity constraints

$$P_i = C_1 \wedge C_2 \wedge \cdots C_i.$$

The set of *prioritized integrity constraints* is specified as

$$ICP = \{\overleftrightarrow{\Box}(P_i \supset \Box P_i) : i \leq n\}.$$

Definition 5.10 M is a *revision model for K with prioritized integrity constraints* $C_1, \cdots, C_n$ iff M is a revision model for K and $M \models ICP$.

Theorem 5.11 *Let M be a revision model for K with prioritized integrity constraints $C_1, \cdots, C_n$. Then $K_A^{*^M} \models C_i$ whenever A is consistent with the conjunction of all constraints C_j, $j \leq i$.*

Example 5.12 Let $KB = \{\texttt{chair(Derek,DCS)}\}$ and $C = \{C_1, C_2\}$, where

$$C_1 = \texttt{chair(x,d)} \wedge \texttt{chair(y,d)} \supset \texttt{x=y}$$
$$\text{and} \quad C_2 = \texttt{chair(x,DCS)} \equiv \texttt{teachnocourse(x)}.$$

From $\{O(KB)\} \cup ICP$ we can derive in CO*

$$\texttt{teachnocourse(Ken)} \wedge \texttt{chair(Maria,DCS)}$$
$$\xrightarrow{\text{KB}} \texttt{chair(x,DCS)} \equiv \texttt{x = Maria}.$$

It may be the case that certain constraints should have equal priority, that none in a certain subset of C have priority over others. It should be easy to see that the strong version of integrity constraints and the prioritized version can be combined. One just needs to assert the premises IC for this subset of equal-priority constraints and adjust the set ICP to reflect this. We leave the details to the reader.

6 Concluding remarks

We have presented a modal logic for subjunctive reasoning that, unlike current logics, can account for the effect of *only knowing* a knowledge base. In this sense, the logic can also be viewed as an axiomatization of AGM revision. Furthermore, it characterizes revision without making the Limit Assumption and allows integrity constraints to be expressed naturally *within* the logic.

In [4; 3] we show that CO*, with its ability to reason about knowledge, can be viewed as a generalization of autoepistemic logic. Thus we can constrain the revision process with autoepistemic statements. We also discuss how the notions of plausibility and epistemic entrenchment can be expressed in CO* and used in the same way as subjunctive premises and integrity constraints. The relationship to possibilistic logic has been explored in [5] where degrees of plausibility are shown to correspond to degrees of possibility in the sense of Dubois and Prade [10]. Finally, the very close relationship to default reasoning is explored in [6; 3].

In [6; 8] we show that the triviality result of Gärdenfors [14] is avoided in our logic at the expense of postulate (R4), which we claim cannot be correct for belief sets that include conditionals. The triviality result has also led to the distinction between revision and update [31; 22; 16]. In fact, Grahne and Mendelzon [17] have presented a model for subjunctives based on update rather than revision. This seems to provide a very distinct semantics for subjunctives. An interesting avenue of research would be to pursue the connection between the two, to examine the extent to which update can be captured by unary modal operators, and the extent to which either problem can be formulated so that one subsumes the other. The generalizations of revision afforded by the modal approach (e.g., weaker notions of accessibility, lack of a Limit Assumption, integrity constraints) may also apply to update.

Finally, this model of revision and subjunctive queries can be extended to iterated revision and therefore nested conditional queries. This extension of the AGM theory has not been well-developed, though Rott [28] has pursued this avenue of research.[15] Some preliminary investigations of iterated revision in our modal framework can be found in [7] and [9].

Acknowledgements

Thanks to Gösta Grahne, Alberto Mendelzon, and Ray Reiter for helpful discussion and bringing to my attention the conditional aspect of revision. Thanks also to Peter Gärdenfors for his comments.

References

[1] Carlos Alchourrón, Peter Gärdenfors, and David Makinson. On the logic of theory change: Partial meet contraction and revision functions. *Journal of Symbolic Logic*, **50**:510–530, 1985.

[2] Anthony J. Bonner. A logic for hypothetical reasoning. In *Proceedings of the Seventh National Conference on Artificial Intelligence*, pp. 480–484, St Paul, 1988.

[3] Craig Boutilier. *Conditional Logics for Default Reasoning and Belief Revision.* Technical Report KRR-TR-92-1, University of Toronto, Toronto, January 1992. Ph.D. thesis.

[4] Craig Boutilier. Epistemic entrenchment in autoepistemic logic. *Fundamenta Informaticae*, **17**(1–2):5–30, 1992.

[5] Craig Boutilier. Modal logics for qualitative possibility and beliefs. In *Proceedings of the Eighth Conference on Uncertainty in AI*, pp. 17–24, Stanford, 1992.

[15] We should point out that nesting is unproblematic for the theories of update mentioned above.

[6] Craig Boutilier. Normative, subjunctive and autoepistemic defaults: Adopting the Ramsey test. In *Proceedings of the Third International Conference on Principles of Knowledge Representation and Reasoning*, pp. 685–696, Cambridge, 1992.

[7] Craig Boutilier. Revision sequences and nested conditionals. In *Proceedings of the Thirteenth International Joint Conference on Artificial Intelligence*, pp. 519–525, Chambery, 1993.

[8] Craig Boutilier. Unifying default reasoning and belief revision in a modal framework. *Artificial Intelligence* 1994 (to appear).

[9] Craig Boutilier and Moisés Goldszmidt. Revision by conditional beliefs. In *Proceedings of the Eleventh National Conference on Artificial Intelligence*, pp. 649–654, Washington, D.C., 1993 (to appear).

[10] Didier Dubois and Henri Prade. An introduction to possibilistic and fuzzy logics. In Glenn Shafer and Judea Pearl, editors, *Readings in Uncertain Reasoning*, pages 742–761. Morgan-Kaufmann, San Mateo, 1990.

[11] Ronald Fagin, Jeffrey D. Ullman, and Moshe Y. Vardi. On the semantics of updates in databases: Preliminary report. In *Proceedings of SIGACT-SIGMOD Symposium on Principles of Database Systems*, pp. 352–365, 1983.

[12] André Fuhrmann. Reflective modalities and theory change. *Synthese*, **81**(1):115–134, 1989.

[13] Peter Gärdenfors. Belief revisions and the Ramsey test for conditionals. *The Philosophical Review*, **95**:81–93, 1986.

[14] Peter Gärdenfors. *Knowledge in Flux: Modeling the Dynamics of Epistemic States.* MIT Press, Cambridge, 1988.

[15] Matthew L. Ginsberg. Counterfactuals. *Artificial Intelligence*, **30**(1):35–79, 1986.

[16] Gösta Grahne. Updates and counterfactuals. In *Proceedings of the Second International Conference on Principles of Knowledge Representation and Reasoning*, pp. 269–276, Cambridge, 1991.

[17] Gösta Grahne and Alberto O. Mendelzon. Updates and subjunctive queries. In *Proceedings of Workshop on Nonstandard Queries and Nonstandard Answers*, volume 1, pp. 33–52, Toulouse, 1991.

[18] Gösta Grahne, Alberto O. Mendelzon, and Ray Reiter. On the semantics of belief revision systems. In *Proceedings of Theoretical Aspects of Reasoning about Knowledge*, Pacific Grove, 1992.

[19] Adam Grove. Two modellings for theory change. *Journal of Philosophical Logic*, **17**:157–170, 1988.

[20] I. L. Humberstone. Inaccessible worlds. *Notre Dame Journal of Formal Logic*, **24**(3):346–352, 1983.

[21] Peter Jackson. On the semantics of counterfactuals. In *Proceedings of the Eleventh International Joint Conference on Artificial Intelligence*, pp. 1382–1387, Detroit, 1989.

[22] Hirofumi Katsuno and Alberto O. Mendelzon. On the difference between updating a knowledge database and revising it. In *Proceedings of the Second International Conference on Principles of Knowledge Representation and Reasoning*, pp. 387–394, Cambridge, 1991.

[23] Hirofumi Katsuno and Alberto O. Mendelzon. Propositional knowledge base revision and minimal change. *Artificial Intelligence*, **52**:263–294, 1991.

[24] Hector J. Levesque. All I know: A study in autoepistemic logic. *Artificial Intelligence*, **42**:263–309, 1990.

[25] David Lewis. *Counterfactuals.* Blackwell, Oxford, 1973.

[26] Raymond Reiter. *What Should a Database Know?* Technical Report KRR-TR-90-5, University of Toronto, Toronto, July 1990.

[27] Hans Rott. Conditionals and theory change: Revisions, expansions, and additions. *Synthese*, **81**(1):91–113, 1989.

[28] Hans Rott. A nonmonotonic conditional logic for belief revision. In A. Fuhrmann and M. Morreau, editors, *The Logic of Theory Change*, pp. 135–181. Springer-Verlag, Berlin, 1990.

[29] Robert C. Stalnaker. A theory of conditionals. In W.L. Harper, R. Stalnaker, and G. Pearce, editors, *Ifs*, pp. 41–55. D. Reidel, Dordrecht, 1968. 1981.

[30] Robert C. Stalnaker. *Inquiry.* MIT Press, Cambridge, 1984.

[31] Marianne Winslett. Reasoning about action using a possible models approach. In *Proceedings of the Seventh National Conference on Artificial Intelligence*, pp. 89–93, St Paul, 1988.

[32] Marianne Winslett. *Updating Logical Databases.* Cambridge University Press, Cambridge, 1990.

Appendix

Proofs of representation results

Theorem 3.5 *Let M be a full revision model and $*^{\mathrm{M}}$ the revision function determined by M. Then $*^{\mathrm{M}}$ satisfies postulates (R1) through (R8).*

PROOF. This follows almost immediately given the derived theorems presented at the beginning of Section 3.3.1 (**RCM** through **CKI**) and the definition of $*^{\mathrm{M}}$. ■

Theorem 3.6 *Let $*$ be a revision function satisfying postulates (R1) through (R8). Then for any theory K there exists a full revision model M such that $K_A^* = K_A^{*^{\mathrm{M}}}$ for all A.*

PROOF. The proof of the theorem will be similar to the proof of the representation result given by Grove [19], and uses the observation that a system of spheres can be considered to be a totally preordered relation on possible worlds.

Let $*$ be an AGM revision operator. We use several well-known facts about such operators (see [14]).

We will construct a full revision model $M = \langle W, \geq, \varphi\rangle$ which corresponds to $*$ for any given consistent K. M is given by:

1. $W = \{w : w \text{ is a maximal consistent set of } \mathbf{L}_{CPL}\}$. We use w to also denote the obvious propositional valuation associated with the set of formulae (so $w \models A$ iff $A \in w$; and $w \in \|S\|$ iff $S \subseteq w$ for any set of sentences S).

2. $v \geq w$ iff there exists a sentence $A \in w \cap v$ such that $K_A^* \subseteq w$, or there is no consistent A such that $K_A^* \subseteq v$.

3. $\varphi(w, A) = 1$ iff $A \in \varphi$ for any atomic A.

We will show that M is a K-revision model by demonstrating each of the necessary properties.

(a) $\geq$ Is reflexive: That $w \geq w$ for all $w \in W$ follows easily in either the case where $w \in \|K_A^*\|$ or not, for some consistent A.

(b) $\geq$ Is totally-ordered: Suppose $w \not\geq v$ and $v \not\geq w$. Then for some consistent A and B, $v \in \|K_A^*\|$ and $w \in \|K_B^*\|$. So $A \vee B \in v \cap w$, and (by (R7) and (R8)) we have $K_{A\vee B}^* = K_A^*$ or $K_{A\vee B}^* = K_B^*$ or $K_{A\vee B}^* = K_A^* \cap K_B^*$. Thus one of v or w is in $K_{A\vee B}^*$, contradicting the fact that neither $v \geq w$ or $w \geq v$.

(c) $\geq$ Is transitive: Suppose $u \leq v$ and $v \leq w$. Assume that there are consistent B, C such that $B \in w$ and $v \in \|K_B^*\|$, $C \in v$ and $u \in \|K_C^*\|$

(otherwise $u \leq w$ holds trivially). Now $\neg C \notin K^*_B$, so by (R7) and (R8) we have $\neg C \notin K^*_{B\vee C}$. This means (by (R8)) that $K^*_{(B\vee C)\wedge C} = (K^*_{B\vee C})^+_C$. In other words, $K^*_C = (K^*_{B\vee C})^+_C$. Hence, $\|K^*_C\| \subseteq \|K^*_{B\vee C}\|$ and $u \in \|K^*_{B\vee C}\|$. But $B \vee C \in w \cap u$, so $u \leq w$.

(d) All K-worlds are minimal: Suppose $w \in \|K\|$. For any world v there exists some $A \in w \cap v$ such that $K \cup \{A\}$ is consistent (e.g., let A be a tautology). By (R3) and (R4), $K^*_A = K^+_A$. Since $w \in \|K^+_A\|$, we have $w \in \|K^*_A\|$. Then by definition of $\geq$, $w \leq v$.

(e) Only K-worlds are minimal: Suppose $w \in \|K\|$, while $v \notin \|K\|$. Choose some $A \in v \cap w$ (such an A exists, for example any tautology). Since $A \in w$, we have $K \cup \{A\}$ is consistent, and by (R3) and (R4), $K^*_A = K^+_A$. But $v \notin \|K\|$ so $v \notin \|K^+_A\|$. Hence $v \notin \|K^*_A\|$ and $v \not\leq w$.

(f) All truth valuations are in W: This is obvious given the definition of M.

Thus M is a K-revision model. It remains to be shown that the revision function determined by M is $*$. For inconsistent A this is clear, since $K^*_A = Cn(\bot)$ in both cases (for $*$ and $*^{\mathrm{M}}$). So assume that A is consistent. We must show

$$B \in K^*_A \text{ iff there is some } w \in W,\ \ M \models_w A \wedge \Box(A \supset B).$$

Lemma 6.1 *If $v \leq w$, $w \in \|K^*_A\|$, and $v \models A$, then $w \leq v$.*

Proof. Since $A \in w \cap v$, $w \in \|K^*_A\|$. The definition of $\leq$ ensures $v \leq v$. ∎

Lemma 6.2 *$w \in \|K^*_A\|$ iff $w \in \min(A)$, where $\min(A) = \{v \in W : v \models A$ and if $u < v$ then $u \not\models A\}$.*

Proof. Suppose $w \in \|K^*_A\|$ and $v \in \|A\|$. By Lemma 6.1 $w \leq v$, hence $w \in \min(A)$. (Thus the existence of $\min(A)$ is demonstrated.)

Suppose $w \in \min(A)$ and $w \notin \|K^*_A\|$. Since A is consistent, there is some $v \in \|K^*_A\|$. By supposition, $w \leq v$, since $v \models A$. This means that there is a $B \in w \cap v$ such that $w \in \|K^*_B\|$. But then we have

$$w \in \|(K^*_B)^+_A\| = \|K^*_{A\wedge B}\| = \|K^*_{B\wedge A}\| = \|(K^*_A)^+_B\| \subseteq \|K^*_A\|.$$

Thus $\|K^*_A\| = \min(A)$. ∎

Suppose $B \in K^*_A$. Then for all $w \in \|K^*_A\|$, $w \models B$ and (by Lemma 6.2) for all $w \in \min(A)$, $w \models B$. By definition of $\min(A)$,

$$M \models_w A \wedge \Box(A \supset B).$$

So $M \models A \xrightarrow{\text{KB}} B$.

Suppose $M \models A \stackrel{\text{KB}}{\longrightarrow} B$. Then there is a v such that

$$M \models_v A \wedge \Box(A \supset B).$$

By definition of $\min(A)$, $v \geq w$ for all $w \in \min(A)$. So for $w \in \|K_A^*\|$ we have $w \models A \supset B$; and then $B \in K_A^*$.

Thus, $K_A^* = K_A^{*^{\mathrm{M}}}$. ∎

10

Updates and subjunctive queries

Gösta Grahne and Alberto O. Mendelzon

Abstract

A subjunctive query of the form $\phi > \psi$ means 'if ϕ were true in the knowledgebase, would ψ also necessarily be true?' We propose the following semantics for subjunctive queries: $\phi > \psi$ will hold in the current knowledgebase T if ψ holds in the result of updating T with ϕ. This is known as the *Ramsey test* in philosophy. We adapt the *model checking approach* of Halpern and Vardi: a knowledgebase is a finite set of finite sets of positive facts interpreted in a closed world setting. We then use Winslett's possible models approach to give semantics to knowledgebase updates, and we introduce a query language which is essentially propositional logic, augmented with a subjunctive conditional that has an intensional interpretation in our model. We show that query answering and update can be performed in polynomial time in the size of the knowledgebase. However, query equivalence is shown to be complete in polynomial space, and this is also the complexity of query answering as a function of query size. We give a sound axiomatization of query equivalence and show that the update operator satisfies the postulates for updates adapted by Katsuno and Mendelzon from the Alchourrón–Gärdenfors–Makinson belief revision postulates.

1 Introduction

Imagine the following queries. 'If I place a gate at this particular position in the integrated circuit I am designing, will the design rules be violated?', or 'If my child is born in Canada, will I be eligible for Canadian citizenship?', or 'Is there any single course I can take which will let me graduate this year?', or 'If I were to make flight connections, could I fly to the Rockies?'

The above are examples of *subjunctive queries*; they ask the database what would happen if the world were a certain way. Let us represent by formula $\phi > \psi$ the sentence 'if the world were such that ϕ, it would necessarily also be such that ψ'. As philosophers have abundantly shown, giving semantics to such statements is not without its intricacies [20, 27]. A very natural approach was proposed by F. P. Ramsey [30]. Consider all 'closest' worlds to the current one in which ϕ holds, and see if they all satisfy ψ. If so, say $\phi > \psi$ holds in the current world. The difficulty now is to define what are the closest worlds in which ϕ holds.

The first thing we have to settle to attack this difficulty is how our knowledge about the current world is represented. The standard approach in knowledge representation (and in much of database theory) is to assume that a certain set of sentences $\mathtt{T}$ in a formal language represents the set of possible current worlds. Given a new sentence ϕ, we need to find a modified theory $\mathtt{T}'$ that describes the closest worlds wherein ϕ holds. Formulated in this way, the problem of defining the closest worlds where a certain sentence holds becomes what in artificial intelligence is known as the *belief revision* problem [1] and in database theory as the *update semantics* problem [2, 13, 9]. Hence, the semantics of a subjunctive query should be clear: update the database with sentence ϕ, and then check whether ψ holds in the result. There are two problems with this. The first problem is to define a comprehensible semantics of updates under arbitrary sentences ϕ, taking into account in particular the cases where ϕ is inconsistent with $\mathtt{T}$. The second problem is that reasonable proposals for such semantics lead to update mechanisms which are of infeasible data complexity, i.e., exponential on the size of the theory $\mathtt{T}$.

Let us examine more closely the semantic problem, that is, what should be the result of updating a theory $\mathtt{T}$ with a sentence ϕ? The departure point of recent work in belief revision is the *rationality postulates* proposed by Alchourrón, Gärdenfors, and Makinson [1] and colloquially known as the the *AGM postulates.* These are principles that every adequate belief revision operator should be expected to satisfy. For example: the new fact ϕ must be a consequence of the revised theory. And: if the new fact ϕ is consistent with $\mathtt{T}$, then the result should be logically equivalent to $\mathtt{T}\wedge\phi$.

Katsuno and Mendelzon [26] pointed out that these postulates are not universally desirable for all kinds of belief revision applications. In particular, they distinguished two kinds of theory change operations, *update* and *revision.* Update consists of bringing the knowledgebase up to date when the world described by it changes. For example, most database updates are of this variety, e.g. 'increase Joe's salary by 5%'. The second type of modification, *revision,* is used when new information is obtained about a static world. For example, we may be trying to diagnose a faulty circuit and want to incorporate into the knowledgebase the results of successive tests, where newer results may contradict old ones. Katsuno and Mendelzon came to the conclusion that the *AGM* postulates describe only revision, and they give a modified set of postulates that characterize update operators.

For example, suppose two robot vehicles V and W are orbiting Venus. We have received the message 'I have landed,' but due to noise we could not determine whether it came from V or W. Let v be the proposition 'V has landed' and w 'W has landed'. After receiving the message, the knowledgebase $\mathtt{T}$ is the sentence

$$(v \wedge \neg w) \vee (\neg v \wedge w).$$

Suppose we now send the command 'Land immediately' to V, and V replies 'I have landed'. This change can be modelled by incorporating the sentence v into $\mathtt{T}$. Since v is consistent with $\mathtt{T}$, the *AGM* postulate cited above says the result should be equivalent to $\mathtt{T} \wedge v$, which is equivalent to $v \wedge \neg w$. But upon reflection it becomes clear that this is incorrect. After V has landed, all we know is that V has landed; there is no reason to conclude that W has not. The correct answer should be v. To coin a phrase of J. Biskup [3], we are 'opening up the world'.

Going back to our original question of how to give semantics to subjunctive queries of the form 'does $\phi > \psi$?', it seems we now have a choice of using update or revision to define the closest worlds where ϕ holds. But, as it turns out, Gärdenfors [17] has shown that using revision to define the semantics of subjunctive statements leads to triviality, while Grahne [21] has constructed a non-trivial, decidable propositional system in which update is used to define subjunctive implication.

In sum, we propose the following semantics for subjunctive queries: $\phi > \psi$ will hold in the current database $\mathtt{T}$ if the result of updating $\mathtt{T}$ with ϕ has ψ has a logical consequence. All update operators which satisfy the postulates of [26] will be acceptable; in particular, Winslett's *possible models approach* [33] seems a reasonable candidate.

But now we have to face the computational consequences of this definition. If $\mathtt{T}$ is a propositional theory, computing the result of updating $\mathtt{T}$ with ϕ using Winslett's operator is at least *NP-hard* on the size of $\mathtt{T}$ [33]. One way of dealing with this computational complexity would be to look for worst-case exponential time algorithms that may perform well in some practical situations. This is the approach taken by Del Val [10]. He gives algorithms for updating arbitrary propositional knowledgebases in conjunctive normal form and discusses in detail their running time in certain situations, citing experimental results.

Our approach is different. We observe that the source of the complexity is conciseness. Very short theories can describe very large sets of possible worlds. On the other hand, it is not *a priori* given that any practical set of possible worlds has such a concise theory. Suppose now, that instead of storing theories, we actually store worlds. We can then replace theorem proving by *model checking*, as suggested by Halpern and Vardi [23]:

> We argue that rather than representing an agent's knowledge as a collection of formulas, and then doing theorem proving to see if a given formula follows from an agent's knowledgebase, it may be more useful to represent an agent's knowledge by a semantic model, and then do model checking to see if the given formula is true in that model.

This is the approach we take. We define a world as a finite set of atomic facts, and a knowledgebase as a finite set of worlds. The approach is somewhat similar to the use of *flocks* of theories by Fagin *et al.* [12]; however, flocks are sets of theories, while knowledgebases are sets of models. We follow the *closed world assumption*: only the facts that are explicitly stored are true in a world [31, 29]. Thus defined, a knowledgebase could also be seen as a propositional formula in disjunctive normal form, equipped with the axioms for Minker's *generalized closed world assumption.* These axioms—the *circumscription axioms*—would, however, require quantification over infinite sets of propositions (see Cadoli and Lenzerini, [7]). By adopting the model checking approach we achieve the advantage of not having to resort to the stronger quantified language in expressing the knowledgebase (see [23]).

We propose a query and update formalism that allows the expression of general subjunctive queries on knowledgebases. Our approach allows us to develop query answering algorithms that run in polynomial time in the size of the knowledgebase. The price we pay is that certain updates can cause the knowledgebase to grow much faster than the corresponding propositional theory.

Our language is related to that of [4, 5] and [6], who study intuitionistic database languages in which it is possible to have subjunctions of the form $\phi > \psi$, where ϕ is a conjunction of atomic formulas, and where ψ is atomic, embedded in the the bodies of clauses. When negated literals are used in these languages, negation is, however, interpreted as failure.

The proposal of Ginsberg [19] is related to the 'syntactic school' of Fagin [13, 12]. According to Ginsberg, the subjunction $\phi > \psi$ is entailed by a theory $\mathtt{T}$, if ψ is entailed by all maximal subsets of $\mathtt{T}$ that are consistent with p. Naturally, this definition is sensitive to the syntactic form of $\mathtt{T}$. Insensitivity to syntax is required both in the Alchourrón–Gärdenfors–Makinson belief revision postulates and the Katsuno–Mendelzon update postulates. It has also recently been shown by Eiter and Gottlob [11] that the syntactic approaches are computationally more expensive than approaches satisfying the belief revision or update postulates.

Other approaches to subjunctive queries are also reported in e.g. [15] and [16].

Section 2 of this chapter contains the definition of subjunctive queries and updates in knowledgebases. In Section 3 we study the data complexity of the operators, and show that queries and updates can be computed in time polynomial in the size of the knowledgebase. The expression complexity of queries and updates is the topic of Section 4. We show that, from this point of view, query evaluation is complete in polynomial space, and that the size of the updated knowledgebase can be exponential in the size of the formula to be inserted. Section 5 contains a discussion on query optimization. We present a sound axiomatization for query transformation, and show that testing for query equivalence is complete in polynomial space. Finally, in Section 6 we consider general properties of change operators, and show that our update operator satisfies the postulates of Katsuno and Mendelzon [26].

2 The framework

Let T be a countably infinite set of *facts*, also called *terms*. We use the name $\mathcal{R}_T$ for the set $\{R : R \subset_{fin} T\}$. Since T is tacitly understood, we will write $\mathcal{R}_T$ simply as $\mathcal{R}$. Each $R \in \mathcal{R}$ is called a *world*.

For each world R we define a binary relation $\leq_R$ over $\mathcal{R}$, given by

$$S \leq_R S' \text{ iff } (S \setminus R) \cup (R \setminus S) \subseteq (S' \setminus R) \cup (R \setminus S').$$

In other words, $S \leq_R S'$ iff the symmetric difference between S and R is a subset of the symmetric difference between S' and R. It is easily verified that $\leq_R$ is a partial order on $\mathcal{R}$. We shall also use a relation $<_R$. The relation $S <_R S'$ holds, iff $S \leq_R S'$ holds, and S is not equal to S'.

Let $\mathcal{S} \subseteq \mathcal{R}$, and $\{R, S\} \subseteq \mathcal{R}$. Then we say that S is *$\leq_R$-minimal in $\mathcal{S}$*, if S is in $\mathcal{S}$, and if $S' \in \mathcal{S}$ and $S' \leq_R S$, then $S' = S$. [1]

$\mathcal{KB}$ is the set $\{KB : KB \subset_{fin} \mathcal{R}\}$. Each $KB \in \mathcal{KB}$ is called a *knowledgebase.* Note that each world in a KB stores only positive information; all terms not explicitly asserted in a world are assumed to be false in that world in our query semantics.

We say that each $t \in T$ is a *term.* From terms we can build *formulas* using the Boolean connectives $\bot, \wedge, \neg$, and the intensional connective $>$. The 0-ary connective $\bot$ denotes the constant *false.* Letters such as ϕ and ψ will be used for formulas. Intuitively, $\phi > \psi$ means 'if ϕ *were* true, ψ *would* be true'. The set of all formulas is denoted Φ (T is understood). The *interpretation* of a formula ϕ is denoted $[\![\phi]\!]$, and defined as follows.

$$[\![\bot]\!] = \emptyset \tag{1}$$

[1] Note that as a consequence of the fact that $\mathcal{R}$ consists of finite worlds, each nonempty subset of $\mathcal{R}$ contains at least one $\leq_R$-minimal element.

$$
\begin{aligned}
[\![t]\!] &= \{R \in \mathcal{R} : t \in R\} && (2)\\
[\![\phi \wedge \psi]\!] &= [\![\phi]\!] \cap [\![\psi]\!] && (3)\\
[\![\neg\phi]\!] &= \mathcal{R} \setminus [\![\phi]\!] && (4)\\
[\![\phi > \psi]\!] &= \{R \in \mathcal{R} : \mu(\phi, R) \subseteq [\![\psi]\!]\}, \text{where} &&\\
\mu(\phi, R) &= \{S \in \mathcal{R} : S \text{ is } \leq_R \text{-minimal in } [\![\phi]\!]\} && (5)
\end{aligned}
$$

For convenience, we will introduce the following abbreviations: $\top$ abbreviates $\neg\bot$, $\phi \vee \psi$ abbreviates $\neg((\neg\phi)\wedge(\neg\psi))$, $\phi \to \psi$ abbreviates $(\neg\phi)\vee\psi$, $\phi \leftrightarrow \psi$ abbreviates $(\phi \to \psi) \wedge (\psi \to \phi)$, and $\phi \supset \psi$ abbreviates $\neg(\phi > \neg\psi)$. The intuitive meaning of the intensional connective $\supset$ is the following: $\phi \supset \psi$ is read 'if ϕ *were* true, ψ *might* be true'. These defined connectives have the following semantic characterizations.

Lemma 2.1

$$
\begin{aligned}
[\![\top]\!] &= \mathcal{R} && (6)\\
[\![\phi \vee \psi]\!] &= [\![\phi]\!] \cup [\![\psi]\!] && (7)\\
[\![\phi \to \psi]\!] &= (\mathcal{R} \setminus [\![\phi]\!]) \cup [\![\psi]\!] && (8)\\
[\![\phi \leftrightarrow \psi]\!] &= ([\![\phi]\!] \cap [\![\psi]\!]) \cup ((\mathcal{R} \setminus [\![\phi]\!]) \cap (\mathcal{R} \setminus [\![\psi]\!])) && (9)\\
[\![\phi \supset \psi]\!] &= \{R \in \mathcal{R} : \mu(\phi, R) \cap [\![\psi]\!] \neq \emptyset\} && (10)
\end{aligned}
$$

Equations (5) and (10) are illustrated diagrammatically in Figure 1 below.

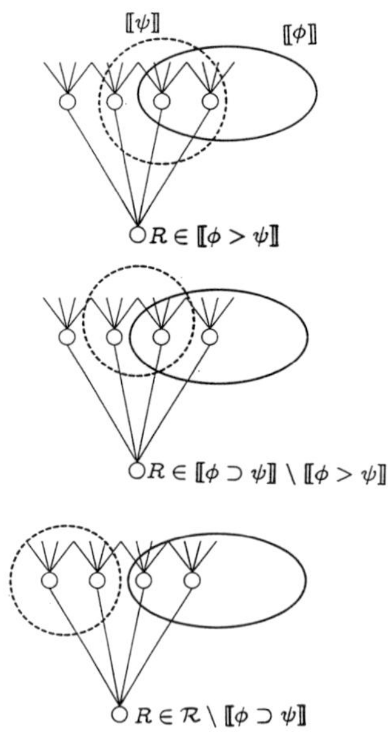

Figure 1: Interpretations of subjunctive sentences.

The first case shows a world R, such that all the $\leq_R$-minimal worlds in $[\![\phi]\!]$ are ψ-worlds, so R belongs to $[\![\phi > \psi]\!]$, and hence also to $[\![\phi \supset \psi]\!]$. The second case shows a world R, such that some $\leq_R$-minimal worlds are ψ-worlds, but not all; hence R belongs to $[\![\phi \supset \psi]\!]$, but not to $[\![\phi > \psi]\!]$. The third case shows a world R, such that no $\leq_R$-minimal world is a ψ-world. Hence R does not belong to $[\![\phi \supset \psi]\!]$ (and consequently not to $[\![\phi > \psi]\!]$ either).

Let us now introduce two *interface functions*, *Ask* and *Tell*. Formally, *Ask* is a function from $\Phi \times \mathcal{KB}$ to $\{yes,\ no,\ possible\}$, and *Tell* is a function from $\Phi \times \mathcal{KB}$ to $\mathcal{KB}$, defined as follows:

$$Ask(\phi, KB) = \begin{cases} yes & \text{if } KB \subseteq [\![\phi]\!] \\ no & \text{if } KB \cap [\![\phi]\!] = \emptyset \\ possible & \text{otherwise} \end{cases} \tag{11}$$

$$Tell(\phi, KB) = \bigcup_{R \in KB} \mu(\phi, R) \tag{12}$$

In Theorem 3.2 we will show that the range of *Tell* is indeed $\mathcal{KB}$.

We can now show that our language satisfies the Ramsey property.

Ramsey's lemma 2.2 $Ask(\phi > \psi, KB) = Ask(\psi, Tell(\phi, KB))$.

As to the properties of the *Tell* function, we will show in Section 6 that *Tell* satisfies the update postulates of Katsuno and Mendelzon [26].

A diagram of the *Tell*-function appears in Figure 2 below. The diagram shows how *KB*-worlds are mapped to their closest ϕ-worlds by $Tell(\phi, KB)$. The diagram only shows the case where none of the KB-worlds is itself a ϕ-world, that is, the *KB* and ϕ are inconsistent. If the *KB* is consistent with ϕ, then every ϕ-world in the *KB* is mapped to itself by $Tell(\phi, KB)$.

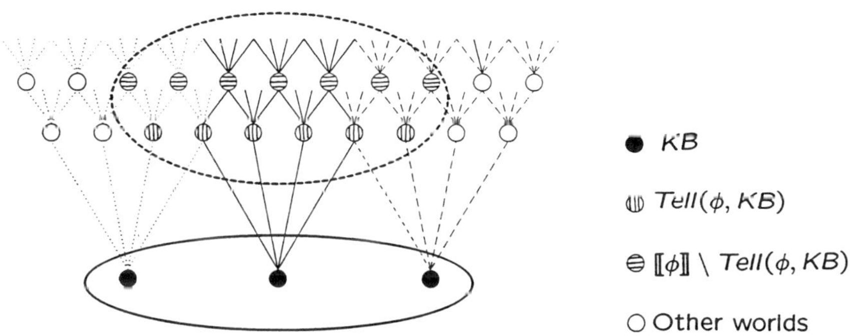

Figure 2: The *Tell*-function.

Let us now return to the two vehicles orbiting Venus. The set of all facts T includes the facts v, 'vehicle V has landed', and w, 'vehicle W has landed'. Suppose that before receiving the message the knowledgebase—we will call it KB_0—contains the four possible worlds $\{v\}$, $\{w\}$, $\{v, w\}$, and $\emptyset$. Note that, for any propositional formula ϕ, $Ask(\phi, KB_0) = yes$ if and only if ϕ is a tautology on the propositional letters v and w, and $Ask(\phi, KB_0) = no$ if and only if ϕ is unsatisfiable. On learning that exactly one of the vehicles has landed, we update this knowledgebase to

$$KB_1 = Tell((v \wedge \neg w) \vee (\neg v \wedge w), KB_0) = \{\{v\}, \{w\}\}.$$

We shall now evaluate *Ask* for some queries on KB_1:

$$Ask(v, KB_1) = Ask(w, KB_1) = possible,$$

$$Ask(\neg v, KB_1) = Ask(\neg w, KB_1) = possible,$$

$$Ask(v \wedge w, KB_1) = no,$$

$$Ask((v \wedge \neg w) \vee (\neg v \wedge w), KB_1) = yes.$$

Now consider the subjunctive query $Ask(v > \neg w, KB_1)$. That is, if V lands, will W necessarily still be orbiting? To answer the query, we need to test membership in $[\![v > \neg w]\!]$. Conceptually, $[\![v > \neg w]\!]$ is the set of worlds R in $\mathcal{R}$ such that, if we update R to make v hold, we obtain a world where $\neg w$ also holds. The world $\{v\}$ is such a world, but the world $\{w\}$ is not; we conclude that $Ask(v > \neg w, KB_1) = possible$. That is, if V lands, W may or may not have landed. Note that, as indicated by Ramsey's lemma, this is the same as evaluating the query $Ask(\neg w, Tell(v, KB_1))$. The update $Tell(v, KB_1) = \{\{v\}, \{v, w\}\}$ is the one that we computed in the introduction.

It is straightforward to incorporate *integrity constraints* in our framework. (See [25].) Suppose that the set of possible worlds is constrained to be among $[\![\iota]\!]$, for some $\iota \in \Phi$. Then the *update under constraint* ι is defined as

$$Tell^{\iota}(\phi, KB) = Tell(\phi, KB) \cap [\![\iota]\!].$$

That is, only those models of $Tell(\phi, KB)$ that satisfy the constraints are retained. Since $\mu(\phi, R) \cap [\![\iota]\!] = \mu(\phi \wedge \iota, R)$, it follows that $Tell^{\iota}(\phi, KB) = Tell(\phi \wedge \iota, KB)$. Thus updating with a formula that is inconsistent with the integrity constraint results in an empty knowledgebase. In practice, such updates are rejected or cause an exception.

3 Data complexity

In this section we show that $Ask(\phi, KB)$ and $Tell(\phi, KB)$ can both be computed in time polynomial in the size of KB, for any formula $\phi \in \Phi$.

We proceed 'bottom–up', by some technical results. The first objective is to show that membership of a world in $[\![\phi]\!]$ depends only on the terms mentioned explicitly in the sentences ϕ. We start by some technical lemmas.

We shall 'overload' the symbol $\supset$. It should be clear from the context whether $\supset$ stands for the intensional 'might' connective, or whether $\supset$ denotes the the usual proper superset relation.

Lemma 3.1 *$S' \leq_R S$ iff $(S' \setminus R) \subseteq (S \setminus R)$ and $(R \setminus S') \subseteq (R \setminus S)$.*

Lemma 3.2 (i). *$S \cap U \leq_{R \cap U} S$.*
(ii). *$S \cup V \leq_{R \cup V} S$.*

PROOF. (i) We have $((S \cap U) \setminus (R \cap U)) \subseteq (S \setminus (R \cap U))$, and $((R \cap U) \setminus (S \cap U)) = ((R \cap U) \setminus S)$.

(ii) $((S \cup V) \setminus (R \cup V)) \cup ((R \cup V) \setminus (S \cup V)) = (S \setminus (R \cup V)) \cup (R \setminus (S \cup V)) \subseteq (S \setminus (R \cup V)) \cup ((R \cup V) \setminus S)$. ∎

Lemma 3.3 *(i) If $S' \leq_R S$, then $S' \cap U \leq_{R \cap U} S \cap U$, and*
(ii) If $S' \leq_R S$, then $S' \cup V \leq_{R \cup V} S \cup V$.

PROOF. (ii) Taking the fact that $(A \cup C) \setminus (B \cup C) = A \setminus (B \cup C)$, Lemma 3.1, and the symmetrical nature of the two cases, it is sufficient to show that $(S' \setminus R) \subseteq (S \setminus R)$ only if $(S' \setminus (R \cup V)) \subseteq (S \setminus (R \cup V))$.

For a contradiction, suppose that $t \in (S' \setminus (R \cup V)) \setminus (S \setminus (R \cup V))$. Since $(S' \setminus (R \cup V)) \subseteq (S' \setminus R) \subseteq (S \setminus R)$, we obtain $t \in (S \setminus R) \setminus (S \setminus (R \cup V))$, which implies that $t \in V$, and thus $t \in (R \cup V)$; a contradiction to the assumption that $t \in (S' \setminus (R \cup V))$.

(i) Let $t \in ((S' \cap U) \setminus (R \cap U))$, i.e. $t \in (S' \setminus R) \cap U$, i.e. $t \in S' \setminus R$, and $t \in U$. We now have $t \in S \setminus R$, and $t \in U$, that is, $t \in ((S \cap U) \setminus (R \cap U))$. ∎

For the next result we shall need a definition: for each $\phi \in \Phi$, let L_ϕ be the set of all terms mentioned in ϕ, i.e. $L_\perp = \emptyset$, $L_t = \{t\}$, $L_{\neg\phi} = L_\phi$, and $L_{\phi \wedge \psi} = L_{\phi > \psi} = L_\phi \cup L_\psi$.

Theorem 3.4 *If $R \in [\![\phi]\!]$, then*

(i) $(R \cap U) \in [\![\phi]\!]$, for all $U \supseteq L_\phi$, and

(ii) $(R \cup V) \in [\![\phi]\!]$, for all (finite) $V \subseteq (T \setminus L_\phi)$.

PROOF. We proceed by an induction on the structure of ϕ.

(*Base*). Let $t \in T$, and suppose $R \in [\![t]\!]$, i.e. $t \in R$. If $t \in U$, then obviously $t \in (R \cap U)$, i.e. $(R \cap U) \in [\![t]\!]$. Obviously also, $t \in R$ implies that $t \in (R \cup V)$.

For the other base case, we note that the antecedent $R \in [\![\bot]\!]$ of the theorem is always false.

(*Inductive step*). Suppose $R \in [\![\psi \wedge \chi]\!]$. Thus $R \in [\![\psi]\!]$, and $R \in [\![\chi]\!]$. By the inductive hypothesis, we have $(R \cap U) \in [\![\psi]\!]$, for all $U \supseteq L_\psi$, and thus in particular for all $U \supseteq (L_\psi \cup L_\chi)$. Using a symmetric argument for $[\![\chi]\!]$, and the fact that $(L_\psi \cup L_\chi) = L_{\psi\wedge\chi}$, we obtain $R \cap U \in [\![\psi \wedge \chi]\!]$, for all $U \supseteq L_{\psi\wedge\chi}$.

By the inductive hypothesis we also obtain that $R \cup V \in [\![\psi]\!]$, for all $V \subseteq (T \setminus L_\psi)$, and thus in particular for all $V \subseteq (T \setminus L_{\psi\wedge\chi})$. The claim follows.

For the next case, suppose $R \in [\![\neg\psi]\!]$. First note that $L_{\neg\psi} = L_\psi$. Then, towards a contradiction, suppose that there is a $U \supseteq L_\psi$, such that $R \cap U \notin [\![\neg\psi]\!]$. Thus $R \cap U \in [\![\psi]\!]$. Since $(R \setminus U) \subseteq (T \setminus L_\psi)$, the inductive hypothesis yields $((R \cap U) \cup (R \setminus U)) \in [\![\psi]\!]$, i.e. $R \in [\![\psi]\!]$; a contradiction.

Towards the next contradiction, suppose that there is a $V \subseteq (T \setminus L_\psi)$, such that $R \cup V \notin [\![\neg\psi]\!]$. Then $R \cup V \in [\![\psi]\!]$. Now $(R \cup L_\psi) \supseteq L_\psi$, so by the inductive hypothesis $((R \cup V) \cap (R \cup L_\psi)) \in [\![\psi]\!]$. Since $V \cap L_\psi = \emptyset$, we obtain $((R \cup V) \cap (R \cup L_\psi)) = R$, which gives the desired contradiction.

For the final case, suppose that $R \in [\![\psi > \chi]\!]$. Note here that $L_{\psi>\chi} = L_\psi \cup L_\chi$. We claim that if $U \supseteq L_{\psi>\chi}$, then $(R \cap U) \in [\![\psi > \chi]\!]$. This amounts to showing that if $\mu(\psi, R) \subseteq [\![\chi]\!]$, then $\mu(\psi, R \cap U) \subseteq [\![\chi]\!]$. Let, therefore, $S \in \mu(\psi, R \cap U)$. From Lemma 3.2 (i), and the fact that $\leq_{R\cap U}$ is a partial order, it follows that $S = (S \cap U)$.

Now S is in $[\![\psi]\!]$, so if S is $\leq_R$-minimal in $[\![\psi]\!]$, we are done.

Suppose, therefore, that there is a $S' <_R S$, where $S' \in \mu(\psi, R)$. Now Lemma 3.3 (i) gives $S' \cap U \leq_{R\cap U} S \cap U$. Since $S \in \mu(\psi, R \cap U)$, and $S = (S \cap U)$, we obtain $S = (S' \cap U)$. By the inductive hypothesis, we have $(S' \cap U) \in [\![\chi]\!]$, and therefore $S \in [\![\chi]\!]$.

To conclude, we show that if $R \in [\![\psi > \chi]\!]$, and $V \subseteq (T \setminus L_{\psi>\chi})$, then $(R \cup V) \in [\![\psi > \chi]\!]$. Again, we show that if $\mu(\psi, R) \subseteq [\![\chi]\!]$, then $\mu(\psi, R \cup V) \subseteq [\![\chi]\!]$.

Let, therefore, $S \in \mu(\psi, R \cup V)$. Then it must be that $V \subseteq S$, since Lemma 3.2 (ii) gives $S \cup V \leq_{R\cup V} S$, and S is $\leq_{R\cup V}$-minimal in $[\![\psi]\!]$. By the inductive hypothesis, $S \cap (S \setminus V) = (S \setminus V)$ is in $[\![\psi]\!]$.

If $(S \setminus V) \in \mu(\psi, R)$, then, by the inductive hypothesis, $S = ((S \setminus V) \cup (V \cap S)) \in [\![\chi]\!]$.

If $(S \setminus V) \notin \mu(\psi, R)$, there must be an S', such that $S' <_R (S \setminus V)$, and $S' \in \mu(\psi, R)$. Now Lemma 3.3 (ii) gives us the fact that $S' \cup V \leq_{R\cup V} S$.

Since S is in $\mu(\psi, R \cup V)$, and $\leq_{R \cup V}$ is a partial order, it must be that $(S' \cup V) = S$. Again, since $S' \in [\![\chi]\!]$, the inductive hypothesis gives the fact that $S = (S' \cup V) \in [\![\chi]\!]$. ∎

The following key result shows that $\mu(\phi, R)$, the set of worlds in $[\![\phi]\!]$ that are 'closest' to world R, is essentially independent of any terms not mentioned in ϕ. We will use the following notation. Let U be a subset of T. By $\mu^U(\phi, R)$ we mean the set

$$\{S : S \text{ is an } \leq_{R \cap U} \text{ minimal element, such that } S \subseteq U \text{ and } S \in [\![\phi]\!]\}.$$

Theorem 3.5 $\mu(\phi, R) = \{S \cup (R \setminus L_\phi) : S \in \mu^{L_\phi}(\phi, R)\}$.

PROOF. Let $S \in \mu^{L_\phi}(\phi, R)$. By Theorem 3.1 (ii) we have $(S \cup (R \setminus L_\phi)) \in [\![\phi]\!]$. Suppose then to the contrary that $(S \cup (R \setminus L_\phi)) \notin \mu(\phi, R)$. Then there is an $S' \in \mu(\phi, R)$, such that $S' <_R (S \cup (R \setminus L_\phi))$. From Lemma 3.3 (i) it follows that $S' \cap L_\phi \leq_{R \cap L_\phi} (S \cup (R \setminus L_\phi)) \cap L_\phi = S$. Since $S \in \mu^{L_\phi}(\phi, R)$, we have $S' \cap L_\phi = S$.

We will now derive a contradiction. From $S' <_R (S \cup (R \setminus L_\phi))$ it follows that either $S' \setminus R \subset S \setminus R$, or $R \setminus S' \subset R \setminus (S \cup (R \setminus L_\phi))$.

Consider the first case. We have $S' \setminus R = ((S' \cap L_\phi) \setminus R) \cup ((S' \setminus L_\phi) \setminus R)$, and since $S' \cap L_\phi = S$, we obtain $S' \setminus R = (S \setminus R) \cup ((S' \setminus L_\phi) \setminus R)$. Therefore, the first case is not possible.

Then consider the second case. We have $R \setminus S' = ((R \cap L_\phi) \setminus (S' \cap L_\phi)) \cup ((R \setminus L_\phi) \setminus (S' \setminus L_\phi))$. On the other hand we have $R \setminus (S \cup (R \setminus L_\phi)) = (R \cap L_\phi) \setminus S = (R \cap L_\phi) \setminus (S' \cap L_\phi)$. Thus the second case is not possible either. Consequently, it must be our counterassumption that is wrong.

For inclusion in the other direction, let $S \in \mu(\phi, R)$. We shall first show that $S \setminus L_\phi = R \setminus L_\phi$. Suppose on the contrary that there is a $t \in (S \setminus L_\phi)$, such that $t \notin (R \setminus L_\phi)$. But this would imply that $S \setminus \{t\} <_R S$; a contradiction. Likewise, the existence of a $t \in (R \setminus L_\phi) \setminus (S \setminus L_\phi)$ would imply $S \cup \{t\} <_R S$. Therefore, it must be that $S \setminus L_\phi = R \setminus L_\phi$.

We will now proceed to show that $S \cap L_\phi \in \mu^{L_\phi}(\phi, R)$. The desired inclusion then follows, since we are now in a position to conclude that $(S \cap L_\phi) \cup (R \setminus L_\phi) = S$

By Theorem 3.1 (i) we have $S \cap L_\phi \in [\![\phi]\!]$. If, as a counterassumption, $S \cap L_\phi \notin \mu^{L_\phi}(\phi, R)$, there must be an $S' \in [\![\phi]\!]$, such that $S' \subseteq L_\phi$, and $S' <_{R \cap L_\phi} S \cap L_\phi$. From Lemma 3.3 (ii) it then follows that $S' \cup (R \setminus L_\phi) \leq_R S$. Since $S \in \mu(\psi, R)$, we obtain $S' \cup (R \setminus L_\phi) = S$, and consequently that $S' = S \cap L_\phi$; a contradiction. ∎

Consider now the following two algorithms and the procedures they use:

```
ALGORITHM 1.   Evaluation of Ask(φ, KB).

INPUT.         A formula φ ∈ Φ, and a knowledgebase KB ∈ 𝒦ℬ.

OUTPUT.        The value of Ask(φ, KB).

METHOD.        if and({ eval(φ, R) : R ∈ KB}) = true
               then output('yes')
               else if or({ eval(φ, R) : R ∈ KB}) = true
                    then output('possible')
                    else output('no');

END OF ALGORITHM 1.
```

```
ALGORITHM 2.   Computation of Tell(φ, KB).

INPUT.         A formula φ ∈ Φ, and a knowledgebase KB ∈ 𝒦ℬ.

OUTPUT.        The value of Tell(φ, KB).

METHOD.        output( ⋃_{R∈KB} mu(φ, R));

END OF ALGORITHM 2.
```

```
function eval(φ, R) : boolean;
begin
     case the form of φ of :
          ⊥      : eval := false;
          t      : eval := t ∈ R;
          ¬ψ     : eval := not( eval(ψ, R));
          ψ ∧ χ  : eval := and({ eval(ψ, R), eval(χ, R)});
          ψ > χ  : eval := and({ eval(χ, S) : S ∈ mu(ψ, R)});
     end case;
end;
```

```
function mu(φ, R) : set;
begin
      closest := {S : S ⊆ L_φ};
      for each U ∈ closest do
            if not( eval(φ, U)) then closest := closest \ {U};
      for each U ∈ closest do
            for each V ∈ closest do
                  if V <_{R∩L_φ} U then closest := closest \ {U};
      for each S ∈ closest do
            closest := (closest \ {S}) ∪ {S ∪ (R \ L_φ)};
      mu := closest;
end;
```

Since the function **mu**(ϕ, R) clearly computes the set $\{S \cup (R \setminus L_\phi) : S \in \mu^{L_\phi}(\phi, R)\}$, an easy induction on the structure of the sentence ϕ yields the following.

Corollary 3.6 *Algorithm 1 correctly computes Ask(ϕ, KB), and Algorithm 2 correctly computes Tell(ϕ, KB).*

Let us now turn to the computational complexity of the two algorithms. As a notational convenience, for a sentence $\phi \in \Phi$, we denote by $|\phi|$ its length counted in occurrences of symbols from $T \cup \{\neg, \wedge, >\}$. For a set A, we denote by $|A|$ the number of elements in it. Note that for any $\phi \in \Phi$, we have $|L_\phi| \leq |\phi|$.

Lemma 3.7 *Let ϕ be a fixed sentence from Φ. Then the running time of function* **mu**(ϕ, R) *is $\mathcal{O}(|R|)$.*

PROOF. Since $|\texttt{closest}| = 2^{|L_\phi|} \leq 2^{|\phi|}$, the total number of iterations in the loops in **mu** is bounded by a constant. Also, for each $U \in$ `closest`, we have $|U| \leq |L_\phi| \leq |\phi|$. Therefore the computation of **eval**(ϕ, U) within **mu** does not depend on $|R|$ at all, i.e. it can be carried out in constant time.

In the nested **for each**-loop we test whether $V <_{R \cap L_\phi} U$. Clearly, this can be done in time proportional to $|R|$. Likewise, the step in the last loop takes time proportional to $|R|$. ∎

Lemma 3.8 *Let ϕ be a fixed sentence from Φ. Then the running time of function* **eval**(ϕ, R) *is $\mathcal{O}(|R|)$.*

PROOF. We proceed by an induction on the structure of ϕ.

Base. If ϕ is $\perp$ the claim is obvious. If ϕ is of the form t, we have to test whether $t \in R$. This takes time proportional to $|R|$.

Inductive step. If ϕ is of the form $\neg\psi$ or $\psi \wedge \chi$, then the claim is obvious. Suppose, therefore, that ϕ is of the form $\psi > \chi$.

First we compute $\mathbf{mu}(\psi, R)$. Since $|\psi| < |\phi|$, Lemma 3.4 tells us that this computation requires time proportional to $|R|$. Next, the number of elements in $\mathbf{mu}(\psi, R)$ is less than $2^{|L_\psi|} \leq 2^{|\phi|}$ and is therefore bounded by a constant, say c. We thus have to compute **eval** no more than c times. The size of each S in $\mathbf{mu}(\psi, R)$ is at most $|R| + |\psi| < |R| + |\phi|$. Since $|\chi| < |\phi|$, the inductive hypothesis yields the fact that the computation of $\mathbf{eval}(\chi, S)$ can be carried out in time $\mathcal{O}(|R| + |\phi|) = \mathcal{O}(|R|)$. ∎

By the size of a knowledgebase we mean the sum of the sizes of the worlds in it. We now have the following straightforward consequence of the two previous lemmas.

Theorem 3.9 *Algorithms 1 and 2 both run in time linear in the size of KB.*

4 Expression complexity

In this section we will study the complexity of computing $Ask(\phi, KB)$ and $Tell(\phi, KB)$, as a function of $|\phi|$, the length of ϕ.

It is clear that Algorithm 2 takes time that is exponential in $|\phi|$. The following theorem says that the bound cannot be improved. We note that Fagin *et al.* [12] mention a similar result.

Theorem 4.1 *There is a knowledgebase KB and a family $\{\phi_n\}_{n\in\omega}$ of formulas, such that the size of $Tell(\phi_n, KB)$ is exponential in the length of ϕ_n.*

PROOF. Let $KB = \{\emptyset\}$, and let ϕ_n be the formula $(t_1 \vee u_1) \wedge \ldots \wedge (t_{n+1} \vee u_{n+1})$. Then $\mu(\phi_n, \emptyset) = \{\{v_1, \ldots, v_{n+1}\} : v_i \in \{t_i, u_i\}, i \in \{1, \ldots, n+1\}\}$. ∎

On the other hand, if ϕ is a propositional formula in disjunctive normal form, then the size of $Tell(\phi, KB)$ is linear in the length of ϕ. We also note that for updates of the form ϕ_n above, the *model trees* of Fernández and Minker [14] might provide a compact representation of the resulting *KB*. This question would, however, require further investigation.

In order to characterize the expression complexity of *Ask*, we will study the problem of deciding whether $Ask(\phi, KB) = yes$, for a fixed *KB*. We provide a constructive upper bound that actually also computes the value of $Ask(\phi, KB)$. We also provide a matching lower bound for the decision problem.

Formally, by the *expression complexity* of *Ask wrt KB* we mean the complexity of the set

$$Query_{KB} = \{\phi \in \Phi : Ask(\phi, KB) = yes\}.$$

First we interest ourselves in the *satisfiability* problem, that is, the problem of determining if $[\![\phi]\!] \neq \emptyset$, for a given ϕ, in which case we say that ϕ is satisfiable. Formally, we are interested in the set

$$Sat_{\Phi} = \{\phi \in \Phi : [\![\phi]\!] \neq \emptyset\}.$$

Our first result concerns decidability.

Lemma 4.2 *Sat_{Φ} is effectively decidable.*

PROOF. We will show that $\phi \in Sat_{\Phi}$ if and only if $[\![\phi]\!] \cap \{S : S \subseteq L_{\phi}\} \neq \emptyset$. The latter problem is decidable as a consequence of Corollary 3.1.

The if direction of the above claim is obvious. For the only if direction, let $R \in [\![\phi]\!]$. By Theorem 3.1 (i), we have $(R \cap L_{\phi}) \in [\![\phi]\!]$, and obviously $(R \cap L_{\phi}) \in \{S : S \subseteq L_{\phi}\}$. ∎

The next problem to tackle is the computational complexity of Sat_{Φ}. For this, consider the following variant of the function **eval**(ϕ, R):

```
function eval(φ, R) : boolean;
begin
    case the form of φ of :
        ⊥     : eval := false;
        t     : eval := t ∈ R;
        ¬ψ    : eval := not( eval(ψ, R));
        ψ ∧ χ : eval := and({ eval(ψ, R), eval(χ, R)});
        ψ > χ : begin
                    temp := true;
                    for each U ⊆ L_ψ do
                        if eval(ψ, U) then
                        begin
                            close := true;
                            for each V ⊆ L_ψ do
                                if and( {eval(ψ, V),
                                V <_{R∩L_ψ} U}) then
                                  close := false;
                            if close then
                                temp := and( {temp,
                                eval(χ, U ∪ (R \ L_ψ) )});
                        end;
                    eval := temp;
                end;
    end case;
end;
```

This version of **eval** is a depth-first search. The depth of the recursion is clearly bounded by $|\phi|$, the length of ϕ. In an implementation, the stack will therefore have at most as many nodes as there are subformulas of ϕ. In each node we need to store the current subformula, and when the subformula is $\psi \wedge \chi$ we need to record whether we are evaluating ψ or χ. In the case where the current subformula is $\psi > \chi$, we need, in addition to the values of variables `temp` and `close`, to record which subset of L_ψ is under consideration. We also need a marker that tells us where in the block for $\psi > \chi$ we are. None of these pieces of information requires more amount of space than a polynomial of the current subformula.

In order to test if ϕ is in Sat_Φ, as in the proof of Lemma 4.1 we cycle through all subsets S of L_ϕ, and for each S we run the modified version **eval**(ϕ, S). Since $|S| \leq |\phi|$ we are thus lead to the following result.

Theorem 4.3 *Sat_Φ is in* PSPACE.

We will now provide a matching lower bound for Sat_Φ. For this we will use a reduction from the Quantified Boolean Formula problem (QBF, Garey and Johnson [18], see also Hopcroft and Ullman [24]). Formally, QBF is the set of all expressions of the form

$$Q_n t_n(\ldots(Q_1 t_1(\phi))),$$

where $n \geq 0$, where each $Q_i \in \{\forall, \exists\}$, where each $t_i \in T$, and where ϕ is a propositional formula in Φ, such that $L_\phi = \{t_1, \ldots, t_n\}$.

The value of a QBF $Q_n t_n(\ldots(Q_1 t_1(\phi)))$ is *true* or *false*. The value is defined recursively as follows. A QBF $\forall t_i(Q_{i-1}t_{i-1}(\ldots(Q_1 t_1(\psi))))$ is *true* if and only if both QBFs $Q_{i-1}t_{i-1}(\ldots(Q_1 t_1(\top_i(\psi))))$, and $Q_{i-1}t_{i-1}(\ldots(Q_1 t_1(\bot_i(\psi))))$ are *true*. By $\top_i(\psi)$ we mean the formula ψ with each occurrence of t_i replaced by $\top$. Likewise, $\bot_i(\psi)$ denotes ψ with each occurrence of t_i replaced by $\bot$. Also, the QBF $\exists t_i(Q_{i-1}t_{i-1}(\ldots(Q_1 t_1(\psi))))$ is *true* if and only if at least one of the QBFs $Q_{i-1}t_{i-1}(\ldots(Q_1 t_1(\top_i(\psi))))$, and $Q_{i-1}t_{i-1}(\ldots(Q_1 t_1(\bot_i(\psi))))$ is *true*. In the base case of the recursion we will have a formula, say χ, that contains only Boolean connectives, $\top$ and $\bot$. This QBF is *true* if $[\![\chi]\!] = \mathcal{R}$, and *false* if $[\![\chi]\!] = \emptyset$.

Theorem 4.4 *Sat_Φ is* PSPACE*-hard.*

PROOF. Let $Q_n t_n(\ldots(Q_1 t_1(\phi))) \in$ QBF. We will construct a formula $\rho \in \Phi$, such that $Q_n t_n(\ldots(Q_1 t_1(\phi)))$ is *true* if and only if $\rho \in Sat_\Phi$. We will have $L_\rho = \{t_1, \ldots, t_n, u_1, \ldots, u_n\}$, where

$$\rho = \sigma_n \wedge \rho_n.$$

Here

$$\sigma_n = \bigwedge_{i \in \{1,\ldots,n\}} \neg t_i \wedge \neg u_i,$$

and σ_0 is $\top$. The formula ρ_n as well as each ρ_i is defined recursively as follows:

$$\rho_i = \begin{cases} (t_i \vee u_i) > \rho_{i-1} & \text{if } Q_i = \forall \\ (t_i \vee u_i) \supset \rho_{i-1} & \text{if } Q_i = \exists \end{cases}$$

The formula ρ_0 is simply ϕ. Clearly, the length of ρ is linear in the length of $Q_n t_n(\ldots (Q_1 t_1(\phi)))$.

As an illustration of the transformation, consider the QBF

$$\forall t_3(\exists t_2(\forall t_1((t_3 \wedge t_2) \to t_1))).$$

We now have

$$\rho = \sigma_3 \wedge ((t_3 \vee u_3) > ((t_2 \vee u_2) \supset ((t_1 \vee u_1) > ((t_3 \wedge t_2) \to t_1)))).$$

We will now show that $Q_n t_n(\ldots (Q_1 t_1(\phi)))$ is *true* if and only if ρ is satisfiable. We start by some notation. Let $R \in \mathcal{R}$, and $i \in \{0, \ldots, n\}$. By ϕ_i^R we mean the formula ϕ with each occurrence of t_j, where $i+1 \leq j \leq n$, replaced by $\top$, if $t_j \in R$, and replaced by $\bot$, otherwise. Note that $\phi_n^R = \phi$, and that ϕ_0^R contains only Boolean connectives, $\top$ and $\bot$.

Now we claim that for all $i \in \{0, \ldots, n\}$, if $R \in [\![\sigma_i]\!]$, then

$$Q_i t_i(\ldots (Q_1 t_1(\phi_i^R))) \text{ is } \textit{true} \text{ iff } R \in [\![\rho_i]\!].$$

We verify the claim by an induction on i.

(*Base*). Clearly, $[\![\phi_0^R]\!] = \mathcal{R}$ if and only if $R \in [\![\phi]\!]$. Thus the QBF ϕ_0^R is *true* if and only if $R \in [\![\rho_0]\!]$. The value of R is irrelevant here, since $[\![\sigma_0]\!] = \mathcal{R}$.
(*Inductive step*). First note that if $R \in [\![\sigma_i]\!]$, then $\mu(t_i \vee u_i, R) = \{R \cup \{t_i\}, R \cup \{u_i\}\} \subseteq [\![\sigma_{i-1}]\!]$. Let Q_i be $\forall$ (resp. $\exists$). Then we have

$$R \in [\![\rho_i]\!]$$

iff

$$(R \cup \{t_i\}) \in [\![\rho_{i-1}]\!], \text{ and (resp. or) } (R \cup \{u_i\}) \in [\![\rho_{i-1}]\!]$$

iff (by the inductive hypothesis)

$$Q_{i-1}t_{i-1}(\ldots (Q_1 t_1(\phi_{i-1}^{R\cup\{t_i\}}))) \text{ is } \textit{true},$$
$$\text{and (resp. or) } Q_{i-1}t_{i-1}(\ldots (Q_1 t_1(\phi_{i-1}^{R\cup\{u_i\}}))) \text{ is } \textit{true}$$

iff

$$(Q_{i-1}t_{i-1}(\ldots Q_1 t_1(\top_i(\phi_i^R)))) \text{ is } \textit{true},$$
$$\text{and (resp. or) } (Q_{i-1}t_{i-1}(\ldots Q_1 t_1(\bot_i(\phi_i^R)))) \text{ is } \textit{true}$$

iff

$$Q_i t_i(\ldots (Q_1 t_1(\phi_i^R))) \text{ is } \textit{true}.$$

Thus the claim is proved. Suppose then that $\sigma_n \wedge \rho_n$ is satisfiable. As in Lemma 4.1, we can restrict our attention to worlds that are subsets of $\{t_1, \ldots, t_n, u_1, \ldots, u_n\}$. Thus we have that $\sigma_n \wedge \rho_n$ is satisfiable iff $\emptyset \in [\![\rho_n]\!]$ iff $Q_n t_n(\ldots(Q_1 t_1(\phi_n^\emptyset)))$ is *true* iff $Q_n t_n(\ldots(Q_1 t_1(\phi)))$ is *true*. ■

It is clear that the modified version of procedure **eval** also gives an algorithm for computing $Ask(\phi, KB)$ in space polynomial in the length of ϕ. For the decision problem, we conclude the following.

Corollary 4.5 *For all* $KB \in \mathcal{KB}$, $Query_{KB}$ *is in* PSPACE.

For a lower bound, it is easy to see that, in the notation of the proof of Theorem 4.3, $Ask(\rho_n, \{\emptyset\}) = yes$ if and only if the QBF ϕ is *true*. Thus we have the following result.

Corollary 4.6 $Query_{\{\emptyset\}}$ *is* PSPACE-*complete.*

We note that some further complexity-theoretic results for updates have recently been obtained by Eiter and Gottlob [11]. Instead of data and expression complexity, they study (among other things) the *combined complexity* of unnested subjunctive queries, which, in the notation of the present chapter, would be the complexity of the set

$$\{\langle KB, \phi > \psi\rangle : Ask(\phi > \psi, KB) = yes\},$$

where ϕ and ψ are propositional sentences. Eiter and Gottlob show that this set is Π_2^p-complete. They also show that if the knowledgebase is *represented* by a set of propositional Horn clauses $\mathtt{T}$, and if ϕ and ψ are also propositional Horn clauses, then the problem of verifying whether $Ask(\phi > \psi, [\![\mathtt{T}]\!]) = yes$ is *co-NP* complete (in the size of the input $\langle \mathtt{T}, \phi, \psi\rangle$). If, furthermore, the size of ϕ is bounded by a constant, then this problem can be solved in polynomial time.

5 Query transformation

In this section we provide a sound axiomatization of query equivalence, and show that the problem of testing whether two queries are equivalent is *PSPACE*-complete.

Formally, we say that ϕ and ψ are *equivalent*, denoted $\phi \equiv \psi$, and defined as

$$\phi \equiv \psi \text{ iff } Ask(\phi, KB) = Ask(\psi, KB),$$

for all $KB \in \mathcal{KB}$.

Let Θ be the smallest subset of Φ that contains all formulas of the following form

All truth-functional axioms,

$\phi \rightarrow (\psi > \phi)$, where $L_\phi \cap L_\psi = \emptyset$,

$\phi > \phi$,

$(\phi > \neg\phi) \rightarrow (\psi > \neg\phi)$,

$((\phi > \chi) \wedge (\psi > \chi)) \rightarrow ((\phi \vee \psi) > \chi)$,

$(\phi > \psi) \rightarrow (\phi \rightarrow \psi)$,

$(\phi \wedge \psi) \rightarrow (\phi > \psi)$,

and that it is closed under modus ponens and the following rule:

For any $n \geq 1$,
$((\chi_1 \wedge \ldots \wedge \chi_n) \rightarrow \psi) \mapsto ((\phi > \chi_1 \wedge \ldots \wedge \phi > \chi_n) \rightarrow (\phi > \psi))$.

We can now show that the axiomatization is *sound.*

Theorem 5.1 *If* $\phi \leftrightarrow \psi \in \Theta$, *then* $\phi \equiv \psi$.

The proof of this theorem is straightforward and is thus omitted. We are currently investigating the completeness of the axiomatic system.

As to the computational complexity of equivalence, we are interested in the complexity of the set

$$Equ_\Phi = \{(\phi, \psi) \in \Phi \times \Phi : \phi \equiv \psi\}.$$

The equivalence problem is a variation of the satisfiability problem, since it is easily shown that $(\phi, \psi) \in Equ_\Phi$ if and only if $\neg(\phi \leftrightarrow \psi) \notin Sat_\Phi$. Therefore, we have the following result.

Corollary 5.2 Equ_Φ *is* PSPACE-*complete.*

6 Change algebras

Our *Tell* function is a *change* operator, and represents a particular solution to the change problem. The change problem appears in many guises, such as data and knowledgebase updates, view updates, belief revisions, truth maintenance, abduction, defeasible reasoning, and so forth. Generally, change is a form of non-monotonic reasoning (see e.g. Makinson and Gärdenfors, [28]).

In order to fit our *Tell* operator into a more general pattern, we will introduce some notation. Henceforth, Let T' be a fixed finite subset of T, and let Φ' be the set of all propositional formulas ψ in Φ, such that $L_\phi \subseteq T'$. Furthermore, let $\circ$ be a mapping from $\Phi' \times \Phi'$ to Φ'. Then the tuple

$$\langle \Phi', \circ \rangle$$

is called a (free) *change algebra*, and for ϕ and ψ in Φ', $\phi \circ \psi$ is meant to represent the formula obtained by changing ϕ with ψ.

Properties of change operators that have appeared in the literature are examined in Katsuno and Mendelzon [25]. In particular, two classes of change algebras have recently been identified: revision algebras (Alchourrón *et al.* [1]), and update algebras (Katsuno and Mendelzon [26]). A revision corresponds to a change in our knowledge about a static world, whereas an update corresponds to a change in the world. The conditions characterizing these algebras will be given below. We first need some additional notation.

Let $\{\phi, \psi\} \subseteq \Phi'$, and define $[\![\phi]\!]' = [\![\phi]\!] \cap \{S : S \subseteq T'\}$. Then we say that ϕ is *satisfiable*, if $[\![\phi]\!]' \neq \emptyset$ (as before), that ϕ *implies* ψ, if $[\![\phi]\!]' \subseteq [\![\psi]\!]'$, that ϕ is *equivalent* to ψ, if $[\![\phi]\!]' = [\![\psi]\!]'$ (as before), and that ϕ is *complete*, if $[\![\phi]\!]'$ is a singleton. We now have the following definitions.

A tuple $\langle \Phi', \circ \rangle$ is a *revision algebra* if it is a change algebra and the following conditions hold (Alchourrón *et al.*, [1] and Katsuno and Mendelzon, [26]):

(R1) $\phi \circ \psi$ implies ψ

(R2) If $\phi \wedge \psi$ is satisfiable, then $\phi \circ \psi$ is equivalent to $\phi \wedge \psi$.

(R3) If ψ is satisfiable, then $\phi \circ \psi$ is satisfiable.

(R4) If ϕ is equivalent to ξ and ψ to χ, then $\phi \circ \psi$ is equivalent to $\xi \circ \chi$.

(R5) $(\phi \circ \psi) \wedge \chi$ implies $\phi \circ (\psi \wedge \chi)$.

(R6) If $(\phi \circ \psi) \wedge \chi$ is satisfiable, then $\phi \circ (\psi \wedge \chi)$ implies $(\phi \circ \psi) \wedge \chi$.

For an intuitive account of these conditions or postulates, see [1] and [26].

It is clear that changes in the knowledge about a static world, i.e. revisions, do not capture all change operators. In particular, most database changes are changes in the world. Such changes are called updates. Formally, a tuple $\langle \Phi', \circ \rangle$ is an *update algebra* if it is a change algebra and the following conditions hold (Katsuno and Mendelzon, [26]):

(U1) $\phi \circ \psi$ implies ψ.

(U2) If ϕ implies ψ, then then $\phi \circ \psi$ is equivalent to ϕ.

(U3) If both ϕ and ψ are satisfiable, then $\phi \circ \psi$ is satisfiable.

(U4) If ϕ is equivalent to ξ and ψ to χ, then $\phi \circ \psi$ is equivalent to $\xi \circ \chi$.

(U5) $(\phi \circ \psi) \wedge \chi$ implies $\phi \circ (\psi \wedge \chi)$.

(U6) If $\phi \circ \psi$ implies χ, and $\phi \circ \chi$ implies ψ, then $\phi \circ \psi$ is equivalent to $\phi \circ \chi$.

(U7) If ϕ is complete, then $(\phi \circ \psi) \wedge (\phi \circ \chi)$ implies $\phi \circ (\psi \vee \chi)$.

(U8) $(\phi \vee \varphi) \circ \psi$ is equivalent to $(\phi \circ \psi) \vee (\varphi \circ \psi)$.

These conditions are given intuitive motivation in Katsuno and Mendelzon, [26], which paper also gives model theoretic characterizations of revision and update operators.

In order to embed our *Tell* operator into a change algebra we will need some more notation. Let $\mathbf{S} = \{S_1, \ldots, S_n\}$ be a set of subsets of T'. Then $\varphi_{\mathbf{S}}$ denotes the formula $\varphi_{S_1} \vee \ldots \vee \varphi_{S_n}$, where

$$\varphi_{S_i} = (\bigwedge_{t \in S_i} t) \wedge (\bigwedge_{t \in \{T' \setminus S_i\}} \neg t).$$

Also, if $\phi \in \Phi'$, then we define

$$KB_\phi = [\![\phi]\!]'.$$

Now define a change operator $\circ_{Tell}$ as follows:

$$\phi \circ_{Tell} \psi = \varphi_{Tell(\psi, KB_\phi)}.$$

An examination of the space example in Section 2, reveals that $\circ_{Tell}$ does not satisfy condition (R2). We conclude the following.

Theorem 6.1 *$\langle \Phi', \circ_{Tell} \rangle$ is not a revision algebra.*

On the other hand, the next theorem shows that our *Tell* mapping indeed reflects a change in the world, i.e. it is an update.

Theorem 6.2 *$\langle \Phi', \circ_{Tell} \rangle$ is an update algebra.*

This fact is proved using a representation theorem of Katsuno and Mendelzon, [26] which states that any update algebra can alternatively be characterized by partial orders on worlds, of which the partial orders $\leq_K$ of this chapter are an instance.

7 Conclusion

We have given a framework for subjunctive queries, defining their semantics from the point of view of belief revision theory. By taking a model checking approach, we obtain queries and updates of polynomial data complexity. From an expression complexity point of view, it turns out that an update can increase the size of the knowledgebase exponentially, and that query evaluation is complete in polynomial space, as is also query equivalence, i.e. the problem of testing whether two queries returns the same answer for all knowledgebases. For query equivalence we have provided a sound axiomatization.

The following direction now suggests itself: the language for Φ can be extended with variables, equality, and quantification. The natural question to study is, then, the expressive power of such extended knowledgebase languages, since it seems that our μ-operator can be made to generalize the fixpoint queries of Chandra and Harel, [8]. This direction is pursued in Grahne, Mendelzon and Revesz, [22].

Acknowledgements

Many thanks to Hirofumi Katsuno and the anonymous referees for their comments.

References

[1] C. E. Alchourrón, P. Gärdenfors, and D. Makinson. On the logic of theory change: partial meet contraction and revision functions. *Journal of Symbolic Logic* **50**, 510–530, 1985.

[2] F. Bancilhon and N. Spyratos. Update semantics of relational views. *ACM Transactions on Database Systems* **4**, 557–575, 1981.

[3] J. Biskup. A foundation of Codd's relational maybe-operations. *ACM Transactions on Database Systems* **8**, 608–636, 1983.

[4] A. J. Bonner. Hypothetical datalog: complexity and expressibility, in *Proceedings of the Second International Conference on Database Theory*, pp. 144–160, 1988.

[5] A. J. Bonner. A logic for hypothetical reasoning, in *Proceedings of the Seventh AAAI National Conference on Artificial Intelligence*, pp. 480–484, 1988.

[6] A. J. Bonner, L. T. McCarty, and K. Vadaparty. Expressing database queries with intuitionistic logic, in *Proceedings of the North American Conference on Logic Programming*, pp. 831–850, 1989.

[7] M. Cadoli and M. Lenzerini. *The Complexity of Propositional Closed World Reasoning and Circumscription.* Technical report, Dipartimento di Informatica e Sistemica, Università di Roma 'La Sapienza', 1991.

[8] A. K. Chandra and D. Harel. Structure and complexity of relational queries. *Journal of Computer and System Sciences* **25**, 99–28, 1982.

[9] S. S. Cosmadakis and C. H. Papadimitriou. Updates of relational views. *Journal of the Association for Computing Machinery* **31**, 742–760, 1984.

[10] A. Del Val. Computing knowledge base updates. To appear in *Proceedings of the Third Conference on Principles of Knowledge Representation*, 1992.

[11] T. Eiter and G. Gottlob. On the complexity of propositional knowledge base revision, updates, and counterfactuals, in *Proceedings of the Eleventh ACM SIGACT–SIGMOD–SIGART Symposium on Principles of Database Systems*, pp. 261–273, 1992.

[12] R. Fagin, G. M. Kuper, J. D. Ullman, and M. Y. Vardi. Updating logical databases, in *Advances in Computing Research, vol. 3: The Theory of Databases,* (P. C. Kanellakis and F. P. Preparata, eds.), pp. 1–18, JAI Press, Greenwich, Ct, 1986.

[13] R. Fagin, J. D. Ullman, and M. Y. Vardi. On the semantics of updates in databases, in *Proceedings of the Second ACM SIGACT–SIGMOD–SIGART Symposium on Principles of Database Systems,* pp. 352–365, 1983.

[14] J. A. Fernández and J. Minker. Bottom-up evaluation of hierarchical disjunctive databases, in *Proceedings of the Seventh International Conference on Logic Programming,* pp. 660–675, 1991.

[15] D. M. Gabbay. N-Prolog: an extension of Prolog with hypothetical implications. II. Logical foundations and negation as failure. *Journal of Logic Programming* **2**, 251–283, 1985.

[16] D. M. Gabbay and U. Reyle. N-Prolog: an extension of Prolog with hypothetical implications. I. *Journal of Logic Programming* **1**, 319–355, 1984.

[17] P. Gärdenfors. *Knowledge in Flux: Modeling the Dynamics of Epistemic States,* Bradford Books, MIT Press, Cambridge, MA, 1988.

[18] M. R. Garey and D. S. Johnson. *Computers and Intractability: A Guide to the Theory of NP-Completeness,* Freeman, San Francisco, 1979.

[19] M. L. Ginsberg. Counterfactuals. *Artificial Intelligence* **30**, 35–79, 1986.

[20] N. Goodman. *Fact, Fiction, and Forecast,* Harvard University Press, Cambridge, 1955.

[21] G. Grahne. Updates and counterfactuals, in *Proceedings of the Second International Conference on Principles of Knowledge Representation and Reasoning,* pp. 269–276, 1991.

[22] G. Grahne, A. O. Mendelzon, and P. Z. Revesz. Knowledgebase transformations, in *Proceedings of the Eleventh ACM SIGACT–SIGMOD–SIGART Symposium on Principles of Database Systems,* pp. 246–260, 1992.

[23] J. Halpern and M. Y. Vardi. Model checking vs. theorem proving: a manifesto, in *'Proceedings of the Second International Conference on Principles of Knowledge Representation and Reasoning,* pp. 325–334, 1991.

[24] J. E. Hopcroft and J. D. Ullman. *Introduction to Automata Theory, Languages and Computation,* Addison-Wesley, 1979.

[25] H. Katsuno and A. O. Mendelzon. Propositional knowledge base revision and minimal change. *Artificial Intelligence* **52**, 263–294, 1991.

[26] H. Katsuno and A. O. Mendelzon. On the difference between updating a knowledge base and revising it, in *Proceedings of the Second International Conference on Principles of Knowledge Representation and Reasoning,* pp. 387–394, 1991.

[27] D. K. Lewis. *Counterfactuals,* Blackwell, Oxford, 1973.

[28] D. Makinson and P. Gärdenfors. Relations between the logic of theory change and nonmonotonic logic, in *Lecture Notes in Artificial Intelligence*, Vol. 465 : *The Logic of Theory Change,* (A. Fuhrmann and M. Morreau, eds.), pp. 185–205, Springer Verlag, Berlin, 1991.

[29] J. Minker. On indefinite databases and the closed world assumption, in *Proceedings of the Sixth International Conference on Automated Deduction,* pp. 292–398, 1982.

[30] F. P. Ramsey. General propositions and causality, in *Foundations of Mathematics and Other Logical Essays,* (R. B. Braithwaite, ed.), pp. 237–257, Routledge and Kegan Paul, New York, 1950.

[31] R. Reiter. On closed world databases, in *Logic and Databases,* (H. Gallaire and J. Minker, eds.), pp. 55–76, Plenum Press, New York, 1978.

[32] M. Winslett. A framework for comparison of update semantics, in *Proceedings of the Seventh ACM SIGACT–SIGMOD–SIGART Symposium on Principles of Database Systems,* pp. 315–324, 1988.

[33] M. Winslett. Reasoning about action using a possible models approach, in *Proceedings of the Seventh National Conference on Artificial Intelligence,* pp. 89–93, 1988.